Lady Blanche Murphy

On the Rhine, and other Sketches of European Travel

Lady Blanche Murphy

On the Rhine, and other Sketches of European Travel

ISBN/EAN: 9783743316034

Manufactured in Europe, USA, Canada, Australia, Japa

Cover: Foto ©Andreas Hilbeck / pixelio.de

Manufactured and distributed by brebook publishing software (www.brebook.com)

Lady Blanche Murphy

On the Rhine, and other Sketches of European Travel

AND OTHER SKETCHES OF

EUROPEAN TRAVEL.

BY

LADY BLANCHE MURPHY, T. ADOLPHUS TROLLOPE,
Mrs. SARAH B. WISTER, EDWARD KING, Etc.

WITH NUMEROUS ILLUSTRATIONS.

PHILADELPHIA:
J. B. LIPPINCOTT & CO.
1881.

CONTENTS.

		PAGE
DOWN THE RHINE	*Lady Blanche Murphy.*	5
BADEN AND ALLERHEILIGEN	*T. Adolphus Trollope.*	75
WHY DO WE LIKE PARIS?	*Sarah B. Wister.*	86
AMONG THE BISCAYANS	*George L. Catlin.*	111
TROUVILLE	*L. Lejeune.*	121
THE ITALIAN LAKES	*Robert A. McLeod.*	133
EASTER ON THE RIVIERA	*W. D. R.*	149
A MONTH IN SICILY	*Alfred T. Bacon.*	167
GLIMPSES OF SWEDEN	*J. A. Harrison.*	208
TRY NORWAY!	*Olive Logan.*	230
HUNGARIAN TYPES AND AUSTRIAN PICTURES	*Edward King.*	246
ODD CORNERS OF AUSTRIA	*Edward King.*	276
ALONG THE DANUBE	*Edward King.*	293
DANUBIAN DAYS	*Edward King.*	311

DOWN THE RHINE.

PART I.

![Merchants' Exchange at Constance]

MERCHANTS' EXCHANGE AT CONSTANCE, WHERE THE COUNCIL MET.

LIKE a certain old, eternally-young, and dearly-monotonous subject, the Rhine has been an inexhaustible theme for song, legend and romance. Old as is its place in literature, familiar as are its shores not only to the traveler in Europe, but to the least well-read of the stay-at-homes, there is always something new to be said about it, or at least it can be viewed in a new aspect. Its early stages are certainly less well known than its middle portion—*the* Rhine of poetry and legend—but they are equally beautiful, and especially characterized by natural scenery of the most picturesque kind. Historical memories are not lacking either, even within fifty miles of its rise in the glaciers of the Alps, while its early beauty as a mountain-torrent, dashing over the rocks of the Via Mala, has for some a greater charm than even its broad lake-like waters fringed with cathedrals, abbeys, and stately guildhalls, or its windings among "castled crags."

One branch of the river bursts from under a tumbled mass of ice and rock—one of those marvelous "seas" of ice which are the chief peculiarity of the Alps, and which sometimes, as in the case of the glacier of the Rheinwald, present among other features that of an immense frozen waterfall. Passing through the village of Hinterrhein, whose inhabitants are the descendants of a colony planted there by Barbarossa to guard the old military road over the Alps, and which boasts of a Roman temple and other less well-defined remains of human dwellings of the same period, the Rhine enters the grand gorge of the Via Mala, between Andeer and Rongella, on the road below the Splügen Pass and village. Every such pass has its Devil's Bridge or its "Hell" or its "Bottomless Pit," and tradition tells of demons who pelted each other with the riven masses of rock, or giants who in malice split the rocks and dug the chasms across which men dared no longer pass. But it needs no such figures of speech to make a mountain-gorge one of the sublimest scenes in Nature, one which thrills the beholder with simple admiration and delight. The Via Mala is one of the most splendid of these scenes. A sheer descent of two thousand feet of rock, with clinging shrubs, and at the bottom the trunks of pines and firs that have lost their hold and grown into mossy columns stretched across the stream and often broken by its force; a winding, dizzy road leading over single-arched bridges and half viaducts built into the black rock; a foam-white stream below; a succession of miniature waterfalls, rapids and whirlpools; spray and rainbow poised over the stream at intervals, and here and there the narrowing rocks bending their ledges together and wellnigh shutting out the sun; the "Lost Hole," where tall firs, with their roots seemingly in space, stand up like a forest of lances, and the very formation of the rocks reminds one of gigantic needles closely-wedged together,—such are the features of the gorge through which the Rhine here forces its way. Then comes Zillis, a regular Swiss village, at the entrance of the valley of Thusis, which is a broad green meadow dotted with chalets, a picturesque, domestic, rural landscape, a bit of time set in the frame of eternity, and holding in its village chronicles memories to which distance lends enchantment, but which, in view of the scenes we have just described, seem wonderfully bare of dignity. Here is the castle of Ortenstein, the warrior-abbey of Katsis, the Roman Realta, the castle of Rhäzünz, the bridge of Juvalta, and many castles on the heights overlooking the valley, which at the time of the "Black League" of the nobles against the "Gray Confederation" of the citizens (which gave its name to this canton, the Grisons) were so many rallying-points and dens of murder. There is romance in the legends of these castles, but one seldom stops to think of the robbery and lawlessness hidden by this romance. For these knights of the strong hand were no "Arthur's knights," defenders of the weak, champions of the widow and the orphan, gentle, brave and generous, but mostly oppressors, Bedouins of the Middle Ages, ready to pounce on the merchandise of traveling and unarmed burghers and defy the weak laws of an empire which could not afford to do without their support, and consequently winked at their offences.

A legend of this part of the Rhine, less well known than those of the Loreley, Drachenfels or Bishop Hatto's Tower, belongs to Rhäzünz. After the feud had lasted long years between the nobles and the citizens, the young lord of this castle was captured in battle by the Gray Confederates, and the people's tribunal

ZILLIS.

condemned him to death. The executioner stood ready, when an old retainer of the prisoner's family asked to be heard, and reminded the people that although the youth's hot blood had betrayed him into many a fray, yet some of his forefathers had been mild and genial men, not unwilling to drink a friendly glass with their humbler neighbors. For old associations' sake let this custom be renewed at least once before the execution of this last of the race of Rhäzünz: it was the first and last favor the youth, in his dying moments, requested of them.

JUVALTA.

Stone drinking-vessels were brought: a regular carousal followed, and good-humor and good fellowship began to soften the feelings of the aggrieved citizens. Then the faithful old servant began to speak again, and said it would be a pity to kill the young man, a good swordsman too, who, if they would spare his life, would join the Gray Confederacy and fight for instead of against the people—be their champion, in a word, in all their quarrels, instead of their foe and their oppressor. He prevailed, and the youth, it is said, religiously kept the promise made for him.

Passing the Toma Lake, a small mountain-tarn, whence rises one of the feeders of the Vorder-Rhein, and Dissentis, whose churches are crowned with Greek-looking cupolas set upon high square towers, and whose history goes back to the ravages of Attila's barbarian hordes and the establishment of the Benedictine monastery that grew and flourished for upward of a thousand years, and was at last destroyed by fire by the soldiers of the first French republic, we follow the course of the increasing river to where the smaller and shorter Middle Rhine falls into the main branch at Reichenau. The Vorder-Rhein has almost as sublime a cradle as the other branch. Colossal rocks and a yet deeper silence and solitude hem it in, for no road follows or bridges it, and it comes rolling through the wildest canton of Switzerland, where eagles still nest undisturbed and bears still abound, and where the eternal snows and glaciers of Erispalt, Badus and Furka are still unseen save by native hunt-

CITY GATE AT ILANZ.

ers and herdsmen whose homes are far away. Here is the great Alpine watershed, dividing the basin of the North Sea from that of the Mediterranean. But at Reichenau *the* Rhine absorbs the individuality of each of these mountain-torrents, and here we meet with memories of the mediæval and the modern world curiously mingled in the history of the castle, which has been an episcopal fortress of the bishops of Chur, its founders, a lay domain when the lords of Planta owned it, and an academy or high school when Monsieur Chabaud, the director, gave fourteen hundred francs a year salary to a young teacher of history, geography, mathematics and French who was afterward the citizen-king, Louis Philippe. Here is Martinsloch, where Suwarrow shamed his mutinous Cossacks who refused to attempt the passage of the Alps, by ordering a grave to be dug for him, throwing off his clothes and calling to his men to cast him in and cover him, "since you are no longer my children and I no longer your father."

TAMINA SPRING.

Ilanz is the first town on the Rhine, and has all the picturesqueness one could desire in the way of quaint architecture, bulbous cupolas, steep roofs with windows like pigeon-holes, covered gateways, and a queer mixture of wood and stone which gives a wonderfully old look to every house. Chur—or Coire, as it is more commonly called out of Germany and Switzerland—is of much the same character, an old episcopal stronghold, for its bishops were temporal lords of high renown and still higher power. Then the Rhine winds on to another place, whose present aspect, that of a fashionable watering-place, hardly brings its history as a mediæval spa to the mind. The healing springs at Ragatz were discovered by a hunter of the thirteenth century on the land belonging to the great and wealthy Benedictine abbey. For centuries the spring, whose waters come from Pfäffers and Tamina, and are brought half a mile to Ragatz through iron pipes, was surrounded by mean little huts, the only homes of the local health-seekers, except of such—and they were the majority—as were the guests of the abbey; but when crowds increased and times changed, the abbey built a large guest-house at the springs. Now the place has passed into the hands of a brotherhood no less well known the world over, and who certainly, however well they serve us, give no room for romance in their dealings with us. The promenade and hotels of the place rival Baden and Homburg, but the old spring of Tamina, in its wild beauty, still remains the same as when the mediæval sportsman stumbled upon it, no doubt full of awe and trembling at the dark, damp walls of rock around him, where visitors now admire and sketch on the guarded path. The only other interest of Ragatz, except its scenery, is Schelling's grave and monument put up by Maximilian II. of Bavaria, his scholar and friend.

Everywhere, as the Rhine flows on, the tourist notices its wonderful coloring, a light, clear green, which characterizes it at least as far as the Lake of Constance, in whose neighborhood the vines first begin to bloom and become an important item in the prosperity of the country. Here too the river first becomes navigable, and the heavy square punt that ferries you over at Rüthi, and the pictures of the old market-ships that preceded the first American steamer of 1824, and carried the vine produce to other and dryer places (for in Constance the land lay so low that cellars could not be kept dry, and the surplus of the vintage was at once exchanged for corn and fruit, etc.), are the first signs of that stirring commercial life which is henceforth inseparably connected with the great German stream.

ISLAND OF MAINAU.

Five different governments crowd around and claim each a portion of the shores of the "great lake" of Germany. Yet it is not much more than forty miles long, with a breadth at its widest part of nine. In old Roman times its shores were far more beautiful and worthy of admiration than now. Then it was fringed by forests of birch, fir and oak, and its islands were covered with dense groves. The chief beauty of lowland is in its forests: when they are gone the bareness of the landscape is complete. Rocky mountains can afford to be treeless, but to an artist's eye there is little beauty in treeless plains, and all the boasting of German enthusiasts about this lake cannot hide the fact that its shores are singularly low and bare. But if the landscape is tame, the historical recollections of the Lake of Constance are rich and interesting. The oldest town on its shores is Bregenz, the *Brigantium* mentioned by Pliny and Strabo, and Christianized by Saint Gall and Saint Columbanus, the Irish missionaries whose wanderings over Europe produced so many world-famous monasteries. The great abbey of St. Gall was not far from the lake, and Columbanus established his last monastery at Bobbio in Italy. Lindau ("the field of linden-trees"), almost as old a city as Bregenz, built on an island and connected with the mainland by a long bridge over which the railway runs, was founded by the Germans, and some of the earliest Christian converts built its churches and convents, while later on its commerce grew to be one of the most important in Germany,

CASTLE OF HOHENTWIEL.

and raised the status of the city to the level of the members of the Hanseatic League; but all this was lost in the Thirty Years' War, when it was devastated and partly burnt: now it ranks as a third-rate Bavarian town. But it is impossible to string together all the remembrances that distinguish these lake-towns, many of them now refuges for Englishmen in narrow circumstances, their commerce dwindled, their museums the thing best worth seeing in them.

We pass Arbon; Friedrichshafen, the summer palace of the kings of Würtemberg, a sturdy, warring city in the Carlovingian times; Meersburg, now a fishing-centre, once a stronghold of its martial bishops, and famous in later times as the residence of the baron of Lassberg, a modern *savant* and *virtuoso* of whom Germany is justly proud; and lastly Constance, the city of the Roman emperor Constantius, still beautiful and stately in its buildings. Charlemagne tarried here on his way to Rome on the occasion of his coronation, and many German kings spent Christmas or Easter within its walls. Here, in the large but low hall of the Kaufhaus, or Merchants' Exchange, the council of 1414 met, and never did the Greek councils of the primitive Church present more varied and turbulent scenes. The walls are paneled and frescoed by Philip Schwören, an artist of Munich, and Frederick Pecht, a native of Constance, with representations of these scenes, but it was rather a rough place in those days, and tapestries and dais, weapons and costly hangings, concealed the unfinished state of walls, floor and roof. The old city has other buildings as intimately connected with the council as this hall—the convents of the Dominican and Franciscan friars, each successively the prison of John Huss, the first containing a dungeon below the water-level and foul in the extreme, the second a better and airier cell for prison-

HANS HOLBEIN.

ers, as well as a great hall in which several sessions of the council took place, and where Huss was examined and condemned; the house where Huss first lodged with a good and obscure widow; and three miles from the town the castle of Gottlieben, also a prison of the Reformer, and for a short time of the deposed pope, John XXIII. Little more than a century later the Reformation had grown powerful in Constance, and Charles V. besieged and, notwithstanding the desperate resistance of the burghers, took the town, but not before a most murderous defence had been made on the Rhine bridge, the picture of which, after the unsuccessful fight, reminds one of the heroic defence of the dyke at Antwerp against the Spaniards, and even of that other memorable event in Spanish history, the Noche Triste of Mexico.

As we leave the lake two islands come in sight, Mainau and Reichenau, the latter having a legend attached to it connected with the foundation of its abbey which is the counterpart of that of Saint Patrick and the snakes and vermin of Ireland. The "water was darkened by the multitude of serpents swimming to the mainland, and for the space of three days this exodus continued," whereupon Saint Firmin founded the abbey, which grew to such wealth and power, both as a religious house, a school for the nobility and a possessor of broad feudal domains, that the abbots used to boast in the twelfth and thirteenth centuries that they could sleep on their own land all the way to Rome. The Rhine issues from the lake at Stein, a picturesque little town of Merovingian times, which has seen as many "tempests in a tea-cup" as any of its grander and more progressive rivals; and not far off is the castle of Hohentwiel, built into a towering rock, once the home of the beautiful and learned Hedwige, duchess of Swabia. We need not dwell on Schaffhausen, one of the best-known points of the river, an ancient town overgrown with modern excrescences in the way of fashionable hotels and Parisian dwellings. One of the features of these river-towns, when they are not "improved," is the crowding of houses and garden-walls sheer into the stream, leaving in many places no pathway on the banks, which are generally reached by steep, mossy steps leading from old streets or through private yards.

We are nearing the four "forest towns" of the Habsburgs, at the first of which, Waldshut—where stood in Roman times a single fort to command the wilderness, much as the pioneers' outposts used to stand on the edge of the Western forests peopled with hostile Indians—the Aar, the Rhine's first tributary of any consequence, joins the great stream. Lauffenburg, Säckingen and Rheinfelden, the three other forest towns, each deserve a page of description, both for their scenery and their history, their past architectural beauties, and their present sleepy, museum-like existence; but rather than do them injustice we will pass on to Bâle—or Basel, as it should be written, for the French pronunciation robs the name of its Greek and royal etymology from *Basileia*. Basel was never lagging in the race of intellectual progress: her burghers were proud and independent, not to say violent; her university was eager for novelties; her merchants spent their wealth in helping and furthering art and literature. The Rathhaus or guildhall is a gauge of the extent of the burgher supremacy: all over Germany and the Low Countries these civic buildings rival the churches in beauty and take the place of the private palaces that are so especially the boast of Italian cities. Among the great men of Basel are Holbein and the scarcely less worthy, though less well-known artist, Matthew Merian, the engraver. Of the former's designs many monuments remain, though injured by the weather—a fountain with a fresco of the dance of the peasants, and some houses with mural decorations ascribed to him. Basel has its own modern excitements—races and balls and banquets—although the private life of its citizens is characterized by great simplicity. The profession of teaching is in such repute there that many rich men devote themselves to it, and among the millionaires of the old city may be found not a few schoolmasters. As in Geneva, learning and a useful life are the only things on which the old families pride themselves.

From Basel, whose every reminiscence is German, and whose Swiss nationality dates only from the epoch of the Reformation, the Rhine flows through the "storied" Black Forest, peopled with nixies and gnomes, the abode of the spectre woodcutter, who had sold all power of feeling human joys for the sake of gold, and who spent every night cutting down with incredible swiftness and ease the largest fir trees, that snapped like reeds under his axe. Old Breisach, with its cathedral of St. Stephen, and its toppling, huddled houses clustering around the church, is the most interesting town before we reach Freiburg. The tendency of mediæval towns to crowd and heighten their houses contrasts sharply with the tendency of our modern ones to spread and broaden theirs. Defence and safety were the keynote of the old architecture, while display is that of ours, but with it has come monotony, a thing unknown to the builders of the Middle Ages. Houses of each century, or each period of art, have, it is true, a family likeness, but, like the forms of Venetian glass, a pair or a set have minute differences of ornamentation which redeem the objects from any sameness. So it was with all mediæval art, including that of building the commonest dwelling-houses: there was congruity, but never slavish uniformity.

The first sight of Freiburg—we include it among Rhenish towns, though it is not *on* the Rhine—presents a very German picture. Old dormer windows pierce the high-pitched roofs; balconies and garden trellises hang in mid-air where you least expect them; the traditional storks, the beloved of Hans Andersen, are realities even here on the tall city chimneys; and no matter where you look, your eye cannot help falling on the marvelously high and attenuated spire of one of the finest cathedrals in the world. Artistically speaking, this church has the unique interest of being the only completed work of ecclesiastical architecture that Ger-

INTERIOR OF FREIBURG CATHEDRAL.

many possesses. The height of the spire and its position immediately above the great gateway produce here the same illusion and disappointment as to the size of the church which is proverbial as regards St. Peter's at Rome. This impression soon disappears, and every step reveals new beauties. Each cluster of simple tall gray columns, supporting massive fourteenth-century arches, is adorned with one carved niche and its delicate little spire sheltering the stone statue of an apostle or evangelist; the chancel is filled with the canons' stalls, each a masterpiece of wood-carving; and at the eastern end, beneath the three higher windows and separated from the wall, stands the mediæval high altar with its three carved spires surmounting the reredos, and just below this a "triptych" of enormous size, a pictured altar-piece with folding-doors, the latter being painted both inside and out with scriptural subjects as quaintly interpreted by the devout painters of the early German school. But not only the nave, with its carved pulpit and canopy, its old dark benches, not renewed since the seventeenth century at least, and its crowds of worshipers, is interesting to the sight-seer, but each side chapel, rich with what in our times would be thought ample decoration for a large church, is enough to take up one's day. In these and in the aisles lie buried the patrons, founders, defenders and endowers of the cathedral, while in the chapel of the university are laid the masters and doctors whose fame reached over the learned and civilized world of the Middle Ages, and whose labors Holbein no doubt flatteringly hinted at when he chose for the subject of his great altarpiece in this chapel the visit of the Wise Men of the East to the infant Saviour. In each of these chapels are wood-carvings of great beauty and variety, and stained glass windows whose colors are as vivid as they were four hundred years ago; and in one is still preserved a heavy Byzantine cross of chased silver, the gift (or trophy) of a crusading knight, for Freiburg too "took the cross" under the enthusiastic direction of that great man, Bernard of Clairvaux. It is not often that such a building as this cathedral has such a worthy neighbor and companion as the beautiful exchange, or Kaufhaus, that stands opposite on the "platz." This, though of later date and less pure architecture, is one of the most beautiful buildings of its kind in Germany. The lower part reminds one of the doges' palace at Venice—a succession of four round arches on plain, strong, Saxon-looking pillars; at each corner an oriel window with three equal sides and a little steep-pointed roof of its own shooting up to the height of the main roof. The great hall on the same level has a plain balcony the whole length of the building, and five immense windows of rather nondescript form and mullioned like Elizabethan windows, between each of which is a statue under a carved canopy; and these are what give the characteristic touch to the house. They represent the emperor Maximilian, lovingly called "the last knight," Charles V., "on whose dominions the sun never set," Philip I. and King Ferdinand. The color of the material of which this exchange is built (red sandstone) increases the effect of this beautiful relic of the Middle Ages. But, though we should be glad to linger here and admire it at our leisure, there are other houses in the city that claim our attention as showing, in their less elaborate but perfectly tasteful decoration, the artistic instincts of those burghers of old. And the fountains too! Not the bald, allegorical, monotonous and rarely-found (and when found only useless and ornamental) fountains of our new cities, but the lavishly-carved, artistic creations of an art-imbued age—the water free to all and flowing for use as well as for show, and the statues of civic patron-saints and occasionally men of local renown; as, for instance, the single statue of a meditative monk, his left hand supporting his chin, and a closed book in his right hand, Berthold Schwarz, the inventor of gunpowder.

From this inland side-trip we go back to the now broadening river, the part of the Rhine where the "watch" has been so often kept as well as sung—that part, too, where Roman forts were thickly strewn, and where the Merovingian and

THE "DREI EXEN."

Carlovingian emperors fought and disputed about the partition of their inheritances. But everywhere in this land of Upper-Alsace 1870 has effaced older memories, and modern ruins have been added to the older and more romantic ones. No foreigner can impartially decide on the great question of the day—i. e., whether German or French sentiment predominates—while the interested parties themselves each loudly ignore the no doubt *real* claims of the other. As a simple matter of fact, Alsace is German by blood and by language, but race-differences are so often merged in other feelings, the product of kind treatment and domestic ties, that the sympathies of nations may be materially changed in less than a century. We certainly come across a good deal that is very French in the villages between New Breisach and Colmar: the *blouse* is the costume of the men; the houses are painted in light colors, in contrast to their steep gray roofs; the women bring refreshments out to the wagoners, and stop for a coquettish gossip in a light-hearted, pleasant, vivacious way not seen in other places, whose matrons seem graver and more domestic. But Colmar, in its streets, the names over the shops, the old corner-windows, is as German and antique, as good a "specimen" city, as Nüremberg or Augsburg. Here is the artist's delight and the antiquary's mine. Colmar, contemptuously styled "a hole" by the great Napoleon, was living enough at the time of the emperor Frederick II., and was one of the prosperous, haughty, freedom-loving burgher cities to which the sovereigns so gratefully gave the name and privileges of an "imperial" town. This city of ancient Germany is now one of the most stagnant among modern towns, just "advanced" enough to possess corner "loafers," and, we hope, to be ashamed of having publicly burnt the works of Bayle in the market-place; but its architectural beauties are such and so many that if you are on your way to Strassburg you had better deny yourself the pleasure of stopping here. Balconies and galleries strike the eye at every turn; irregular houses, their beams often visible; doorways of wonderful beauty; and a population nearly as antique, the women carrying loads on their heads and wearing short dark stuff gowns, thick blue worsted stockings and wooden shoes. Of course the cathedral is the pride of the town, and it has some rather rare characteristics distinguishing it from the rest of the churches of this neighborhood, chiefly its simplicity of decoration. The impression of a noble simplicity is specially borne in upon us by the aspect of the dark, broad chancel with its carved stalls, and little else in the way of ornament: the sculptured door leading to the sacristy unfortunately hides a remarkable work of early German art, the *Virgin of the Rose-hedge*, by Martin Schön. The tower of the cathedral has above it only a small building with a steep, irregular, tapering roof, and here sits the watchman whistling on his cobbler's stool in a place that would be the envy of many a scholar pestered in his lower dwelling by inconsiderate visitors; as, for instance, that perfect type of scholars, Isaac Casaubon, whose journal bears witness to his yearning after more time and fewer admiring, consulting and tormenting friends. Not far from Colmar is a castle-ruin with three towers, the "Drei Exen," illustrating an old Alsatian proverb, the translation of which is, in substance,

> Three castles on one hill;
> Three churches in one churchyard;
> Three cities in one valley,—
> Such is Alsace everywhere.

Other castles crown the heights above the villages of Kaisersberg and Rappoltsweiler, but we are getting tired of castles, and this region is abundant in old houses, the shell of the old home-life which has changed so little in the country. What difference is there between this ruddy, blue-eyed girl, with thick plaits of fair hair and utter innocence of expression, the mother of a future generation as healthy and sturdy and innocent as herself, and her own grandmother at the same age three generations back? Neither the village interests nor the village manners have changed: placidly the life flows on, like that of the Rhine water itself, in these broad, level, fruitful plains between the Black Forest and the Vosges. And so we seem, in these various houses with wide gables turned to the street, cross-beams and galleries and unexpected windows, outside stairs of stone or wood climbing up their sides, wide low doorways, tiny shrines set in the rough wall, and dizzy roofs pierced like dovecotes—houses that remind us of Chester, the old English town that has suffered least from innovation,—in these we seem to see some part of the old tranquil home-life of this Alsatian people renewed and re-acted before our eyes. Again the same variety of beautiful houses will meet us at Strassburg. But the woods are no less lovely: old trees round the ruins of St. Ulrich, and on the way to the abbey of Dusenbach, and round the shores of the "White" and the "Black" Lake, bring to the mind a yet older picture of German life, that of the free Teutons of Tacitus, the giant men who made it so important to the Romans to have the Rhine, the great natural highway, strongly fortified from its sources to its mouth.

Hoh-Königsburg, a splendid ruin, said to be the loveliest in Alsace, is now the property and the pride of the commune of that name, so that the victory of the present over the past is also represented in these living panoramas before us, for there is deep meaning in the possession by the people, as an artistic show, of the very stronghold which was once their bane and their terror. Then we run through Schlettstadt, with its sedgy banks, among which herons and storks are picking up their daily bread: deep shadows of old trees hide the blank walls on the river-side, and its cathedral towers high above the mingled steeples and cupolas and nearly as high roofs of some of the larger buildings, while we think of its successful warfare with the bishops of Strassburg, its firm adherence in the thirteenth and fourteenth centuries to the imperial cause, of its sieges and fires, and also its famous "academy" and library; not forgetting, however, its shame in the

ST. THOMAS'S CHURCH, STRASSBURG.

sixteenth century, when the Jews were more signally persecuted here than in many other towns—at a time, too when the fanaticism that had driven so many to change their faith should have taught both parties of Christians some home-lessons. Its neighbor, Strassburg, has nearly as bad a record, but what with the beauty of the latter and its recent

FERKELMARKT (PIG-MARKET) AT STRASSBURG.

stormy history, its sins are the last things a traveler thinks of. Its cathedral and its clock have been fully described, but other churches of the old city are well worth a visit, that of St. Thomas being a specimen of an architecture essentially Christian and anterior to the Gothic, the same whose perfection is seen in many churches in Umbria and Tuscany and Romagna, before the miserable mania of the Renaissance style grew up. What was pardonable in a palace was monstrous in a church, but there was an evil age just before the Reformation, when, if certain learned and elegant and *pagan* prelates had had their way, Christianity would have been condemned as "barbarism." They were the Voltaires of their day, the disciples of a cultured infidelity which brought on the great rent between Latin and Teutonic Christianity.

In Strassburg we have the river Ill and its canal joining the Rhine, and Venice-like scenes, narrow quays, clumsy, heavy punts, fanciful chimney-stacks, crazy, overhanging balconies, projecting windows, a stirring human tide, voices and noises breaking the silence, an air of unconsciousness of beauty and interest, an old-world atmosphere; but there is a newer side, less attractive, the Place Broglie, crowded with Parisian cafés with all their tawdry paraphernalia, and prim white square houses, proud of their wretched uniform, like a row of charity-school children in England. Here is the fashionable centre, the lounging, gossiping dandyism and pretension of the modern world; but, thank Heaven! it is only an excrescence. Burn down this part, and the town would look as large and as important, for at every turn of more than two-thirds of the old area you are met by the living pictures that make these market-places, crooked streets and hidden chapels so familiar to the heart. The Ferkelmarkt, or "pig-market," though not in the most famous quarter of the town, is remarkable for its old gabled, galleried houses, while the view of the great spire of the cathedral is also good: not far, again, is a thirteenth-century house, with two stories in the gable and three below, besides the ground-floor, which is a shop; and even many of the common houses, not specially pointed out to the tourist, are beautified by some artistic ironwork about the doors, some carved gateway or window, some wall-niche with a saint's statue, or a broad oak staircase as noble in proportions and beautiful in detail as if it were in a princely abode. The absence of all meanness, of all vulgarity, of all shams, is what strikes one most in examining mediæval domestic architecture. Would we could go to school again in that regard! Just outside Strassburg we come upon a path leading through beech-woods upward toward rocky ledges and walls and a convent; not a ruined one this time, but a most frequented and friendly place, built on the top of a hill and presided over by a hospitable sisterhood. This is the scene of the life-history and legends of Saint Ottilia, and the spring for eye-diseases has been from time immemorial connected with her. The little chapel over the spring has the charm of small, unpretending, common places, where no show is made and no conventional admiration expected. Just as a speaker pauses here and there in his speech, expecting applause for such and such a popular phrase or striking sensationalism, so is our admiration as travelers regulated and bespoken beforehand. Here no man with any pretension to education dare pass in silence or let out a criticism: some things are sacred, like the tradition of the beauty of a faded society-queen. "What has been must always be." But what a relief to find some places you are not expected to go into ecstasies about! And they are generally worthy of more attention than they get, and if churches they are invariably more likely to move you to devotion. This has been my experience in Europe. The great pageants, gorgeous processions, etc. leave the soul cold, but an empty church, a sparsely-attended service, a lack of music, a quiet frame of mind, unstrained by rushing after this or that picture, this or that monument,—such are the things one remembers with thankfulness.

DOWN THE RHINE.

PART II.

"RHEIN-SCHNAKEN."

PAST the ruins of Madenburg, we follow the emperor Rudolph's road to Spires (German *Speyer*), whose cathedral is the Westminster Abbey of the German Empire. The tombs of emperors and empresses and their children— Swabians, Habsburgs, Nassaus—line the aisles of the cathedral, whose massive Romanesque style shows through the more elaborate, fanciful and somewhat disappointing restoration of Louis I. of Bavaria; for under his hands the old, grim, stately church has come to wear something of a modern look. But the historic recollections are many, and in St. Afra's chapel we recognize the spot where for five years lay the coffin of Henry IV., the vault where his forefathers slept being closed to his body by the ecclesiastical censures he had incurred after his forced reconciliation with his nobles and the Church.

And now comes the quick-flowing Neckar, rushing into the Rhine, and bidding us go a little up its course to where Heidelberg, its castle, its university, its active life and its beautiful past, make altogether a place that I should be inclined, from my own recollections, to call the pleasantest in Germany, and ical, boast of Bunsen and Vangerow, and speak proudly of "our" professors and of the last examinations. They do more than merely make money out of their show-city, as do the good-natured but slower-witted Munichers, but some enthusiastic Rhinelanders claim for this difference of temperament a reason not wholly æsthetic — *i. e.*, the influence of Rhine wine, transformed generation after generation into Rhine blood. The foreign traveler probably misses all these details, and for him Heidelberg is the student-city and the city of the most renowned ruin in Germany. He will find that all the beauty he has read of is real: the castle *is* all that has been said and sung of it, with its tower shattered and crumbling; its various façades, particularly the Friedrichsbau and that named after Emperor Otto Henry; its courtyard with pointed arches; its ivy-grown fountain; its elaborate Renaissance niches and

THE GREAT TUN, HEIDELBERG CASTLE.

which is certainly not one of the least important in the life that distinguishes Germany at this time. And what kind of impression does it make at first on a stranger? A German traveler says that it presented to him a marked contrast with Munich, where, although it is an art-centre, a sort of deadness to intellectual concerns characterizes all but the art-students and foreign visitors. Even the Heidelberg porters are lively and crit- armor-clad statues; its modern loungers sitting over their Rhine wine in chairs that English collectors would give three or four guineas apiece for; its tangle of flowers and bushes; its crimson flush when English tourists spend their money in illuminating it with Bengal lights; its adjacent gardens, where a nearly perfect band plays classical music to critics who are none the less discerning because they look lost in tobacco-smoke and beer-fumes; its background of Spanish chestnut woods, where I saw the pale-green tassels of the blossoms still hanging among the broad leaves that had just reached their summer depth of color, and where wild legends place a "Devil's Den" and a Wolf Spring, a brook where a wolf is said to have torn to pieces the enchantress Zetta;—above all, its matchless view sheer down a wall of rock into the rushing Neckar flood, over the vast plain beyond, and over a wilderness of steep roofs of thirteenth- and fourteenth-century houses. All this is but a faint description of the impression Heidelberg leaves on the mind. It would be leaving out an important "sight" not to mention the famous "tun," still stored, but empty, in the cellars of the castle, and the little guardian of the treasure, the gnome carved in wood, whose prototype was the court-fool of one of the Nassau sovereigns, and whose allowance was no less than fifteen bottles a day.

But the place has other interests, which even the donkey-riders, whom the natives portray as rather eccentric in dress and behavior, must appreciate. The high school, which has survived all the desolations and wrecks of the Thirty Years' war and the still more cruel French war under Louis XIV. and his marshal Turenne, dates as far back as 1386, and the university into which it has grown has been since the beginning of this century the cause of the upward growth and prosperous restoration of the town. The German student-life has been as much described, though perhaps never so truly, as the life of the Western frontiers and prairies, and I will give but one glimpse, because it is all I know of it, though that glimpse is probably but the outcome of

THE SHATTERED TOWER, HEIDELBERG.

an exceptional phase of student-life. The person who described the scene and saw it himself is trustworthy. He had been living some months at Heidelberg, on the steep slope leading up to the castle (the short cut), and one night, on looking out of his window, he saw the glare of torches in a courtyard below, several houses, perhaps even streets, off, for the town is built on various levels up the rock. Here were several groups of young men, evidently students, dancing in rings and holding torches, and the scene looked wild and strange and somewhat incomprehensible. Next day the spectator found out that this was the peculiar celebration of a death by a club whose rules were perhaps unique. It was an inner sanctum of the ordinary student associations, something beyond the common dueling brotherhoods, more advanced and more reckless — a club in which, if any member quarreled with another, instead of settling the matter by a duel, the rivals drew lots to settle who should commit suicide. This had happened a day or so before, and a young man, instead of standing up as usual to be made passes at with a sword that would at most gash his cheek or split his nose, had shot himself through the head. Even in that not too particular community great horror prevailed, and the youth was denied Christian burial; so that his father had to come and take away the body in secret to convey it to his own home. This heathenish death led to an equally heathenish after-carousal, the torchlight dance winding up the whole, not perhaps inappropriately.

Heidelberg has a little Versailles of its own, a prim contrast to its noble chestnut-groves, yet not an unlovely spot — the garden of Schwetzingen, where clipped alleys and *rococo* stonework make frames for masses of brilliant-colored flowers; but from here we must skim over the rest of the neighborhood — gay, spick-and-span Mannheim, busy Ludwigshafen and picturesque, ruin-crowned Neckarsteinach, where, if it is autumn, we catch glimpses of certain vintage-festivals, the German form of thanksgiving and harvest home. But of this we shall see more as we journey downward and reach the far-famed Johannisberg and Rüdesheim. Still, we cannot forget the vineyard feature of Rhine and Neckar and Moselle scenery, for it follows us even from the shores of the Lake of Constance, and the wine keeps getting more and more famous, and the wine-industry and all its attendant trades more important, as we go on. The ruins of monasteries are sprinkled among the vine-terraces, for the monks were the earliest owners, introducers and cultivators of the grape — greatly to their credit at first, for it was a means of weaning the Christianized barbarians from hunting to tilling the earth, though in later years there grew terrible abuses out of this so-called "poetic" industry. If I were not pledged to eschew moralizing, I should like to have my say here about the nonsense written from time immemorial about "wine, woman and song" — rather worse than nonsense, because degrading to both the latter — but in speaking of the Rhine one cannot but glance at its chief trade, though one *can* refrain from rhapsodies about either the grape or the juice. The fact is, the former is really not lovely, and the artificial terraces of slaty débris, the right soil and the right exposure for the crop, are indeed quite unsightly. The *beauty* of the vine is far better seen, and is indeed ideal, in Southern Italy, where the grapes hang from luxuriant festoons, cordages of fruit swinging like hammocks from young poplars, and sometimes young fruit trees, while beneath grow corn and wheat. The wine, I believe, is mediocre — and so much the better — but the picture is beautiful. In Northern Italy the thrifty, practical German plan is in vogue, and the ideal beauty of vines is lost. But where is the vine loveliest to my mind? Out in the forests, where it grows wild, useless and luxuriant, as I have seen it in America, the loveliest creeper that temperate climes possess — a garden and a bower in itself.

Following the course of the Neckar, and broadening for forty miles before reaching the Rhine, lies the Odenwald, the "Paradise of Germany" — a land of legends, mountains and forests, whose

PILGRIMS ON THE CASTLE HILL.

very name is still a riddle which some gladly solve by calling the land "Odin's Wood," his refuge when Christianity dis- placed him. Here, under the solemn beeches, the most beautiful tree of the Northern forests, with smooth, gray, column-like trunk and leaves that seem the very perfection of color and texture, lie the mottled deer, screened by those rocks that are called the waves of a "rock ocean," and lazily gazing at the giant trunk of a tree that for many years has lain encrusted in the earth till as many legends have accumulated round it as mosses have grown over it—a tree that California might not disown, and which is variously supposed to have been part of a Druidical temple or part of an intended imperial palace in the Middle Ages. But as we climb up Mount Melibocus, and look around from the Taunus to the Vosges, and from Speyer to Worms and golden Mayence, we see a ruined castle, that of Rodenstein, with a more human interest in its legend of a rival Wild Huntsman, whose bewitched hounds and horns were often heard in the neighborhood, and always before some disaster, chiefly a war, either national or local. This huntsman wore the form of a black dog in the daytime, and was the savage guardian of three enchanted sisters, the youngest and loveliest of whom once tried to break the spell by offering her love, her hand and her wealth to a young knight, provided he could, next time he saw her, *in the form of a snake*, bear her kiss three times upon his lips. He failed, however, when the ordeal came, and as the serpent-maiden wound her cold coils around him and darted out her forked tongue, he threw back his head and cried in an agony of fear, "Lord Jesus, help me!" The snake disappeared: love and gold were lost to the youth and freedom to the still spellbound woman. The legend goes no further, unless, like that of the ruined castle of Auerbach, it hints at the present existence of the forlorn enchanted maidens, yet waiting for a deliverer; for at Auerbach the saying is that in the ruins dwells a meadow-maiden whose fate it is to wait until a child rocked in a cradle made of the wood of a cherry tree that must have grown on the meadow where she was first mysteriously found, came himself to break her invisible bonds; and so every good German (and not seldom the stranger) that visits Schloss Auerbach does so with a pious intention of delivering the maiden in case he himself may unawares have been rocked in a cradle made of the wonder-working cherry-wood. If the reader is not tired of legends, this neighborhood affords him still another, though a less marvelous one, of a young girl of the noble Sickingen stock who lost herself in a great wood, and who, after being searched for in vain, was guided homeward late at night by the sound of the convent-bell of St. Gall's (not the famous monastery of that name); in thanksgiving for which the family offered for all coming ages a weekly batch of wheaten loaves to be distributed among the poor of the parish, and also made it customary to ring the great bell every night at eleven o'clock, in remembrance of the event, and likewise as an ear-beacon to any benighted traveler who might happen to be in the neighborhood.

At Ladenburg we pass one of those churchyards that are getting familiar to us at this stage of Rhine-journeying, full of crosses and crucifixes with quaint little roofs over them; and at Weinheim we come upon as antiquated a spot as any that exists in our day, a wilderness of old houses, each one of which is worth a detailed picture; then at Unterlandenbach we find the most famous of the Bergstrasse wines; and hurrying through modern Darmstadt, with its Munich-rivaling theatre, museum and galleries, and its heart-core of old houses smothered among "classicalities" in white plaster, we come to the old episcopal city of Worms, where no beautiful scenery distracts the mind from the mighty human recollections of Luther and the Diet and the first strong symptoms of life in the Reformation. The Jews' burial-place, however, brings to mind the one-sidedness of the freedom of conscience proclaimed by the Reformers, who could be as intolerant as their forerunners, the powerful bishops of Worms and the persecutors of the Jews in the Middle Ages, as the Lutherans were in the days of the Renaissance. The massive Roman character of the cathedral is mingled with something airier and more Gothic, but still remains

FRIEDRICHSBAU (OR FREDERICK'S BUILDING), HEIDELBERG CASTLE.

chiefly a model of the basilica style, with its low, strong round arches, and grafted on these the later, yet not mediæval, figures of distorted, dwarfed, monstrous animal forms, supposed to represent the demons of heathendom conquered by, and groaning in vain under the yoke of, the Christian Church. But no amount of vague description will bring before the mind's eye these great cathedrals, whereas slighter and lesser subjects are easily made lifelike with the pen ; so, passing by the fountains, the market-places, the ancient fortifications and the splendid modern monument of Luther surrounded by his brother Reformers and their supposed predecessors (altogether, a rather fanciful and motley grouping, morally speaking), we come to the everyday life of the city of to-day. It is strange how many of these old German towns are "resuscitated" (I wish I could find a better word for the meaning), having been wholly crushed in the terrible French war under Louis XIV., and having slowly sunk into a seemingly hopeless state of stagnation, and yet within the last fifty years having gathered up their fragments anew and started into life again. Commerce, railways, etc. had much to do with this new lease of life, but intellectual progress has had almost as large a part in this new birth of the dead cities. Learning grew popular—what a significant difference there is between this fact and that of learning growing *fashionable!*—and men awoke to the need as well as the glory of knowledge—a weapon which, far more than the sword, quietly prepared Germany for the onward stride she has now taken. If the mental progress had not been going on so steadily for so many years, the late political triumphs could not have happened.

The old dominions of Worms had the poetic name of *Wonnegau*, or the "Land of Delight;" and since the flat, sedgy meadows and sandy soil did not warrant this name, it was no doubt given on account of the same ample, pleasant family-life and generous hospitality that distinguishes the citizens of Worms to this day. There were—and are—merchant-princes in Germany as well as in Genoa, Venice, Bruges, Antwerp and London of old, and though life is even now simpler among them than among their peers of other more sophisticated lands, still it is a princely life. The houses of Worms are stately and dignified, curtained with grapevines and shaded by lindens : the table seems always spread, and there is an air of leisure and rest which we seldom see in an American house, however rich its master. The young girls are robust and active, but not awkward, nor is the house-mother the drudge that some superfine and superficial English observers have declared her to be. We have begun to set up another standard of woman's place in a household than the beautiful, dignified Hebrew one, and even the mediæval one of the times whence we vainly think we have drawn our new version of chivalry toward womankind. But in many places, even in the "three kingdoms," the old ideal still holds its place, and in the Western Highlands the ladies of the house, unless demoralized by English boarding-school vulgarities, serve the guest at table with all the grace and delicacy that other women have lost since they have deputed all hospitality save that of pretty, meaningless speeches to servants. In Norway and Sweden the old hospitable, frank customs still prevail, and in all simplicity your hostess, young or old, insists on doing much of your "valeting;" and while we need not imitate anything that does not " come natural " to us, we should surely refrain from laughing at and stigmatizing as barbaric any social customs less artificial than our own. And indeed Germany is blest in the matter of good housekeepers, who are no less good wives, and especially discerning, wise and sympathizing mothers. A few of the lately-translated German novels show us the most delightful and refined scenes of German home-life, and now and then, though seldom, a stranger has a glimpse of some of these German homes, whether rich or not, but generally not only comfortable, but cultured. To some English minds—and we fear also to some American ones—of the "hot-house" order there is something absolutely incompatible between

THE COURTYARD, HEIDELBERG CASTLE.

grace and work, study and domestic details; but, letting practical Germany alone, have they ever read Eugénie de Guérin's life and journal, to admire which is almost as much a "hall-mark" of culture as to enjoy Walter Scott and appreciate Shakespeare? And if they have, do they not remember how the young housekeeper sits in the kitchen watching the baking and roasting, and reading Plutarch in the intervals? And do they not remember her washing-days? Every thrifty housewife is not an Eugénie de Guérin, but that any absolute incongruity exists between housework and brainwork is a notion which thousands of well-educated women in all countries must, from experience, emphatically deny.

Nor is elegance banished from these German homes: if there are libraries and museums within those walls, there are also drawing-rooms full of knick-knacks, and bed-rooms furnished with inlaid foreign woods and graceful contrivances covered by ample curtains, pretty beds shaped cradlewise, devoid of the angles we seem to find so indispensable to a bed, and corner closets fluted inside with silk or chintz and ornamented with airy vallances or bowed-out gilt rods. Glass doors leading into small, choicely-stocked conservatories are not uncommon, or even that crowning device of artistic luxury, an immense window of one undivided sheet of plate-glass, looking toward some beautiful view, and thus making a frame for it. All this sounds French, does it not? but Aix and Cologne and Mayence and Frankfort and Bremen are genuine German cities, and it is in the burgher houses that you find all this. Even very superficial observers have noticed the general air of health, prosperity and comeliness of the people. Washington Irving, who traveled in the Rhineland fifty-five years ago, when critical inquiry into home-life was not yet the fashion for tourists, speaks in his letters of the peasantry of the Bergstrasse being "remarkably well off," of their "comfortable villages buried in orchards and surrounded by vineyards," of the "country-people, healthy, well-clad, good-looking and cheerful." Once again he speaks of the comeliness of the Rhine peasants, "particularly on the lower part of the Rhine, from Mayence downward," and elsewhere of the cottages as so surrounded by garden and grass-plat, so buried in trees, and the moss-covered roofs almost mingling and blending with the surrounding vegetation, that the whole landscape is completely rustic. "The orchards were all in blossom, and as the day was very warm the good people were seated in the shade of the trees, spinning near the rills of water that trickled along the green sward." This, however, was in Saxony, where the landscape reminded him much of English scenery. Then of the higher middle classes, the bankers of Frankfort, he speaks as cultured, enlightened, hospitable, magnificent in their "palaces, . . . continually increasing." And these are but cursory pencilings, for everywhere he was rather on the watch for the antique than mindful of human and progressive peculiarities.

Mayence, by the bye (or *Mainz*, as it is in the mother-tongue), was once called the "golden," partly for its actual wealth of old, partly for its agricultural and vineyard riches, and partly as the centre of an immense river-trade that enriched every city on the Rhine, from Worms to Cologne especially. Here the archbishops reigned paramount sovereigns, and here were fought many hard battles between what called itself the Church and the people. Mayence once cut itself off for several years from all Christian services, and held its spiritual sovereign at bay, though now its religious spirit is undeniable; but then how much have the representatives of the Church changed! To-day they are humble, poor and accessible to all: then they were haughty, warlike, despotic and rich. To-day, they are wellnigh persecuted, and the hearts of the people generously turn to them, and if principle and policy can ever be said to go together, it is so in this case. But let the circumstances be reversed: I wonder would the lesson be remembered? Here, where Archbishop Willigis in the tenth century persecuted the Jews, and made up to the city for it by building the grand St. Stephen's and the earliest part of the cathedral; here, where terrific invasions of barbarians and massacres of Christians gave color to the legends that ascribe the foundation of the city to a Trojan hero, Moguntius, or to an exiled wizard of Trèves, fourteen hundred years *before* the Christian era; here, where ecclesiastical quarrels and popular tumults were things of daily occurrence, and where one of the best minnesingers, Henry, count of Meissen, surnamed *Frauenlob*, or "Ladies' Praise," was carried to his grave in the cathedral by twelve maidens of the town,—there stirs to-day a spirited though commonplace life, the link of which with the old life lies in the invention commemorated by Gutenberg's monument, one of Thorwaldsen's best works. Old and new jostle each other in our bewildered minds. There are drawbridges, towers and gates still to be seen; the old city is a future important military dépôt; the Carnival scenes merrily take us back to the costume if not the manners of the Middle Ages; and some of the old *Meenzer* dialect is still preserved among the quaint knitting-women with frilled caps and ungainly baskets who drive a small trade in stout stockings for the country-people as they jog in to market. Then we pass St. Alban's church, where Charlemagne's wife Fastrada is buried, and where her husband drew from her dead finger an enchanted ring which he was glad afterward to throw into the moat at his castle of Nieder-Ingelheim; and here now is a procession coming out of the church, and the people devoutly following, all chanting the solid old hymns, hundreds of years old, which are still the musical A, B, C of every German child. How different to what *we* call hymn-singing! The Rhineland is intensely Catholic in this neighborhood, and since the unwise "Falk laws" many who were before indifferent have rallied to their childhood's faith and stood forth as its fiercest champions. Perhaps just now you would not meet a procession, but a few years ago they were common in the streets of Mayence. The cathedral, spite of all political drawbacks, is being carefully restored, and the choir, which I remember as especially fine, is looked upon as a triumph of reverent and congruous restoration.

On the shores of the river we come upon purely modern life again—the ho-

AN ALLEY IN THE GARDEN OF SCHWETZINGEN.

tels, the quays, the tourists, the steamers, and the *Rhein-schnaken*, a species of "loafer" or gossip who make themselves useful to passengers when the boats come in. These are often seen also at Biebrich, the old palace of the Nassaus, now become the property of the city, and partly a military school, while the gardens have become the fashionable promenade of Mayence. The formal alleys and well-kept lawns, with the distant view of the Taunus and the Odenwald on one side, and a glimpse of the opening Rheingau, a famous gorge of the Rhine, on the other, make it a beautiful resort indeed, exclusive of the interest which the supposed derivation of its name gives it—*i. e.*, the "place of beavers," an animal that abounded there before man invaded these shores. And now the eye can follow the course of the Rhine (from the roof of the palace) as far as Ingelheim, Ehrenfels, the Mouse Tower, Johannisberg and Rüdesheim, and vineyards climb up the rocks and fight their way into the sunshine; and we begin to feel that these little shrines we sometimes come across, and huts of vineyard-keepers, and queerly-shaped baskets like some of the Scotch fish "creels," all force on our attention the fact that the growing and making and selling of wine are the most characteristic features of Rhine-life, at least outside the cities. Though the vineyards are not as picturesque as poets insist on making them, yet the vintage-season is full of picturesque incidents. This is a "movable festival," and occurs any time between the beginning of September and the middle of November. What applies to one district does not to another, and there are a thousand minute differences occasioned by soil, weather and custom; so that none of the following observations is to be taken as a generalization. At the outset it is worth notice that the German word *Weinberg* ("Wine-hill") is much more correct than our equivalent, for even in the flatter countries where the grape is grown the most is made of every little rise in the ground. The writer

CATHEDRAL OF WORMS.

of a recent magazine article has exploded the commonly-received idea that in the United States alone more Rhine wine is drunk than the whole Rhine wine-region really produces. The truth is, that it is a problem how to get rid of all that is made. The wine is drunk new by every one in the neighborhood, and sells at prices within the means of all; and this because there are vineyards by the hundred whose exposure does not fit them for the production of the fine wines eagerly bought by foreign merchants, and also because many of the small wine-

LUTHER'S MONUMENT AT WORMS.

growers have no means of getting their wares to the right market. The great traffic is confined chiefly to wholesale growers, rich men who can tide over half a score of bad years and afford to sell the whole crop of those years for next to nothing; and *their* wine it is which with us represents the whole Rhine vintage. It is, however, hardly more than a third, and the rest of the wine made on the Rhine is to the untutored taste just as good and just as pleasant. It is said by connoisseurs that all the difference between the wine of good and bad years is in its "bouquet," and the juice of the same grapes brings four dollars and a half a gallon *at the vineyard* one year and can be bought in another year for twenty cents. The wine-trade has developed an odd profession, that of wine-taster, and these skillful critics command high wages and great consideration. But of course each locality has its own knot of oracles, and the ludicrous gravity with which these village "tasters" decide on the merits of mine host's purchases—or perhaps growths—is a subject not unworthy the pencil of Ostade, Teniers or Hogarth. The parish priest is not the least learned among these local connoisseurs, and one or two official personages generally form, with him, the jury that decides on the worth of the year's crop. Professional buyers and commissioners from German and foreign firms crowd to the markets where the wine is sold, and after being open to inspection for a week the crop of each grower is generally sold in a lump to some one firm, probably an old customer, for a sum that sounds fabulous; but then the bad years, when just as much expense is lavished on the vines and no returns bring the growers a reward, have to be considered as a counterweight. Of course there is a monstrous deal of "doctoring," and even the purest of the wines are not as they came from Nature's hand; but in the bad years it is notorious that fortunes are made out of wine sold for a few cents a gallon and exported at a profit of a hundred per cent. Thence, perhaps, comes the byword about our drinking more wine than the vineyards produce.

But, leaving the commercial aspect of the trade, let us take a glance at the picturesque side. Like the fisheries, this business, that looks commonplace in cellars and vaults, has its roots in free, open-air life, and is connected with quaint historical details and present customs hardly less novel to us. The aspect of the country in autumn, as described in a letter written last year, is lovely—"the exuberant quantity of fine fruit; . . . the roads bordered by orchards of apples and pears, where the trees are so loaded that the branches have to be supported by stakes lest they should break; . . . men, women and children busy in the vineyards on the sides of the hills; the road alive with peasants laden with baskets of fruit or tubs in which the grapes were pressed. Some were pressing the grapes in great tubs or vats on the roadside. In the afternoon there were continual firing of guns and shouting of the peasants on the vine-hills, making merry after their labor, for the vintage is the season when labor and jollity go hand in hand. We bought clusters of delicious grapes for almost nothing, and I drank of the newly-pressed wine, which has the sweetness of new cider. . . . Every now and then we passed wagons bearing great pipes of new wine, with bunches of flowers and streamers of ribbons stuck in the bung." The last cask of the vintage is always honored by a sort of procession—Bacchanalia, an artist might call it—the three or four youngest and prettiest girls mounted on it in a wagon, their heads crowned with grapes and leaves and a heap of fruit in their laps. The men lead the horses slowly home, stopping often to drink or offer to others the new wine, and brandishing aloft their clubs for beating the fruit with; the children run alongside with armfuls of the fruit, and their faces stained all over with the juice, while in some nook, perhaps a stone arbor trellised with vines, sits the portly, jolly owner, with his long-jointed pipe, an incarnation of a German Bacchus, smiling at the pretty maidens, who pelt him with his own grapes. But before the season a very different scene takes place in the "locked" vineyards, closed by law even to their owners, and where at night no one but a lonely watchman, with gun loaded and wolfish dog at his heels, sits in a little straw-thatched, tent-shaped hut to ward off thieves and intruders. When the vineyards are declared open, the best policy is to get in the harvest at once, unless you are rich enough to have your crops carefully watched every hour for a week, when the grapes will certainly be better and the wine more precious. For it is a custom that after the opening, but as long as the vintage is not actually begun in any vineyard, the grapes are free to visitors. The guests of the owner are privileged to pluck and eat all through the vintage; but again custom ordains that if you eat only half a plucked cluster, you should hang the remainder on the trellis, that it may not be trodden under foot and wasted. Donkeys and women carrying those odd, heavy baskets that decorate the cottages convey the grapes to the pressing-vats in endless and recrossing processions, and not one grape that has been plucked is left on the ground till the morrow: all must be stowed away the same day before dusk. The vintage-days themselves are busy, and the hot and tired workers would wonder to see poets and painters weave their hard labor into pictures and sonnets. But the opening day, as well as the closing one, is a festival, often a religious one, and a procession winds its way where laden animals tread all the rest of the week. A sermon is generally preached, and after the ceremony is over the day becomes a kind of holiday and picnic affair. Groups of workers during the vintage sit on the hot slate terraces, shrinking close to the walls for the sake of a coolness that hardly exists save underground in the wide, gloomy catacombs that undermine the hillside; and these caverns, filled with great casks, are not the least curious sight of the Rhine wine-regions. Above ground, you come on little shrines and stone crosses embowered in fruit, the frame of the sorry picture far more beautiful than the picture itself, yet that daub means *so* much to the simple, devout peasant who kneels or rests under it! The process of picking and pressing is simple and quick. The grapes are picked from the stalks and dropped into little tubs, then shaken out into baskets with a quick double movement, and pressed with "juice-clubs" on the spot, whereupon the load is quickly carried off (sometimes carted in large casks) to the great wine-presses in the building provided for this purpose. There is an overseer to each group of workers, who regulates the rate and quantity of fruit to be thrown at once into the first tubs, and who takes note of the whole day's harvest, which is reckoned by the basketful When we come to the far-famed Johannisberg vineyards, whose origin lies back in the tenth century, when Abbot Rabanus cultivated these hillsides that are now partly the property of some of the Metternich family, we learn the value of these basket-

MAYENCE KNITTING-WOMEN.

fuls, each containing what goes to make a gallon; which quantity will fill four bottles, at eight thalers the bottle among friends who take no percentage and give you the pure juice. After that, does any one suppose that he gets Johannisberg, Steinberg or Rüdesheim, or Brauneberg and Bernkasteler Doctor, two of the best Moselle wines, when he pays two or three dollars a bottle for this so-called wine in a restaurant? Better call for what the restaurant-keeper would protest was not worth buying, but which the real connoisseur would agree with the Rhine peasantry in drinking and enjoying—the new, undoctored wine that is kept in the wood and drawn as the needs of customers require.

One of the prettiest vintage-sights is the feast of St. Roch, held yearly near Bingen in the Rheingau, on the grounds of the Villa Landy, now belonging to Herr Braun. St. Roch is here considered the patron of the wine-industry, and the festival is held on the Sunday following the 16th of August, the day of the restoration of the old chapel. Against the exterior eastern wall is put up a temporary pulpit; the hill is clothed with white tents gayly decked with leaves, grapes, flowers and ribbons; refreshments are sold; all the bells of the neighborhood peal and jingle; the country-folk in costume come up in merry groups or in devout processions with their parish clergy, school banners and crosses, singing hymns or reciting the rosary, and after the sermon and prayers scattering through the vineyards and spending the day in what we will hope is no worse a manner than appears to the artist eye.

There is one peculiarity about the Rüdesheim vintage-season—its lateness. It begins about the 3d of November, sometimes a little earlier, but still later than most others. Two years ago it took place in this way, after a fortnight's steady fog and weather more like that of a wild northern sea-coast than of the "sunny" Rhine. But this gray, damp air was the very thing wanted, for it slowly rots the grapes and produces from this corruption the most delicious wine. It is said that this Rüdesheim custom of a late vintage is due to a fortunate fit of forgetfulness of the abbot of Fulda, who once neglected to give the necessary permission to open the Johannisberg vineyards, and did not remedy his mistake till early in November, when the despairing vine-dressers fancied the crop wholly spoilt; but another version tells us that it once happened that the vintage was delayed through the circumstances of a war that laid waste most of the neighborhood and claimed the service of every able-bodied man, so that the vine-growers in disgust sold the crop for a mere nothing, and found out afterward what a prize they had let slip through their fingers. It is said to be for the sake of producing this rottenness in the grape before gathering it that in some Greek and Armenian vineyards the vines are sometimes pinned down to the hot earth and allowed to creep like ivy over the soil. So at Rüdesheim the vintage went on in glee and high expectations, in contrast to the sullen sky and clinging mist, while the foggy nights were disturbed by blazing fires, continuous shots and hymns of joy and jollity sung by the home-going workers.

DOWN THE RHINE.

PART III.

EVENING CONCERT AT WIESBADEN.

WIESBADEN (the "Meadow-Bath"), though an inland town, partakes of some of the Rhine characteristics, though even if it did not, its notoriety as a spa would be enough to make some mention of it necessary. Its promenade and Kurhaus, its society, evening concerts, alleys of beautiful plane trees, its frequent illuminations with Bengal lights, reddening the classic peristyles and fountains with which modern taste has decked the town, its airy Moorish pavilion over the springs, and its beautiful Greek chapel with fire-gilt domes, each surmounted by a double cross connected with the dome by gilt chains—a chapel built by the duke Adolph of Nassau in memory of his wife, Elizabeth Michaelovna, a Russian princess,—are things that almost every American traveler remembers, not to mention the Neroberger wine grown in the neighborhood.

Schlangenbad, a less well-known bathing-place, is a favorite goal of Wiesbaden excursionists, for a path through dense beech woods leads from the stirring town to the quieter "woman's republic," where, before sovereigns in incognito came to patronize it, there had long been a monopoly of its charms by the wives and daughters of rich men, bankers, councilors, noblemen, etc., and also by a set of the higher clergy. The waters were famous for their sedative qualities, building up the nervous system, and, it is said, also beautifying the skin. Some credulous persons traced the name of the "Serpents' Bath" to the fact that snakes lurked in the springs and gave the waters their healing powers; but as the neighborhood abounds in a small harmless kind of reptile, this is the more obvious reason for the name. I spent a pleasant ten days at Schlangenbad twelve or thirteen years ago, when many of the German sovereigns preferred it for its quiet to the larger and noisier resorts, and remember with special pleasure meeting with fields of Scotch heather encircled by beech and chestnut woods, with ferny, rocky nooks such as —when it is in Germany that you find them—suggest fairies, and with a curious village church, just restored by a rich English Catholic, since dead, who lived in Brussels and devoted his fortune to religious purposes all over the world. This church was chiefly interesting as a specimen of what country churches were in the Middle Ages, having been restored in the style common to those days. It was entirely of stone, within as well as without, and I remember no painting on the walls. The "tabernacle," instead of being placed on the altar, as is the custom in most churches now, and has been for two or three hundred years, was, according to the old German custom, a separate shrine, with a little tapering carved spire, placed in the corner of the choir, with a red lamp burning before it. Here, as in most of the Rhine neighborhoods, the people are mainly Catholics, but in places where summer guests of all nations and religions are gathered there is often a friendly arrangement by which the same building is used for the services of two or three faiths. There was, I think, one such at Schlangenbad, where Catholic, Lutheran and Anglican services were successively held every Sunday morning; and in another place, where a large Catholic church has since been built, the old church was divided down the middle of the nave by a wooden partition about the height of a man's head, and Catholic and Protestant had each a side permanently assigned to them for their services. This kind of practical toleration, probably in the beginning the result of poverty on both sides, but at any rate creditable to its practicers, was hardly to be found anywhere outside of Germany. I remember hearing of the sisters of one of the pope's German prelates, Monsignor Prince Hohenlohe, who were Lutherans, embroidering ecclesiastical vestments and altar-linen for their brother with as much delight as if he and they believed alike; and (though this is anything but praiseworthy, for it was prompted by policy and not by toleration) it was a custom of the smaller German princes to bring their daughters up in the vaguest belief in vital truths, in order that when they married they might become whatever their husbands happened to be, whether Lutheran, Anglican, Catholic or Greek. The events of the last few years, however, have changed all this, and religious strife is as energetic in Germany as it was at one time in Italy: people must take sides, and this outward, easy-going old life has disappeared before the novel kind of persecution sanctioned by the Falk laws. Some persons even think the present state of things traceable to that same toleration, leading, as it did in many cases, to lukewarmness

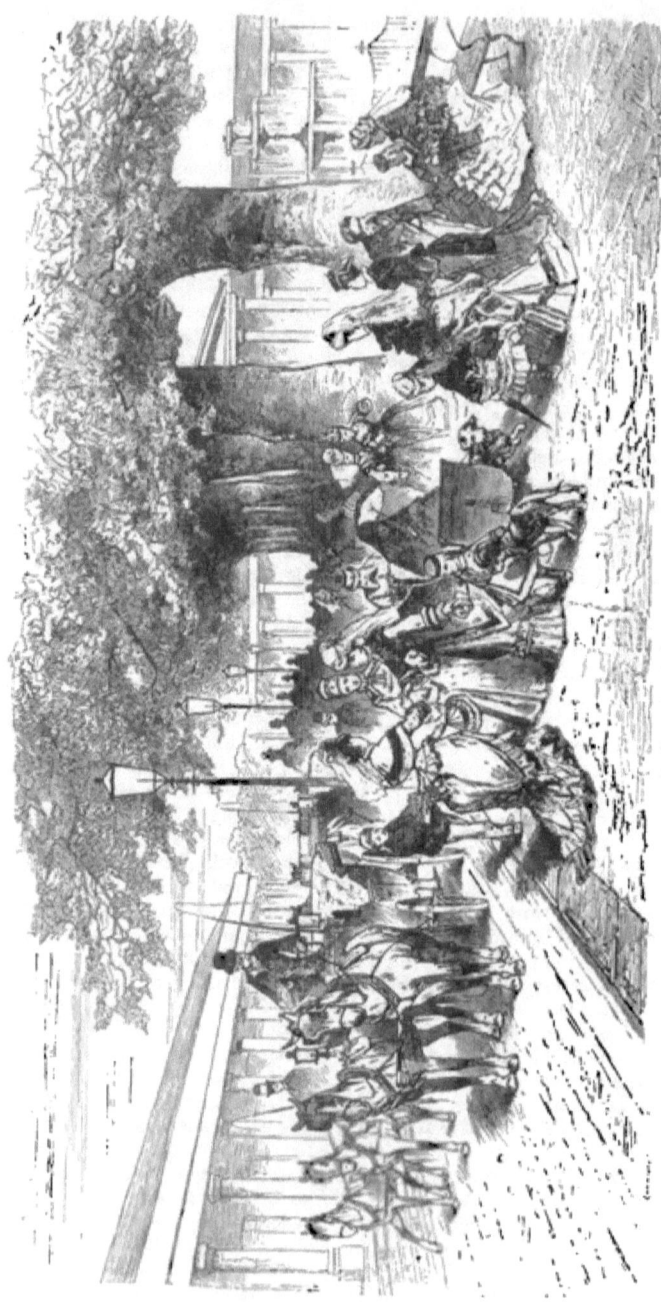

PROMENADE AT WIESBADEN.

and indifferentism in religion. Strange phases for a fanatical Germany to pass through, and a stranger commentary on the words of Saint Remigius to Clovis, the first Frankish Christian king: "Burn that which thou hast worshiped, and worship that which thou hast burnt"!

Schwalbach is another of Wiesbaden's

LUTHER'S HOUSE AT FRANKFORT.

handmaidens — a pleasant, rather quiet spot, from which, if you please, you can follow the Main to the abode of sparkling hock or the vinehills of Hochheim, the property of the church which crowns the heights. This is at the entrance of the Roman-named Taunus Mountains, where there are bathing-places, ruined castles, ancient bridges, plenty of legends, and, above all, dark solemn old chestnut forests. But we have a long way to go, and must not linger on our road to the free imperial city of Frankfort, with its past history and present importance. Here too I have some personal remembrances, though hurried ones. The hotel itself — what a relief such hotels are from the modern ones with electric bells and elevators and fifteen stories! — was an old patrician house ample, roomy, dignified, and each room had some individuality, notwithstanding the needful amount of transformation from its old self. It was a dull, wet day when we arrived, and next morning we went to the cathedral, Pepin's foundation, of which I remember, however, less than of the great hall in the Römer building where the Diets sat and where the "Golden Bull" is still kept — a hall now magnificently and appropriately frescoed with subjects from German history. Then the far-famed Judengasse, a street where the first Rothschild's mother lived till within a score of years ago, and where now, among the dark, crazy tenements, so delightful to the artist's eye, there glitters one of the most gorgeously-adorned synagogues in Europe. A change indeed from the times when Jews were hunted and hooted at in these proud, fanatical cities, which were not above robbing them and making use of them even while they jeered and persecuted! The great place in front of the emperor's hall was the appointed ground for tournaments, and as we lounge on we come to a queer house, with its lowest corner cut away and the oriel window above supported on one massive pillar: from that window tradition says that Luther addressed the people just before starting for Worms to meet the Diet. This other house has a more modern look: it is Goethe's birthplace, the house where the noted housekeeper and accomplished hostess, "*Frau Rath*"—or "Madam Councilor," as she was called—gathered round her those stately parties that are special to the great free cities of olden trade. Frankfort has not lost her reputation in this line: her merchants and civic functionaries still form an aristocracy, callings as well as fortunes are hereditary, and if some modern elements have crept in, they have not yet superseded the old. The regattas and boating-parties on the Main remind one of the stir on the banks of the Thames between Richmond and Twickenham, where so many "city men" have lovely retired homes; but Frankfort has its Kew Gardens also, where tropical flora, tree-ferns and palms, in immense conservatories, make perpetual summer, while the Zoological Garden and the bands that play there are another point of attraction. Still, I think one more willingly seeks the older parts—the Ash-tree Gate, with its machicolated tower and turrets, the only remnants of the fortifications; the old cemetery, where Goethe's mother is buried; and the old bridge over the Main, with the statue of Charlemagne bearing the globe of empire in his hand, which an innocent countryman from the neighboring village of Sachsenhausen mistook for the man who invented the *Aeppelwei*, a favorite drink of Frankfort. This bridge has another curiosity—a gilt cock on an iron rod, commemorating the usual legend of the "first living thing" sent across to cheat the devil, who had extorted such a promise from the architect. But although the ancient remains are attractive, we must not forget the Bethmann Museum, with its treasure of Dannecker's *Ariadne*, and the Städel Art Institute, both the legacies of public-spirited merchants to their native town; the Bourse, where a business hardly second to any in London is done; and the memory of so many great minds of modern times—Börne, Brentano, Bettina von Arnim, Feurbach, Savigny, Schlossen, etc. The Roman remains at Ober-

JOHN WOLFGANG GOETHE.

ürzel in the neighborhood ought to have a chapter to themselves, forming as they do a miniature Pompeii, but the Rhine and its best scenery calls us away from its great tributary, and we already begin to feel the witchery which a popular poet has expressed in these lines, supposed to be a warning from a father to a wandering son:

To the Rhine, to the Rhine! go not to the Rhine!
  My son, I counsel thee well;
For there life is too sweet and too fine, and every
  breath is a spell.

The nixie calls to thee out of the flood; and if thou
  her smiles shouldst see,
And the Lorelei, with her pale cold lips, then 'tis all
  over with thee:

For bewitched and delighted, yet seized with fear,
Thy home is forgotten and mourners weep here.

This is the Rheingau, the most beautiful valley of rocks and bed of rapids which occurs during the whole course of the river—the region most crowded with legends and castles, and most frequented by strangers by railroad and steamboat. The right bank is at first the only one that calls for attention, dotted as it is with townlets, each nestled in orchards, gardens and vineyards, with a church and steeple, and terraces of odd, overhanging houses; little stone arbors trellised with grapevines; great crosses and statues of patron saints in the warm, soft-

GOETHE'S BIRTHPLACE.

toned red sandstone of the country; fishermen's taverns, with most of the business done outside under the trees or vine-covered piazza; little, busy wharfs and works, aping joyfully the bustle of large seaports, and succeeding in miniature; and perhaps a burgomaster's garden, where that portly and pleasant functionary does not disdain to keep a tavern and serve his customers himself, as at Walluf.

At Rauenthal (a "valley" placed on high hills) we find the last new claimant to the supremacy among Rhine wines, at least since the Paris Exhibition, when the medal of honor was awarded to Rauenthal, which has ended in bringing many hundreds of curious

JUDENGASSE AT FRANKFORT.

connoisseurs to test the merits of the grape where it grows. Now comes a whole host of villages on either side of the river, famous through their wines— Steinberg, the "golden beaker;" Scharfenstein, whose namesake castle was the refuge of the warlike archbishops of Mayence, the stumbling-block of the archbishops of Trèves, called "the Lion of Luxembourg," and lastly the prey of the terrible Swedes, who in German stories play the part of Cossacks and Bashi-Bazouks; Marcobrunnen, with its classical-looking ruin of a fountain hidden among vineyards; Hattenheim, Hallgarten, Gräfenberg; and Eberbach, formerly an abbey, known for its "cabinet" wine, the hall-mark of those times, and its legends of Saint Bernard, for whom a boar ploughed a circle with his tusks to show the spot where the saint should build a monastery, and afterward tossed great stones thither for the foundation, while angels helped to build the upper walls. Eberbach is rather deserted than ruined. It was a good deal shattered in the Peasants' War at the time of the Reformation, when the insurgents emptied the huge cask in which the whole of the Steinberg wine-harvest was stored; but since 1803, when it was made over to the neighboring wine-growers, it has remained pretty well unharmed; and its twelfth-century chapel, full of monuments; its refectory, now the press-house, with its columns and capitals nearly perfect; its cellars, where every year more wine is given away than is stored—*i. e.*, all that which is not "cabinet-worthy"— as in the tulip-mania, when thousands of roots were thrown away as worthless, which yet had all the natural merit of lovely coloring and form,—make Eberbach well worth seeing.

Next comes Johannisberg, with its vineyards dating back to the tenth century, when Abbot Rabanus of Fulda cultivated the grape and Archbishop Ruthard of Mayence built a monastery, dedicated to Saint John the Baptist, which for centuries was owner and guardian of the most noted Rhine vintage; but abuses within and wars without have made an end of this state of things, and Albert of Brandenburg's raid on the monks' cellars has been more steadily supplemented by the pressure of milder but no less efficient means of destruction. When Napoleon saw this tract of land and offered it to General Kellermann, who had admired its beauty, he is said to have received a worthy and a bold answer. "I thank Your Majesty," said the marshal, "but the receiver is as bad as the thief." The less scrupulous Metternich became its owner, giving for it, however, an equivalent of arable and wood land. The Metternich who for years was Austrian ambassador at Paris during the brilliant time of the Second Empire, and whose fast and eccentric wife daily astonished society, is now owner of the peerless Johannisberg vineyards, among which is his country-house. Goethe's friends, the Lade and Brentano families, lived in this neighborhood, and the historian Nicholas Vogt lies buried in the Metternich chapel, though his heart, by his special desire, is laid in a silver casket within the rocks of Bingen, with a little iron cross marking the spot. At Geisenheim we are near two convents which as early as 1468 had printing-presses in active use, and the mysterious square tower of Rüdesheim, which brings all sorts of suppositions to our mind, though the beauty of the wayside crosses, the tall gabled roofs, the crumbling walls, the fantastically-shaped rocks, getting higher and higher on each side, and the perpetual winding of the river, are enough to keep the eye fixed on the mere landscape. At the windows, balconies and arbors sit pretty, ruddy girls waving their handkerchiefs to the unknown "men and brethren" on board the steamers and the trains; and well they may, if this be a good omen, for here is the "Iron Gate" of the Rhine, and the water bubbles and froths in miniature whirlpools as we near what is called the "Bingen Hole."

As we have passed the mouth of the Stein and recollected the rhyme of Schrödter in his *King Wine's Triumph*—

Wreathèd in vines and crowned with reeds comes the Rhine,
And at his side with merry dance comes the Main,

RÜDESHEIM.

While the third with his steady steps is all of stone
   (Stein),
And both Main and Stein are prime ministers to the
   Lord Rhine—

so now we peer up one of the clefts in the rocks and see the Nahe ploughing its way along to meet the great river. Just commanding the mouth is Klopp Castle, and not far warlike Bingen, a rich burgher-city, plundered and half destroyed in every war from those of the fourteenth to those of the eighteenth century, while Klopp too claims to have been battered and bruised even in the thirteenth century, but is better known as the scene of the emperor Henry IV.'s betrayal to the Church authorities by his son, who treacherously invited him to visit him here by night. A little way up the river Nahe, where the character of the people changes from the lightheartedness of the Rhine proper to a steadiness and earnestness somewhat in keeping with the sterner and more mountainous aspect of the country, is Kreuznach, (or "Crossnear"), now a bathing-resort, and once a village founded by the first Christian missionaries round the first cross under whose shadow they preached the gospel. Sponheim Castle, once the abode of Trithemius, or Abbot John of Trittenheim, a famous chronicler and scholar, reminds us of the brave butcher of Kreuznach, Michael Mort, whose faithfulness to his lawful lord when beset by pretenders to his title in his own family won for the guild of butchers certain privileges which they have retained ever since; and Rheingrafenstein, where the ruins are hardly distinguishable from the tossed masses of porphyry rock on which they are perched, tells us the story of Boos von Waldeck's wager with the lord of the castle to drink a courier's top-boot full of Rhine wine at one draught—a feat which he is said to have successfully accomplished, making himself surely a fit companion for Odin in Walhalla; but his reward on earth was more substantial, for he won thereby the village of Hüffelsheim and all its belongings. In a less romantic situation stands Ebernburg, so called from the boar which during a siege the hungry but indomitable defenders of the castle paraded again and again before the eyes of the besiegers, whose only hope lay in starving out the garrison —the property of the Sickengens, whose ancestor Franz played a prominent part in the Reformation and gave an asylum in these very halls to Bucer, Melanchthon, Œcolampadius and Ulrich von Hütten. Past Rothenfels, where towering rocks hem in the stream, like the Wye banks in Arthur's country on the Welsh borders; the scattered stones of Disibodenberg, the Irish missionary's namesake convent, which afterward passed into the hands of the Cistercians; Dhaum Castle and Oberstein Church, these two with their legends, the first accounting for a bas-relief in the great hall representing an ape rocking a child, the heir of the house, in the depths of a forest, and giving him an apple to eat,—we come to a cluster of castles which are the classical ground of the Nahe Valley. The very rocks seem not only crowned but honeycombed with buildings: chapels stand on jutting crags; houses, heaped as it were one on the roof of the other, climb up their rough sides, and the roofs themselves have taken their cue from the rocks, and have three or four irregular lines of tiny windows ridging and bulging them out.

Taking boat again at Bingen, and getting safely through the Rhine "Hell Gate," the "Hole," whose terrors seem as poetic as those of the Lorelei, we pass the famous Mouse Tower, and opposite it the ruined Ehrenfels; Assmanshausen, with its dark-colored wine and its custom of a May or Pentecost feast, when thousands of merry Rhinelanders spend the day in the woods, dancing, drinking and singing, baskets outspread in modified and dainty pic-nic fashion, torches lit at night and bands playing or mighty choruses resounding through the woods; St. Clement's Chapel, just curtained from the river by a grove of old poplars and overshadowed by a ruin with a hundred eyes (or windows), while among the thickly-planted, crooked crosses of its churchyard old peasant-women and children run or totter, the first telling their beads, the second gathering flowers,

BINGEN, FROM KLOPP CASTLE.

and none perhaps remembering that the chapel was built by the survivors of the families of the robber-knights of Rheinstein (one of the loveliest of Rhine ruins) and three other confederated castles, whom Rudolph of Habsburg treated, rightly enough, according to the Lynch law of his time. They were hung wherever found, but their pious relations did not forget to bury them and atone for them as seemingly as might be.

Bacharach, if it were not famed in Germany for its wine, according to the old rhyme declaring that

> At Würzburg on the Stein,
> At Hochheim on the Main,
> At Bacharach on the Rhine,
> There grows the best of wine,

would or ought to be noticed for its wealth of old houses and its many architectural beauties, from the ruined (or rather unfinished) chapel of St. Werner, now a wine-press house, bowered in trees and surrounded by a later growth of crosses and tombstones, to the meanest little house crowding its neighbor that it may bathe its doorstep in the river—houses that when their owners built and patched them from generation to generation little dreamt that they would stand and draw the artist's eye when the castle was in ruins. Similarly, the many serious historical incidents that took place in Bacharach have lived less long in the memory of inhabitants and visitors than the love-story connected with the ruined castle—that of Agnes, the daughter of the count of this place and niece of the great Barbarossa, whom her father shut up here with her mother to be out of the way of her lover, Henry of Braunschweig. The latter, a Guelph (while the count was a Ghibelline), managed, however, to defeat the father's plans: the mother helped the lovers, and a priest was smuggled into the castle to perform the marriage, which the father, after a useless outburst of rage, wisely acknowledged as valid. The coloring of many buildings in this part of the Rhineland is very beautiful, the red sandstone of the neighborhood being one of the most picturesque of building materials. Statues and crosses, as well as churches and castles, are built of it, and even the rocks have so appealed by their formation to the imagination of the people that at Schönburg we meet with a legend of seven sisters, daughters of that family whose hero, Marshal Schomburg, the friend and right hand of William of Orange, lies buried in Westminster Abbey, honored as marshal of France, peer of Great Britain and grandee of Portugal, and who, for their haughtiness toward their lovers, were turned into seven rocks, through part of which now runs the irreverent steam-engine, ploughing through the tunnel that cuts off a corner where the river bends again.

Now comes the gray rock where, as all the world knows, the Lorelei lives, but as that graceful myth is familiar to all, we will hurry past the mermaid's home, where so much salmon used to be caught that the very servants of the neighboring monastery of St. Goar were forbidden to eat salmon more than three times a week, to go and take a glimpse of St. Goarshausen, with its convent founded in the seventh century by one of the first Celtic missionaries, and its legend of the spider who remedied the carelessness of the brother cellarer when he left the bung out of Charlemagne's great wine-cask by quickly spinning across the opening a web thick enough to stop the flow of wine. A curious relic of olden time and humor is shown in the cellar—an iron collar, grim-looking, but more innocent than its looks, for it was used only to pin the unwary visitor to the wall while a choice between a "baptism" of water and wine was given him. The custom dates back to Charlemagne's time. Those who, thinking to choose the least evil of the two, gave their voice for the water, had an ample and unexpected shower-bath, while the wine-drinkers were crowned with some tinseled wreath and given a large tankard to empty. On the heights above the convent stood the "Cat" watching the "Mouse" on the opposite bank above Wellmich, the two names commemorating an insolent message sent by Count John III. of the castle of Neu-Katzellenbogen to Archbishop Kuno of Falkenstein, the builder of the castle of Thurnberg, "that he greeted him and hoped he would take good care of his mouse, that his (John's) cat might not eat it up." And now we pass a chain of castles, ruins and villages; rocks with such names as the Prince's Head; lead, copper and silver works, with all the activity of modern life, stuck on like a puppet-show to the background of a solemn old picture, a rocky, solitary island, "The Two Brothers," the twin castles of Liebenstein and Sternberg, the same which Bulwer has immortalized in his *Pilgrims of the Rhine*, and at their feet, close to the shore, a modern-looking building, the former Redemptorist convent of Bornhofen. As we step out there is a rude

RHEINGRAFENSTEIN.

quay, four large old trees and a wall with a pinnacled niche, and then we meet a boatful of pilgrims with their banners, for this is one of the shrines that are still frequented, notwithstanding many difficulties — notwithstanding that the priests were driven out of the convent some time ago, and that the place is in lay hands; not, however, unfriendly hands, for a Catholic German nobleman, married to a Scotch woman, bought the house and church, and endeavored, as under the shield of "private property," to preserve it for the use of the Catholic population of the neighborhood. Last summer an English Catholic family rented the house, and a comfortable home was established in the large, bare building attached to the church, where is still kept the *Gnadenbild*, or "Grace image," which is the object of the pilgrimage—a figure of the Blessed Virgin holding her dead Son upon her knees. These English tenants brought a private chaplain with them, but, despite their privileges as English subjects, I believe there was some trouble with the government authorities. However, they had mass said for them at first in the church on weekdays. A priest from Camp, the neighboring post-town, was allowed to come once in a week to say mass for the people, but with locked doors, and on other days the service was also held in the same way, though a few of the country-people always managed to get in quietly before the doors were shut. On Sundays mass was said for the strangers and their household only in a little oratory up in the attics, which had a window looking into the church near the roof of the chancel. One of them describes "our drawing-room in the corner of the top floor, overlooking the river," and "our life . . . studying German, reading and writing in the morning, dining early, walking out in the evening, tea-supper when we come home. . . . There are such pretty walks in the ravines and hills, in woods and vineyards, and to the castles above and higher hills beyond! We brought one man and a maid, who do not know German, and found two German servants in the house, who do everything. . . . It is curious how cheaply we live here; the German cook left here does everything for us, and we are saying she makes us much better soups and omelettes and souffles than any London cook." Now, as these three things happen to be special tests of a cook's skill, this praise from an Englishman should somewhat rebuke travelers who can find no word too vile for "German cookery."

The time of the yearly pilgrimage came round during the stay of these strangers, "and pilgrims came from Coblenz, a four hours' walk (in mid-August and the temperature constantly in the nineties), on the opposite side of the river, singing and chanting as they came, and crossed the river here in boats. High mass was at half-past nine (in the morning) and benediction at half-past one, immediately after which they returned in boats down the stream much more quickly. The day before was a more local pilgrimage: mass and benediction were at eight, but pilgrims came about all the morning." Later on, when the great heat had brought "premature autumn tints to the trees and burnt up the grass," the English family made some excursions in the neighborhood, and in one place they came to a "forest and a large tract of tall trees," but this was exceptional, as the soil is not deep enough to grow large timber, and the woods are chiefly low underwood. The grapes were small, and on the 22d of August they tasted the first plateful at Stolzenfels, an old castle restored by the queen-dowager of Prussia, and now the property of the empress of Germany. "The view from it is lovely up and down the river, and the situation splendid—about four hundred feet above the river, with high wooded hills behind, just opposite the Lahn where it falls into the Rhine." Wolfgang Müller describes Stolzenfels as a beautiful specimen of the old German style, with a broad smooth road leading up over drawbridges and moats, with mullioned windows and machicolated towers, and an artistic open staircase intersected by three pointed arches, and looking into an inner courtyard, with a fountain surrounded by broad-leaved tropical water-plants. The sight of a combination of antique dignity with correct modern taste is a delight so seldom experienced that it is worth while dwelling on this pleasant fact as brought out in the restoration of Stolzenfels, the "Proud Rock." And that the Rhinelanders are proud of their river is no wonder when strangers can talk about it thus: "The Rhine is a river which grows

MOUSE-TOWER (OR BISHOP HATTO'S TOWER) AND EHRENFELS.

upon you, living in a pretty part of its course: . . . its less beauteous parts have their own attractions to the natives, and its beauties, perhaps exaggerated, unfold greatly the more you explore them, not to be seen by a rushing tourist up and down the stream by rail or by boat, but sought out and contemplated from its heights and windings . . . In fact, the pretty part of its course is from Bingen to Bonn. Here we are in a wonderfully winding gorge, containing nearly all its picturesque old castles, uninterrupted by any flat. The stream is rapid enough, four miles an hour or more—not equal to the Rhone at Geneva, but like that

THE LORELEI ROCK.

river in France. One does not wonder at the Germans being enthusiastic over their river, as the Romans were over the yellow Tiber."

Other excursions were made by the Bornhofen visitors, one up a hill on the opposite side, over sixteen hundred feet high, whence a fine distant view of the Mosel Valley was seen, and one also to the church of St. Apollinaris, at Remagen, at some distance down the river, where are "some fine frescoes by German artists covering the whole interior of the church. One artist painted four or five large ones of the Crucifixion, Resurrection and other events relating to the life of Our Lord; a second several of the life of St. Apollinaris, and two others some of Our Lady and various saints, one set being patron saints of the founder's children, whom I think we saw at Baden—Carl Egon, Count Fürstenberg-Stammheim.... The family-house stands close to the church, or one of his houses, and seems to have been made into a Franciscan convent: the monks are now banished and the church deserted, a *custode* (guardian) in charge. We went one day to Limburg to see the bishop of this diocese, a dear old man who only speaks German, so E—— and C—— carried on all the conversation. The cathedral is a fine old Norman building with seven towers: it is undergoing restoration, and the remains of old frescoes under the whitewash are the groundwork of renewed ones. Where an old bit is perfect enough it is left."

Camp, a mile from Bornhofen, is an insignificant place enough, but claiming to have been a Roman camp, and having an old convent as picturesque as those of far-famed and much-visited towns. The same irregular windows, roofed turrets springing up by the side of tall gables, a corner-shrine of Our Lady and Child, with vines and ivy making a niche for it,

A STREET IN LIMBURG.

mossy steps, a broken wall with trailing vines and steep stone-roofed recess, probably an old niche,—such is a sketch of what would make a thoroughly good picture; but in this land there are so many such that one grows too familiar with them to care for the sight. Nearly opposite is Boppard, a busy ancient town, with a parish church beautiful enough for a cathedral—St. Severin's church, with carved choir-stalls and a double nave—and the old Benedictine monastery for women, now a cold-water cure establishment. Boppard has its legend of a shadowy Templar and a faithless bridegroom challenged by the former, who turned out to be the forsaken bride herself; but of these legends, one so like the other, this part of the Rhine is full. The next winding of the stream shows us Oberspay, with a romantic tavern, carved pillars supporting a windowed porch, and a sprawling kind of roof; the "King's Stool," a modern restoration of the mediæval pulpit or platform of stone supported by pillars, with eighteen steps and a circumference of forty ells, where the Rhenish prince-archbishops met to choose the temporal sovereigns who were in part their vassals; Oberlahnstein, a town famous for its possession in perfect repair of the ancient fortifications; Lahneck, now a private residence, once the property of the Templars; Stolzenfels, of which we have anticipated a glimpse; the island of Oberwörth, with an old convent of St. Magdalen, and in the distance frowning Ehrenbreitstein, the fortress of Coblenz.

Turning up the course of the Lahn, we get to the neighborhood of a small but famous bathing-place, Ems, the cradle of the Franco-Prussian war, where the house in which Emperor William lodged is now shown as an historic memento, and effaces the interest due to the old gambling Kursaal. The English chapel, a beautiful small stone building already ivied; the old synagogue, a plain whitewashed building, where the service is conducted in an orthodox but not very attractive manner; the pretty fern- and heather-covered woods, through which you ride on donkeyback; the gardens, where a Parisian-dressed crowd airs itself late in the afternoon; all the well-known adjuncts of a spa, and the most delightful baths I ever saw, where in clean little chambers you step down three steps into an ample marble basin sunk in the floor, and may almost fancy yourself a luxurious Roman of the days of Diocletian,—such is Ems. But its environs are full of wider interest. There is Castle Schaumburg, where for twenty years the archduke Stephen of Austria, palatine of Hungary, led a useful and retired life, making his house as orderly and seemly as an English manor-house, and more interesting to the strangers, whose visits he encouraged, by the collections of minerals, plants, shells and stuffed animals and the miniature zoological and botanical gardens which he kept up and often added to. I spent a day there thirteen years ago, ten years before he died, lamented by his poor neighbors, to whom he was a visible providence. Another house of great interest is the old Stein mansion in the little town of Nassau, the home of the upright and patriotic minister of that name, whose memory is a household word in Germany. The present house is a comfortable modern one—a *château* in the French sense of the word—but the old shattered tower above the town is the cradle of the family. At the village of Frücht is the family-vault and the great man's monument, a modern Gothic canopy, somewhat bald and characterless, but bearing a fine statue of Stein by Schwanthaler, and an inscription in praise of the "unbending son of bowed-down Fatherland." He came of a good stock, for thus runs his father's funeral inscription, in five alliterative German rhymes. I can give it but lamely:

> His nay was nay, and steady,
> His yea was yea, and ready;
> Of his promise ever mindful,
> His lips his conscience ne'er belied,
> And his word was bond and seal.

Stein was born in the house where he retired to spend his last years in study: his grave and pious nature is shown in the mottoes with which he adorned his home: "A tower of strength is our God" over the house-door, and in his library, above his books and busts and gathering of life-memorials, "Confidence in God, singleness of mind and righteousness."

His contemporaries called him, in a play upon his name which, as such things go, was not bad, "The foundation-*stone* of right, the stumbling-*stone* of the wicked, and the precious *stone* of Germany." Arnstein and its old convent, now occupied by a solitary priest: Balduinenstein and its rough-hewn, cyclopean-looking ruin, standing over the mossy picturesque water-mill; the marble-quarries near Schaumburg, worked by convicts; Diez and its conglomeration of houses like a puzzle endowed with life,—are all on the way to Limburg, the episcopal town, old and tortuous, sleepy and alluring, with its shady streets, its cathedral of St. George and its monument of the lion-hearted Conrad or Kuno, surnamed Shortbold (Kurzbold), a nephew of Emperor Conrad, a genuine woman-hater, a man of giant strength but dwarfish height, who is said to have once strangled a lion, and at another time sunk a boatful of men with one blow of his spear. The cathedral, the same visited by our Bornhofen friends, has other treasures—carved stalls and a magnificent image of Our Lord of the sixteenth century, a Gothic baptismal font and a richly-sculptured tabernacle, as well as a much older image of *St. George and the Dragon*, supposed by some to refer to the legendary existence of monsters in the days when Limburg was heathen. Some such idea seems also not to have been remote from the fancy of the mediæval sculptor who adorned the brave Conrad's monument with such elaborately monstrous figures: it was evidently no lack of skill and delicacy that dictated such a choice of supporters, for the figure of the hero is lifelike, dignified and faithful to the minute description of his features and stature left us by his chronicler, while the beauty of the leaf-border of the slab and of the capitals of the short pillars is such as to excite the envy of our best modern carvers.

CONRAD'S MONUMENT, LIMBURG CATHEDRAL.

DOWN THE RHINE.

CONCLUDING PART.

CASTLE OF ELTZ.

COBLENZ is the place which many years ago gave me my first associations with the Rhine. From a neighboring town we often drove to Coblenz, and the wide, calm flow of the river, the low, massive bridge of boats and the commonplace outskirts of a busy city contributed to make up a very different picture from that of the poetic "castled" Rhine of German song and English ballad. The old town has, however, many beauties, though its military character looks out through most of them, and reminds us that the Mosel city (for it originally stood only on that river, and then crept up to the Rhine), though a point of union in Nature, has been for ages, so far as mankind was concerned, a point of defence and watching. The great fortress, a German Gibraltar, hangs over the river and sets its teeth in the face of the opposite shore: all the foreign element in the town is due to the deposits made there by troubles in other countries, revolution and war sending their exiles, *émigrés* and prisoners. The history of the town is only a long military record, from the days of the archbishops of Trèves, to whom it was subject, to those of the last war. It has, however, some pleasanter points: it has long been a favorite summer residence of the empress of Germany, who not long before I was there had by her tact and toleration reconciled sundry religious differences that threatened a political storm. Such toleration has gone out of fashion now, and the peacemaking queen would have a harder task to perform now that the two parties have come to an open collision. There is the old "German house" by the bank of the Mosel, a building little altered outwardly since the fourteenth century, now used as a food-magazine for the troops. The church of St. Castor commemorates a holy hermit who lived and preached to the heathen in the eighth century, and also covers the grave and monument of the founder of the "Mouse" at Wellmich, the warlike Kuno of Falkenstein, archbishop of Trèves. The Exchange, once a court of justice, has changed less startlingly, and its proportions are much the same as of old; and besides these there are other buildings worth noticing, though not so old, and rather distinguished by the men who lived and died there, or were born there, such as Metternich, than by architectural beauties. Such houses there are in every old city. They do not invite you to go in and admire them: every tourist you meet does not ask you how you liked them or whether you saw them. They are *homes*, and sealed to you as such, but they are the shell of the real life of the country; and they have somehow a charm and a fascination that no public building or show-place can have. Goethe, who turned his life-experiences into poetry, has told us something of one such house not far from Coblenz, in the village of Ehrenbreitstein, beneath the fortress, and which in familiar Coblenz parlance goes by the name of "The Valley"—the house of Sophie de Laroche. The village is also Clement Brentano's birthplace.

The oldest of German cities, Trèves (or in German *Trier*), is not too far to visit on our way up the Mosel Valley, whose Celtic inhabitants of old gave the Roman legions so much trouble. But Rome ended by conquering, by means of her civilization as well as by her arms, and *Augusta Trevirorum*, though claiming a far higher antiquity than Rome herself, and still bearing an inscription to that effect on the old council-house—now called the Red House and used as a hotel—became, as Ausonius condescendingly remarked, a second Rome, adorned with baths, gardens, temples, theatres and all that went to make up an imperial capital. As in Venice everything precious seems to have come from Constantinople, so in Trier most things worthy of note date from the days of the Romans; though, to tell the truth, few of the actual buildings do, no matter how classic is their look. The style of the Empire outlived its sway, and doubtless symbolized to the inhabitants their traditions of a higher standard of civilization. The Porta Nigra, for instance—called Simeon's Gate at present—dates really from the days of the first Merovingian kings, but it *looks* like a piece of the Coliseum, with its rows of arches in massive red sandstone, the stones held together by iron clamps, and its low, immensely strong double gateway, reminding one of the triumphal arches in the Forum at Rome. The history of the transformations of this gateway is curious. First a fortified city gate, standing in a correspondingly fortified wall, it became a dilapidated granary and storehouse in the Middle Ages, when one of the archbishops gave leave to Simeon, a wandering hermit from Syracuse in Sicily, to take up his abode there; and another turned it into a church dedicated to this saint, though of this change few traces remain. Finally, it has become a national museum of antiquities. The amphitheatre is a genuine Roman work, wonderfully well preserved; and genuine enough were the Roman games it has witnessed, for, if we are to believe tradition, a thousand Frankish prisoners of war were here given in one day to the wild beasts by the emperor Constantine. Christian emperors beautified the basilica that stood where the cathedral now is, and the latter itself has some basilica-like points about it, though, being the work of fifteen centuries, it bears the stamp of successive styles upon its face. To the neighborhood, and also to strangers, one of its great attractions lies in its treasury of relics, the gift of Constantine's mother, Saint Helena, for many hundred years objects of pilgrimage, and even to the incredulous objects of curiosity and interest, for the robe of a yellowish-brown — supposed to have been once purple—which is shown as Our Lord's seamless garment, has been pronounced by learned men to be of very high antiquity. But what possesses the Rhine tourist to moralize? He is a restless creature in general, more occupied in staring than in seeing —a gregarious creature too, who enjoys the evening table d'hôte, the day-old *Times* and the British or American gossip as a reward for his having conscientiously *done* whatever Murray or Baedeker bade him. Cook has only transformed the tourist's mental docility into a bodily one: the guidebook had long drilled his mind before the tour-contractor thought of

RUINS OF THE CASTLE OF AUERBACH.

drilling his body and driving willing gangs of his species all over the world.

There is a funny, not over-reverent,

legend afloat in Trier to account for the queer dwarf bottles of Mosel wine used there: it refers to a trick of Saint Peter, who is supposed to have been travelling in these parts with the Saviour, and when sent to bring wine to the latter drank half of it on his way back, and then, to conceal his act, cut the cup down to the level of the wine that remained. These measures are still called *Miserâbelchen*, or "wretched little remainders."

The Mosel has but few tributary streams of importance: its own course is as winding, as wild and as romantic as that of the Rhine itself. The most interesting part of the very varied scenery of this river is not the castles, the antique towns, the dense woods or the teeming vineyards lining rocks where a chamois could hardly stand—all this it has in common with the Rhine—but the volcanic region of the Eifel, the lakes in ancient craters, the tossed masses of lava and tufa, the great wastes strewn with dark boulders, the rifts that are called valleys and are like the Iceland gorges, the poor, starved villages and the extraordinary rusticity, not to say coarseness, of the inhabitants. This grotesque, interesting country —unique, I believe, on the continent of Europe—lies in a small triangle between the Mosel, the Belgian frontier and the Schiefer hills of the Lower Rhine: it goes by the names of the High Eifel, with the High Acht, the Kellberg and the Nürburg; the Upper (*Vorder*) Eifel, with Gerolstein, a ruined castle, and Daun, a pretty village; and the Snow-Eifel (*Schnee Eifel*), contracted by the speech of the country into Schneifel. The last is the most curious, the most dreary, the least visited. Walls of sharp rock rise up over eight hundred feet high round some of its sunken lakes—one is called the Powder Lake—and the level above this abyss stretches out in moors and desolate downs, peopled with herds of lean sheep, and marked here and there by sepulchral, gibbet-looking signposts, shaped like a rough T and set in a heap of loose stones. It is a great contrast to turn aside from this landscape and look on the smiling villages and pretty wooded scenery of the valley of the Mosel proper; the long lines of handsome, healthy women washing their linen on the banks; the old ferryboats crossing by the help of antique chain-and-rope contrivances; the groves of old trees, with broken walls and rude shrines, reminding one of Southern Italy and her olives and ilexes; and the picturesque houses in Kochem, in Daun, in Trarbach, in Bernkastel, which, however untiring one may be as a sightseer, hardly warrant one as a writer to describe and re-describe their beauties. Klüsserath, however, we must mention, because its straggling figure has given rise to a local proverb—"As long as Klüsserath;" and Neumagen, because of the legend of Constantine, who is said to have seen the cross of victory in the heavens at this place, as well as at Sinzig on the Rhine, and, as the more famous legend tells us, at the Pons Milvium over the Tiber.

The Mosel wine-industry has much the same features as that of the Rhine, but there is a great difference between the French wines, which are mostly red, and the German, which are mostly white. Among the latter hundreds of spurious, horrible concoctions for the foreign market usurp the name of Mosel wine. It is hardly necessary even to mention the pretty names by which the real wines are known, and which may be found on any wine-card at the good, unpretending inns that make Mosel travelling a special delight. The Saar wines are included among the Mosel, and the difference is not very perceptible.

The last glance we take at the beauties of this neighborhood is from the mouth of the torrent-river Eltz as it dashes into the Eifel, washing the rock on which stands the castle of Eltz. The building and the family are an exception in the history of these lands: both exist to this day, and are prosperous and undaunted, notwithstanding all the efforts of enemies, time and circumstances to the contrary. The strongly-turreted wall runs from the castle till it loses itself in the rock, and the building has a home-like, inhabited, complete look; which, in virtue of the quaint irregularity and magnificent natural position of the castle,

VIEW OF COBLENZ FROM PFAFFENDORF.

standing guard over the foaming Eltz, does not take from its romantic appearance, as preservation or restoration too often does.

Not far from Coblenz, and past the island of Nonnenwerth, is the old tenth-century castle of Sayn, which stood until the Thirty Years' War, and below it, quiet, comfortable, large, but unpretending, lies the new house of the family of Sayn-Wittgenstein, built in 1848, where, during a stay at Ems, we paid a visit of two days. The family were great Italian travellers, and we had met in Rome more than twenty years before, when the writer and the boys, whom I met again—the one as an officer of the Prussian army, and the other as a Bonn student—were children together. At dinner one evening at this new Sayn house, as we were tasting some Russian dish of soured milk (the mother was a Russian), we reminded each other of our ball on Twelfth Night at Rome, when the youngest of these boys happened to become king "by the grace of the bean," and spent some hours seated in state with gilt-paper crown and red-velvet mantle till he was too sleepy to oversee his subjects' revels any longer; of a day when the pope was to "create" several cardinals, and of the young "king's" unshaken belief that *he* would have the scarlet hat sent him if he only waited long enough at the window to look out for the messengers, and of his consequent watch all day, seeing the carriages pass and repass and the bustle of a *festa* go on, till the sunset flushed over St. Peter's in the distance, and the disappointment became certain at last. Of not much more manly pastimes did the Bonn student have to tell, for the slitting of noses was then in high favor, and a bit of advice was gravely recounted as having come from a doctor to an obstinate duellist, "not to get his nose cut off a *fifth* time, as the sewing had got so shaky by repetition that he could not answer for the nose sticking on if touched once more." The house was really beautiful, and furnished with a taste which had something Parisian, and yet also something individual, about it. The parquet floors of inlaid and polished wood used in Germany were here seen to their greatest perfection in some of the rooms; but what most struck me was a Moorish chamber lighted from above—a small, octagon room, with low divans round the walls and an ottoman in the centre, with flowers in concealed pots cunningly introduced into the middle of the cushions, while glass doors, half screened by Oriental-looking drapery, led into a small grotto conservatory with a fountain plashing softly among the tropical plants. There was also a good collection of pictures in a gallery, besides the paintings scattered through the living rooms; but the garden was perhaps as much a gem to its owner's mind as anything in the house, as an "English" garden always is to a foreigner. There, in the late afternoon of that day, came one of the Prussian royal family and paid the mistress of the house an informal friendly visit, taking "five-o'clock tea" in the English fashion, and with a retinue of two or three attendants making the tour of the close-shaven lawns, the firm gravelled walks and the broad and frequent flights of steps that led from one terraced flower-garden to another. These were courtly and educated descendants of terrible scourges of mankind in old days—of Sayns who were simply robbers and highwaymen, levying bloody toll on the Coblenz merchants' caravans, and of Brandenburgs who were famous for their ravages and raids. Times have changed no less than buildings, and the houseful of pictures and treasures is no more unlike the robber-nest destroyed in war by other robbers than the young Bonn student is unlike his rough-and-ready forefathers.

As we push our way down the Rhine we soon come to another such contrast, the little peaceful town of Neuwied, a sanctuary for persecuted Flemings and others of the Low Countries, gathered here by the local sovereign, Count Frederick III. He gave them each a plot of land, built their houses and exempted them from all dues and imposts, besides granting them full freedom of worship; but not for them alone was this boon, for as other wars made other exiles, so were all and every welcome to Neuwied, and the place even now contains Catholics, Lutherans, Calvinists, Mennonites and Quakers, all living in peace together. The United Brethren (or Moravians) founded a colony here in 1750. The honesty of these people is proverbial, their simplicity of life is patriarchal, and the artist at least will not object to their manners, for the sake of the pleasing costume of their women, whose white caps look akin to the peaceful, rural background of their life, red and blue bands on these caps respectively distinguishing the married from the unmarried women. The little brook that gives its name to the village runs softly into the Rhine under a rustic bridge and amid murmuring rushes, while beyond it the valley gets narrower, rocks begin to rise over the Rhine-banks, and the scenery after Andernach becomes again what we so admired at Bingen and Bornhofen.

Andernach is the Rocky Gate of the Rhine, and if its scenery were not enough, its history, dating from Roman times, would make it interesting. However, of its relics we can only mention, *en passant*, the parish church with its four towers, all of tufa, the dungeons under the council-house, significantly called the "Jews' bath," and the old sixteenth-century contrivances for loading Rhine-boats with the millstones in which the town still drives a fair trade. At the mouth of the Brohl we meet the volcanic region again, and farther up the valley through which this stream winds come upon the retired little watering-place of Tönnistein, a favorite goal of the Dutch, with its steel waters; and Wassenach, with what we may well call its dust-baths, stretching for miles inland, up hills full of old craters, and leaving us only at the entrance of the beech-woods that have grown up in these cauldron-like valleys and fringe the blue Laachersee, the lake of legends and of fairies. One of these Schlegel has versified, the "Lay of the Sunken Castle," with the piteous tale of the spirits imprisoned; and Simrock tells us in rhyme of the merman who sits waiting for a mortal bride; while Wolfgang Müller sings of the "Castle under the Lake," where at night ghostly torches are lighted and ghostly revels held, the story of which so fascinates the fisherman's boy who has heard of these doings from his grandmother that as he watches the enchanted waters one night his fancy plays

ORTENSTEIN.

him a cruel trick, and he plunges in to join the revellers and learn the truth. Local tradition says that Count Henry II. and his wife Adelaide, walking here by night, saw the whole lake lighted up from within in uncanny fashion, and founded a monastery in order to counteract the spell. This deserted but scarcely-ruined building still exists, and contains the grave of the founder: the twelfth-century decoration, rich and detailed, is almost whole in the oldest part of the monastery. The far-famed German tale of Genovefa of Brabant is here localized, and Henry's son Siegfried assigned to the princess as a husband, while the neighboring grotto of Hochstein is shown as her place of refuge. On our way back to the Rocky Gate we pass through the singular little town of Niedermendig, an hour's distance from the lake—a place built wholly of dark gray lava, standing in a region where lava-ridges seam the earth like the bones of antediluvian monsters, but are made more profitable by being quarried into millstones. There is something here that brings part of Wales to the remembrance of the few who have seen those dreary slate-villages—dark, damp, but naked, for moss and weeds do not thrive on this dampness as they do on the decay of other stones—which dot the moorlands of Wales. The fences are slate; the gateposts are slate; the stiles are of slate; the very "sticks" up which the climbing roses are trained are of slate; churches, schools, houses, stables, are all of one dark iron-blue shade; floors and roofs are alike; hearthstones and threshold-stones and gravestones, all of the same material. It is curious and depressing. This volcanic region of the Rhine, however, has so many unexpected beauties strewn pellmell in the midst of stony barrenness that it also bears some likeness to Naples and Ischia, where beauty of color, and even of vegetation, alternate surprisingly with tracts of parched and rocky wilderness pierced with holes whence gas and steam are always rising.

Sinzig, on the left bank of the last gorge of the Rhine, besides its legend of Constantine has a convent said to have been built by the empress Helena; and in this convent a mummied body of a long-dead monk, canonized by popular tradition, and remarkable for the journey to Paris which his body took and returned from unharmed in the days of Napoleon I. On the opposite shore, not much lower down, is another of the numberless pilgrimage-chapels with which the Rhine abounds, and the old city of Linz, with an authentic history dating from the ninth century, telling of an independence of any but nominal authority for some time, and at last of a transfer of the lordship of the old town from the Sayns to the archbishops of Cologne. This supremacy had to be kept up by the "strong hand," of which the ruined fortress is now the only reminder; but there is a more beautiful monument of old days and usages in the thirteenth-century church of St. Martin, not badly restored, where the stained-glass windows are genuinely mediæval, as well as the fresco on gold ground representing the "Seven Joys of Mary," painted in 1463. Just above Remagen lies the Victoria-berg, named after the crown-princess of Prussia, the princess-royal of England, and this is the evening resort of weary Remageners—a lovely public garden, with skilfully-managed vistas, and a "Victoria temple," placed so as to command the five prettiest views up and down the stream, as well as over the woodland behind the town. Let not the classic name of "temple" deceive us, however, for this is a genuine German arbor, picturesque and comfortable, with a conical roof of stately and rustic pillars, seats and balustrade rising from the steep bank on which the "lookout" is perched. The winding Ahr, coming from the tufa-plateau of the Eifel and watering a pretty valley full of old castles and churches, rolls its waters into the Rhine in this neighborhood, and in summer no trip is so pleasant to the citizens of Bonn and Cologne, and indeed to many tourists if they have time to breathe. But in winter the scenery is worthy of the New World. The dark rocks and narrow slits of valleys piled with snow and crusted with ice, the locked waterfalls and caves with portcullises of icicles let down across their mouths, make a pendant for the splendid and little-known scenery of American mountains in January. By one of the castles, a ruin belonging to the Steins of Nassau, poetically called *Landskröne*, or the

"Land's Crown," from its beautiful situation on a basalt hill, is a perfectly-preserved chapel perched on the top of the rock, where, says the legend, the daughter of the besieged lord of the castle once took refuge during a local war. The sacristy has an unusual shape, and is hewn out of the rock itself; and here it was that the maiden sat in safety, the rock closing over the cleft by which she had crept in, and a dove finding its way in every day with a loaf to feed her, while

COURT OF JUSTICE, AHRWEILER.

a spring within the cave supplied her with water. Legends have grown over every stone of this poetic land like moss and lichen and rock-fern; and at Beul, a small bathing-place with a real geyser and a very tolerable circle of society, we come across the universal story of a golden treasure sunk in a castle-well and guarded by a giant. The old, world-forgotten town has its hall of justice and all the shell of its antique civic paraphernalia, while at present it is a sleepy, contented, rural place, with country carts and country riders by families crowding it on market-days, and making every yard of the old street a picture such as delights the traveller from cities whose plan is conveniently but not picturesquely that of a chess-board. The baths, like those of Schlangenbad, are in great favor with nervous women, and like that neighborhood too, so has this its miniature Olivet and Calvary, the devout legacy of some unknown crusader, who also founded at Ahrweiler the Franciscan monastery called Calvary Hill. These "calvaries," in many shapes and degrees, are not uncommon in Catholic Germany; "stations of the cross"—sometimes groups of painted figures, life-size, sometimes only small shrines with a framed picture within—mark the distances up the hill, at the top of which is a representation of the crucifixion; and as the agony in the garden is not included in the "stations," there is generally at the foot of the hill an additional shrine in a natural cave or surrounded by artificial rock-work. The prettiest part of the Ahr valley is at and about Walporzheim, which the Düsseldorf artists have, by reason of its famous wine quite as much as of its romantic scenery, chosen for the place of their frequent feasts, half picnic, half masque, when their get-up rivals that of any carnival, not even excepting that of the "Krewe of Komus" or those other displays peculiar to Belgium and Holland of which the late celebration of the "Pacification of Ghent" was an example.

The Rhine once more! and now indeed we shall hardly leave it again, but this is the last part in which we can enjoy the peculiar beauties that make it different from any other river in the world. The Swiss Rhine is a mountain-torrent, the Dutch Rhine a sluggish mud puddle, but the German Rhine is an historic river. Quite as legendary as historic, however; and perhaps that has made its charm in the eyes of foreigners even more than its national associations, dear to the native mind; and here, between Rolandseck, Nonnenwerth and Drachenfels, poetry takes precedence of history, and we do not want the antiqua-ry to come and shatter the legend of Roland of Roncesval's fidelity to the Lady of Drachenfels, even after her vows in Nonnenwerth convent, with his pitiless array of dates and parade of obvious impossibilities. But I pass over the legendary details that make this region so interesting. What will better bear repetition is some description of the scenery lying inland from the shores, the natural Quadrilateral, containing minor mountains, such as the Siebengebirge (or the Seven Hills) and the Bonner Alps, and encircling also the volcanic region between Honnef and Dollendorf. These hills with their step-and-terrace formation were once fortified by Valentinian against the formidable Frankish hordes, and German poetry early began to find scenery in them worthy of its national epic, and so laid the scene of the Saga of Wilkina among these mountains and valleys. Here, above the legends of Roland and Siegfried and the Christian captive, who, exposed to the dragon of the rock, vanquished him by the cross, so that he fell backward and broke his neck, is the solid remembrance of castles built on many of these Rhine-hills, defences and bulwarks of the archbishops of Cologne against the emperors of Germany. But Drachenfels keeps another token of its legend in its dark-red wine, called "dragon's blood." (Could any teetotaller have invented a more significant name?) One has often heard of the unbelieving monk who stumbled at the passage in Scripture which declares that a thousand years are but as one day to the Lord, and the consequent taste of eternity which he was miraculously allowed to enjoy while he wandered off for a quarter of an hour, as he thought, but in reality for three hundred years, following the song of a nightingale. The abbey of Heisterbach claims this as an event recorded in its books, and its beautiful ruins and wide naves with old trees for columns are, so says popular rumor, haunted by another wanderer, an abbot with snow-white beard, who walks the cloisters at night counting the graves of his brethren, and vainly seeking his own, which if he once find

DRACHENFELS.

his penance will be over. This part of the Rhine was the favorite home of many of the poets who have best sung of the national river: a cluster of townlets recalls no less than five of them to our mind—Unkel, where Freiligrath chose his home; Menzerberg, where Simrock lived; Herresberg, Pfarrins's home; Königswinter, Wolfgang Müller's birthplace; and Oberkassel, that of Gottfried Kinkel. Rhondorf shows us a monument of one of the last robber-lords of Drachenfels, and Honnef a smiling modern settlement, a very Nice of the North, where the climate draws together people of means and leisure, *littérateurs*, retired merchants and collectors of art-treasures, as well as health-seekers. These little colonies, of which most of the large cities on the Rhine have a copy in miniature, even if it be not a bathing-place, are the places in which to seek for that domestic taste and refinement which some hasty and prejudiced critics have thought fit to deny to the Fatherland.

The scenery of the Rhine begins to lose its distinctive features as we near Bonn: plains replace rocks, and the waters flow more sluggishly. Bonn is alive enough: its antiquities of Roman date are forgotten in its essentially modern bustle, for the heart of its prosperity is of very recent date, the university having been founded only in 1777, and after the troubles of the Revolution reorganized in 1818. It has grown with a giant growth, and has reckoned among its professors Niebuhr, Schlegel, Arndt, Dahlmann, Johann Müller, Ritschl, Kinkel, Simrock and other less world-famous but marvellous specialists. Then there is the memory of Beethoven, the honor of the town, which is his birthplace and has put up a monument to him, and the last modern element that has effaced the old recollections—the numerous English colony—not to mention the rich foreigners whom perhaps the university, perhaps the scenery, and perhaps the heedless fashion that sets in a tide now toward this place, now toward that, have drawn to the new Bonn. Poppelsdorf Castle, now the museum of natural history, and the fine groves and gardens attached to it, now a public promenade, have the brisk, business-like look of a "live" place: the building, it is true, is modern, having been built in 1715. But if we are obstinate enough to search for signs of the days when archbishops ruled instead of dukes and kings, we shall find old remains, the cathedral of course included, and nowhere a more curious one than the Kreuzberg, a place of pilgrimage, where the church of 1627 has replaced an old wood-shrine: its rich gateway was intended to represent the front of Pontius Pilate's palace at Jerusalem, and on it are frescoes of the various scenes of the Passion. Within this thirty marble steps lead up into a vestibule in imitation of the *Scala Santa* in Rome, and pilgrims went up these stairs only on their knees. The vaults used until lately to contain a quantity of dried or mummied bodies of Servite monks (that order once had a convent here), reminding one of the ghastly Capuchin crypts in Rome, in Syracuse and in Malta. This neighborhood is rich in pilgrimage-shrines and legends, and Simrock has preserved a tale of the Devil which is a little out of the common run. He and the Wind, it is said, once went by a certain Jesuit church in company, and the former begged the latter to wait a moment for him, as he had some business within. The Devil never reappeared, and the Wind is still blowing perpetually round the building, waiting and calling in vain. The old myth of Barbarossa waiting in his cave, his beard grown round and round the stone table on which he leans his sleepy head, which in another form meets us in the Mosel Valley, repeats itself in Wolfsberg, not far from Siegburg, near Bonn. I wonder whether the English anglers and oarsmen, and the pretty girls ready to flirt with the students and give away the prizes at an archery-meeting or a regatta, ever think of these musty old legends looked up by scholars out of convent chronicles and peasants' fireside talk? The difference between past and present is not greater or more startling than is their likeness, the groundwork of human nature being the same for ever. Especially in these old lands, how like the life of

MARKET-PLACE AT WORMS.

to-day to that of hundreds of years ago in all that makes life real and intense! The same thing in a mould of other shape, the same thoughts in a speech a little varied, the same motives under a dress a little less natural and crude— even the same pleasures in a great degree, for the wine-flask played fully as great a part in old German times as it does now.

"Holy Cologne" seems at first an impersonation of the olden time, but its busy wharves, crowded shipping and tall warehouses tell us another tale. Indeed, Cologne is more rich than holy, and its commercial reputation is quite as old as its religious one. The country around is flat and uninteresting, but Cologne merchants have made Brühl a little paradise in spite of this; and their country-houses of all styles, with balconies, verandas, porches, piazzas, English shrubbery and flower-gardens, conservatories and gay boats, lawns and statues, make even the monotonous banks of the sluggish Rhine beautiful in spite of Nature. Then comes a reminder of old times — the towers and fortifications, which are still standing, though now turned into public gardens and drives that stretch out both on the river and the land side; but the former, *Am Thürmchen*, forming a sort of parapeted quay, crossed by massive battlemented gateways, is the most fashionable and commands the best views. The trees almost hide the shipping, as their predecessors no doubt did eighteen hundred years ago and more, when the Ubier tribe of barbarians, a commercial as well as warlike people, undertook to ferry over the whole of Cæsar's army to the right bank of the Rhine in their own boats. The quays swarm now with hotels, and these in summer swarm with strangers from all countries—pilgrims of Art and Nature, if no longer of religion — and the old town becomes in their eyes less a solid, real city with a long history than a museum opened for their special behoof. And indeed these German places seem to take kindly to this part, for they rival each other in modern amusements and gauds set out to lure the light-minded. Music-halls and beer-gardens, theatres and cafés, illuminated promenades and stalls full of tempting flagons labeled "genuine eau de Cologne," are cunningly arrayed to turn away the mind from the stately antique churches and houses of Cologne. Every one has heard of the cathedral, many have seen it, and more have seen at least photographs of great accuracy, and pictures of it which, if less strict in detail, give it a more lifelike look and include some of its surroundings. The church of St. Gereon, a martyr of the Theban Legion massacred at Cologne to a man for refusing to worship the imperial ensigns, under which no one denied that they had fought like lions, is a massive Romanesque building older than the cathedral, dating from the days of Constantine and Saint Helena. The church of the Holy Apostles is a basilica with rounded apse and four octagon towers, one at each corner of the nave. St. Peter's church, the interior terribly modernized by the Renaissance, has for an altar-piece Rubens's picture of the *Crucifixion of Saint Peter*. The Gürzenich House, now used for public balls and imperial receptions, is a magnificent fifteenth-century building, adorned with dwarf towers at each corner, a high, carved and stone-roofed niche with statue over the round-arched door, transom windows filled with stained glass, and carvings of shields, animal heads, colonnettes and other devices between and above these windows. The councilhouse or town-hall has a beautiful colonnade supporting arches, and a quaint nondescript creature whose abyss-like maw opens wide and gapes horribly at the beholder each time the clock strikes. A bas-relief in the hall represents a curious incident in the civic history of the town, the successful struggle of Burgomaster Gryn with a lion, the show and pet of some treacherous nobles who invited Gryn to dinner, and under pretence of showing him their very unusual acquisition, pushed him into the stone recess and closed the gate upon him. The burgomaster thrust his hand and arm, wrapped in his thick cloak, down the animal's throat, while he pierced him

RHEINFELS.

through and through with the sword in his other hand. The struggles between Cologne and her archbishops were hot and incessant, much as they were in other ecclesiastical sovereignties. Of these there is no longer a trace in the present, though the might of the burghers exists still, and the city that was once called the kernel of the Hanseatic League, and boasted of its Lorenzo de' Medici in the person of the good and enlightened Matthias Overstolz, has now almost as proud a place among merchants as Hamburg or Frankfort. Before we pass to more modern things let us not forget the shrine of the Three Kings in the cathedral, which is simply a mass of gold and jewelry, in such profusion as to remind one of nothing less than the golden screen studded with uncut gems called the *Palla d'Oro* at San Marco, directly behind the high altar, and the Golden Frontal of St. Ambrose at Milan—golden altar it might more fitly be named, as each side of the altar is a slab of solid gold, almost hidden by its breastplate of precious stones. The same warrior-archbishop, Conrad of Hochstaden, who, driven from Cologne, transferred his see to Bonn, was the first founder of the cathedral, though in those days of slow and solid building to found was not to finish. The cathedral is not *finished* even yet. The present scenes in which Cologne shines are many—for instance, its lively market on the Neumarkt, and the country costumes one sees there each week as the stalls and carts, easily drawn by dogs and donkeys, are set up in the square; the parade of the old guard, called the "Sparks of Cologne" from their scarlet uniforms; and the Carnival, a high opportunity for fun and display, and specially seized upon to reproduce historic figures and incidents, such as the half-comic *Gecker-Berndchen*, a typical figure in red and white, the colors of the town, with a shield in one hand and a wooden sabre in the other, shouting the traditional warning cry, "*Geck los Geck elans!*" the antique procession of burgher youths and maidens, the latter with large white caps and aprons, and the former in three-cornered hats, black breeches and stockings and thick low shoes. Then follows a fancy ball in the Gürzenich House, in which the lineal descendants of the burgomasters and councillors of old come out in ancient family trappings of black cloth or velvet, stiff white ruff and heavy gold chain from shoulder to shoulder, which their forefathers once wore in earnest. Among the museums and other additions of modern taste is the beautiful botanical garden and large conservatory, where flourish tropical plants in profusion—a thing we find in many even of the secondary German towns.

The Rhine itself is becoming so uninteresting that it is hardly worth while lingering on its banks, and as we get near thrifty Holland the river seems to give itself up wholly to business, for between Cologne and Aachen (Aix-la-Chapelle) are miles upon miles of manufactories, workshops and mills; warehouses connected with coal-mines; dirty barges blackening the water; iron-works and carpet-mills; cloth and paper-mills and glass-works—a busy region, the modern translation of the myth of gnomes making gold out of dross in the bowels of the earth.

Aachen has a double life also, like many Rhine towns: it is the old imperial coronation city, the city of Charlemagne, with a corona of legends about it; and it is also the modern spa, the basket of tempting figs with a concealed asp somewhere within, a centre of fashion, gossip and gambling. How is it that people who profess to fly from the great capitals for the sake of a "little Nature" are so unable to take Nature at her word and confess her delights to be enough for them? They want a change, they say; yet where is the change? The table is the same, high-priced, choice and varied; the society is the same, the gossip is the same, the amusements are the same, the intrigues the same; the costume equally elaborate and expensive; the restless idleness as great and as hungry for excitement: all the artificiality of life is transported bodily into another place, and the only difference lies in the frame of the picture. Exquisites from the capital bring their own world with them,

"AM THÜRMCHEN," COLOGNE.

and their humbler imitators scrape together their hard winter's earnings and spend them in making an attempt cavalierly to equal for a short time the tired-out "man of the world" and "woman of fashion." Some come to find matches for sons and daughters; others to put in the thin end of the wedge that is to open a way for them "into society;" others come to flirt; others to increase their business relations; others to out-dress and out-drive social rivals; others to while away the time which it is unfashionable to spend cheaply in the city; others for—shall we say higher? because—political causes: few indeed for health, fewer still for rest. You see the same old wheel go round year after year, with the same faces growing more and more tired and more and more hopeless.

Of Aachen's legendary, historical, romantic side who has not heard?—of the castle of Frankenburg on the outskirts, where Charlemagne's daughter carried her lover Eginhardt through the snow, that their love might not be betrayed by a double track of footsteps; of Charlemagne's palace, where his school, the Palatine, presided over by English Alcuin, was held; and the baths where a hundred men could swim at ease at one time; and Charlemagne's cathedral, of which the present one has preserved only the octagonal apse; of his tomb, where he sat upright after death in imperial robes and on a marble throne (the latter is still shown); of the columns brought from Rome and Ravenna; of the marvellous and colossal corona of wax-lights which hangs by a huge iron chain from the vaulted roof; of the bronze doors of the western gateway, now closed, but whose legend of the Devil is commemorated by the iron figure of a she-wolf with a hole in her breast, and that of a pineapple, supposed to represent her spirit, of which she mourns the loss with open jaws and hanging tongue? The Devil is always cheated in these legends, and one wonders how it was that he did not show more cleverness in making his bargains. The cathedral still claims to possess precious relics—of the Passion, the Holy Winding-sheet, the robe of the Blessed Virgin and the blood-stained cloth in which the body of Saint John the Baptist was wrapped. These involve a yearly pilgrimage from the nearer places, and a great feast every seventh year, when a holy fair is kept up for weeks round the cathedral. There is no better living specimen of the Middle Ages than such gatherings, and no doubt then, as now, there was some undercurrent of worldly excitement mingling with the flow of genuine devotion. Aachen's old cornhouse, the bridge gate and the many houses full of unobtrusive beauties of carving and metal-work lead us by hook and by crook — for the streets are very winding—out on the road to Burtschied, the hot-water town, whose every house has a spring of its own, besides the very gutters running mineral water, and the cooking spring in the open street boiling eggs almost faster than they can be got out again in eatable condition. This is another of the merchant *villeggiaturas* of Germany; and a good many foreigners also own pretty, fantastic new houses, planted among others of every age from one to eight hundred years.

It is so strange to come upon a purely modern town in this neighborhood that Exefeld strikes us as an anachronism. It is wholly a business place, created by the "dry-goods" manufactures that have grown up there, and are worth twenty million thalers a year to the enterprising owners, who rival French designs and have made a market for their wares in England and America. This is a great foil to old Roman Neuss, with its massive gates, its tower attributed to Drusus—after whom so many bridges and towers on the Rhine are named—and even to Düsseldorf, which, notwithstanding its modern part, twice as large as its old river front, has some beautiful antique pictures to show us, both in the costumes of its market-women, who wear red petticoats with white aprons and flapping caps, and stand laughing and scolding in a high key by their dog-drawn carts, and in its council-house, an early Renaissance building with square, high-roofed turrets overlooking the market-place. In that little house, in a narrow street leading to the market, Heine was born; in that wretched little architectural abortion, the theatre, a critical audience listened to Immermann's works; and in the Kurzenstrasse was born Peter von Cornelius, the restorer of German art. Schadow succeeded him at the head of the Academy, and a new school of painting was firmly established in the old city, which had energy enough left in it to mark out another successful path for itself in trade. The new town is handsome, monotonous, rich and populous, but the galleries and museums somewhat make up for the lack of taste in private architecture. One of the most beautiful of the town's possessions is the old Jacobi house and garden, rescued from sale and disturbance by the patriotic artist-guild, who bought it and gave the garden to the public, while the house where Goethe visited his friend Jacobi became a museum of pictures, panelling, tapestry, native and foreign art-relics, etc., all open to the public. The gardens, with their hidden pools and marble statues, their water-lilies and overarching trees, their glades and lawns, have an Italian look, like some parts of the Villa Borghese near Rome, whose groves of ilexes are famous; but these northern trees are less monumental and more feathery, though the marble gods and goddesses seem quite as much at home among them as among the laurel and the olive.

LADY BLANCHE MURPHY.

BADEN AND ALLERHEILIGEN.

BEFORE the change which has recently befallen the chief German watering-places, Baden — or, as it was more commonly called, Baden-Baden — was the most frequented, the most brilliant and the most profitable "hell" in Europe. Its baths and medicinal waters were a mere excuse for the coming thither of a small number of the vast concourse which annually filled its hotels. In any case, they sank into comparatively utter insignificance. It was not for water — at least not for the waters of any other stream than that of Pactolus — that the world came to Baden. Of course, the sums realized by the keepers of the hell were enormous; and they found it to be their interest to do all that contributed to make the place attractive on a liberal scale. Gardens, parks, miles of woodland walks admirably kept, excellent music in great abundance, vast salons for dancing, for concerts, for reading-rooms, for billiard-rooms, etc. — all as magnificent as carving and gilding and velvet and satin could make them — were provided gratuitously, not for those only who played at the tables, but for all those who would put themselves within reach of the temptation to do so. And this liberal policy was found to answer abundantly. Very many of the water-cure places in the smaller states of Germany had their hells also, and did as Baden did, on a more modest scale. Then came the German unification and the great uprising of a German national consciousness. And German national feeling said that this scandal should no longer exist. A certain delay was rendered necessary by the contracts which were running between the different small governments and the keepers of the gambling-tables. But it was decreed that when the two or three years which were required for these to run out should be at an end, they should not be renewed. It was a serious resolution to take, for some half dozen or so of these little pleasure-towns believed, not without good reason, that the measure would be at once fatal to their prosperity and well-nigh to their existence. And of course there were not wanting large numbers of people who argued that the step was a quixotic one, as needless and fallacious in a moral point of view as fatal on the side of economic considerations. Could it be maintained that the governments in question had any moral duty in the matter save as regarded the lives and habits of their own people? And these were not imperilled by the existence of the gambling-tables. For it was notorious that each of these ducal and grand-ducal patrons of the blind goddess strictly forbade their own subjects to enter the door of the play-saloons. And as to those who resorted to them, and supplied the abundant flow of gold that enriched the whole of each little state, could it be supposed that any one of these gamblers would be reformed or saved from the consequences of his vice by the shutting up of these tables? It was difficult to answer this question in the affirmative. No liquor law ever prevented men from getting drunk, nor could it be hoped that any closing of this, that or the other hell could save gamblers from the indulgence of their darling passion. Nevertheless, it can hardly be seriously denied that the measure was the healthy outcome of a genuinely healthy and highly laudable spirit. "Ruin yourself, if you will, but you shall not come here for the purpose, and, above all, we will not touch the profit to be made out of your vice." This was the feeling of the German government, and, considering the amount of self-denial involved in the act, Germany deserves no small degree of honor and praise for having accomplished it.

And now it is time to ask, Has Baden —for we will confine our attention to this ci-devant queen of hells—has Baden suffered that ruin which it was so confidently predicted would overtake her? *Baden Revisited*, by one who knew her well in the old days of her wickedness and wealth, supplies the means for replying to the question. Unquestionably, in the mere matter of the influx of gold the town has suffered very severely. How were some four-and-twenty large hotels, besides a host of smaller ones, which often barely sufficed to hold the crowds attracted by the gambling-tables, to exist when this attraction ceased? It might have been expected that a large number of these would at once have been shut up. But such has not been the case. I believe that not one has been closed. Nevertheless, a visitor's first stroll through the town, and especially in the alleys and gardens around the celebrated "Conversations-Haus," as it hypocritically called itself, is quite sufficient to show how great is the difference between Baden as it was and Baden as it is—between Baden the wealthy, gaudy, gay, privileged home of vice, and Baden moralized and turned from the error of its ways. And it cannot be denied that, speaking merely of the impression made upon the eye, the difference is all in favor of vice. "As ugly as sin" is a common phrase. But, unfortunately, the truth is that sin sometimes looks extremely pretty, especially when well dressed and of an evening by gaslight. And it did, it must be owned, look extremely pretty at Baden. The French especially came there in those days in great numbers, and they brought their Parisian toilettes with them. And somehow or other, let the fact be explained as it may—and, though perhaps easily explicable enough, I do not feel called upon to enter on the explanation here—one used in those wicked old days to see a great number of very pretty women at Baden, which can hardly be said to be the case at Baden moralized. The whole social atmosphere of the place was wholly and unmistakably different, and in outward appearance wicked Baden beat moral Baden hollow. It would not do in the old time to examine the gay scene which fluttered and glittered before the eyes much below the absolute exterior surface. The little town in those old days, as regarded a large proportion of the crowd which made it look so gay, was—not to put too fine a point upon it —a sink of more unmitigated blackguardism than could easily be found concentrated within so small a compass on any other spot of the earth. A large number of the persons who now congregate in this beautiful valley look, to tell the truth, somewhat vulgar. Vulgar? As if the flaunting crowds which seemed to insult the magnificent forests, the crystal streams and the smiling lawns with their

IN FRONT OF THE KURSAAL AT BADEN.

finery were not saturated with a vulgarity of the most quintessential intensity ! Yes, but that only showed itself to the moral sense of those who could look a little below the surface, whereas the vulgarity that may be noted sunning itself in the trim gardens and sprawling on the satin sofas which are the legacy of the departed wickedness is of the sort that shows itself upon the surface. In a word, moral Baden looks a little *dowdy*, and *that* wicked Baden never looked.

The general determination at Baden when the terrible decree which put an end to its career of wealth and wickedness came upon it like a thunderbolt was of the kind expressed by the more forcible than elegant phrase, " Never say die !" The little town was determined to have a struggle for its existence. It still had its mineral waters, so highly valued by the Romans. The Romans, it may be remarked *en passant*, seem to have discovered and profited by every mineral spring in Europe. Hardly one of the more important springs can be named which cannot be shown, either by direct historic testimony or by the still existing remains of baths and the like, to have been known to the universal conquerors. Well, Baden still had its waters, good for all the ills to which flesh is heir—*capiti fluit utilis, utilis alveo*. It still had its magnificent forests—pine and oak and beech in most lovely juxtaposition and contrast. It had the interesting and charmingly picturesque ruins of its ancient castle on the forest-covered hill above the town, perched on one mighty mass of porphyry, and surrounded by other ranges of the same rock, thrown into such fantastic forms that they seem to assume the appearance of rival castellated ruins built on Nature's own colossal plan, and such a world of strange forms of turrets and spires and isolated towers and huge donjons that the Devil has " pulpits " and " bridges " and " chambers " there, as is well known to all tourists to be his wont in similar places. It had its other mediæval baronial residences situated in the depths of the forest at pleasant distances for either driving or walking. It had its delicious parks and gardens, beginning from the very door of the "Conversations-Haus," with brilliantly-lighted avenues, gay with shops and gas-lamps, and gradually wandering away into umbrageous solitudes and hillside paths lit by the moon alone—so gradually that she who had accepted an arm for a stroll amid the crowd in the bright foreground of the scene found herself enjoying solitude *à deux* before she had time to become alarmed or think what mamma would say. Then it had still the gorgeous halls, the ball-rooms, the concert-rooms, the promenading-rooms, with their gilding and velvet and satin furniture, which had been created by a wave of the wand of the great enchanter who presided at the green table. Why should not all these good things be turned to the service of virtue instead of vice? Why should not respectability and morality inherit the legacy of departed wickedness? Why should not good and virtuous German Fraüleins, with their pale blue eyes and pale blond hair, do their innocent flirting amid the bowers where the Parisian demi-monde had outraged the chaste wood-nymphs by its uncongenial presence? The loathsome patchouli savor of the denizens of the Boulevard would hardly resist the purifying breezes of one Black Forest winter. The notice to quit served on Mammon would be equally efficacious as regarded the whole of his crew. The whole valley would be swept clean of them, and sweetened and restored to the lovers of Nature in her most delicious aspect. Baden, emerging from the cold plunge-bath of its first dismay, determined that it should be so. The hotel-keepers, the lodging-house-keepers, the livery-stable-keepers, the purveyors of all kinds, screwed their courage to the sticking-place and determined to go in for virtue, early hours and moderate prices. Well, yes! moderate prices! This was the severest cut of all. But there was no help for it. Virtue does prefer moderate prices. There could be no more of that reckless scattering of gold, no more of that sublime indifference to the figure at the foot of the bill, which characterized their former customers. What mattered a napoleon or so more or less in their daily expense to him or her whose every evening around the green table left them some thousands of francs richer or poorer than the morning had found them? There can be no doubt, I fear, that Baden would have much preferred a continuance in its old ways. But the choice was not permitted to it. It is therefore making a virtue of necessity, and striving to live under the new régime as best it may. And I am disposed to think that better days may yet be in store for it. At present, the preponderating majority of the visitors are Germans. There are naturally no French, who heretofore formed the majority of the summer population. There are hardly any Americans, and very few English. Those of the class which used to find Baden delightful find it, or conceive that they would find it, so no more. And English and Americans of a different sort seem to have hardly yet become aware that they would find there a very different state of things from that which they have been accustomed to associate in idea with the name of the place. It must be supposed, however, that they will shortly do so. The natural advantages and beauties of the place are so great, the accommodation is so good, and even in some respects the inheritance of the good things the gamblers have left behind them so valuable, that it is hardly likely that the place will remain neglected. Where else are such public rooms and gardens to be found? The charge made at present for the enjoyment of all this is about six or eight cents a day. Such a payment could never have originally provided all that is placed at the disposal of the visitor. He used in the old times to enjoy it all absolutely gratuitously, unless he paid for it by his losses at the tables. Play provided it all. But it is to be feared that the very modest payment named above will be found insufficient even to keep up the establishment which Mammon has bequeathed to Virtue. The ormolu and the carved cornices, and the fresco-painted walls and the embroidered satin couches and divans, and the miles upon miles of garden-walks, have not indeed disappeared, as, according to all the orthodox legends, such Devil's gifts should do, but they will wear out; and I do not think that any eight cents a day will suffice to renew them. But in the mean time you may avail yourself of them. You may lounge on the brocade-covered divans which used to be but couches of thorns to so many of their occupants, undisturbed by any more palpitating excitement than that produced by the perusal of the daily paper. The lofty ceilings echo no more the hateful warning croak of the croupier, "Faites votre jeu, messieurs. Le jeu est fait!" which used to be ceaseless in them from midday till midnight. There are no more studies to be made on the men and women around you of all the expressions which eager avarice, torturing suspense and leaden despair can impart to the human countenance. The utmost you can hope to read on one of those placidly stolid German burgher faces is the outward and visible sign of the inward oppression caused by too copious a repast at the one-o'clock *table d'hôte*. It is the less disagreeable and less unhealthy subject of contemplation of the two. But the truth remains that virtuous Baden does look somewhat dowdy.

Just seventy-three years ago a change as great as that which has transformed Baden happened to an establishment which represented the old-world social system of Europe as completely and strikingly as Baden the "watering-place" —that is the modern phrase—did the Europe of the latter half of the nineteenth century. In another green valley of this region, as beautiful as, or even more beautiful than, that of Baden, there existed a gathering-place of the sort produced by the exigencies of a different stage of social progress — the convent of Allerheiligen, or, as we should say, All Saints or Allhallows. It is within the limits of an easy day's excursion from Baden, and no visitor who loves "the merry green wood" should omit to give a day to Allerheiligen, for he will scarcely find in his wanderings, let them be as extensive as they may, a more perfect specimen of the loveliest forest scenery. It is an old remark, that the ancient ecclesiastics who selected the sites of the monastic establishments that were multiplied so excessively in every country in Europe showed very excellent judgment and much practical skill in the choice of them. And almost every visit made to the spot where one of these cloister homes existed confirms the truth of the observation, more especially as regards the communities belonging to the great Benedictine family. The often-quoted line about seeking " to merit heaven by making earth a hell," however well it may be applied to the practices of some of the more ascetic orders, especially the mendicants, cannot with any reason be considered applicable to the disciples of St. Benedict. In point of fact, at the time when the great and wealthy convents of this order were founded it was rather outside the convent-wall that men were making the world a hell upon earth. And for those who could school themselves to consider celibacy no unendurable evil it would be difficult to imagine a more favorable contrast than that offered by "the world" in the Middle Ages and the retreat of the cloister. A site well selected with reference to all the requirements of climate, wood and water, and with an appreciative eye to the beauties of Nature, in some sequestered but favored spot as much shut in from war and its troubles as mountains, streams and forests could shut it in; a building often palatial in magnificence, always comfortable, with all the best appliances for study which the age could afford; with beautiful churches for the practice of a faith entirely and joyfully believed in; with noble halls for temperate but not ascetic meals, connected by stairs by no means unused with excellent and extensive cellars; with lovely cloisters for meditative pacing, and well-trimmed gardens for pleasant occupation and delight,—what can be imagined more calculated to ensure all the happiness which this earth was in those days capable of affording?

Such a retreat was the convent of Allerheiligen. It was founded for Premonstratensian monks at the close of the twelfth century by Uta, duchess of Schawenburg, who concludes the deed of foundation, which still exists, with these words: "And if anybody shall do anything in any respect contrary to these statutes, he will for ever be subject to the vengeance of God and of all saints." Poor Duchess Uta! Could her spirit walk in this valley, as lovely now as when she gave it to her monks, and look upon the ruins of the pile she raised, she would think that the vengeance of God and all saints had been incurred to a considerable extent by somebody. The waterfalls—seven of them in succession—made by the little stream that waters the valley immediately after it has passed through the isolated bit of flat meadow-land on which the convent was built, continue to sing their unceasing song as melodiously as when the duchess Uta visited the spot and marked it out for the "Gottes Haus" she was minded to plant there. Her husband, the duke Welf, who had married her when she was a well-dowered widow, had been a very bad husband, which naturally tended to lead his neglected lady wife's mind in the direction of founding religious houses. He was duke of Altorf and Spoleto, the one possession lying on the shores of the Lake of Lucerne, and the other among the ilex-woods that overlook the valley of the Tiber—a strange conjunction of titles, which is in itself illustrative of the shape European history took in that day, and of the preponderating part which Germany played in Italy and among the rulers of its soil. Being thus duke of Spoleto, Welf resided much in Italy, but does not seem to have found it necessary to take his German wife with him to those milder skies and easier social moralities. Uta stayed at home amid the dark-green valleys of her native Black Forest, and planned cloister-building. Before the chart, however, which was to give birth to Allerheiligen was signed, Duke Welf came home, and having had, it would seem, his fling to a very considerable extent, had reached by a natural process that time of life and that frame of mind which inclined him to join in his long-neglected wife's pietistic schemes. So they planned and drew up the statutes together, and the con-

RUINS OF THE ABBEY OF ALLERHEILIGEN.

vent was founded and built, a son of Uta by her first husband being, as is recorded, the first prior.

It was not long before the young community became rich. Such was the ordinary, the almost invariable, course of matters. Property was held on very unstable conditions even by the great and powerful. The most secure of all tenures was that by which the Church held what was once her own. And in a state of things when men were persuaded both that it was very doubtful whether they would be able to keep possession of their property, especially whether they would be able to secure such possessions to those who were to come after them, and that the surest way to escape that retribution in the next world which they fully believed to have been incurred by their deeds in this world was to give what they possessed to some monastic institution, it is not difficult to understand how and why monasteries grew rich. And it is equally intelligible that the result should have followed which did, as we know, follow almost invariably. As the monasteries became rich the monks became corrupt—first comfortable, then luxurious, then licentious. The Benedictines escaped this doom more frequently than the other orders. Even after their great convents had become wealthy and powerful landlords they were often very good landlords, and the condition of their lands and of their tenants and vassals contrasted favorably with that of the lands and dependants of their lay neighbors. The superiority of the Benedictines in this respect was doubtless due to their studious and literary habits and proclivities. It is constantly urged that the cause of learning and of literature owes a great debt of gratitude to the monks, but it should be said that this debt is due almost exclusively to the sons of St. Benedict.

But something more than this may be said for the community founded by Duchess Uta, the beautiful ruins of whose dwelling now complete the picturesque charm of this most exquisite valley. By a rare exception history has in truth nothing to say against them. Their record is quite clear. All remaining testimony declares that from their first establishment to the day of their dissolution the Allerheiligen monks lived studious and blameless lives. Possibly, the profound seclusion of their valley, literally shut in from the outer world by vast masses of thick roadless forests, may have contributed to this result, though similar circumstances do not in all cases seem to have ensured a similar consequence. Good fortune probably did much in the matter. A happy succession of three or four good and able abbots would give the place a good name and beget a good tradition in the community; and this in such cases is half the battle. "Such and such goings-on may do elsewhere, but they won't suit Allerheiligen"—such a sentiment, once made common, would do much for the continuance of a good and healthy tradition.

Accordingly, it was long before the sentence of dissolution went forth against the monastery of Allerheiligen—that sentence which was to produce a change in the place and all around it as momentous as that other sentence which some seventy years later went forth against Baden-Baden. It was not till 1802 that the monastery of Allerheiligen was dissolved; and its extinction was due then not to any reason or pretext drawn from the conduct of the inmates, but to the religious dissensions and political quarrels of princes and governments. But the doom was all the more irrevocably certain. In all the countries in which monasteries have been abolished and Church property confiscated tales eagerly spread, and by no means wholly disbelieved even by the spoilers themselves, are current of the "judgments" and retribution which have sooner or later fallen on those who have been enriched by the secularization of Church property or who have taken part in the acts by which the Church has been dispossessed. But rarely has what the world now calls "chance" brought about what the Church would call so startlingly striking a manifestation of the wrath of Heaven against the despoilers of "God's house." St. Norbert was the original founder of the Premonstratensian rule. And it was precisely on St. Norbert's Day next after the dissolution of the monastery of Allerheiligen that a tremendous and—the local chroniclers say—unprecedented storm of thunder, lightning and hail broke over the woodland valley and the devoted fabric in such sort that the lightning, more than once striking the buildings, set them on fire and reduced the vast pile to the few picturesque ruins which now delight the tourist and the landscape painter. Could the purpose and intent of the supernal Powers have been more strongly emphasized or more clearly marked? Truly, the scattered monks may have been excused for recalling with awe, not unmingled with a sense of triumph, the prophetic denunciation of their foundress Uta, which has been cited above, against whoso should undo the pious deed she was doing. For more than six hundred years her work had prospered and her will had been respected, and now after all those centuries the warning curse was still potent. Neither thunder nor lightning, nor the anger of St. Norbert, however, availed to rebuild the monastery or recall the monks. Their kingdom and the glory thereof has passed to another, even to Herr Mittenmeyer, *Wirth und Gastgeber*, who has built a commodious hostelry close by the ruins, which are mainly those of the church, and on the site of the monastic buildings, and who distributes a hospitality as universal, if not quite so disinterested, as that practised by his cowled predecessors. There, for the sum of six marks—about a dollar and a half—per diem you may find a well-furnished cell and a fairly well-supplied refectory, and may amuse yourself with pacing in the walks where St. Norbert's monks paced, looking on the scenes of beauty on which they gazed, and casting your mind for the nonce into the mould of the minds of those who so looked and mused. You may do so, indeed, thanks to Herr Mittenmeyer, with greater comfort, materially speaking, than the old inmates of the valley could have done. For the most charming and delicious walks have been made through the woods on either side of the narrow valley, and skilfully planned so as to show you all the very remarkable beauties of it. These, in truth, are of no ordinary kind. The hillsides which enclose the valley are exceedingly steep, almost precipitous indeed in some places, though not sufficiently so to prevent them from being clothed with magnificent forests. Down this narrow valley a little stream runs, and about a quarter of a mile from the spot on which the convent stood, and the ruins stand, makes a series of cascades of every variety of form and position that can be conceived. All these falls, together with the crystalline pools in huge caldrons worn by the waters out of the rocks at their feet, were no doubt well known to the vassal fishermen who brought their tribute of trout to the convent larder. But the majority of the holy men themselves, I fancy, lived and died without seeing some of the falls, for they would be by no means easily accessible without the assistance of the paths which by dint of long flights of steps, constructed of stones evidently brought from the ruins of the abbey, carry the visitor to every spot of vantage-ground most favorable for commanding a view of them. If, however, you have the advantage over the monks in this respect, your retreat will be less adapted to the purposes of retirement in another point of view. Ten or a dozen carriages a day filled with German tourists, all in high spirits and all very thirsty ("Thanks be!" says Herr Mittenmeyer), are not appropriate aids to the indulgence of contemplation. Scott advised his readers if they "would view fair Melrose aright, to visit it by the pale moonlight." And to those who would view Allerheiligen aright I would add the recommendation that the moon should be an October moon. The usual holiday-making months in Germany are by that time over. The professors have gone back to their chairs in the different universities; the *privat-docents* have reopened their courses; the substantial burghers have returned to their shops; and the *raths* of all sorts and degrees have ensconced themselves once more behind their official desks, and have ceased to "babble of green fields" any more till this time twelvemonth. The tourists will have gone, and the autumnal colors will have come into the woods. There is much beech mixed with the pine in these forests, and the beech in October is as gorgeous a master of color as Rubens or Veronese. Herr Mittenmeyer's mind, too, will have entered into a more placid and even-tempered phase. A stout, thickset man is Herr Mittenmeyer, with broad, rubicund face and short bull neck, of the type that suggests the possibility of an analogous shortness of temper under the pressure of being called in six different directions at once. Altogether, it is better in October. The song of the waterfall will not then be the only one making the woods melodious. There will be a fitful soughing of the wind in the forest. There will be a carpeting of dry, pale-brown oak-leaves on all the paths which "will make your steps vocal." Again and again, when slowly and musingly climbing the steep homeward path up the valley in the dark hour, when the sun has set and before the moon has yet risen, you will fancy that you hear the tread among the leaves of a sandalled foot behind you. But it is well that the path leads you, for there is no more any vesper-bell flinging its sweet and welcome notes far and wide over hill and vale to guide the returning wanderer through the forest.

Then the whole of this Black Forest region is full of legends and traditional stories, which live longer and are more easily preserved among a people where the sons and the daughters live and marry and die for the most part under the shadow of the same trees and the same thatch beneath which their fathers and mothers did the same. Of course, the Black Huntsman is as well known as of yore, though perhaps somewhat more rarely seen. But his habits and specialties have become too well known to all readers of folk-lore to need any further notice. Less widely known histories, each the traditional subject of inglenook talk in its own valley, may be found at every step. There is a rather remarkable grotto or cavern in the hill above Allerheiligen, the main ridge which divides that valley from Achern and the Rhine. It is, you are told, the Edelfrauengrab (the "Noble Lady's Grave"). And you will be further informed, if you inquire aright, how that unhallowed spot came to be a noble lady's grave, and something more than a grave. 'Twas at the time of the Crusades—those mischief-making Crusades, which, among all the other evil which they produced, would have absolutely overwhelmed the divorce courts of those days with press of business if there had then been any divorce courts. This noble lady's lord went to the Crusades. How could a gallant knight and good Christian do aught else? Of course he went to the Crusades! And of course his noble lady felt extremely dull and disconsolate during his absence. What was she to do? There was no circulating library; and even if there had been, she would not have been able to avail herself of its resources, for, though tradition says nothing upon the subject, it may be very safely assumed that she could not read. And needlework in the company of her maids must have become terribly wearisome after a time. She could go to mass, and to vespers also. Probably she did so at the new church of the recently-established community nestling in so charming a spot of the lovely valley beneath her. Let us hope that it was not there that she fell in with one whom in an hour of weakness she permitted to console her too tenderly for the absence of her crusading lord. Had she waited with patience but only nine months longer for his return, all would have been well. For he did return as nearly as possible about that time; and, arriving at his own castle-door, met one whom he at once recognized as his wife's confidential maid coming out of the house and carrying a large basket. The natural inquiry whither she was going, and what she had in her basket, was answered by the statement—uttered with that ingenuous fluency and masterly readiness for which ladies' maids have in all countries, and doubtless in all ages, been celebrated—that the basket contained a litter of puppies which she was taking to the river to drown. Alas! the girl had adhered but too nearly to the truth. There *were* seven living and breathing creatures in the basket, and the confidential maid had been sent on the very confidential errand of drowning them. Woe worth the day! They were seven little unchristened Christians, doomed to die one death as they had been born at one birth —the result of that erring noble lady's fault. The methods of injured husbands were wont to be characterized by much simplicity and directness of purpose in those days. The noble crusader invoked the aid of no court, either spiritual or lay. He happened to remember the existence of a certain dismal cavern in the sandstone rock not far from his dwelling. The entrance to it was very easily walled up. That cavern became the noble lady's prison and deathbed, as well as her grave! And a valuable possession has that lady's death and grave become to the descendants of her lord's vassals, for many a gulden is earned by guiding the curious to see the spot and by retailing the tragic history.

Well! and of the two changes, the two abolitions, which have been here recorded, which was the most needed, which the most salutary, which the least mingled in its results with elements of evil? Poor Baden piteously complains that it does not take half the money in the course of the year that it used to receive as surely as "the season" came round in the old times. And the poor, wholly unconverted by maxims of political economy, declare that there have been no good times in the land since the destruction of the monasteries. After all, Abbot Fischer (that was the name of the last of the long line) and his monks were less objectionable than M. Benazet and his croupiers. Could we perhaps keep the scales even and make things pleasant all round by re-establishing both the abolished institutions—restoring the croupiers and "makers of the game" to their green table, and requiring them out of their enormous gains to re-endow the convent? "C'est une idée, comme une autre!" as a Frenchman says.

T. ADOLPHUS TROLLOPE.

WHY DO WE LIKE PARIS?

PART I.

THE RUE DE RIVOLI AND THE TOUR ST. JACQUES.

"ALL roads lead to Paris," said the wise and witty Doudan: "it is the Rome of the new era." I will not offend my readers by repeating a native witticism which has become a proverb. Americans—good and bad—are not the only foreigners who congregate in Paris. Paris was the first stage in the *grand tour* of the last century; French comedies and caricatures of fifty years ago abound in representations of the English; some of the noblest names of Great Britain are now more identified with Paris than with London. The Irish Jacobites who emigrated in a body after the triumph of William of Orange were soon incorporated into the French Legitimist society. That which now stands for the court of Poland has its seat in Paris: the Hôtel Lambert is occupied by the Czartoryskis, who represent the extinct royalty in virtue of their descent from kings of Poland of their own name and from the Sapiehas, who also sat upon that rickety throne. They form a centre for the Polish society of Paris, amidst which they preserve a semblance of regal dignity and the etiquette of a court, reproducing the Stuart court at St. Germains in the seventeenth century. There is also a high Spanish society, with Queen Isabella at its head. Much foreign royalty finds a home and holds a certain state there. The emperor Julian the Apostate liked Paris because it was quiet: it may be doubted whether many people have resorted to it since his time for that reason, yet it draws and holds the grave as well as the gay. Chopin went thither on a visit, and remained there for ever after: it was a joke of his to the last that he was merely passing through Paris. Heine found himself moored there for life: his yearnings for the Fatherland always produced a reaction toward France. In his night thoughts sleepless fancy brings before him the oaks and lindens of Germany and his old mother, whom he has not seen for ten years; but it ends—

> Thank Heaven! through my window streams
> The Frankish sun with gladsome beams:
> Here comes my wife, as fresh as day,
> To laugh my German griefs away.

It is hard to say wherein this universal charm lies. Paris is the least cosmopolitan of great cities—she is only French: the complaint of the nation has been that Paris stands for the whole country, whereas there is much of France which is not Parisian, much of it which shows the influence of Paris less than some circles of American society did ten years ago (just now they take their tone from Marlborough House and Sandringham). Yet, though it is true that Paris is not all France, she is French, essentially French; and there must be something in the nature of her inhabitants which offers points of sympathy to the variety of nations and dispositions gathered together there. There is extreme diversity in the range of French character, which may easily be observed in the difference of their public men, the reserved scholarly type being as distinct as the theatrical or the satirical. Notwithstanding a proneness to violence in the national temperament, which breaks out in times and in ways at which all Christendom stands aghast, and other tendencies peculiarly repugnant to the Anglo-Saxon, the French possess qualities which raise their standard to a higher level than that of their decorous neighbors. The notions of honor and glory which have been turned into a scoff by people incapable of understanding the ideal are familiar to them from the cradle: such seed, falling on good soil, brings forth flowers of chivalry like Larochejacquelin and some of the men who fought for us a hundred years ago. But there are homelier virtues which the French practise more assiduously than any other people —thrift, for instance. There is nothing which strikes us open-handed, over-careless Americans more disagreeably on going abroad than the perpetual wrangle over candle-ends and cheese-parings, farthings and halfpence. I am not speaking now of the customary fleecing of foreigners and travellers, but of the habitual economy; and the form which this takes in England is what we call "meanness"—a parsimony which, besides pinching itself, makes use of every small and shabby trick for saving at the expense of others. In Germany also this necessity, though more self-respecting, has a sordid aspect. In Italy it gayly sacrifices the necessaries of life to the luxuries, and induces the majority of the middle class, and not a few of the nobility, to stint themselves in food and fuel for the sake of opera-tickets, an afternoon drive, a holiday suit of clothes —not from ostentation, but from a preference for what is amusing to what is substantial. But in France the sense of order and fitness is perpetually gratified by the proportion and relation preserved between people's means and their lives; by the unusual neatness and grace with which even poverty can be invested; by the cheerfulness with which lifelong toil and a hard lot are borne; by the spirit and good sense which season much work with a little play. Courtesy of the finest

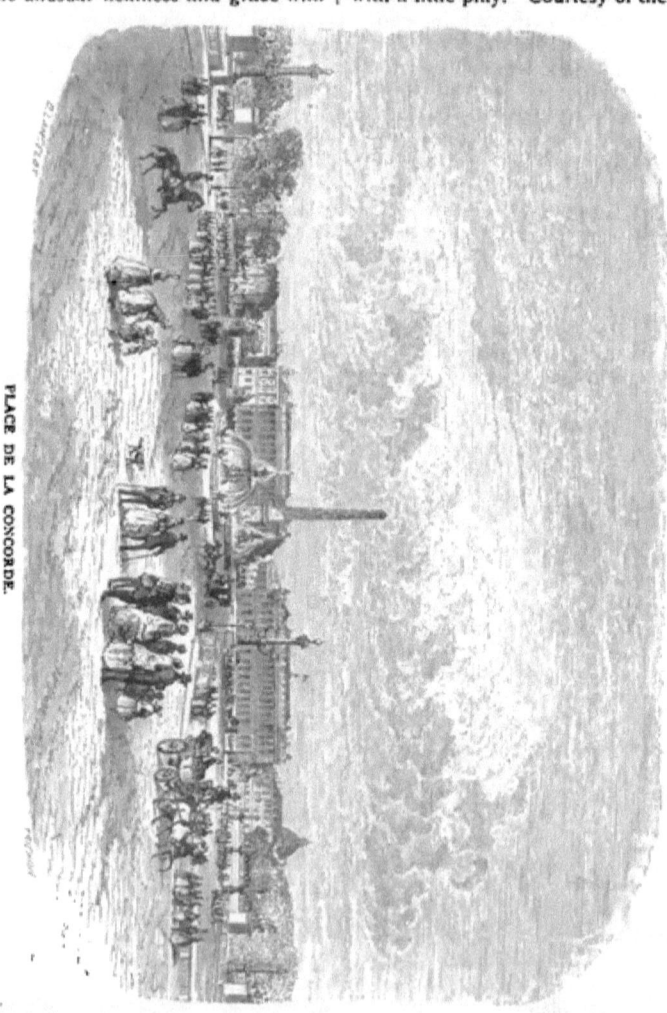

PLACE DE LA CONCORDE.

kind is an almost invariable rule, in spite of threadbare stories of Frenchmen who take the wing of a chicken and the best seat in the railway-carriage: the Englishman or German who will not take the whole chicken or the only seat is the exception. The American criterion of good-nature and good manners must not be carried across the Atlantic. Another hackneyed reproach against the French which we have taken up from the English is, that they have no home-life, because they live on flats and eat at restaurants. The reply is now almost as familiar as the accusation, yet it must be repeated as long as the accusation is brought: The family tie is a warmer and closer bond in France than in England, or even with us; the grandfather or grandmother is the cherished and revered centre of a circle which often includes a bachelor uncle or spinster cousin; and cold pudding for poor relations is unknown. There is a sort of unselfishness practised among all classes in France of which we have very little knowledge: it is a common act for a sister to renounce her share of the parental inheritance to give a brother the means of starting in life, or for several members of a family to unite in the same sacrifice to make up a sister's dower: this generally implies for all but the chosen one straitened means and single lives—for women often a convent—while that one, if a man, becomes in return the stay and support of the rest; if a woman, their good angel. A comparison of the virtues of the Latin and other races might explain much of the charm of Latin countries. These amiable qualities, although unknown to the greater number of strangers who frequent Paris, or denied by them, help to produce that agreeable temperature of cheerfulness and satisfaction which goes for a great deal in one's enjoyment of a place. But the positive resources for tastes of every sort are inexhaustible.

To begin with, there is scarcely a pursuit, whether serious or frivolous, which may not be followed to greater advantage in Paris than in any other European city. There is not such an accumulation of amusements as in London during the season, but, on the other hand, there is no dead season in Paris, as in almost all other capitals. The great galleries are open the whole year round, and so, practically, are the theatres and opera-houses, for their short vacations do not occur simultaneously: good music and acting are always to be found. The rush of social gayety is over before the spring exhibition of paintings opens; there is no custom among the richer people of leaving town in a body, such as prevails in London and our great cities, so that Paris never wears a dreary, deserted aspect; the display in the shop-windows does not lose its sheen, nor the Champs Élysées their life, nor the Bois de Boulogne its fashion, at any time of year. Most people like a place the outward aspect of which puts them in good spirits.

This feature of Paris must have been less prominent before the reign of Napoleon III. and M. Haussmann. Those who love the architectural expression of what is venerable, picturesque and encrusted with historical associations watched the progress of their improvements with grief. It was curious to observe as the emperor's popularity declined how the tone of the people and the press changed in regard to this magnificent clearing out. At first it was spoken of as the "embellishments," then as the "alterations," then as the "demolition:" an illustrated paper constantly published woodcuts of buildings which were disappearing under the title of "Paris qui s'en va." It was natural that many Parisians should bewail the destruction of so much that was old and beautiful, and that many visitors like myself should have mourned to find the goal of a pilgrimage only the site of a former shrine. But the grand avenue beginning at the beautiful old church of St. Germains l'Auxerrois, embracing the palace and courts of the Louvre, the palace, pavilions and gardens of the Tuileries, the Place de la Concorde with its fountains and obelisk, the festive Champs Élysées, all sunshine and leafy shade, is worth a great many old bits and odd corners. Let us remember, too, that the immense life of a million and a half of inhabitants and the incalculable currents of travel were forced into those narrow, crooked streets, blind alleys, dark passages, and we shall admit the need of the straight channels and the open thoroughfares. The modernization of ancient and picturesque cities is a constant and natural subject of lamentation, but modern life requires modern accommodation: it is impossible that the capital of Austria or Italy in the nineteenth century should remain as it was in the Middle Ages. Paris, as was inevitable, has changed far more than Vienna, far more than the Eternal City will ever change, let us hope, but she is not bereft of all her ancient ornaments. If we are most interested by the far past, as the citizens of a new country are apt to be, let us begin by looking around at some of the relics which still remain, without departing from the beaten track.

No street is so inseparably connected with the modern and American idea of Paris as the Rue de Rivoli, a broad, light-colored vista of hotels, handsome houses and sparkling shop-windows: following it to the end, we come to the Tour St. Jacques, a fine fragment of late Gothic rising nearly two hundred feet from the pavement, like a steep rock from a plain. It is the last vestige of a church begun under Louis XII., finished in the palmy days of Francis I. and demolished by the mob in 1789. Under the pointed arch of the lowest story stands a statue of Pascal, who made some of his philosophical experiments in this tower. From its summit, once crowned by a lovely spire, there is a magnificent view of Paris. From that height the Seine seems to flow almost at our feet, dividing around the island on which stands Notre Dame, whose mighty towers are close over against us. We look down into the little, narrow streets near the cathedral, and they swarm with shadowy historical figures, but the personages of Victor Hugo's novel *Notre Dame de Paris* — or, as we call it, *The Hunchback of*

THE STE. CHAPELLE.

Notre Dame — drive out the real and rightful ghosts. It is a handbook for this part of Paris, in which one may find the city restored as it was three centuries ago and as great part of it remained until recent times. The island seems one to us looking down, but it is several islets pieced together and bridged across. Still gazing from the Tour St. Jacques, we see with a shudder how hardly the exquisite Ste. Chapelle escaped the flames of the Commune: when the fire had all but reached the walls it stopped as if by a miracle, and this gem of early florid architecture survived. A special providence watches over this little church, small in comparison with its great neighbor. It was built by the royal St. Louis to receive relics of peculiar sacredness from Palestine, part of the true cross and the crown of thorns. The two octagonal towers are encircled halfway up by a crown of thorns in stone: the same fancy has carved and bristled the pinnacles with little spikes which mingle with the foliage of the crockets and produce a luxuriant decoration. In 1618 the Ste. Chapelle was endangered by a fire which destroyed one of the finest halls of the adjacent Palais de Justice; twelve years later its own beautiful spire was burnt, and not replaced until 1853; in 1776 all the buildings actually adjoining it were consumed; in 1781 the conflagration raged about it, sweeping away monuments and mementos of every period, but sparing the splendid reliquary: the jewel-like glass of the windows, coeval with the church, escaped the fury of the Revolution. The church has been restored with extreme care from remains of the old wood-carving, frescoes and sculpture, so that we look upon its beauties as they delighted the devout heart of its royal founder on the eve of departure for his first ill-starred crusade. Notwithstanding the flaws in his character, Louis IX., like St. Elizabeth of Hungary, is one of those mediæval physiognomies whose enthusiasm and childlike simplicity, unspotted through life, make us forget their shortcomings: in those days the great of the earth, whatever their faults, had often an unworldliness which imparts a singular purity and luminousness to their memory.

The island well illustrates how crowded every rood of the old city is with places of interest. In this small space alone there are the cathedral, the Ste. Chapelle, the Palais de Justice, the church of St. Louis en l'Île—a small church built in 1664, but interesting from its connection with the University of Paris; the Hôtel Dieu, the most ancient hospital in Paris, the origin of which dates from Merovingian times; the Hôtel Lambert, a lordly mansion which appears in the memoirs of the seventeenth and eighteenth centuries, and now, by the occupancy of the Czartoryskis, represents the court of Poland; the Conciergerie. Many of the oldest edifices are built over still more venerable ones, of which the foundations and other portions are still visible: many contain smaller independent structures, like the ancient church of St. Julien des Pauvres within the precincts of the Hôtel Dieu. Paris may be studied like a huge palimpsest in stone and mortar, where beneath the new is something old, and beneath the old something older. The superb brand-new Tribunal de Commerce is a case in point: between the antique piles of the Palais de Justice and the Hôtel Dieu its modern Corinthian architecture is strikingly out of place. The grandiose, heavily-handsome staircase and cupola and the Cour d'Honneur, built like the court of an Italian palace of the Renaissance, have neither stateliness nor meaning in their present position: the building belongs to the new quarters, to the city of Napoleon III. and M. Haussmann; but it stands on the site of a Roman prison and of the mediæval church and convent of St. Bartholomew.

There never were such people as the French for literally tearing themselves to pieces. Between Notre Dame and the river, where there are an open walk and a modern fountain, stood not fifty years ago the splendid palace of the archbishops of Paris, rich with the ecclesiastical treasures of seven centuries. During the political disturbances which attended the accession of Louis Philippe the palace was sacked by the mob, headed, it is said, by officers of the National Guard: everything in it was broken, stolen or thrown into the river, and the building itself was so nearly destroyed that it could not be rebuilt. The archbishop of that time, Monseigneur de Quelen, a man eminent for piety, courage and every other virtue, twice narrowly escaped death at the hands of that most awful of all mobs, the mob of Paris, who were clamoring for his head on the strength of absurd reports of arms and ammunition concealed in the vaults of Notre Dame. His life was shortened by these agitations and revulsions of feeling. Within the last hundred years four archbishops of Paris have died a violent death, beginning with the unworthy Gobel, who was guillotined in 1794. They have been a

THE PONT NEUF.

line of martyrs: Mgr. de Quelen was a martyr in all but the mere fact; Mgr. Affre fell in attempting to persuade the insurgents of the Faubourg St. Antoine to disperse in the revolution of 1848: he was shot on the barricade with words of peace on his lips and the olive-branch in his hand. He had put aside entreaties and warnings with the words, "The Good Shepherd gives his life for the sheep:" his dying ejaculation was, "May my blood be the last to be shed!" His successor, Mgr. Sibour, was assassinated by a renegade priest in 1857 as he was performing the great annual service in honor of Ste. Geneviève, the patroness of Paris. The blood of the last archbishop, Mgr. Darboy, is scarcely dry in the ditch of the Grande Roquette, where he was shot by the Communists in May, 1871. The humblest missionary to African savages is in less danger than these magnif-

PORTE ROUGE, NOTRE DAME.

icent prelates. We do not like Paris so much when we think of all the blood that has been shed here: the blood-stains of the Commune are still fresh, and, going back as far as we can, we find the damned spot everywhere. One of the most beautiful bits of Notre Dame is the Porte Rouge on the north side, which may be translated the "Door of Blood," and which was built by John the Fearless, duke of Burgundy, in expiation of the murder of the duke of Orleans in 1407. The valor and other princely qualities of Jean sans Peur and the odious character of his victim, who was the very curse of France, bias us in favor of the former notwithstanding the treachery of his deed. Their enmity had been bitter and of long standing, but they met for formal and public reconciliation, attended mass and received the sacrament together, and ended the day by a banquet. On his way home the duke of Orleans was surrounded and assassinated: the story goes that one wrapped in a mantle and scarlet hood, so as to conceal his face and figure, suddenly came out of a house and struck the final, fatal blow, and that this was the duke of Burgundy. The duke of Orleans had offered him an unpardonable insult by placing the likeness of the duchess of Burgundy among the portraits of his mistresses. It is further said that the duke of Burgundy had received intelligence of a plot to assassinate himself, and merely got the start of his foe. His atonement was splendid, according to the notions of those times. About ten years afterward he paid the natural penalty of his great crime, and was slain in his turn on the bridge of Montereau during a parley with the dauphin, afterward Charles VII. His tomb is at Dijon, the place of his birth, beside that of his father, Philippe le Hardi; his duchess Margaret lies by his side coroneted and in daisy-sprinkled robe; around the base of the monument troops of little monks mourn the death of their prince with every demonstration of grief. But under the rich Gothic canopy which forms the porch of the Porte Rouge the duke and duchess of Burgundy kneel in perpetual repentance amid a crowd of divine and sacred figures.

The combination of richness in detail and simplicity of general plan is the characteristic beauty of Notre Dame. The eye comprehends its grand proportions at the first glance: it is pervaded by a sublime repose which is undisturbed by the prodigality of sculpture on the triple portal, the flying buttresses, the rose-windows, the three galleries. Pointed Gothic cannot go further in the union of majesty and grace.

Even amid these magnificent landmarks of the old French monarchy the imagination of a traveller, tracing the footprints of history, is preoccupied by recollections of the First Revolution. His path is constantly crossing the seared, ensanguined track. In 1872 the marks of the Commune hardly seemed fresher than those of 1792. Here, in the island, the round turrets of the Conciergerie, flanking its arched gateway facing the river and seen from the opposite quay, divide our thoughts with the Gothic magnificence, with the holy, heroic, fierce, romantic traditions of earlier times. The Conciergerie was a dungeon ages ago, when the Palais de Justice was a royal residence: it had its terrors, its executions, its *oubliettes;* but it is as the prison of the Revolution that it keeps its horrible fame. Nor is it only that the Conciergerie was the prison, but the prison of the doomed — one huge condemned cell. Here the Girondists supped together on the night before their execution with jest and song and speech, with some show of theatrical bravado, with noble acts of real courage, like Vergniaud's throwing away the poison of which there was not enough for his friends: hither came Charlotte Corday and Madame Roland from the Abbey, Marie Antoinette from the Temple, the Jacobins from the Luxembourg — one last journey more for them all. These went forth to death, but hundreds were perfidiously discharged and sent back to life, to meet a more appalling fate at the gates by the hands of the mob. Twice the apartment in which Marie Antoinette spent her last two months on earth has been consecrated to her memory by paintings, inscriptions, relics: they were torn out and dispersed in 1830; it was again restored and restocked during the Second Empire, when the empress Eugénie had set a fashion of enthusiasm for the unfortunate queen; but it was again pillaged by the fury of the Commune, and the very cell itself destroyed in May, 1871.

There are occasional exhibitions of ferocity in the lives of individuals and nations on which it is wise not to dwell if we wish to keep our faith in human nature. It is better to leave the island and its still unvisited curiosities and cross to the left bank of the Seine. This is the Rive Gauche, which many think the most interesting and agreeable part of Paris, and where they find the best reasons for a sojourn there. The quays are the favorite haunt of bric-à-brac lovers, collectors of old books and rare engravings. New books too may be bought at the second-hand stalls for a song: I have seen a complete edition of Sainte-Beuve, near forty volumes, as fresh as if just from Hachette's shop, for something between fifteen and sixteen dollars. The Pont St.

CHAPEL OF THE HOTEL DE CLUNY.

Michel leads from the island to the Latin Quarter, so well known to students, especially students of medicine. It is a labyrinth of streets with learned names, the Rue Gerson, Rue Amyot, Rue Descartes, Rue Laplace: the stranger expects sermons from their stones and supposes every house to be an abode of learning. Here are the Sorbonne, or theological seminary, the Collége de France, the École Polytechnique, the École Normale, while *colléges* and *lycées* by the score shoulder one another. But this scholastic realm is the centre of the *vie de Bohème,* that country without confines, the land of the prodigal and ne'er-do-weel, where many a sober citizen, many a member of the learned professions in the Old and New Worlds, have sowed their wild oats, and some have made them into pipes and blown blithely and tunefully thereupon. Victor Hugo is cicerone for the Île de la Cité, and to Henri Murger belongs the Pays Latin, with its larks, its devil-may-care laughter, its wit, poetry, pathos, its transient yet sometimes tragic loves, its harrowing and horrible destinies. Parisians assert that there is no longer such a life, such a country; that it has been divided like Poland and its autonomy destroyed; that Murger's and Musset's novels are tales from ancient history. If this be true, so much the better: idleness, improvidence and vice are less dangerous when they do not wear sentimental faces and assume idyllic attitudes. For one man who came scot-free out of the ordeal, how many left health, happiness, wholesome habits behind them! The preface to Murger's *Vie de Bohème* and Musset's *Frédéric et Bernerette* are the best homilies on the subject—Murger's own sad story the best moral.

The outward aspect of the quarter, although not new, is prosaic enough until suddenly we come upon a Gothic gateway in an old wall; and here are the ancient Lutetia and mediæval Paris again. It is the entrance to the Hôtel de Cluny, a noble specimen of fifteenth-century domestic architecture. It may be called the city palace of the abbots of Cluny, as Lambeth is the London house of the archbishops of Canterbury. Down in Burgundy, on the quiet banks of the Saône, stand the magnificent ruins of the abbey of Cluny, founded in the solitude by a duke of Aquitaine in 920. It rose rapidly in importance and influence, and the abbot became one of the great ecclesiastical powers of Europe. About a hundred years from its foundation, Hildebrand—afterward the great pope Gregory VII.—retired thither to find a stricter rule of life than in his convent at Rome. In another hundred years the post of abbot was filled by Peter the Venerable, an erudite, generous, zealous man, a prominent Church politician.

He accomplished a great work for the abbey, reforming its loosened manners and relaxed rule, obtaining valuable privileges and strengthening its prerogatives by the favor of kings and popes. All this makes no difference now to any human being alive, but Peter the Venerable is remembered as the friend of Abelard and Héloïse, the most famous pair of lovers the world has ever known. He gave shelter and sympathy to Abelard when that thrice-unhappy man was silenced, banished and threatened with excommunication for his independent thinking and speaking. The compassion of Peter the Venerable survives with the sorrows of Héloïse and Abelard: the tears which he shed over the recital of their misfortunes, his letter of condolence to Héloïse on Abelard's death, his tenderness for the latter's memory, are preserved in the heavy, correct, unclassical tomes of the *Bibliotheca Veterum Patrum*, where few people will look for them; but everybody may see the beautiful tomb in the cemetery of Père la Chaise at Paris which was made by Peter's order for Abelard. Modern lovers still make sentimental journeys to the tomb: it is covered with wreaths on All Souls' Day—most of them, sad to say, crowns of everlasting flowers or still more frightful ones of black and white beads. After Peter's death the abbey continued to flourish until it became the head of nearly two thousand religious houses and had a revenue of sixty thousand dollars a year. No wonder that the abbot required a town-house at the capital for greater convenience in looking after so many interests, temporal and spiritual; and toward the close of the fifteenth century this stately palace arose. It was far from being dedicated exclusively to clerical use, however. Soon after it was finished, Mary Tudor, the sister of Henry VIII. of England, lived here while widow of Louis XII. of France, previous to her marriage to Brandon, duke of Suffolk—the unromantic heroine of a romantic love-story. Her bedroom bears the pretty but misleading title of "Chambre de la Reine blanche," in allusion to the white mourning which the queens of

France wore as weeds. Here too James V. of Scotland, superfine, poetical, chivalrous, ill-fated personage, was married to Madeleine, the daughter of Francis I. Later, the Guises made a stronghold of the place: it served as a refuge of the doves of Port Royal and their abbess; as the barracks of a company of actors; as the head-quarters of Marat in '93, until Charlotte Corday's knife stopped

INTERIOR OF STE. GENEVIÈVE (THE PANTHÉON).

the murderous business which was doing there. Its late purpose, horrible as it is to remember, probably saved the Hôtel de Cluny from the destruction which overtook the mother-house. On the banks of the Saône two ruined towers and a dilapidated wall are all that remain of the glorious abbey of Cluny; but the hôtel was spared by the sans-culottes, and its regeneration after Marat's occupancy began by its being used in part as a stable, in part as a cooper's shop and for similar harmless purposes. At length it was bought by the accomplished and enthusiastic M. de Sommerard, author of *Les Arts au Moyen Age*, to receive his collection of historical specimens and relics of the early arts in France. The government bought it of his heirs in 1843, and keeps it as a museum of national antiquities. The lofty rooms with mullioned windows are filled with splendid old furniture, tapestry, lace, pottery, armor, weapons, trinkets and curiosities too various to classify. They are haunted by students and connoisseurs of bric-à-brac; by artists making sketches of the gorgeous Arras and Gobelin hangings or of those magnificent carved and sculptured mantelpieces which figure in so many watercolor drawings and on so many canvases; by actors careful of accuracy in the costume of an historical part; but most of all by lovers of the past and the picturesque. It is a grand old curiosity-shop. One of the strangest relics in the collection is a set of crowns belonging to the Gothic period in Spain: they consist of a king's, a queen's, and those of six royal infants: any well-read child will immediately remember Hop-o'-my-Thumb's host, the ogre, in whose family a crown was also an indispensable article of attire.

The gem of the building is a chapel adjoining the apartment of Mary Tudor: its vaulted roof is supported by a single slender, octagonal column; the fan-tracery of the roof is filled in with a profusion of delicate leafage; the lectern, credence and other pieces of church furniture are carved in the most elaborate manner; the walls are enriched with Gothic niches of exquisite form and design; grace and elegance control the proportions and decorations, yet the whole effect is cold and depressing. A church in which men no longer worship can no more retain its aspect of a sanctuary than an uninhabited house the atmosphere of a home; arm-chairs, tables, sofas, chairs, books, writing-materials cannot preserve an apartment from the mildew of desertion which overspreads it when human life no longer abides there; and so, in spite of the altar and its appointments, the Divine Presence seems to depart from the temple no longer warmed by prayer and praise.

From the chapel a winding stone staircase leads down to the older building, the palace of the emperor Julian and of the Merovingian and Carlovingian kings —the Palais des Thermes, as it is called, nothing but the great Roman bathing-establishment being left. The principal chamber is a vast vaulted hall, with walls as thick as a fortress, which has been converted into a museum of Roman antiquities. This opens upon a little grassy area, as quiet, trim and green as a convent-garden, which is also filled with fragments of sculpture. It is a common practice abroad to convert the waste spaces in and about fine ruins into gardens, and the charm of these spots is indescribable. One sits on the capital of a fallen pillar or the head of a gargoyle imbedded in close-shorn turf, with brilliant, formal flower-beds on every side like the trays of a jewel-case; the lights and shadows of the greenery overhead waver on gray crumbling battlements or sculptured tracery; and whether a vision of old builders and denizens fills the place, or nothing moves except the silently-shifting sunlight and the birds which hop and peek, the moments glide away like flowing water in these retreats where time has come to a stop. The longer we stay the harder it is to get up and go away, and many an hour slips by in this tranquil enclosure, which contains an epitome of the history of Paris, and the foot lingers as we pass through the old Gothic monastery-porch, which lets us through to the Hôtel Cluny and out into the streets of modern Paris again. It was by another of those hair-breadth escapes which saved the Ste. Chapelle that these precious monuments and treasures missed being blown to atoms in 1871. It was a question of hours: the vaults of the neighboring Panthéon were full of gunpowder, but the troops got possession of the building before the Communists could explode their mines, or the whole quarter, with its hoards of antiquities, art, books, manuscripts, scientific apparatus, military trophies—all that piety, learning, valor, taste, intelligent industry, patriotism, delight in—would have been reduced to a heap of rubbish.

The Panthéon looks as modern as any building in Paris, and it is as difficult to admire its eighteenth-century Renaissance as the eighteenth-century Corinthian of the Madeleine. The original church was built by Clovis early in the sixth century at the instance of his queen, Clotilde, through whom he was converted to Christianity, and of Ste. Geneviève, the gentle shepherdess and patron saint of Paris. It was first dedicated to Sts. Peter and Paul, but on Ste. Geneviève's death she was buried there and the church renamed in her honor. Nothing of stone and mortar lasts thirteen hundred years except ruins: even a church requires renovation after a millennium. The first church of Ste. Geneviève was burned by the Northmen A. D. 857, and rebuilt; in the last century it had to be rebuilt again; and the present edifice was begun once more by command of a king, Louis XV., and at the request of a woman, Madame de Pompadour! The chaste shades of Ste. Geneviève and Queen Clotilde probably fled before this unhallowed reconstruction, and there is nothing to call them back to the present fane, superb as it is in dimensions and decoration. One traveller at least must confess to finding neither edification nor enjoyment in the redundant modern statuary representing France and her peculiar virtues and attributes, her great representative men, her goddesses and genii, nor in the showy historical and allegorical paintings, although they are signed by the hands of Gros and Gérard. Every step that one takes suggests a sardonic reflection. On the piers which support the dome are bronze tablets to those who fell in the revolution of 1830: their monuments will endure longer than brass, for they are protected and entirely hidden by the wainscoting which has been placed over them. There is something ludicrous as well as hideous in the way in which each political party in France, as it gets the upper hand, flings the relics of its predecessor out of window, like a ghastly parody of Box and Cox's breakfast. The Revolution rushes in; out goes the dust of saints and kings, that philosophers, atheists and sans-culottes may be solemnly entombed in their stead: back comes authority, albeit a National Convention; away with the bones of Voltaire, Rousseau, Mirabeau, Marat, the last — who can wonder? — to the common sewer: royalty returns and scrapes together its scattered ashes and restores the broken noses of its effigies; the Commune comes and blows everything to indiscriminate sherds. These parallels obtrude themselves too pertinaciously at the Panthéon.

WHY DO WE LIKE PARIS?

CONCLUDING PART.

PALACE OF THE LUXEMBOURG.

LET us go on to the palace of the Luxembourg, which is close at hand; not without painful memories, it is true—where in Paris, where on earth, can one escape them?—but with pleasant ones too, and a host of agreeable suggestions and recollections. On this ground in the sixteenth century stood the handsome house and gardens of Harlay-Sancy, a great political and financial personage in those days. After passing through the hands of a duke d'Épinay-Luxembourg, who gave the habitation his name, which it has kept in spite of half a dozen other appellations, it was bought by Marie de Medicis when queen-regent. In memory of her home she caused a palace to be constructed on the model of the Pitti Palace at Florence, but, although the general plan and style of the two are alike, the Luxembourg is a poor reproduction of its massive Italian prototype. Marie de Medicis bequeathed it to her son, Gaston of Orleans, and although the property frequently changed owners, it as constantly reverted to the Orleans family up to the time of the First Revolution. Then for a brief terrible time it was used as a prison. "Nightly come the Tumbrils to the Luxembourg with the fatal Roll-call—list of the batch of to-morrow. Men rush toward the gate; listen if their name be in it. One deep-drawn breath when the name is not in: we live still one day! And yet some score or scores of names were in. Quick there! They clasp their loved ones to their heart one last time; with brief adieu, wet-eyed or dry-eyed, they mount and are away. This night to the Con-

THE PAVILLON DE FLORE OF THE TUILERIES.

ciergerie; through the Palais misnamed of *Justice* to the Guillotine to-morrow."* Government in the shape of the Directory took its seat there, to be succeeded by the Consulate: then it became a parliamentary building, Palace of the Senate, the Chamber of Peers, Palace of the Senate again, according to the order or disorder of the day, until, on the destruction of the Hôtel de Ville in 1871, it had to be appropriated to the Municipal Council and the offices of the department of the Seine, otherwise the municipality of Paris.

On my first visit to the Luxembourg it was the wife of the prefect of the Seine for the nonce who graciously showed our party over the palace, which was not then open to the public. She was a trig little woman, with fine dark eyes, nice teeth and that charm of courtesy and readiness which does duty so often and so well in France for wit and beauty. The lively little lady considered her residence in the Luxembourg as exile, and

* Carlyle's *History of the French Revolution.*

when we admired the spacious rooms, the really royal lodging, she shrugged her shoulders gracefully and assured us that her own hôtel on the other side of the river was much more attractive. It might be more homelike and more in the taste of the present day, but the Luxembourg struck us as at once stately and cheerful —a very pleasant palace. The paintings and statues are by the best artists of the century, and there is a succession of pillared halls with cupolas, of lofty, light saloons with painted ceilings profusely carved and gilded, of corridors and galleries lined

TOMB OF NAPOLEON I.

with busts and statues — all bright and airy, not gloomy and dull like many monarchs' homes. Marie de Medicis's own suite of rooms is splendid and luxurious, befitting a queen of France and daughter of the Italian Renaissance; the furniture is gold and crimson velvet; the pictures are by Poussin, Philippe de Champagne and Rubens, who might be called her painter-laureate. There is a miserable contrast between her life here and her end in the dismal lodgings at Cologne. Adjoining the principal palace there is a small one— or more properly a *hôtel* in the French acceptation of the word as a private house of some pretension — called Le Petit Luxembourg: it was built by Cardinal Richelieu, and given to his niece, the duchess d'Aiguillon, one of the great ladies and great beauties of her time, and it was the scene of brilliant assemblies and secret councils in that gay, arrogant, aristocratic life of Paris in which social frivolity and the momentous issues of the day were intermixed. Attached to this building there is a little cloister—part of a convent that disappeared long ago— which has been roofed over with glass and turned into a conservatory: it makes the most charming of winter-gardens, and a cool resort for summer evenings too, when its stone arches are open to the night air and the fountain plashes in the centre of the quadrangle. The Petit Luxembourg has its own private garden with fine old trees, and the feudal rural appendage of a dovecote.

Our amiable conductress took leave of us after doing the honors of the palace and its dependencies, and we found our way into the picture-gallery. It was originally formed by Louis XV. in 1750 to exhibit paintings and other works of art which were packed away in the garrets of the Louvre and the cabinets of Versailles. But the number of these is not large, and the interest of the collection, which is two-thirds modern, may be inferred from the fact that it is made up of recognized masterpieces. If I remember rightly, the pictures have all taken a first prize at the annual exhibition known as the *Salon:* they belong to the government, and are kept here during the artist's life, to be after his death eventually transferred to the Louvre, or, if their popularity does not stand the test of time, to be sent into honorable retirement in one of the provincial galleries. Here, then, we see the most celebrated canvases of the French contemporary school. Among others are *La Source*, by Ingres, a cool, chaste nymph issuing from a rock: her lovely naked body has all the pearly freshness of dew; the gray cliff and a garland of humid green make up a picture of exquisite purity and refinement. Couture's *Décadence* covers an immense surface of wall: it shows the influence of the Venetian school, which first roused his genius in childhood. It is an historical painting, typifying the decline of the Roman Empire by a huge orgy, steeped in sensuality, but not revolting: men and women with beautiful forms and faces press grapes into golden cups, scatter roses, recline on ivory couches and purple draperies, burn incense for the perfume, not for worship; two philosophers stand apart smiling and moralizing; somewhere in the background, I think, a Christian is brought in. It is a theatrical, scenic picture, of which this is but a skeleton description. Hébert's *Malarie* depicts a boatload of Italian peasants slowly falling down the imperceptible current of a stream which traverses the Pontine Marshes: the fever has laid its hot hand on their drooping heads, on the sluggish stream, on its parched yellow banks, on the heavy air. It is a picture full of sentiment and melancholy: the doom of a race is there. Regnault is the latest idol of the French artist and literary world: he was good, gifted, brave, handsome, young; he threw away his life and his blossoming promise in the trenches at the siege of Paris; he was killed by the last volley the Prussians fired. The Luxembourg has two of his pictures—the equestrian portrait of General Prim, a wonderfully strong, spirited performance, which shows the influence of Velasquez and the noble Spanish school; the other is a ghastly Eastern execution.

FONTAINE MOLIÈRE.

From the picture-gallery to the garden it is but a step—the beautiful, celebrated old garden, full of great chestnut trees and marbles and twittering birds. This is not a gay garden, a fashionable lounge, like the promenade of the Tuileries, with its orange trees in tubs before the Commune. It is a garden of bygone days, and a spirit of seclusion broods over the walks and groves, although they are not deserted. Studious youths from the benches of the neighboring colleges come here book in hand; old soldiers from the asylums sun themselves on the terrace; fond couples meet by stealth under the trees; white-capped nurses gossip with each other while the children toddle and skip along the gravel. The grounds have been ruthlessly sliced and shaved by the new streets and boulevards, but even in their reduced condition they retain so much dignity and charm that their obliteration, which is sometimes talked of, would rob one side of Paris of its chief beauty.

The painters of the great pictures in the gallery of the Luxembourg are almost without exception pupils of the École des Beaux Arts. That famous school has its seat in a large modern building, a patchwork of relics and reminiscences of the most distant countries and ages: Grecian porticos of recent erection are clapped against sculptured Gothic walls of the thirteenth and fourteenth centuries; scraps of the most exquisite French Renaissance, if so we may call that graceful and original style which Italian architects devised for the Valois kings, are intercalated with genuine antiques; yet the external effect is fine and agreeable, and within the discrepancies belong to every academy of fine arts.

LA MAISON DE MOLIÈRE.

In the amphitheatre where the prizes are awarded is Delaroche's great composition, as familiar in this country as in Europe by the engravings and photographs which were at one time to be seen in every print-shop. I first made its acquaintance in this form with secret scepticism as to the merits of the original. It looks finely when seen in its right place, which is, after all, the true way to see every work of art, and it is a comprehensive muster of all the great—and many of the lesser—artists of the world. Their physiognomies may be accentuated to bring out their individuality, but that very fact enables one to pick out the faces like names in a directory. But the room of capital interest is that called the Gallery of Prizes, containing the works which have gained the *grand prix de Rome*, which entitles the successful competitor to a four years' sojourn in Rome, or, if he prefer it, to two years there and two of travel and study at the expense of the government. The whole work of the school is competitive: the pupil is expected to study alone; at certain intervals a session is held and a subject for illustration is given; the students are required there and then to produce a study of it, whether in painting, sculpture or architecture; the best attempts are rewarded by an honorable mention or prizes of different degrees; once a year comes the great struggle for the prix de Rome; the study which takes that prize remains in this hall. It is very curious to compare these first assertions of genius with the mature productions of the same hands: in many the divine spark gleams unmistakably, in others by no less celebrated names we are forced to admire the sharpness of sight which could discern it. But how many of these efforts, some of them giving evidence of remarkable talent, are signed by names unknown to fame! What becomes of all this promise? What is the obscure and melancholy end of these disappointed hopes and ambitions, these unredeemed pledges? The whole world knows the history of a Corot or a Meissonier, but who were the candidates of the year before or the year after? If they died young, the gods loved them, and it is well; but if they have lived, where and what are they now?

From the Palais des Beaux Arts we turn out upon the quays, and the river-view bursts upon the sight. Up the stream are the towers of Notre Dame, downward the bridges in close succession, until the curving channel brings the trees of the two banks together. Opposite are the Louvre, the Tuileries — the Tuileries, alas! no more — the ruins of the beautiful Pavilion of Flora, the fountains and obelisk of the Place de la Concorde. We are on the Quai d'Orsay, the edge of the Faubourg St. Germain, where it is in bad taste to allude to the "Marseillaise," the assumption being that everybody's grandfather was beheaded to that tune: it is the last retreat of conservatism, Ultramontanism, aristocracy — the old aristocracy, which looks down upon the Napoleonic courts and the nobility of Louis Philippe as parvenus, and on the sovereigns themselves as pretenders. Here are the streets so familiar in novels of Parisian life, Balzac's, About's, Feuillet's— the Rue de Bellechasse, Rue de Varenne, Rue St. Dominique, Rue de Grenelle; here is the Rue du Bac, named from the ferry at its foot which plied across the Seine before Mansard built his bridge, the Pont Royal, not two hundred years ago. Madame de Staël in exile on the Lake of Geneva sighed for the gutter of the Rue du Bac, for which countless fair Americans likewise sigh, as on its margin stand the famous shops of the Bon Marché and Petit St. Thomas, two of the prime attractions of Paris to a large class of our countrywomen. Why the latter should be so called I never could divine, unless it takes its name from the neighboring church of St. Thomas Aquinas, who may be called the Less in respect to Thomas surnamed Didymus, although the Angelic Doctor was the superior in faith, and appears never to have doubted anything. The European custom of giving names to shops as well as inns puzzles Americans at first, but there is something specially incongruous in buying gewgaws, or even plain dry goods, under the patronage of a saint.

The principal feature of this part of Paris is the Hôtel des Invalides, the great military asylum, an immense, airy, cheerful, uninteresting building, and its church, containing the tomb of Napoleon I. Whatever may be the rank of Mansard as an architect of palaces—and I am inclined to think that much of the beauty and dignity are due to his peculiar style—it must be a strange taste that can tolerate his ecclesiastical buildings. Everything at the church of the Invalides corresponds to its architecture— the sculpture, paintings and monuments. The crypt occupies the same position in the church that the ladies' cabin does in an ocean-steamer, part above, part below, deck. There is nothing imposing or beautiful in the interior; the square pillars do not suit the round vault; Pradier's colossal statues, representing twelve of Napoleon's victories, are big but not great. The tomb alone and the thought of it make the place solemn, awful. There are certain phrases to which no Frenchman is insensible. "The sun of Austerlitz," "the cannon of Arcola," are words which thrill a chord in the coldest heart of even a Legitimist. It is trite to say that glory is what all Frenchmen prize above everything on earth and in heaven, and that Napoleon is the incarnation of Glory: no nation, almost no individual, is inaccessible to the same enthusiasm. There is a magic in the names of conquerors—Alexander, Cæsar, Charlemagne, William of Normandy; the most dauntless courage, the highest military talent do not possess it; there must be victory besides. For the space of a generation this man's life was a gigantic victory, a prolonged triumph: the imagination cannot resist the impression. The execration of Byron and Wordsworth could find no comparison for his overthrow but the fall of the archangel. It is not the hero of the French nation, but something more tremendous, which rests in that sarcophagus—one of the Titanic race, who strides across the earth, leaving a memory to endure as long as time. It is to be remembered, above all things,

GRAND STAIRCASE OF THE TRIBUNAL DE COMMERCE.

that this man slew the Revolution. It is true that the monster was gorged with the blood of her own children, the Gironde, the Mountain, the Convention, and that many blows and wounds had been dealt her by the exasperated nation; but the death-stroke was given by Napoleon when he fired on the mob on the 5th of October, 1795, and he stamped out the last spark of life four years later, when he seized upon the divided government and cried, "I will have no more factions."

It was but a week or two after that fateful 13th Vendémiaire that the Place de la Révolution (formerly Place de Louis XV.), purged of its guillotine, was renamed Place de la Concorde.* Leaving vast splendid square. The fountains bulge like great crystal goblets in the sunshine, the obelisk of Luxor cuts sharp against the blue sky, the marble horses prance in eternal struggle with their marble grooms: on one hand is the river, beyond it the façade of the Legislative Palace, above which looms the dome of the Invalides; on the other, between two palaces with arcades and porticos, the broad Rue Royale displays the pillared Corinthian front of the church of the Madeleine; before us is the verdure of the Champs Élysées. All the gay life of Paris is glancing through this arena on the way to and from the Bois de Boulogne, yet who can see it for the first time and forget that hither the tumbrils brought their load; that here stood the guillotine like a Moloch which France fed with her children by hecatombs; that here fell the head of an innocent king and queen, of their saintly sister Madame Elizabeth, of countless men and women whose only crime was being holy or brave or noble, of many who had already shed their blood for their country? Let Frenchmen remember it, and let others forget it if they can; but this is not easy with the ruins of the Tuileries in sight, with "Liberté, Égalité et Fraternité" of the Commune, that "brotherhood of Cain,"

FOYER OF THE NEW OPERA-HOUSE.

the Rive Gauche without exploring a tithe of its noteworthy places, we cross the Pont de la Concorde and return to the Rive Droite, entering at once the

* Galignani's *Guide-book* says in 1800; Mignet's *History*, 28th October, 1795, or 4th Brumaire.

stamped like a red hand everywhere on walls and parapets. Order and taste are always busy in France repairing the ravages perpetrated by the love of destruction which seems inherent in the people: it seems as if France had two hands, one of which is for ever undoing the work of the other. It is not easy to say how long it will be before the deft and diligent hand can heal and hide the gashes and scars of that spring of 1871. One of the most pitilessly devastated and disfigured regions is the Bois de Boulogne, and here Nature alone can recreate the beauty of the place: she takes time for her tasks; the next generation will never know the enchantment of that spot under the Second Empire. The lake, the islets, the cascades, the lawns, the shrubberies still make it the prettiest and most fairy-like of public parks in its artificial features; but the woods, the noble trees which with patient energy had twice within a century spread their branches over its heights and hollows, are gone: the stumps which cover the long bare hillsides are all that remain of them. In some directions there are still thick copses through which the rider turns his horse's head and canters along as solitary as on a forest-path; but he soon emerges upon a scene of desolation which turns him back to the frequented parts of the park, among the barouches and landaus and crowds of people on foot and on horseback, to ask for beer at one of the chalets or for milk at the dairy of the Pré Catalan.

STREET OF OLDEN PARIS, BY G. DORÉ.

Of the infinite variety of amusement and pastime which Paris offers I have heard my country-people speak most often and lovingly of the theatres, including the opera: as comparatively few of them mentioned concerts, it is to be supposed that the dramatic and scenic elements of the performance count at least for as much as the music in their enjoyment. This preference would not seem strange if it were not so often expressed by Americans who do not understand French. Yet even with this limitation it will not surprise anybody who has been much at the French theatres. The part of every actor in the drama, the very plot of the play, can be guessed by our quick wits, thanks to the perfection with which every one fills his or her character. In spite of Puritanism and Quakerism, we are a playgoing people, and although there is little in the present standard of our stage, as regards either the drama itself or its representation, to cultivate the taste of an audience, the least critical spectator feels the relief from the intolerable inequalities of the star system, the charm of a performance in which every walking gentleman plays his part and preserves his character as carefully as the hero and heroine of the piece. This is true not of the Théâtre Français alone, the Comédie Française, or, as it is proudly and popularly known, Le Français, the foremost theatre of the world, the home of the classics, of high tragedy and genteel comedy, but of any third-rate theatre of Paris. If the Français is to be considered first-rate, if no other is to be included in the same class on account of the choice of subjects, the classic drama is admirably performed at the Odéon, and the range of the Gymnase is good. It is the character of the plays rather than the performance which determines the standing of the theatre in Paris, but the plays in a measure make the performers. The Palais Royal is first-rate of its kind: it was there that the *Grande Duchesse de Gérolstein* made Offenbach famous and set the fashion of the opéra bouffe in 1867. The opéra bouffe was run into the gutter: the old graceful, lively opéra comique has come into favor again, and the Palais Royal entertains its audiences with farces.

"The Comédie Française," says Émile Augier, the author of *Les Fourchambault*, the successful play of last summer, "has the honor of being the sole institution of the old monarchy which has survived it, with the exception of the French Academy: it is already two centuries old, a longevity which is becoming more and more rare with us. It is not only a national monument, but an historical monument intimately connected with the history of our literature." Molière's troupe, performing his plays under his direction, became so popular that the duke of Orleans, brother of Louis XIV., invited them to perform in his palace, the Palais Royal, and the edifice in which their direct dramatic successors perform his comedies to-day is a portion of the Palais Royal, and was begun by another duke of Orleans, the notorious Philippe Égalité, a few years before the Revolution. Molière is the *genius loci*: the neighboring street and fountain bear his name; hard by is the house in which he died, bearing an inscription to commemorate its premature loss: he was but fifty-one years old. He still remains the presiding spirit of the Français: for every play of Corneille's or Racine's they give three at least of Molière's. A classic drama performed by that company is one of the most complete and consummate intellectual enjoyments which civilization affords. In reading *Le Cid*, *Athalie* or *Le Misanthrope* one may fancy that the verse is too stately, too stilted perhaps, the subject too remote from our sympathies to excite emotion of any sort, but hear them at the Français and we are surprised into tears and laughter. There is no subject about which everybody is so ready to turn *laudator temporis acti* as the stage. I was told that Bressant, the Brohan sisters, Mademoiselle Plessy were good, certainly, but that I could form no idea of the way in which certain parts should be given unless I had seen Lafon and Mademoiselle Mars, who died long ago. Augustine Brohan is dead too now, Bressant and Madeline Brohan have retired, Delaunay has given up youthful parts, and I cannot think that Croizette and Mounet-Sully replace them: there is something rough and raw in their acting compared to the perfect finish of the others. They were brought up on a different drama—Sardou's plays, dramatized stories like *Le Sphinx*. There is nothing to train them to personate such noble folly as Bressant's rendering of

Si le roi m'avait donné
Paris, sa grande ville, etc.,

such exquisite tenderness as Delaunay's reading aloud Agnes's love-letter in *L'École des Femmes*, such delicate ridicule as Coquelin's recitation of

Au voleur, au voleur, au voleur.

As the tradition of fine manners is lost in private life, it must decline on the stage, or the latter would cease to fulfil our first demand and hold the mirror up to Nature. If the *grand siècle* is as obsolete as the age of Pericles, its mode and style may be discarded from the stage like mask and cothurn, but it will be vain to expect actors to produce them now and then as a dramatic curiosity: the smooth polish, the fine edge, will be gone. The loss of this training will be destructive of shades in acting, and these are not confined to the older drama, although there are fewer niceties in modern plays. Any one who remembers Bressant's lofty "Misfortune is always respectable" in the tipsy scene of *Le Jeune Mari*, or the combination of dignity and impertinence of his "Je m'appelle Gaston" in *Le Gendre de M. Poirier*, will understand what I mean. It is well known that when from bad lives or failing powers or any other cause great actors lose their general finish and perfection, they fall back upon *points*, the telling speeches and gestures which bring down the house. To produce striking effects becomes their sole aim: the whole quality of their act-

PRINCIPAL FAÇADE OF THE SQUARE OF THE LOUVRE.

ing deteriorates under this fatal system until it becomes as coarse and unnatural as poor scene-painting. What is true of individuals will become true by degrees of the whole stage, and of the drama itself, if the success of a play, whether in the composition or the performance, depends on situations and climaxes. The Théâtre Français is a bulwark against such decline: the fine critical perceptions of the French people maintain its integrity. The government pays the Français and the Odéon a yearly subsidy on the condition of the performance of a certain number of standard dramas and the production of one or more new plays of merit. The regular members of the company are pensioned, which ensures them against want in their old age and protects them from the temptation and degradation of mere money-making by "starring."

The opera too is subsidized by the government. There are three recognized operas in Paris, besides a yearly fungus-growth which takes possession of smaller theatres and disappears at the close of the season. There is the Opéra Comique, the most national of all, standing as it should on the Place Boieldieu, named from the composer of *La Dame Blanche*. The comic opera, though not a native of France, is naturalized there, and long is the list of charming compositions, little masterpieces, which it has produced: some of them are often performed in our country—*Les Diamants de la Couronne* and *Fra Diavolo*—and there are many others which would be equally liked if they were known, the delightful *Pré aux Clercs*, for instance. There is the Italian Opera, the name of which speaks for itself and conjures up a phantom Carnival, a long procession of romantic figures—Norma the Druidess, the Venetian Desdemona, the coquettish Rosina with fan and mantilla, Figaro, Edgardo—and beneath their disguise we recognize the statuesque Pasta, the impassioned Malibran, the glorious Grisi, Lablache, Tamburini, Rubini, Mario—vanished faces, silent voices, which once enraptured nations. The Italian Opera has lately become bankrupt, owing to the change of musical taste. I have proceeded in inverse order, for by rights the Opéra Comique comes last, and first the Grand Opéra, called also the National Academy of Music and French Opera-house. The last achievement, or rather attempt, of Napoleon II. to prop his throne with playthings was the present house, which was not finished until after the fall of the Empire. It fronts on the Boulevard des Capucines, and has sufficient space to be seen on all sides. The building is excessively rich and ornate, covered with statuary and sculptured decoration, but there is great diversity of opinion as to its architectural merit. To me it wants stateliness, grace, character: the groups of statues flinging about their arms and legs have neither meaning nor dignity. Opinions differ also about the auditorium, which has the capital defect of not being good for sound throughout. The staircase and foyer are magnificent: they may not be in faultless taste, but every one finds them splendid and elegant. The paintings by Baudin are real works of art. The polished marble floor, the shining colonnades of this long and lofty hall, remind me, more by freak of fancy than from real resemblance, of the aisles of St. Paul-without-the-Walls at Rome—a superb basilica which has been constructed during the present century on the site of a church of the earliest Christian ages burned down in 1823.

These novelties must not make us forget that the right bank of the Seine has old quarters too—the Marais, a region intersected by streets with delightful names — Rue des Francs Bourgeois, Rue des Manteaux Blancs, Rue Neuve des Petits Champs bringing to mind former struggles for municipal privileges — and convents standing on the green hem of the town. This was the Paris of the Valois dynasty and of the Guises, the principal scene of the Massacre of St. Bartholomew, the centre of the cabals for and against Richelieu and Mazarin. The streets are lined with fine old hôtels spotted with sun-dials, stimulating to curiosity: we should like to go into them all, but there is not time for one. We have not even looked into the Louvre, the finest museum of art in the world, which escaped the destruction that overtook the Tuileries on the 22d of May, 1871, though its fate hung on a breath: it was filled with powder and petroleum: a match, a spark, the slamming of a door, would have been the signal for an explosion. It was saved by the decision and courage of three men — the marquis de Sigoyer, commanding the Twenty-sixth battalion, and two captains of engineers, MM. Delambre and Riondel. To them we owe it that those marvels of beauty and genius remain to instruct and enchant two hemispheres.

In this rapid, disconnected review I have enumerated a few of the attractions of Paris, of her curiosities, her wonders, her sources of interest and enjoyment, yet enough to detect some ingredients of her spell for all minds and moods. To some people the magic lies in what she is, to others in what she has been; to some in what she gives, to others in what she suggests; to most people in the combination of all these, which produce a composite influence acting differently upon different natures. Merely to try and skim the cream of pleasure from the surface of life in Paris by a single article is like nothing but the tiresome old woman of whom we have often heard who tried to bale out the ocean with a pint pot.   SARAH B. WISTER.

AMONG THE BISCAYANS.

APPROACH FROM THE SEA—OFF MOUNT SORRANTO.

THE traveller approaching for the first time the northern coast of Spain from the Bay of Biscay will be surprised and charmed by the grandeur of the mountain-scenery which meets his view. At a distance of seventy miles at sea, on a clear day, the snow-capped peaks of the Cantabrian Pyrenees are visible, first like islands here and there rising out of the bosom of the deep, but gradually shaping themselves, as the beholder draws nearer, into connected portions of a continuous coast-line. Grander still is the effect when, the approach having been made under cover of night, the voyager mounts to the deck in the first cool flush of early morning to find his vessel riding the waves like a sea-bird under the shadow of these giant mountains, which, descending in green cultivated slopes to the very water's edge before him, stretch away in bold bluffs and fantastic promontories to the east and west, seeming to offer an impassable barrier to the farther progress of his journey.

Yet this coast, to all appearance so

inhospitable, is in reality indented with numerous bays and inlets where ocean-vessels may enter and find havens land-locked and secure, amid poplar-lined banks, fertile vineyards and hillsides from which the chimes in hoary church-towers ring out the passing hours and summon the faithful to their devotions. Such is the charming contrast that awaits the voyager who, after having tossed about for a night or two on the Biscay waters, finds his vessel safely moored in the quiet waters of the Bilbao River, a little stream winding in and out among the mountains, and affording navigable

PILOT-TOWER AT THE ENTRANCE TO THE BILBAO RIVER.

communication between the sea and the city of Bilbao, eight miles inland.

It must be admitted that one's impressions of Spain as derived from first contact with her people and civilization in the persons of the pilot and custom-house officer are not as favorable as might be desired. While the arriving steamer is still well out at sea an open boat, pulled by ten or a dozen swarthy oarsmen—picturesque-looking fellows in caps of red or blue flannel, but otherwise conspicuous for their scantiness of habiliments—comes alongside, and one of its occupants clambers up the ladder with the agility of a cat, mutters a greeting to the captain, and proceeds to take command of the ship. There is a troublesome bar at the mouth of the river, and for a paltry matter of five or six dollars, to be divided among them all, this adventurous boat's crew have put out to sea at one or two o'clock in the morning to take their chance of putting a pilot on some incoming vessel. Standing on the bridge, his eye intently fixed on the signal-tower in the river yonder, where, by a flag waved to the right or left, the vessel's course is directed, our pilot has the air of a lazy, good-natured good-for-nothing—a sort of marine Rip Van Winkle, who only works because he has to, and who will probably lie asleep all the afternoon under the shade of some friendly tree, content until the few *pesetas* earned by this morning's work are gone. But, for all that, he brings us safely over the bar, we steam triumphantly past the pilot-tower, the captain passes around a brandy-bottle and glass among the swarthy oarsmen, and a few moments later the pilot has gone and the ship's whistle is blowing for the customs officer, who comes aboard at Portugalete. Although addressed as "Señor Don So-and-So," a rare specimen of the shabby-genteel functionary is the moustached individual in cocked hat, cloak and rusty uniform who steps aboard, follows the captain down to the after cabin, inspects our trunks—or pretends to—signs his name with a magnificent flourish, gulps down a stiff glass of brandy, and leaves again. On his coat-sleeves, covered with tattered lace, one can read the story of all the faded glories of Spain. But he looks happier when he departs than he did when he stepped on board. "*Que voulez-vous?*" says our captain, who is a Frenchman. "The poor fellow's salary is a mere pittance, he tells me he has six children, and—" He shrugs his shoulders. We are left to infer the rest as to what has passed between them.

Portugalete, the little town opposite which we have stopped for a few moments, runs straggling up the hillside, with several steep streets no wider than a Fifth Avenue sidewalk. But they are densely populated with old women, babies and dogs, and but sparse glimpses of blue sky can be seen between the overhanging eaves and windows above.

At the summit of the knoll up which any one of these streets leads, stands, amid a grove of ancestral poplars, the old church of Santa Maria, in which during the late Carlist war some three hundred of Don Carlos's tatterdemalions took refuge when closely pursued by the victorious royalists after the decisive battle of Somorrostro. But vainly did they seek refuge "even at the horns of the altar." The royal troops promptly occupied half a dozen of the neighboring heights with their batteries, knocked away a goodly portion of the church-tower, clock, chimes and all, sent hundreds of shells down through the tiled

DELIVERY OF AMERICAN PETROLEUM IN SPAIN.

roof into the midst of the enforced worshippers within, and finally compelled the surrender of the entire party. Amid the hush and quiet now pervading the interior of this grand old edifice one finds it hard to realize that it has so recently witnessed such a scene of carnage. There are, to be sure, some jagged portions of the bell-tower yet unrepaired, and the parish schoolhouse adjoining it still stands roofless and dismantled. But the chimes have been replaced, the hands once more mark the hours on the dial, and the inscription over the doorway, "*Non est hic aliud nisi Domus Dei et Porta Cœli*," reminds us as we enter that, notwithstanding man's profanation, this is still God's house only.

Santa Maria Church—it is a cathedral in fact—was built late in the fifteenth century, although the earliest inscription visible dates from early in the sixteenth (1532), when, as a tablet informs us, "Don Pedro de Salazar and his beloved wife brought the remains of the former's father to this spot, and caused them to be interred in this chapel." There is another very curious chapel dating from 1560, and a costly bronze *reredos* in scriptural bas-reliefs extending from the floor to the roof in the rear of the chancel, which must have grievously taxed the purses of the faithful.

Under the hill, and fronting directly on the river, is a new Portugalete—a long, terraced avenue with stone balustrade in front, and lined on its inner side with elegant granite dwellings of modern construction, much similar to those seen on upper Fifth Avenue about Central Park. Hither in summer come the wealthy Bilbaoans to enjoy the sea-breezes and forget the cares of city-life. Many of these dwellings, now rebuilt, were destroyed by Don Carlos's artillerists, while others adjoining them, and belonging to adherents of the cause, were left untouched. The Carlists, it seems, knew well at which to direct their aim.

Opposite Portugalete, on the point formed by the river's entrance into the bay, is the bathing-resort of the Bilbao people—Las Arenas, with a gently-sloping beach of fine hard sand and the usual seaside medley of bath-houses, saloons and pavilions, such as one sees at Coney Island, Atlantic City or any other American salt-water resort. A submarine cable from Point Lizard, England, comes in here. The irrepressible Yankee is represented too, by advertisement at least. The writer saw the poster of a well-known American sewing-machine company glaring at him in flaming letters as he sat on the veranda of one of the hotels waiting departure by the horse-railway, which furnishes communication every fifteen minutes during the day between Las Arenas and Bilbao. Advertising, in fact, is conducted on a polyglot basis in this region. All the way up along the river there may be seen over the store doorways signs in Spanish, French and English. The horse-railway track follows the river-bank all the way to Bilbao, the cars being drawn by mules, and resembling in external appearance those in general use in American cities, though the rate of speed is considerably greater. The eight miles are made in about an hour, the mules going at a gallop most of the distance. So well patronized is the road, especially in summer, that the company is taxed to its utmost to provide transportation for the crowds of passengers, and consequently another railway, to follow the opposite bank of the river, is already talked of.

We pay our ten-cent fare to a spruce-looking chap in uniform with the label "Conductor" on his cap, and he in turn "punches with care in the presence of the passengaire" by tearing out from a coupon-book and handing us a ticket entitling the holder to two sections in the first-class compartment of the car. In the second class we discover a motley gathering of workmen, market-women and peasantry, yet, for that matter, the Spanish horse-car is democratic enough throughout. It is no uncommon sight to see a dark-complexioned donna in veil and mantilla standing outside on the rear platform. Inside or outside everybody smokes, regardless of the presence of the gentler sex. The lady who "likes the odor of a good cigar" is altogether a superfluity in Spain.

The roadway skirting the river is well built up for nearly its entire length, if we except two or three intervals where wheat-fields or vineyards come straggling down to its border. At every quarter of a mile is seen a sentry-box, where a *carabinero*, gun in hand, stands watching for any attempt at smuggling. There are several villages on one side or the other, the two principal ones on the opposite bank, San Nicolas and Luchana, being the ore-loading stations or termini of the various railways connecting with the iron-mines in the mountains a few miles back. Farther up, within a mile and a half of the city, is Oleavaga, the station at which petroleum-vessels have to come to anchor. One is almost certain at any time to find an American vessel or two anchored at this point. The writer saw a three-master from Richmond, Virginia, discharging a cargo of oil there. The blue-topped casks, so familiar to the eye of any one who has ever visited the petroleum-region, are lowered over the ship's side into barges, which are towed up to town by lines of women, whose labor can be hired for less than that of mules. The condition of the women of the poorer classes here is abject and pitiable indeed. Women may be seen everywhere, in the fields, on the roads, on the wharves, in the quarries, toiling like cattle, with very little prospect of earning more than the provender necessary to keep them alive.

Far above the housetops at Oleavaga, along the steep mountain-side, over arches and through cuts, runs the dusty turnpike-road connecting Bilbao with Santander. In the morning and evening the diligence—for stage-travel must always remain the principal means of communication in this mountainous country—goes dashing by with three horses tandem, a great snapping of whip-lashes, occasional volleys of oaths, and a cloud of dust enveloping all. He who desires to study Spain and her people from an inside point of view should take one ride in any of these mountain-diligences, but *only* one: he will never want another.

Just before reaching the stone post which marks the city limit one sees on the river-bank the English burial-ground, a shaded enclosure of an acre or so, with a neat chapel and gateway at the entrance, and thickly planted with willows and shrubbery, from the midst of which a snow-white monument or gravestone here and there peeps out. Of late years the iron-ore trade has attracted to Bilbao hundreds of English residents and sailors, and in this quiet spot has been laid to rest, far from home and kindred, many a poor fellow whom the rigid interment-laws of this priest-ridden land have excluded from burial in the public cemetery.

Like Washington, Bilbao may be termed a "city of magnificent distances," her

THE ENGLISH BURIAL-GROUND.

limits extending out into the fields and up the mountain-sides far beyond her thickly-settled centre. This it was that enabled Don Carlos during his siege of the city to boast in turgid rhetoric that he had "captured a portion of Bilbao." His pickets, in fact, were posted on all the country roads in the environs, many of them within the city lines and within talking-distance of the sentries, but none of them ever actually entered the city proper except as prisoners. The siege lasted for one hundred and two days; the inhabitants were reduced to a diet of horse-flesh; upward of five thousand shells were thrown into the city from the forts on the neighboring mountain-tops; houses, churches, and, among other objects, a very handsome wire suspension bridge spanning the river, were demolished; yet the brave Bilbaoans held out, and finally had the satisfaction of seeing Don Carlos and his ragged cohorts beat a precipitate retreat over the adjacent mountains. To-day the Spanish government is replacing at its own expense all buildings destroyed by the besiegers' guns, and Bilbao shows but few traces of her recent trials.

One's impressions of the city on entering it by the horse-railway from down the river are very pleasing. Rows of palatial dwellings, with gardens before them, line the road on the left: to the right, extending along the river-front, is a park with flower-beds, shrubbery and fountains, shaded by a dense growth of forest trees and thronged every afternoon with well-dressed promenaders of both sexes. On the other side of the park can be caught glimpses of steamers, sailing-vessels and smaller craft lying at anchor in the river or discharging their cargoes at the quay; and beyond them, in turn, may be seen the mountain-slope ascending abruptly on the other side.

Most Spanish cities are famous for nothing if not their antiquity, but this one, with its thirty-and-one thousand inhabitants, is an exception to the rule in that it has both an antiquated and a modern side to it. The centres of the

THE GREAT SEAL OF BILBAO.

old and the new town are very clearly defined even to the casual observer. An old New Jersey farm-house with a fanciful Mansard-roofed wing looking haughtily down upon it, or a half-ruined château upon which some ambitious owner of later days has built up a brand-new modern villa, aptly typifies this little city, which in spite of its five or six hundred years of existence is to-day in many respects as wide awake and enterprising in its habits and ideas as any of our live American towns.

Bilbao is built, as it were, in the bend of a figure 5 formed by the river, the more ancient quarter of the city being at the upper end of the curve. At this point the river is spanned by an antiquated stone bridge of two arches, now closed to travel. Yet one looking at its form and architecture, redolent of the past, cannot but picture to himself the pageants of mail-clad horsemen, with all their pennants and blazonry and nodding plumes and martial music, that on many a triumphal occasion in days long gone by have passed over its now crumbling roadway. The old bridge and the large church adjoining it, which is now used as the municipal building, have been adopted as a device for the great seal of Bilbao. A wide quay before the city hall and the arcaded sidewalks adjoining it are used as the public market-place, and at any time before noon the spot is crowded with chattering venders of fish, flesh, fruit, vegetables and a thousand varieties of notions and knickknacks. The river, at this point seems, too, to be utilized as a sort of public washtub, for from sunrise to dark there may be seen at frequent intervals along the banks groups of a dozen or so of barefooted laundresses in gaudy-colored skirts and kerchiefs washing out their family linen or putting it on the rocks to dry.

At every turn in this quarter of Bilbao the stranger meets with much to entertain him. Dark and narrow streets, with family crests and escutcheons quaintly carved over every doorway; long winding stairways straggling up the hillsides, with a resting-place or landing before each door on the way up; alley-ways ending abruptly in walls of rock; a jumble of shops and chapels and convents,—all recall some bit of canvas torn from a mediæval painting, and suddenly reproduced here before the admiring eyes of to-day. But follow the river around for a distance of half a mile, and the scene is changed at once. Here are a modern railway-depôt built in the style of a Swiss chalet, and said to be the finest in Spain; a theatre where you may hear the *Ballo in Maschera* or *Lucia di Lammermoor* sung by an Italian troupe of more than usual merit; a club-house where, if fortunate enough to have the privilege of admission, you may daily read the London *Times* or any of the principal Paris papers; an hotel where for a dollar and a half a day may be found all the comforts of the large hotels in any European capital; a public park, a telegraph-office, and stores stocked with a bewildering and brilliant variety of merchandise. The boulevard and park extending along the river-front before the Hotel d'Inglaterra will prove an attractive place for the visitor. At early morning he may stand there and see the sunrise breaking over the mountains, successively tipping each peak with gold while the base is still swathed in its garment of nocturnal shadows. During the afternoon come throngs of well-dressed ladies and gentlemen promenading, and toward sunset the shaded walks and lawns are resonant with the shouts and laughter of hundreds of joyous children. And when night has settled down upon the scene, and the gas-lamps glimmer through the shade, there may be heard now and then the musical tum-tum of a guitar and a voice trolling out a lively *bolero* as some group of merry-makers go by, with perhaps a couple or two of dancers with joined hands whirling in pirouettes through the dim-lit shadows in advance of them.

To the student in ethnology it is interesting to note the strongly-contrasted types met with in the faces of the people. The swarthy Moorish complexion, black eyes and raven hair predominate,

RIVER-FRONT, SHOWING BOULEVARD AND PARK.

yet the Northern Goths have left their traces too in the clear skin, ruddy cheeks, flaxen locks and blue eyes not unfrequently encountered. Courtliness and dignity of manner, without the excessive *complaisance* of the French, are noticeable everywhere among the "señordons" and "caballeros." Most of the men dress in the fashionable styles usually seen on the Paris boulevards, though here and there the sugar-loaf hat and ample cloak, its folds partially held up before the wearer's face, are still seen. The ladies cling more tenaciously to the traditional costume of their sex, the veil and mantilla, very few of them appearing on the streets with cloaks or bonnets. Housemaids too have their distinguishing *coiffure*, a double braid of hair falling over the back and sometimes reaching nearly to the ground.

French is quite generally spoken, and forms, as almost everywhere else in Europe, the chief means of communication between foreigners and the people themselves. At the *table-d'hôte* dinner at the Hotel d'Inglaterra one day during the writer's stay there were seated twelve guests, ten of whom were conversing together in French on the subject of the New York *Herald's* weather-reports. Yet of those ten, one was a German, two were English, two Moors, two Spaniards, one an American, and only two real Frenchmen; who, by the way, must have relished the babel of varied accents with which their mother-tongue was being served up by the assembled guests.

The churches of Bilbao, while outwardly plain and uninviting, are extremely costly and attractive in their internal decoration. The faithful must, however, forego the luxury of chairs or cushions, and whether rich or poor must alike kneel upon the hard stone floor. As early as five in the morning one finds numerous worshippers, mostly women. But early rising is no difficult matter in Bilbao, thanks to a quaint custom still extant. From midnight to six A. M. the hours, as they are successively rung out by the chimes in the principal cathedral-tower, are repeated by the watchman sta-

A BILBAO MILKMAN.

tioned in the street below, and from him in turn the words are caught up and re-uttered by every other watchman in the city. The effect is indescribably novel and beautiful. The writer chanced to be awakened one morning by hearing the neighboring chimes strike three. An instant afterward a clear, loud, ringing tenor voice in the street below chanted in a strange but not unmusical monotone the words, *Las tres — sereno* ("Three o'clock, and clear"), and a moment later the still air of morning was resonant far and near with re-echoed cries of *Las tres—sereno*, coming back from out the distance like the tinklings of a hundred silver bells.

It is a pity to have to record of Bilbao, with all her churches, that she indulges in the luxury of occasional bull-fights. Four days of every August are set aside for this edifying sport, and during that period the great amphitheatre, seating fourteen thousand people, is daily packed to repletion with men, women and children of all classes, the peasantry coming in by swarms from a distance of twenty or thirty miles around to applaud the *torreadores*, and scream *Bravo!* at the senseless slaughter of scared bulls and jaded horses. Six bulls are daily led into the ring, and as each bull, before being despatched, is allowed to kill five horses, and no more, it is not difficult to figure up the sum-total of quadrupeds, bovine and equine, offered up on the altar of this barbarous custom during its four days' annual duration. But there is an undercurrent of public opinion opposed to all this cruelty. Many Spaniards when the sport is mentioned smile and intimate that, as conducted at the present day, it is an arrant humbug. The horses are poor, used-up creatures, unfit for further service; the bull generally asks no better than, like the "erring sisters," to be allowed to depart in peace; while the gallant *torreador*, so often sung in verse and portrayed on canvas, is a very ordinary sort of fellow — agile, it is true, as any circus-jumper, but never, in reality, exposed to any great danger from his incensed bullship. It is safe to predict that in another half century bull-fighting will have become one of the lost arts in Bilbao.

Street-venders are as numerous and as odd here as anywhere in Europe. The cigar-shops along the sidewalks are neat and convenient, and offer a capital cigar for five cents. The matutinal milkman is perhaps the most interesting character-study in Bilbao. He reminds one of the herdsman Tityrus, that bucolic swain whom Virgil apostrophizes as making the woodlands vocal with strains to his loved Amaryllis. In the early morning hours—and none too early at that—when the slothful housemaid begins to bestir herself and the city awakens to its daily life, a herd of ten or a dozen goats, marshalled by an ill-favored but faithful shepherd-dog and driven by this Spanish Tityrus, may be seen coming lazily down the street. The goatherd is a picture in himself, the very personification of a whole pastoral poem. On his head is a slouch cap of blue flannel; he wears a short blouse; he carries a shepherd's staff in his hand; and ever and anon as he approaches the house of a customer he trolls out a ditty as shrill as a mocking-bird's whistle from a reed flute which he raises to his lips. The goats know where to stop, the door is opened, the servant-maid appears, and the pennyworth or two of milk is served fresh and steaming, the other goats and the dog meantime standing idly by, waiting the signal to resume their march.

A description of the Biscay province would be incomplete without some mention of its inexhaustible iron-mining resources, which have of late years been developed to an extraordinary extent, principally by the aid of a million and a half pounds sterling of British capital. During 1878 over thirty-five hundred vessels, of which upward of two thousand were steamers, came to Bilbao for iron-ore. England's foundries are largely supplied from these mines, the famous Creusot Iron Company of France procures much of its material here, and Krupp, the great German manufacturer of cannon, has four vessels running regularly between this port and Rotterdam. There are direct lines to Cardiff, Swansea, Middleboro' and Newcastle, to Antwerp, to Dunkerque, Boulogne, Bayonne and La Rochelle, and shipments are made even to American ports. A trim Yankee brig, the Eugene Hale, Captain John F. Lord, of Calais, Maine, recently brought out a cargo of wheat from New York, and has long ere this landed her return cargo of Spanish iron-ore at its destination on the Jersey City docks.

RAILROADING IN THE PYRENEES.

When Pliny, the Bayard Taylor of Roman days, wrote home from this region that he had seen "a mountain made of iron," he scarcely exaggerated the truth. The Triano Mountains, to which it is supposed he referred, might with some slight allowance for the tales of a traveller be fairly described in those terms. From time immemorial there have been numbers of little forges or blacksmith-shops scattered through these mountains, but only during the past ten years or so has there been a systematic effort made to develop the resources of the mines. There are now five lines of railway, varying from six to eight miles in length, connecting the river with the mountain-fastnesses where the ore is taken out.

Of these roads, three were built by Englishmen, one by the Franco-Belgian Company and one by Bilbao enterprise. English skill and English industry are visible everywhere, and have dotted these once desolate mountain-sides with populous villages. The locomotives are from Birmingham, the cars from Manchester, the tools from Sheffield, and even the telegraphic-apparatus in many of the stations is found to bear the mark of an English maker. But that which most commands admiration is the bold engineering genius which has carried these roads, with double tracks, tunnels and solid granite embankments, up from the river-level, over gorges, around giddy precipices and through the very bowels of the cliffs, to summits whence one can look down upon other mountain-tops, upon village-dotted vales "stretching in pensive quietness between," and upon the soft blue waters of the Bay of Biscay beyond. Such is the view commanded from the village of Galetta, which has sprung into existence on the mountain-top around the Cæsar and San Miguel mines. Its houses, its walls, its tiny church and its hotel, where "coffee and billiards" are pretentiously announced, are all built of iron-red mud, which by exposure to the sun has become as hard as iron itself. Its streets straggle up and down the mountain-side, anywhere and everywhere, regardless of surveyors' lines; yet it has a mayor, enjoys the honor of being a railway-terminus, and is apparently happy. About six hundred miners, all Spaniards, live here, earning sums equal to a dollar and a dollar and a half a day. The Biscayans are good workmen, industrious, temperate and saving, the English say. Most of them own small farms, which they leave in charge of their wives during their absence here in the mines. When the wet season comes, however, they go home to look after their affairs, and then the mining company is compelled to replace them temporarily by Castilians, who as a rule are quarrelsome, indolent fellows, much given to play and drink. A fair illustration of their character is afforded by an incident that occurred a few months ago. The overseers reported one day that most of the men had quit work or were practically doing nothing. Inquiry was at once ordered, resulting in the discovery that a rivalry had arisen between a couple of workmen and their respective adherents as to which of the two could do the most rock-drilling in a given time. A sum amounting in value to five hundred dollars had been wagered by the competitors and their friends, a day was set apart for the trial for the championship of the Pyrenees, and by general consent work had been suspended to enable the miners to watch the progress of the contest.

One who has any taste for the adventurous will find a rare delight in the return ride by railway down the mountain from Galetta to the river. He must crowd in with the engineer and fireman on the locomotive, for passenger-coaches are a luxury unknown on this line. The rapidly-descending grade of eight hundred feet in six miles renders the use of steam entirely superfluous; and with thirty or forty ore-laden cars adding their impetus, the train, with brakes all on, goes rattling and clattering down the mountain-side at a rate of speed which makes the unaccustomed passenger hold his breath, and perhaps at times fervently wish the journey were over. Yet, with all its spice of danger, the trip is intensely exciting. The fresh, cool mountain-breeze, the unsurpassed scenery, made up on the one side of wild ravines, yawning gorges and bold acclivities, and on the other of a green carpeted landscape bounded by the river far below, — all these combine to elicit an involuntary exclamation of delight from the passenger, and make him forget whatever danger, if any, there may be in the long and rapid descent. And when, having reached once more the river-bank, where the steamer ready for sea is perchance awaiting him, he turns for a farewell glance at the cloud-capped heights from which the iron horse has in safety transported him, it is with a soul filled with new conceptions of the glory of God's creation and the grandeur of man's triumphs.

GEORGE L. CATLIN.

TROUVILLE.

A STREET.

ONE of the characters in *Les Fâcheux*, a sort of disinterested Colonel Sellers of the seventeenth century, had a scheme for increasing the prosperity of France by converting its entire coast-line into seaports. His project was received with that laughter which it is the province of comedies and great inventions to call forth; nevertheless, we have seen it realized, with the difference that the whole French coast from Cape Grisnez to the mouth of the Bidassoa is spangled, not with ports of commerce, but with gay watering-places. Each summer some reigning queen discovers a bit of seaboard, where the shrimps are in their primitive wildness and the bathers have never yet thrown a rope over the arching neck of the wave, and triumphantly takes possession with her little court. An hotel makes its appearance; villas, by ones, by twos, by threes, gather around it; a casino rises from the waves; a mushroom church in the style of the Second Empire springs out of the sand; and the new resort is a fact. The Romulus of one of these summer cities is not infrequently some popular artist or author. Le Puy, near Dieppe, was one of the creations of Alexandre Dumas *fils;* Alphonse Karr presided over the new birth of Etretat; and Trouville was invented somewhere about 1830 by two marine painters, Charles Mozin and Isabey. Rambling along the Norman coast in search of subjects, chance led the two artists one day to a humble fishing-village at the mouth of the Toucques, where the rugged faces and quaint costumes of the inhabitants promised excellent spoil for the brush. They sought entertainment under the sign of the Agneau d'Or, sole inn of the village, where La Mère Auzeraie ruled the roast or its fishy substitute without a rival, and hopefully spread their canvases for the prey. The elder Dumas paid them a visit and gave Mother Auzeraie some lessons in cooking. In the Salon of 1834 some Parisians noticed the new name, Trouville, under that of Mozin on two marines, and the name stuck in their memories. They met with it again in an article by Dumas, and when the hot weather came round they made application for admission to the Agneau d'Or, taking it and Trouville on the trust of the painter and the novelist. Madame Auzeraie—she was Mother Auzeraie no longer—had the temerity to ask three francs a day for board and lodging. Parisian economy, wrathful at being thus fleeced for the benefit of the Golden Lamb, grasped its axe and fell to the erection of villas, thus laying the foundation of Trouville.

It was not, however, till a score of years later, under the Empire, that Fashion smiled upon the new resort. The imperial magistrates and officials were ill at ease on the strand of Dieppe, where the royalists had their summer quarters, and began to look about for a surf in which they could disport themselves with a sense of being at the same time politically in their element. Dieppe had been started by the duchesse de Berry, and was absorbed by the sets of the Faubourg St. Germain and the Faubourg St. Honoré. Its shore was trodden by the feet of the Forty Immortals, who at that time nearly all belonged to the Orleanist party, and by the deposed statesmen of that party, among them M. Thiers. The imperial court had abandoned Dieppe to the opposition, and betaken itself to Biarritz, but Biarritz was too far from Paris for the lesser officials and busy men of the party to follow. Trouville offered them a bathing-place within six hours of the capital, and thither they repaired. Speculation soon became so rife in the village that a square foot of sand on either side of the Honfleur road rose to a price equal to that of a square foot of solid ground in the neighborhood of the Parc Monceaux. Villas sprang up quickly; an hôtel de ville in the style of Louis XIII. was erected, and followed by two parish churches: law and religion were thus installed as adjuvants of fashion. It is a watering-place religion which the faithful practise at Trouville—light, elegant and modish, as suits the season, the place and the toilettes. The elegant and modish architecture of the larger church, Notre Dame de Bon Secours, which is modelled on that of the Trinité in the Chaussée d'Antin, forms an appropriate setting for this religion, and supplies the scenery for masses arranged on the plan of operas, in which groups of priests and choir-boys in rich vestments, with flowers, lights, stained windows, bells and chants, make an *ensemble* of operatic beauty and impressiveness. Notre Dame de Bon Secours is in the business-street of the town, where the butchers and bakers, the vendors of fruit, flowers and other merchandise, carry on their trades. Between this street and the sea is the visitors' quarter, which presents a jumble of hotels, villas, casino, milliners' and pastry-cooks' shops, elbowing each other as closely as if confined by the walls of a city. There is little room for gardens, which do so much to beautify and freshen a watering-place: the Hôtel de Paris, the most expensive in the place, is the only one which offers its guests the luxuries of a little shade and a few flower-beds. This absurd mania for packing the houses together and building upward in narrow aspiration, instead of spreading out comfortably along the shore, makes Trouville resemble a great anthill, and renders it disappointing to those who go there for the unsophisticated object of breathing the sea-air and taking sea-baths. Hence it has always been distasteful to the English, whose open-air instincts cannot comprehend that passion for his native boulevards which leads a Parisian in search of recreation to plunge into another multicolored and many-voiced crowd.

On Sundays this crowd is increased by a cargo of excursionists brought over by the steamer from Havre, and by a freight

THE SANDS.

of busy husbands and fathers whom the Saturday-evening train bears away from their desks and the Bourse to snatch a brief draught of domestic felicity from the whirlpool of froth and fashion in which their better halves are revolving.

During the races the rash stranger who visits Trouville without having engaged a lodging may have to wander a long time without a shelter, and may be thankful if he find one of any quality or at any price The week of the races is to Trouville what the Carnival is to Nice—a climax of gayety, uproar and extravagance. Before the first of August the only summer migrants who have arrived are the occu-

SHRIMP-FISHING.

pants of villas: by the twentieth everybody is there, and the beach has its full complement of children, students and lawyers in the vacation. Travellers who wish to see the most characteristic features of different countries are recommended to visit southern lands in summer and northern ones in winter—to greet Naples under the focus of a June sun, and find St. Petersburg locked in its December frosts. To seize Trouville at the moment when it is most itself, the visitor should drop bravely down upon it in all the discomforts of the racing-week. He will find everything dearer than at any other time; he will be badly served; he will have great difficulty in hiring a carriage, finding a place at the table-d'hôte or getting hold of an unoccupied bathing-house; but he will have the reward of having really seen Trouville. "See Trouville, and—see it no more," is the heartfelt utterance of many a disgusted sojourner as he climbs on the train which is to take him away on the last day of the racing-week. And his dissatisfaction is not without cause. Trouville, like many other fashionable resorts—like Newport and Cowes, for instance—was not made for passing strangers, who have no open sesame to its villas. The real life of the place, with its pleasures and its brightness, is not in the Casino or the large hotels: it is in the salons. To the favored ones who give the watchword of Parisian society, Trouville society opens its store of distractions, filling the hours with concerts, amateur theatricals, improvised balls and charades. But the sojourner at the Hôtel de Paris or the Hôtel des Roches-Noires, if he have no introductions, is restricted to the dissipations of the Casino, which have a certain cheap monotony. The

Casino at Trouville is a large, ugly building, constructed on the plan of a French railway-station. Its chief advantage is its situation close to the sea, and it is one which had nearly cost it its existence in the great tide of October, 1876. It is composed of a covered terrace, where coffee may be sipped in full view of the sea, a billiard-room, a gaming-hall, a reading-room, a dancing-hall and a large saloon surrounded by a gallery which serves for theatrical representations, concerts and large balls. Here one may have the good fortune now and then to see two or three of the company of the Variétés in one of the little *demi-mondaine* plays of Meilhac and Halévy, or the greater treat of watching one of Octave Feuillet's *comédies mondaines* rendered by two or three celebrities from the Français. Mesdames Judic, Theo and Croizette are yearly visitants at Trouville; and it was on its beach that the equestrian portrait of the latter, with its background of sea, was painted by her brother-in-law, Carolus Duran. When there are no dramatic stars at Trouville the evening's entertainment consists of the regular concert, often preceded by a children's hop, which breaks up at half-past nine. The orchestra of the Casino is a good one, and the music is generally well chosen, but it is wellnigh impossible to hear anything, as the habitués consider the concert a mere accompaniment to their conversation. Any stranger who should take exception to this custom, and exhibit an ill-judged desire to hear the *Pastoral Symphony* or the waltz from the *Roi de Lahore*, would be set down as an

MUSSEL-FISHING.

outer barbarian, probably as an Englishman recently imported from Shanghai or Brighton.

The American element introduced the "Boston glide" a few years ago at the Casino balls, where it has happily superseded the *deux temps*. These Casino balls are very pleasant if one has a large acquaintance, but there is nothing free and easy about them: introductions are as necessary as at private entertainments. In spite of its reputation as a "fast" place, Trouville has preserved a touch of exclusiveness peculiar to itself, and has drawn the line with admirable precision between the *monde* and the *demi-monde*—more careful in this regard than Biarritz and other watering-places, where the mixture of the two elements forms a heterogeneous society which might not inaptly be termed *le monde et demi*. Trouville society is not to be arithmetically measured by this mixed number: it solves the great social problem not by addition, but by division, with rigorous proof. It adheres rigidly to the *convenances*, and surrounds its "rosebud garden of girls" with the thorniest hedge of propriety. A man should be aware of danger in order to avoid it: it is easy to recognize one of these damsels. Their hats are simpler, their lap-dogs a trifle larger, their cos-

TYPES OF FISHERMEN IN HOLIDAY COSTUME.

tume and their tone more subdued, than is the case with married women. The latter pass from one dazzling combination to another with a variation of magnificence which leaves the lilies of the field and the monarch-sage in all his glory at equal disadvantage: the train from Paris is not unfrequently delayed, owing to the accumulation at the Gare St. Lazare of the leathery structures wherein all this glory is enshrined. Half a dozen transformations a day is the usual number undergone by the human butterfly of the *beau sexe* at Trouville. First, a morning toilet, to be displayed in strolling on the board walk; this gives place to a driving-costume in the afternoon, which is changed again at four o'clock, when every one adjourns to the beach; at six o'clock, dressing for dinner; and at nine another metamorphosis into full evening-dress. As at Newport, bathing finds little place. A wide board walk extending the whole length of the beach

INTERIOR OF A FISHERMAN'S HUT.

from the pier to the Hôtel des Roches-Noires is the general rendezvous before breakfast, and again before dinner. At these hours the products of worm and Worth sweep over its boards in panoramic changes, unceasingly watched on either side by a sedentary audience, who from the shade of pavilions or of spreading umbrellas well rooted in the sand survey the walkers with vigilant eyes. It is under these umbrella trees that the cabalistic *potins* are held where the birth of each flirtation is registered and its growth measured—where the costumes are subjected to an ordeal of criticism, the rights of each new arrival to the consideration of society are carefully weighed, and questions of etiquette and precedence settled.

Could the smallest part of these comments and decisions become suddenly audible to their objects filing by in stately procession, they would with one accord flee those treacherous boards and regard light umbrellas as toadstools of the Evil One for ever after. But all the heads thus sheltered on the sands at Trouville are not concocting the venomed poison of the *potins*. Some are brought together in milder confidences, and not a few are virtuously poring over the *Revue des Deux-Mondes*, which at this season of the year always prints a novel of Octave Feuillet, the gentle romancer of the Second Empire and a prime favorite with the ladies who summer at Trouville. It is for them that the new novel is written: it forms a regular part of their regimen, like the baths and the sea-air. It is soothing, invigorating, and, above all, it is the fashion. *Un Mariage dans le Monde* and the *Journal d'une Femme* have been decried by some persons as false in tone and setting up a false ideal. It is to be feared that their critics did not read them at Trouville, in which case their carpings are of no account, for Feuillet's novels were made to be read at Trouville, as mangoes were made to be eaten in Cuba.

Below the promenade, on a firm, smooth beach which slopes almost imperceptibly into the sea, are the bathing-houses, so arranged that the two sexes are kept at a puritanical distance from each other, the ladies' quarters being guarded by a vigilant sentinel who bears the nickname of Père la Pudeur. The beach looks to the north, and is in some respects an excellent one. Its chief defect is its flatness. Even at high tide the bather who wishes to stand up to his neck in water must walk a long way before he can accomplish his end. There are not many, however, who are fired with such ambition. Good swimmers sometimes like to gain more exhilaration and a sense of being wet by striking out for the boats and diving from them. The majority of faint-hearted bathers — and they are in a larger majority on the coast of Normandy than on the sands of New Jersey—dabble placidly in the saucer-like shallowness near the water's edge, tethered by ropes to the shore, looking as contented and as out of place as ducks upon dry land. This method of bathing has, besides its tameness, the inconvenience of displaying plenty of models for a Daumier, but few enough for a Canova. Sensitive bathers, who may wish to preserve their anatomy from the searching examination of the numerous glasses levelled seaward, have the privilege of hiring a *cabine à flot*, and being drawn through the waves to a deeper bathing-place. The French ladies imprison their hair most scrupulously in the unbecoming turban of oilskin, having a deeply-rooted conviction that salt water changes its color or causes it to fall out. American ladies know better, and the Greek maidens submitted their locks without injury to the caresses of the waves, following the example of their sea-born goddess:

Quand Venus Astarté, fille de l'onde amère,
Secouait, vierge encore, les larmes de sa mère,
Et fécondait le monde en bordant ses cheveux.

Trouville offers other amusement during the day besides bathing, promenading and dressing. The country in which it is situated, if not exactly picturesque, is smiling and verdant, and excursions are made in all directions by long cavalcades mounted on donkeys. It is the regular thing to go in this way to the château of Bonneville, which is supposed to have been the residence of William the Conqueror. All that is left of its glory is a heap of ruins tumbling over into the moat, an ogive door being still erect, with a single tower, the Tour du Serment, where William is said to have bound Harold by an oath to assist him in the conquest of England. There is a fine view from the foot of the tower over the valley of the Toucques and the beaches of Trouville and Deauville. A woman from the neighboring farm serves as guide to the ruins, and dangles a candle on the end of a string in the black depths of the *oubliette* to chill the souls of visitors by the sight of a ghastly heap of bones at the bottom—bones of feudal knights or of contemporary sheep. When Bonneville has been explored the excursionist may proceed along the road leading to Pont-l'Évêque, cross the Toucques and arrive at the ruins of St. Arnould and of Lassay. The priory of St. Arnould dates from the beginning of the twelfth century: the only part still in existence is the crypt, which is strewn with remains of tombs. Under a group of trees is a more modern chapel, and a spring whose waters are reported to have a miraculous power of healing. They have at least that of refreshing and

THE HARBOR.

cooling, so the spring is not wholly a humbug. Farther on, a venerable staircase, supported by ivy-mantled walls, is all that is left of the château of Lassay, whose history has been narrated by Saint-Simon.

A pleasant drive can be taken to Honfleur, where we see the last of the Seine as it disappears into the Channel. The road thither from Trouville winds along the shore, which is bordered by steep and irregular rocks. In the opposite direction a smoother road leads beside the sea past a string of bright and coquettish little towns, each with its casino, from which lively strains of music issue forth. It takes a whole day to accomplish this excursion pleasantly, driving through Villers, Houlgate, Dives, Cabourg, and halting at Dives to make acquaintance with the excellent dinners which are served up at the Hostellerie de Guillaume le Conquérant. Dives is one of the numerous Norman towns which claim to have speeded the parting Conqueror on his celebrated trip across the Channel. But if this distinction is worn rather threadbare, and strict authenticity denies to our Hostellerie the fame of having provided the farewell feast on that occasion, the homely little Norman inn may still thrive on its good cheer of to-day and its quaint furniture of antique andirons, spits and candlesticks, old Rouen faïence, Middle-Age tables and chairs, wood-carvings, and other curiosities which make its dining-room worthy of being set down intact in the Hôtel de Cluny. The owner of these treasures of bric-à-brac steadfastly refuses to part with a single chip of it, to the despair, no doubt, of scores of longing collectors.

If we allow ourselves to be fascinated into making any sojourn in one of these smaller watering-places, we should carry our entertainment with us or have the power of doing without, for each village is the resort of a particular coterie who rather monopolize its amusement and advantages, leaving but a meagre opportunity of diversion for the casual visitor. If the latter wearies of a tête-à-tête with the sea and the game of looking on, his only resource will be to drive, at the highest speed which his hack will accomplish—about six miles an hour perhaps—back to Trouville.

Here one is not so dependent on so-

THE JETTIES.

ciety to fill up the time: the beach presents a kaleidoscope of life and gayety; there are the intellectual resources of the books at the bookseller's and the newspapers at the Casino; the consolation of an excellent *cuisine* is always at hand; there are the excitements of crab-racing, of catching shrimps and gathering mussels. The mussels—called in the Norman patois *caïeux*—are found clinging to the blackish rocks which are left bare at low tide on the sands between Trouville and Villerville. The mussel is scorned in America: let me say a good word for him, and testify that, cooked *à la marinière*, he is well worthy of regard. The shrimps found at Trouville are small but delicate. They are of the same kind as the river-shrimps at New Orleans. It is not upon shrimps and mussels that the seven hundred native fishermen of Trouville expend their large energies. They have the reputation of being bold and active seamen. Despite the invasion of fashion which they have submitted to—and profited by—for the last forty years, they remain the same as when Charles Mozin painted them in his *Fishermen drawing in their Nets, 1834*. They adhere to the traditional costume—a striped woollen cap, a *suroy* or stout jacket of tarred cloth, trousers of the same, and immense boots, which they replace when on shore by the classic *sabots*. Every night, except on the eve of a fête-day, they put out to sea in a fleet of about a hundred small barques, and every morning, if the weather renders it possible, they come in again with the spoils of their *chaluts*, as the large nets are called. They seem to have no restlessness or desire to escape from the hardships of their life. The money which the summer transformation of their native town brings in to them makes their homes somewhat more comfortable and the fishwives' caps more resplendent with laces than before: that is all the change. Fishermen they will die, and their sons will be fishermen after them. A few here and there have sold their fishing-boats to go into the lucrative profession of bathing-attendants, which enables them to enjoy a double portion of *calvados*, a popular beverage composed of cider and brandy, but the majority stick to their chaluts.

Trouville harbor is formed by the mouth of the Toucques. Outside is a channel fifty mètres wide enclosed between two piers—one two hundred and twenty, the other four hundred, mètres long. In 1860 a floating dock was built at a cost of two and a half millions of francs: its sluice is larger than any other in the country except that of the new dock at Havre. The navigation of the port averages about six hundred vessels, without counting the fishing-boats. The old village of Trouville—the Trouville of Mère Auzeraie and Père Dumas, the nucleus of the brilliant seaside city—lies close to the harbor, and is to be avoided by sensitive nostrils. It has to be gone through, however, in order to reach Deauville on the other side of the river, and most of the Trouville people do go to Deauville several times a week.

Deauville is the Faubourg St. Germain of Trouville. To cross the bridge over the Toucques is like passing into another world—a world wrapped in ennui and stately reserve. From the shades of its ennui it looks with saturnine disdain at the glare and life of its brilliant vis-à-vis. Deauville wears an air of blue-blooded and ancient respectability rather premature, since, in its present stage of existence, it is the younger of the two resorts. In 1860 it was a mere hamlet perched on the brow of a hill, with a church whose brevet of antiquity, dug up in its parsonage garden, consisted of eight hundred gold coins bearing the effigy of Philip the Fair. A new era dawned in the history of the village on the day when the duc de Morny, after an unsuccessful attempt to find a villa at Trouville, crossed the Toucques with a party of friends, came to Deauville, saw and acquired it. A great speculator as well as a great dandy, he no sooner sniffed the air from its shores than he scented the chance which lay in buying up a quantity of that cheap, sandy waste, setting it in vogue, and thus raising its value a hundred-fold. He set the ball of popularity in motion by building a villa there himself, the Villa Morny, which changed its name to Villa Sesto when the duchesse de Morny carried it over, by a second marriage, to the duke of that name. A rich manufacturer, M. Donon, who had joined the scheme, built the next villa, which, with its square battlemented tower, now covered with ivy, is one of the most striking on the *terrasse* at Deauville. M. John Oliffe, the princess Lise Troubetzköi, Prince Demidoff and others followed suit, the fashionable world rallying to the aid of its ingenious leader with no want of alacrity. A race-course was started in the meadows by the Toucques, liberally endowed by the duke and put in the hands of the Jockey Club. Italian palaces with their stately colonnades and statues, Swiss chalets and Dutch cottages, sprang into being as if by enchantment, till the little Norman village could boast of a Street of Nations almost as curious and varied as that at the Champ de Mars last year.

Everything was done to conceal the natural disadvantages of the place. Its patrons imported vegetable earth and transplanted ready-grown trees to the new gardens. They built a casino far exceeding that of Trouville in beauty and convenience. In time, the duc de Morny died, but Deauville was already *lancé:* it paused a moment to raise a statue to its founder, and went on building. It had one enemy, however, and that a powerful one. The sea looked with sullen disfavor upon the new speculation, and droned out an unceasing homily on the text of laying foundations upon sand. Year by year it receded slowly, till the villas, which in the days of the duc de Morny had been caressed by the tide at high water, became in the time of the duc de Sesto green oases in a desert of yellow sand. Deauville is now as proverbially dusty as Pekin or Boston in an east wind. The irate sea has thrown up an immense sandbank which chokes the beach and leaves the bathers to disport themselves in a briny pond not more than three feet deep. The bleaching sands stretch drearily away as far as the eye can reach, with no trees, no sunshades or flashing toilettes to break their monotony, which is as desolate as that of the Ostende beach in midwinter.

Once a year, however, the neglected watering-place has a sudden renewal of animation and brightness. During the races it wakes from its sleep and thrills again with life. Then the huge hotel alongside of the Casino becomes at least half full, and, by levying a double tax on its customers, contrives to make business pay for the week. A well-known "turf"-character, M. Joachim Lefebvre, paid a thousand francs a day for the privilege of sojourning there with his family. Some gentlemen who have got tired of meeting little bills of this kind prefer to visit Deauville in their yachts, and live on board during the *semaine des courses.* The prince of Wales sailed there in 1877, and was carried ashore from his yacht on the shoulders of one of his sailors: this created a rage for that mode of transport which lasted the whole season. The *cabine à flot,* with its harnessed quadruped, was left high and dry on the sand, while the Trouville dandies rode forth into the waves on the shoulders of brawny bathing-attendants.   L. LEJEUNE.

THE ITALIAN LAKES.

MONTE SAN SALVATORE (LAGO DI LUGANO).

THE numerous lakes over which the Alps throw their long shadows offer a striking variety of aspect. Those which lie to the north of this chain have in general an air of rugged and sombre grandeur—a mysterious air, as if accustomed to veil their charms in mountain-mist and obscure their history with doubtful legends—an air, even in midsummer, of uncertain warmth, as if conscious that peaks of eternal snow and leagues of untrodden ice-fields lie between them and the sun. The Italian lakes, on the other hand, stretching to the south of the great mountain-barrier, and shielded by it from the cold winds of the German plain, join to the wildness of Alpine scenery the smile of a genial sky and the luxuriance of a southern vegetation. They have the prestige, too, of an earlier civilization than their northern neighbors. For while Lake Leman was still reflecting the rafts and the uncouth helmets of the Helvetians, and while along the Austrian lakes the rude Pannonian was still hunting the wolf and the bear, the borders of the southern lakes, of Garda and Como, Lugano and Maggiore, were already covered with vineyards and olive-groves and dotted with the luxurious villas of a rich and cultured people. Catullus had his home here, and the two Plinies and many minor lights of Roman letters. Since that day the language, the religion, the government and the manners of the inhabitants of this region have completely changed. Only the rocks and mountains, the waters and the verdure with which Nature yearly renews her youth, remain the same. But there is in those permanent features a rare beauty which has delighted travellers of every age and has been celebrated in the literature of every country.

It was toward the end of last October that I strolled away from my occupations in the French capital to spend a fortnight on the Italian lakes. Of the many routes which from time immemorial have served for the invasion of Italy by the barbarian and the tourist, I chose on this occasion the Brenner. Apart from the pleasing views it offers, this Alpine pass is interesting as being the first over which the Romans ventured to lead their legions, and the first upon which a railway was constructed. I halted at Trent, and it was several days before I could free myself from the charm of the Etruscan city and plan my departure.

One afternoon I was making inquiries at the office of the diligence which runs to Riva on the Lake of Garda, when a newly-married German couple offered to share with me a private carriage which they had just hired for the same journey. I accepted at once, and in an hour we were off. The sober gray suit trimmed with green in which Hans was attired contrasted oddly with the brilliant purple travelling-dress of his fair-haired Gretchen. I wondered at first that they should have been willing to embarrass themselves with a stranger, until I perceived that my presence was no hinderance at all to their demonstrations of affection. We climbed up by a steep and winding road to a narrow defile which the impetuous Vella almost fills. One day, when St. Vigilius was too much pressed for time to walk over the mountain, he wrenched it apart and made this passage. The imprint of his holy hand is still to be seen on the rock. Passing under the cyclopean eyes of scores of Austrian cannon which now defend this important military position, we began to descend the valley of the Sarca. It is a wild region, where every hamlet has a ruined castle and a legend of knight or robber, saint or fairy. The picturesque remains of the Madruzzo Castle bring to mind the celebrated portraits which Titian painted of members of this noble family. The artist's colors have survived the last of a long line, and will doubtless outlive as well the crumbling stones of their stronghold. As we skirted the little Lake of Dobling its still waters reflected rocks and trees, sky and mountain, in an enchanting manner.

"Lovely!" I exclaimed.

"Lovely!" echoed Gretchen, without taking her eyes off Hans.

"Lovely!" answered Hans, still watching the beautiful things reflected in her eyes.

After crossing the rapid Sarca and traversing a desolate tract where rocks of every size, fallen from the overhanging mountain, lie strewn about in chaotic

RIVA (LAGO DI GARDA).

confusion, we reached Arco. This sunny village nestles at the foot of an immense detached boulder whose dizzy summit is crowned by mediæval battlements and towers. Home fit only for birds of prey, this castle was long the nest of a family of robbers. Scarcely had we lost in the distance this greatest wonder of the valley when a sharp turn of the road brought Riva and the Lake of Garda full in view. It was a prospect of singular beauty. The sun had already set except on the highest peaks, and a part of the lake was wrapt in purple shadows. Another part, however, was as clear and light as the sky above it, and all aglow with the images of crimson and orange-tinted clouds. A shrill cry—of delight, I thought—burst from Gretchen's lips. I was mistaken. Hans had pulled off too rudely a ring from her finger, and the fair one was in tears.

Half an hour more of fast driving brought us to Riva, which we entered by the Porta San Michele, one of the four ancient and imposing gateways of which the town boasts. Two good inns offered their hospitality. I chose the Golden Sun, but my romantic companions preferred the Garden. The landlord informed me that the two steamers which daily make the tour of the lake, one along the eastern and one along the western shore, would both start before sunrise. Unwilling to leave Riva so soon, I determined to lie over one day. My windows overlooked the beach, and I fell asleep to the monotonous plash of the wave and to the buzz of noisy talk in the streets, which continued to a late hour.

In the morning I go out to see the local sights. In ten minutes I am satisfied that there is nothing here in the way of painting or architecture worth seeing. But if these are wanting, there are plenty of curious narrow streets, where the houses lean over the way toward each other in a friendly but most unstable manner; there are gardens of blooming oleanders; there are gaudy house-fronts, whose frescoes seem to have waged a hard battle with Time. Above all, there is the animation of the port and the free, happy, open-air life on the beach and in the two large squares. Here every face, every costume, every word, every gesture, is Italian. The harmony between the landscape and the people is perfect, save that over La Rocca, the fortress on the shore, waves the black-and-yellow flag of Franz Joseph, and that here and there an Austrian uniform mars the picture, and that now and then harsh German accents fall on the ear like a discord in a fine strain of music. An unpleasant fact is forced upon the attention. The home of these Italians is as yet no part of Italy: Riva and a small portion of the lake still belong to Austria.

In the afternoon I take the famous walk to the Ponale waterfall. The road thither ascends continually. It has been skilfully led along the ledges of a precipitous cliff which borders the lake to the west of Riva, and occasionally pierces the mountain by short tunnels. After passing through the third tunnel I come to a wooden bridge, under which the Ponale dashes just before taking its final leap into the lake. The frail structure on which I stand trembles and is wet with spray, and the air is full of the roar and gurgle of the waters. But for me the main charm of the walk is not the sight of this noisy torrent, but the superb view of Riva that I get on my way back upon issuing from one of the tunnels. The eye, accustomed for a moment to the darkness, is all the more sensitive to the rich soft light which bathes the mountains and the town. A gentle breeze ripples the lake, and the brightly-painted houses that fringe the beach are seen indistinctly in the water, where they look like a line of waving banners. Half a dozen steeples and bell-towers rise gracefully from among the roofs, and their presence explains the surprising frequency with which the hours of the night are struck. From this height I can distinguish the low walls which surround the town and compress its four thousand inhabitants into the area of a small quadrilateral. But Riva, though still fortified, has a thorough look of peaceful commercial prosperity, and has quite laid aside the warlike air she wore in the Middle Ages. In those troubled times this town saw countless wars and sustained many sieges; belonged now to Venice, now to Milan, now to Austria; and at times was independent and able to defy even a bull of the pope or a rescript of the emperor.

TORBOLE (LAGO DI GARDA).

Two incidents of these wars of the fifteenth century deserve mention. Piccinino, a leader of mercenary troops in the Milanese service, was besieged in Riva by Francis Sforza, who, thirsting for the blood of his adversary, had offered a large reward for his head. Piccinino, seeing that the town was hard pressed and likely to fall, thought it wise to make his escape. First, he had it given out that he had died of the plague: then had himself sewed up in a sack and let down by a rope from the town-wall. There a soldier took the sack on his back and carried it through the enemy's lines, ringing a bell all the while to warn everybody to keep out of the way and avoid contagion. The ruse succeeded, and before it was found out the cunning *condottiere* was out of Sforza's reach.

It was on another occasion, when this same Piccinino held all the lower part of the lake and the Venetians had access only to the upper part, that the other incident occurred. Hannibal crossed the Alps with elephants and Napoleon with cannon, but Sorbolo, a native of Candia, in some sort outdid them both, for he dragged a whole fleet over a mountain which is almost as high as the great St. Bernard Pass. He brought thirty-one Venetian ships as far as he could up the Adige, and then, with the aid of two thousand oxen, hauled them in fifteen days over Monte Baldo and let them down by ropes into the lake.

Torbole, the village where this costly enterprise ended, is about three miles from Riva. It is much visited—by epicureans for its good fish, by artists for its picturesque surroundings, and by enthusiastic climbers, who there begin the ascent of Monte Baldo.

Long before daybreak the next morning the great red and green eyes of two small steamers are looking around for passengers, and their whistles screeching that it is time to get up. I have chosen the boat which skirts the western bank. It starts an hour later than the other, but it is not yet sunrise when we push off. The after-deck is thinly peopled, chiefly by tourists, but the fore-deck, where the seats are cheaper, is crowded. We pass by the tumbling and roaring Ponale, and before many minutes we cross the invisible boundary-line between Austria and Italy. The motion of the boat is hardly felt, for we are sailing with a strong current. The high peaks to the north have already caught the first rays of the sun: masses of white vapor which have been sleeping in the mountain-hollows are roused up and put on a rosy tint. The sky is without a cloud, the lake without a ripple: we seem to be floating in mid-air.

Limone, the first stopping-place, is quite given up to the culture of the fruit from which it takes its name. A row of cypresses gives a gloomy air to the village and awakens a melancholy recollection. It was here that, in 1810, Andreas Hofer, the Tyrolese patriot, was arrested by order of Napoleon. A boat conveyed him to the prison of Peschiera, and he was soon afterward shot in the citadel of Mantua.

We next stop before Tremosine, a village perched high up on a rock, and to which no visible road leads. On the other side of the lake, which is here narrow, the white houses of Malcesine cluster around the base of an imposing castle. This stronghold of the Middle Ages, one of the few in this neighborhood which Time has not been suffered to destroy, was built by Charlemagne, and was formerly the boundary between Austria and the Venetian territory; but it is chiefly interesting from an adventure which here befell Goethe. He had sat down in the courtyard, and was sketching one of the quaint old towers, when the crowd that had gathered around him, taking him for a spy, fell on him, tore his drawings to pieces and sent for the authorities to arrest him. Fortunately, there was in the village a man who had worked in Frankfort and knew the poet by sight, and through his influence Goethe was set free.

Behind Malcesine the ground rises slowly in gentle undulations until the long ridge of Monte Baldo, its summit bare, its sides clothed with chestnut and myrtle and scarred by deep ravines, closes the view. A strong north breeze, which the captain calls the *sover*, has sprung up. It swells the sails of the little barks that dot the lake, and under its influence the water takes a hue of pure ultramarine. Keeping along, close under the wild and steep bank, we arrive at Gargnano, the warmest spot in Northern Italy and the favorite resort of the Brescian aristocracy. Low hills,

BELLAGGIO, SEEN FROM VILLA GIULIA.

covered with lemon-groves and fig trees, form the background of this lovely village, while gay villas and beautiful gardens line the shore. Not far away, at the water's edge, a small column is erected opposite the spot where six members of the same family perished when, in 1866, an Italian gunboat was sunk by the Austrian fleet.

The lake widens fast as we advance. Suddenly the bay of Salo opens to the right, and we enter it to search out the little town of that name, which is quite hidden among orange and mulberry trees. It is ten o'clock when, emerging from this bay, we pass through a narrow strait between a group of islands and the mainland. The breeze gradually dies away, a few minutes of perfect calm succeed, and then fitful gusts agitate the surface of the lake.

"Il lago si volta!" exclaims the captain; and the meaning of the phrase is soon evident, for the south wind sets in strongly and the color of the water changes, first to the deepest possible blue, and then to a bright grass-green. A burly priest at my side tells me that this singular phenomenon occurs in fine weather at the same hour every day. It is a lake in the morning, he says, but a sea in the afternoon; and, quoting Virgil's famous line,

Fluctibus et fremitu assurgens, Benace, marino,

he assures me that in violent storms he has seen the waves run as high here as in any part of the Mediterranean. His conversation occupies my attention for the rest of the journey. Pointing to the town of Garda, faintly seen on the opposite shore, he tells me, among other things, that he was born there; that in the castle there the virtuous Adelaide, queen of Italy, was imprisoned; and that the lake, called *Benacus* by the Romans, assumed its modern name some centuries ago, when it fell under the dominion of the counts of Garda. Just behind Garda is the village where Napoleon gained one of his most brilliant victories and Massena the title of duke of Rivoli.

We are soon abreast of the peninsula of Sermione, on which stood the house of Catullus. This long and narrow strip of land, in shape like an arrow, divides the southern end of the lake into two bays, on each of which is situated an important town. Peschiera, to the east, is one corner of the famous Italian Quadrilateral: to the west lies Desenzano, toward which our steamer is heading—one of the chief grain-markets of Lombardy. Midway on Sermione is a castle with three picturesque towers built by the Scaligers, and at the very end of the peninsula are extensive Roman ruins, now known as the Grotto of Catullus. At the sight of these venerable arches the priest grows enthusiastic.

"Quam te libenter, quamque laetus inviso!
Salve, O venusta Sirmio!"

he exclaimed. "Virgil visited these shores: Dante, when an exile in Verona, accepting the

cortesia del gran Lombardo
Che'n su la scala porta il santo uccello,

made frequent excursions upon and around our lake and drew many pictures of its scenery. But Catullus lived here: this was his home. How often has his eye rested on each point of this wonderful landscape, the mountains, the valleys, this broad expanse of water, the bold headlands and the curving beach! How often has he watched with delight the changes which the hours and seasons work in their appearance! Here he sung his love for Lesbia in words that still thrill us, and here he mourned the death of her sparrow. His whole poetry is but the reflection of the beauty which Nature daily spread before him."

Scarcely are the ruins out of sight when we enter the harbor of Desenzano. After landing I have just time to take lunch and to cast a hurried glance over certain Roman antiquities and relics of the Stone Age found here, before the train starts, and carries me off with it toward Lecco, on the Lake of Como.

The environs of Lecco are not wanting in beauty. The swift Adda rushes by, bearing off the clear waters of the lake; to the east a fantastic mountain, the Resegone or "Great Saw," lifts up its long teeth against the sky; to the

STREET IN TREMEZZO.

west, across the water and at the entrance of the Val Madrera, the village of Malgrate offers a charming prospect. The town itself is given up to iron-foundries, cotton-mills and silk-looms, and has little of interest to detain the traveller except perhaps a museum of instruments of torture. But Manzoni, who placed in this neighborhood some of the best scenes of his *Promessi Sposi*, has endeared the spot for ever to the literary world, and many a tourist now spends a day in Lecco, less to inspect its manufactories or to satisfy his eye with a pleasing landscape than to search out in the streets and the market-place counterparts of the characters of the famous novel.

On the map the Lake of Como looks like an inverted and somewhat irregular Y, or, still more, like a child's first attempt to draw a man, who without arms and with unequal legs is running off to the left. Just at the moment his picture is taken he has one foot on Lecco and the other on the town of Como. The hilly district between the two southern branches of the lake is known as the Brianza, and is noted for its bracing air, its fertile soil and the coolness of its springs. The Brianza ends at the middle of the lake in a dolomite promontory several hundred feet high, on whose western slope lies the village of Bellaggio. This point commands the finest views in every direction: it is near the most interesting of those villas which are open to the public, and it abounds in good hotels. To visit Bellaggio is therefore the aim of every tourist who passes this way. My journey thither it is best to pass over in silence, for I see nothing, and what I feel is indescribable. I am shut up during a furious storm of wind and rain in the cabin of a little steamer which is as nervous and uneasy as if on the Atlantic. I am told, however, that in this part of the lake the banks are lofty and steep, and frequently barren, and that there are marble-quarries to be seen, and cascades and houses and villages crowning the cliffs.

On arriving at Bellaggio, I take lodging in the Villa Serbelloni, one of the many magnificent residences which poverty has induced the Italian nobles to put into the hands of hotel-keepers. The house stands high up on the very end of the promontory, and adjoining it is an extensive park, on which the ruins of a robber's castle look down. The panorama which on a fine day spreads itself out before one who walks in these grounds is of singular beauty. The northern arm of the lake, wider and more regular than the others, opens up a long vista of headlands and bays and red-roofed villages as far as where Domaso peeps out from a grove of giant elms. Beyond, the view is bounded by the snow-covered Alps. Close at hand, near Varenna, the Fiume di Latte, a milk-white waterfall, leaps down from a height of a thousand feet. Toward Lecco huge walls of barren rock arise and wrap every thing near them in sombre shadows. Toward Como the tranquil water is shut in by hills and low mountains, whose flowing lines blend gracefully together. Some of these slopes are dark with pines, some are gray with the olive, some are garlanded with vines which hang from tree to tree, while others are clothed in a rich green foliage, amid which glistens the golden fruit of the orange and the lemon. The banks are lined with bright gardens and noble parks and villas, whose lawns run down to the water's edge and are adorned with fountains, statues, masses of brilliant flowers and clumps of tall trees. Above is a sky of Italian blue, and below is a crystal mirror in which every charm of the landscape is repeated. The impression made by all this loveliness is increased by the air of happiness that pervades the spot. It is the haunt of the rich, the gay, the newly-married: music and song, laughter and mirthful talk, are the most familiar sounds. The smile of Nature seems here to warm men's hearts and drive away the cares they have brought with them.

It is on this site that Pliny the Younger is believed to have had the villa which he called Cothurnus or "Tragedy." The present building is several centuries old. Tradition relates that a certain countess, one of its first occupants, had a habit of throwing her lovers down the cliff when she was tired of them. Making this delightful abode my head-quarters, I spend a week, partly in agreeable sight-seeing and partly in still more agreeable idleness. I visit villas, towers, fossil-beds and waterfalls—in short, everything interesting and accessible—now going on foot, now borne from point to point in one of the sharp-prowed rowboats which are in use here, and now taking the steamer up to Colico or down to Como and back.

At half an hour's walk from here, on the Lecco arm of the lake, is the Villa

BAY OF PALLANZA (LAGO DI LUGANO).

Giulia. It was the favorite residence of the late Leopold, king of Belgium, and, although now a hotel, it is worth a visit for the beautiful grounds that surround it and for the charming view it affords in the direction of Bellaggio. It is here that, while strolling in the garden one afternoon, secretly coveting the wonderful camellias and hortensias, I catch the whisper of familiar voices, and stumble suddenly upon an arbor where, under the shadow of countless roses, I descry a gray-and-green arm around a purple waist. The moment I am seen there is a scream and a flutter, and then a cordial recognition. Hans and Gretchen tell me they are making the same tour that I am, and they hope to meet me again.

Much closer at hand, on the Como arm, is the Villa Melzi. It was built in 1810, in plain but pure style and at great cost, for that Melzi who was publicly embraced by Bonaparte at Lyons and made by him vice-president of the Cisalpine Republic, and afterward duke of Lodi. The interior of the villa is richly decorated, elegantly furnished and adorned with objects of art of every kind. One of the duke's ancestors was the pupil and friend of Leonardo da Vinci, and succeeded him as master in the school he had founded. Four monochromes illustrate this interesting reminiscence. Then there is a bust of Michel Angelo by himself, and various works in marble by those two friends and generous rivals, Canova and Thorwaldsen. The most remarkable painting is a portrait of Bonaparte, taken from life in 1802 by Appiani. The First Consul of France and President of Italy was then thirty-three years old. Richly attired, but pale and thin, he rests his hand upon the map of Italy, the scene of his greatest exploits, and fixes his piercing eye full on the spectator with a glance that recalls the past and seems to predict the future. In the garden the most showy flowers and the rarest trees from every clime are tastefully disposed, while here and there the whiteness of a marble statue contrasts pleasingly with the green of the surrounding vegetation. The bust of Alfieri occupies the highest point of the grounds; those of Madame Letitia and Josephine are half hidden by encroaching vines; Dante and Beatrice, standing together, overlook the lake. At the end of the garden, under the dome of a small chapel encircled by tall cypresses, rest the ashes of the duke of Lodi. His grandson is the present owner of the villa, but he spends here hardly a fortnight in the year. The porter says that his master finds more to amuse him in his town-palaces, of which he has half a dozen in different parts of Italy; but the gardener tells me that this spot awakens too painful memories of a wife tenderly loved and early lost.

Across the lake from here is the Villa Carlotta, called after its former owner, the princess Charlotte of Prussia. Stepping out of his boat, the visitor ascends the marble stairs which lead up from the shore. After a few steps across the garden he reaches the villa, passes through a porch fragrant with jasmine, and is at once ushered into a small room where are some of the finest works of modern sculpture. Canova's *Mars and Venus* and *Palamedes* are here, and they are most admirable, but they are surpassed in charm by the famous group in which Psyche is reclining and Cupid bending fondly over her. The best piece of the collection is the frieze that runs round the room. It is from the chisel of Thorwaldsen, and represents Alexander the Great's triumphal entry into Babylon. Full of the beauty of youth, the conqueror advances in his chariot; Victory comes to meet him; vanquished nations bring presents; while behind him follow his brave Greeks on horse and on foot, dragging along with them the prisoners and the booty. The subject was suggested by Napoleon, who intended the work for the Quirinal. It is in high relief, and in general effect resembles strongly the frieze with which Phidias encircled the Parthenon. It is a pity that these masterpieces are shown first, for after seeing them one does not fully enjoy the statues and paintings in the other rooms.

Two hours may be delightfully spent in making the journey by steamboat from

ROTUNDA OF HERCULES ON ISOLA BELLA.

Bellaggio to Como. Here the lake is so narrow and winding that it seems to be a river. At every moment bold mountain-spurs project into the water, appearing to bar all passage, and one's curiosity is continually excited to find the outlet. The views shift and change with surprising quickness, for the boat stops at a dozen little towns on the way, and for this purpose keeps crossing and recrossing from shore to shore.

The quaint village of Tremezzo is one of the first stopping-places. It is built on the side of a steep hill, and seems to be in constant danger of slipping down. Soon the island of Comacina is passed, now a barren rock with only a small chapel upon it, but once the site of an important town and fortress. Farther on, close to the water's edge, is a pyramid which an obscure Austrian, emulous of the long-lasting fame of the Egyptian kings, caused to be erected to his own memory. To the right rises the lofty Monte Bisbino, the weather-prophet of the neighborhood, for when he puts on his cap of clouds it is sure to rain.

<blockquote>
Se il Bisbin mette il cappello,
Corri a prendere l'ombrello,
</blockquote>

says a local proverb. From this point on to Como both shores are studded with villas of every size and style, but all, with one exception, bright and gay. A rich milliner built one; a great dancer another; a third belongs to Madame Musard, the owner of the open-air concert-grounds at Paris. One was the retreat of Judith Pasta, the famous singer for whom Bellini composed *Norma* and *La Sonnambula;* in another Bonaparte lodged; another was for many years the home of his great-niece, the charming Madame Rattazzi; in another lived the unfortunate Queen Caroline, wife of George IV. The only one among them all that looks gloomy and forbidding is the Villa Pliniana, built three centuries ago by Count Anguissola, one of the four assassins of Duke Farnese. The name it bears was given to it because it stands near a curious spring minutely described in one of Pliny's letters.

Como itself is a quiet, sleepy town. It is justly proud of having given birth to the two Plinies and to Volta. The statue of the electrician stands in the middle of a grass-grown square: those of the great naturalist and his accomplished nephew sit in marble arm-chairs on each side of the cathedral-door. With the ruined castle of Baradello, which looks down on Como, is connected the story of a dreadful retribution. In the thirteenth century the archbishop Otto Visconti, having won a battle and taken his rival, Napo della Torre, prisoner, put him naked into an iron cage which he suspended from the projecting parapet of this castle. After enduring for a few days the jeers of the populace and the pangs of hunger, the unhappy man put an end to his life by beating his head against the bars. One's pity for his sufferings is lessened on learning that he once had a friend of Visconti's in his power and kept him shut up in a wooden cage under the steps of the town-hall at Milan for twelve years.

From Bellaggio to Luino, on the Lago Maggiore, by way of the Swiss town of Lugano, is a short day's journey, thanks to the admirable combination of steamboats and diligences. That part of the Lake of Lugano which is traversed is at first wild and sombre, with inaccessible cliffs rising on either hand. By degrees the landscape softens, and on turning a point Lugano comes in sight, nestling in a hollow between two mountains. One of these, the Monte San Salvatore, has a most graceful outline: it is three thousand feet high, beautifully wooded, of easy ascent, and is said to offer from its summit an enchanting prospect. But neither its charms nor those of the town at its foot induce me to tarry. I hasten on to Luino, gathering on the way, from my seat on top of the diligence, a bewildering series of mountain-pictures, with which mingles the memory of many a smiling village and many a lovely garden—of a pure air and a perfumed breeze, with here and there a pair of bright eyes or a pretty face or a band of sun-browned children hanging on to the coach behind like a cluster of bees.

Luino is neither pretty nor clean, nor has it a single monument or inscription to tell that Bernardo Luini was born here, the celebrated painter whose frescoes adorn many churches and monasteries in the neighborhood. Tired with the day's travel, I climb at an early hour into an enormous bed of state which my landlord has assigned to me and try to forget its grandeur in sleep. I lie awake, however, a great part of the night, listening perforce to a quarrel among certain stage-drivers who have taken their stand under my window. It is carried on by six voices at once in angry tones, but always in polite language. Amiable race! Where a Celt or an Anglo-Saxon would curse and swear, an Italian contents himself with crying out "Pazienza! pazienza!"

In the morning the arguments of an honest-looking boatman persuade me not to wait for the steamer, but to take a small boat with four rowers down to Stresa. Once afloat, it is easy to see why this lake has received the name of *Maggiore*. Though really smaller than the Lake of Garda, it looks larger, for it is in general wider, and there are no precipitious banks to confine the view. The mountains that enclose it are low and retreating, and the eye sweeps over a vast and varied horizon. At my request we gain at once the opposite shore. On an island opposite Cannero the remains of two dismantled castles trace grotesque silhouettes against the sky. One of the boatmen tells me the story of five robber-brothers named Mazzardi who lived there long ago with their followers and ravaged the surrounding country with impunity. He follows this up with other legends of the lake, and dwells especially upon the happy case of a certain Albert Besozzi, a rich profligate, likewise of ancient memory, who, being thoroughly frightened one day by a narrow escape from shipwreck on these waters, dedicated the worthless remainder of his life to Heaven and finished his days in a hermit's cell.

Meanwhile, we have turned into the beautiful bay of Pallanza, and my companions cease rowing for a while to refresh themselves with bread and wine. The steamer comes along, touches at the Pallanza wharf and puts off again. Immediately afterward there is a great commotion. A woman in purple on the deck of the boat is frantically imploring the captain to stop, while a young man on the pier seems to be preparing to jump into the water. Hans has stepped ashore to buy fruit, and has been left behind. The captain is inexorable, the steamer keeps on its course, and every moment the breach becomes wider between those whom no man should put asunder. I take the unhappy man into my boat, and by pulling in a straight line for Stresa we arrive there almost as soon as the steamer, which has followed the wide curve of the bay. What appears in the distance to be a singular monument on the end of the Stresa wharf turns out on nearer approach to be Gretchen standing on a trunk and drying her handkerchief in the breeze.

The four islands that we have passed on the way are known as the Borromean Islands, because they belong for the most part to the rich and powerful Borromeo family. The rare beauty of one of them makes it the wonder of the lake. It was toward the middle of the seventeenth century that Count Vitaliano Borromeo, finding himself the possessor of almost the whole of this island, which was then a barren rock, resolved to make it his residence, and to surround himself with gardens that should rival those of Armida. For more than twenty years architects, gardeners, sculptors and painters labored to give material form to the count's fancies. A spacious palace was erected on one end of the island: on the other ten lofty terraces rose one above the other, like the hanging-gardens of Babylon. The rock was covered with good soil, and the choicest trees and shrubs were brought from every land. Only evergreens, however, were admitted into this Eden, for the count would have about him no sign of winter or death. In 1671 the work was finished. The island was called Isabella, after the count's mother—a name which has since, by a happy corruption, become changed to Isola Bella.

It is on a sunny afternoon that I direct my bark toward the "Beautiful Island."

I look on the landing-place with respect, for it is worn by the footsteps of six generations of travellers. The interior of the palace, which I visit first, is fitted up with princely magnificence and is rich in art-treasures. Mementoes of kings and queens who have accepted hospitality here are shown, and a bed in which Bonaparte once slept. There is a chapel where a priest daily says mass; a throne-room, as in the palaces of the Spanish grandees; and a gallery with numerous paintings. A whole suite of rooms is given up to the works of Peter Molyn, a Dutch artist, fitly nicknamed "Sir Tempest." This erratic man, having killed his wife to marry another woman, was condemned to death. He escaped from prison, however, found an asylum here, and in return for the protection of the Borromeo of that day he adorned his walls with more than fifty landscapes and pastoral scenes.

The garden betrays the epoch at which it was laid out. Prim parterres, where masses of brilliant flowers bloom all the year round, are enclosed by walks along which orange trees and myrtles have been bent and trimmed into whimsical patterns. There are dark and winding alleys of cedars where at every turn some surprise is planned. Here is a grotto made of shells — there an obelisk, or a mosaic column, or a horse of bronze, or a fountain of clear water in which the attendant tritons and nymphs would doubtless disport were they not petrified into marble. There is one lovely spot where, at the middle point of a rotunda, a large statue of Hercules stands finely out against a background of dark foliage. Other Olympians keep him company and calmly eye the visitor from their painted niches. Not far from there is a venerable laurel on which Bonaparte cut the word "Battaglia" a few days before the battle of Marengo. The B is still plainly visible.

Pines and firs planted thickly along the northern side of the island defend it from cold winds. In the sunny nooks of the terraces the delicate lemon tree bears abundant fruit and the oleander grows to a size which it attains nowhere else in Europe. The tea-plant from China, the banana from Africa and the sugar-cane from Mississippi flourish side by side: the camphor tree distils its aromatic essence and the magnolia loads the air with perfume. The cactus and the aloe border walks over which the bamboo bends and throws its grateful shade. Turf and flower-beds carpet each terrace, and a tapestry of ivy and flowering vines conceals the walls of the structure. From the summit a huge stone unicorn looks down upon his master's splendid domain. He overlooks also a corner of the island where his master's authority is not acknowledged. The small patch of land on which the Dolphin Hotel stands has for many centuries descended from father to son in a plebeian family, nor have the Borromeos ever been able to buy it. They have to endure the inn, therefore, as Frederick endured the mill at San-Souci and Napoleon the house he could not buy at Paris.

At last the moment comes when I must quit Stresa, not, however, before I have visited the remaining islands and other points of interest. The steamer puts off, and soon separates me from the landscape that has been my delight for three days—the blue bay with its verdant banks, the softly-shaded hills which enclose it, the snow-covered chain of the Simplon in the background. As we approach the southern end of the lake a colossal bronze statue of San Carlo Borromeo on the summit of a hill near Arona comes into sight. From head to foot the saint measures little less than eighty feet, and the pedestal on which he stands adds to his height half as much more. His face is turned toward Arona, his native town, and one hand is extended to bless it. With my glass I descry a party of liliputian tourists engaged in examining this great Gulliver. Most of them are satisfied when they have reached the top of the pedestal and have ranged themselves in a row on one foot of the statue. Others, more daring, climb up by a ladder to the saint's knee, where they disappear through an aperture in the skirt of his robe. From this point the ascent continues inside of the statue, by means of iron bars, to the head, in which four persons can conveniently remain at once.

At Arona the railway-station and the wharf are near each other, and in a few minutes after I have landed an express-train starts and bears me away from the region of the Italian lakes. When we have passed the last houses of Arona and gained the open plain the statue of the great Borromeo with his outstretched arm comes again for a few moments into view. Perhaps the uncertain light of evening and the jolting of the train deceive me, but I fancy that the good old saint is waving his hand in the familiar Italian way, as much as to say, "A rivederci!"   ROBERT A. MCLEOD.

EASTER ON THE RIVIERA.

ON THE RIVIERA.

A THOUSAND miles in six-and-thirty hours and the blue Mediterranean and sunshine in exchange for London fog and soot! The temptation was irresistible to the Chancery barrister, weary of stuffy courts and sunless chambers; it fascinated the Eton assistant-master, brain-misty with boys' multifarious blunderings; and the very next morning after courts and schools were closed for Easter vacation the pair were seated in the early continental mail from Victoria Station, bound for Mentone. Paris is not reached till half-past six P. M., and the Marseilles express leaves the Gare de Lyons at a quarter after seven; but the *douaniers* are merciful to us, and our *cocher* brisk; so we just catch the train, happily forgetful, in the excitement of the start, that the prosaic but generally necessary ceremony of dinner has somehow got crowded out of the day's programme, and that a night and a long morning lie between us and the flesh-pots of Marseilles.

Day is just breaking when we draw up at Lyons, and the passengers uncurl themselves and tumble sleepily out of their carriages to scarify their throats with scalding chocolate or coffee. In vain the manager of the refreshment-room blandly reiterates the assurance—a perfectly true one—that nobody need hurry. Three minutes of painful deglutition at the cost of a franc a head (what a Tom Tiddler's Ground one of those large French station-restaurants must be!), and the carriages are full again, and our ulsters, cloaks, plaids and wraps of all sorts begin to open and disclose fellow-passengers to one another. This morning the predominant element is military—a cluster of smooth-faced youths, gay in red and blue uniforms, on their way from some military school to pass six months in barracks at Toulon. Speeding due south alongside the brown Rhone, we are perceptibly and visibly passing by rapid stages into a warmer climate. First, mulberry-plantations, the nurseries of the Lyons silk-trade; then olives—starveling specimens the northernmost ones, but gradually increasing in size and number as the Mediterranean is approached; and soon, when Marseilles has been reached and passed, the orange, the pomegranate and the aloe.

Lazily, all a long afternoon, the train dawdles eastward, now skirting the placid sea and playing hide-and-seek with it through a bewildering series of little tunnels—now making a short cut across a peninsula and giving the bent farm-laborers an excuse for the elevating recreation of a stare. Only a two minutes' halt at Fréjus, but it well deserves at least a day to itself. In the days when the masonry of that graceful amphitheatre hard by the station was new, Forum Julii was a port that had received those five hundred galleys which Augustus took at Actium, and as little dreamed of being silted up into an obscure inland town as of having its name shrivelled into Fréjus. But your modern traveller is a Gallio in Old-World matters of this kind, and steams on with a light heart to a more congenial halting-place a score of miles farther on, where there are no associations older than Lord Brougham, who may fairly be said to have invented Cannes. Less than half a century ago the place was an insignificant fishing-village, and now a costly crowd of trim-gardened villas in every style of inappropriate architecture, Gothic, Doric and Castellated, jostle one another jealously, backed up by a satellite town of hotels and *pensions* and doctors. Bright and pretty it looks in the light of the westering sun, and a tempting resting-place indeed after a long, dusty journey in the train. So, obviously, thinks that plethoric little plutocrat travelling with his young wife in the solitary state of a reserved *coupé* under the dominion of a sallow-faced courier. But his pleadings are in vain: the courier has arranged otherwise, and is sole master of the plans, the purse and—the language; so his employer humbly falls back upon petitioning to be allowed a glass of fruit-syrup (which the courier graciously orders and pays for) from the orange-woman on the platform, and is helped back into his coupé to doze away another hour or two of exquisitely beautiful scenery in the comfortable assurance that he is "doing" the Riviera.

There is a good deal of interesting sightseeing to be had in and about Cannes. The oddly-shaped umbrella-pines just on the outskirts of the villadom are a novelty to most people. Within easy reach lie Grasse, most aptly named of villages, where all that's odorous in scents and all that's luscious in *fruits glacés* are manufactured, and Vallauris, where the descendants of a line of potters said to have lasted unbroken from the days of Roman rule turn out bowls and pots and vases of a rough earthenware, simple but excellent both in form and coloring, and indeed everything that could be wished but for an excess of porousness. Then, again, it is but a short sail—or even row—to the island of Ste. Marguérite, where you may realize the scene of Marshal Bazaine's sensational escape from prison and verify the truth of Thackeray's eulogistic ballad by lunching on *bouillabaisse*. Cannes certainly is—at least for everybody except the strangely-constituted beings to whom shops, toilettes, theatres and bustle are the *summum bonum*—a far pleas-

SCENE ON THE SHORE.

anter resting-place than its big neighbor Nice; which latter, too, lying exposed as it does at the foot of a trough in the mountains through which the piercingly cold mistral comes sweeping down from the north-west, is a delusion and a snare to the invalids who come in hopes of finding a mild winter there. Nor is this all. Of late years Nice has suffered from the addition of a very undesirable element to its population — that of the gamblers attending the casino at Monte Carlo, who find in a big town like Nice ample and handy head-quarters, and bring in their train a camp-following of not merely indifferent but offensive characters. People of this class so throng the afternoon and evening trains on the short section of line between Nice and Monte Carlo— the notorious gaming-house moiety of the prince of Monaco's liliputian dominion—as to make the transit positively disagreeable to the ordinary traveller. From the time a party of these *habitués* of the roulette-table enter a carriage till the train stops at their destination their tongues keep up a ceaseless clatter in the jargon of the game. Every one of them seems to remember, with quite marvellous accuracy, all the winning numbers and all the runs upon the red and black of the previous evening. There are jokes too, and laughter in plenty, but — perhaps it is that some are all the time secretly smarting over losses — there is a smack of malice in the fun and an uncomfortable hollowness in the laughter. One is glad when they are gone and one has a few minutes of quiet to gather together the miscellaneous paraphernalia of travel before arriving at Mentone.

Provided only that one's lodging is assured, it is a distinct advantage to reach a journey's end after nightfall. There is a delicious curiosity generated by the shrouding darkness, a weirdness about the silent roads and shapes of trees and buildings, a pleasant excitement as to what to-morrow will disclose, a restful consciousness that the present physical instinct for repose may be indulged not only without loss, but with the certainty of a fresher and more appreciative susceptibility to first impressions in the morning. And in the mean time what an extra zest, after six-and-thirty hours of continuous travelling, in the hearty welcome of hospitality! We can hardly, in the dark, make out the outline of the villa, but the bright-green door, the tile-floored entrance-passage and the slippery stone staircase italicize it unmistakably, while the comfortable curtains and Turkey carpets, the *Nineteenth Century* and *Nation* on the table, the pictures and china on the walls and an indefinable air of coziness in every room, attest quite as plainly an English-speaking home. Of course the new-comers from London have a store of "Skinner's Best Bird's-eye" (a thing quite unpurchasable at Mentone) in their pouches, and equally of course the whereabouts and doings of a host of common friends have to be communicated, and the affairs of the day, certain to gravitate into the interminable Eastern Question, must be discussed; so it is considerably east of midnight before the pipe-ashes are finally shaken out and all is quiet inside the sheltering mosquito-curtains.

Oh the surprise and delight of the scene revealed on throwing open the lattices in the morning!—from the horizon to one's very feet the sunbeams drawing a dazzling golden line athwart the water-way; to the right the rippling wavelets breaking white against the olive-crested point of Cap Martino; in the left foreground the picturesquely huddled buildings of the town running out to the old Genoese fort, and behind them a jagged mountain-screen of Alps, past which the eye can just catch the sunlit walls of Bordighera. Proverb-mongers may prate what they will: I decline to believe that familiarity can breed aught but increased love and admiration for such a spectacle as this.

Quickly out into the garden. Look! the trees all round the house are golden with oranges and lemons; the walks are strewn with the red and yellow fruit, that of almost every tree having a quite distinguishable flavor of its own; a gigantic aloe, right opposite the front door, is thrusting across the drive a lusty sword-

MENTONE.

arm that seems determined soon to block the way; blushing rose and ungainly cactus in juxtaposition, suggestive of Beauty and the Beast; and on the slopes behind terraced vines and figs and patriarchal olive trees—a feast for our eyes in the present, and for the housewife a treasure of unsophisticated marmalade and sun-dried figs and oil in the not distant future.

There will be ample time before *déjeuner* to stroll out to the headland of Cap Martino; and one need not seek a better standpoint from which to get a general panoramic idea of Mentone and its surroundings. The curve of the shore is broken abruptly into two bays by a narrow hump, topped by the remains of a castle (now converted into a cemetery) and crowded with the buildings of the old town, while west and east along the coast stretch the hotels and pensions and villas of these latter days. Half a mile inland rises an isolated knoll crowned by a Capuchin monastery, and to the north, north-west and east the background is closed in by a semicircle of mountains, spurs of the Maritime Alps range, fending off every wind except those from the west and south. The east bay is the more sheltered, so there the wintering invalids abound; and equally of course the robuster ones, residents and transients alike, prefer the west bay, where, too, they get ampler space, more trees, something of a public garden and a daily band into the bargain.

The sea of the Riviera has been stigmatized as fishless, but the accusation must be accepted, if at all, *cum multis granis*. The watcher perched up aloft there in the cross-trees of a sort of bear-pole overhanging the transparent sea is directing the nets of his comrades in the boats below to a glancing shoal of anchovies that, not reddened by pickling, but in their natural gudgeon-like whiteness, will satisfy, or even glut, the market this afternoon; and several other palatable species of the finny tribe—fresh sardines, soles, *loups de mer, bianchetti* (a delicate and diminutive whitebait), and in short all that go to make up bouillabaisse—are sufficiently plentiful. The supply of particular kinds, though, is so variable that anchovies will be three sous the kilogramme one day and two francs another.

Is it the southern sun or the indescribable suggestion of *dolce far niente*, that seems to pervade everything and everybody here, that is the cause? Only a few hours ago I was scanning those sharply-outlined peaks, Le Berceau and the rest, with an Alpine Clubbist's eagerness to assail them all, and already, as we sit after déjeuner with coffee and cigars under a shady carouba in the garden, it seems more pleasant to rest content with looking at them. An English visitor has dropped in with the benevolent object of inducing our host—who is understood to be in incubation over a monograph on Mentonese antiquities—to take some promising young native as an assistant, and is urging his protégé's claims with an amusing confusion of metaphors: "He is a very mine of information about the local archæology, my dear sir. Tap him anywhere, and I'll warrant him to flow. Where you find a real spark of native talent like this, it's a positive duty to water it. And it's indeed a privilege to have all the strata of society rallying round you in your useful task." And so on, till the party attacked surrenders at discretion and escapes from the subject by proposing a visit to Dr. Bennet's garden.

On a steep southward-fronting slope to the east of the town, and close upon the Italian frontier (across which it is a temptingly easy stroll to buy and smuggle a pocketful of those long black acrid, straw-cored cigars in which some smokers find a perverse delight), Dr. Henry Bennet, an English physician resident at Mentone, has formed, evidently with much devotion of time and thought and loving patience, a very notable garden. Up till one o'clock every day it lies freely open to everybody, hospitably challenging a visit by the inscription "*Salvete amici*" carved over its entrance. Here, on a staircase of terrace-walls rising one above another up the hill, a collection of strange fleshy plants that Kew might well envy flourishes in the open air, in

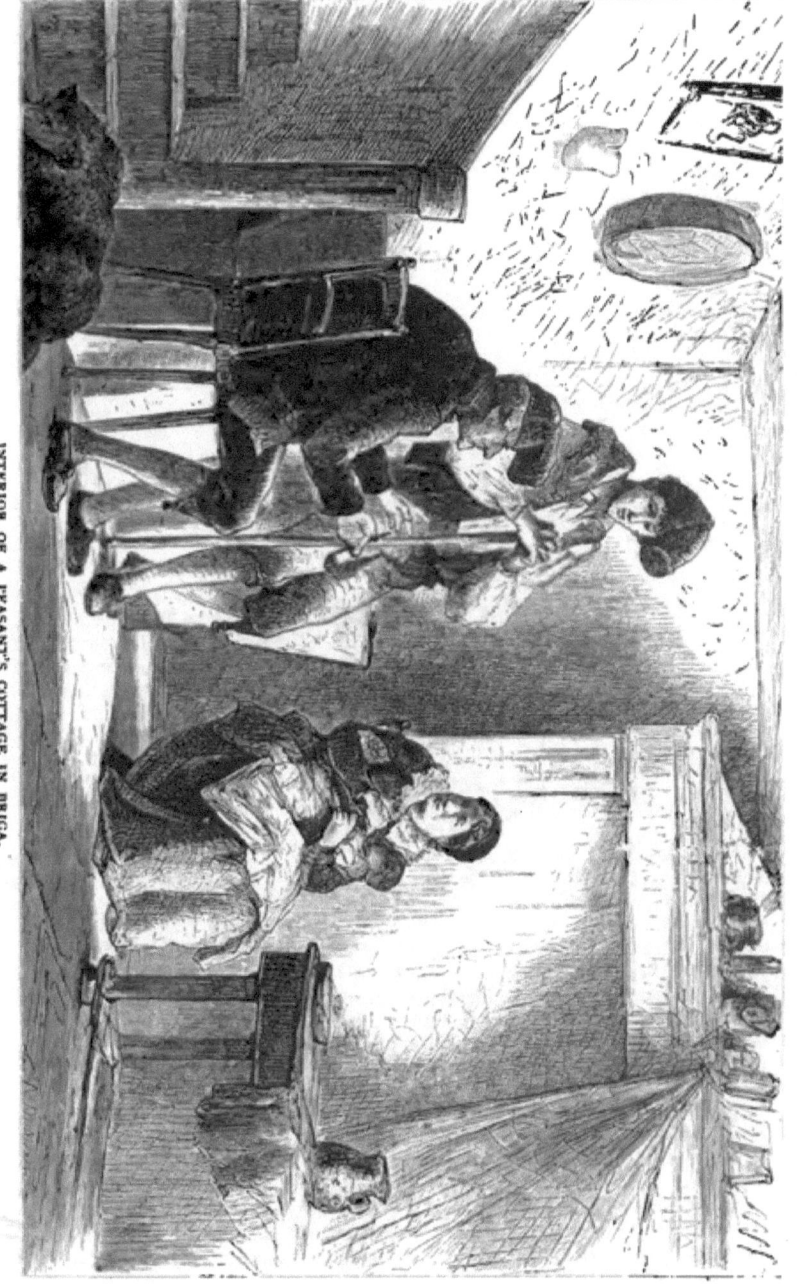

INTERIOR OF A PEASANT'S COTTAGE IN BRIGA.

company with palms, camellias, blood-red ranunculus, the spiny-leaved solanum, delicate creepers of a pink tissue-paper aspect, and a peculiar dull-pink variety of stocks. Goldfish sail about bumptiously in the necessary water-tanks, as if they would cheat you into thinking that the water is stored up there expressly to show them off, and in a cunningly-sheltered corner swings a siesta-bidding hammock. Not against sun so much as against wind this shelter has been devised, for somehow the chilling mistral intrudes even here at times. The gardener propounds, with a fine confidence, his explanation of how this nefarious wind contrives to blow upon his treasures. Sweeping down from the north, it dashes upon the Esterel Mountains, glances off them into the sea, and thence is deflected or refracted back, so that it comes in round the corner, in the deceitful guise of a south-west wind, upon Mentone! An Oxford professor of our party, more skilled maybe in Aristotle and Aldrich than in the physical sciences, is so overcome by the effort requisite to take in this bewildering theory that we have to leave him to seek innocent refreshment in a suburban *vacherie* while we ramble home through the devious streets of the old town. Near the spectacular stairways that lead up to the open space—the only one in the town—in front of the parish church a tablet let into a wall overhanging the narrow thoroughfare piously commemorates the spot from which, "Lutetia Romam redux," a pontifical Pius blessed the assembled crowd. Lower down, the market-place teems with vegetables and volubility. Beans, peas, artichokes, celery and potatoes are recommended by a score of shrill voices, or you may have newly-pressed figs or grapes, or half a dozen kinds of cheese and macaroni. The barrister's eye chances to rest upon some queer-shaped loaves displayed at a bakery-door hard by, and in the twinkling of an eye the lady-bakeress insists upon a purchase. A feeble plea of the impracticability of getting them home is promptly overthrown by "Comme, monsieur est jeune! He will carry them bravely himself;" and Hortensius finds there is nothing for it but to accept the compliment to his youth and lug an armful of bread along the staring promenade.

From early morning till sundown there is always abundance of life in the streets and alleys of Mentone. The genial sunny climate has naturally induced habits of outdoor life. The average native Mentonese gets all the society he wants in the streets (where everybody is on the familiar footing of nicknames with everybody else), and probably keeps up a very limited and frugal establishment at home; and needs every centime of a scanty income to do that. Anyhow, he certainly is not given to hospitality. You may have been for years a resident and *propriétaire*, and on the friendliest terms with all your Mentonese neighbors, but, though habitually kindly, they will never ask you to take bite or sup in their houses. A dinner-party of numerous courses, preceded by five-o'clock tea and Albert biscuits, is veraciously reported to have been given a few years ago at a private house in one of the outlying villages; but the hosts were new-comers from somewhere near Paris, and no doubt in their village they lacked the economical alternative of street society.

The servant-system that obtains at Mentone is in several respects peculiar. A new domestic comes, in the first instance, for eight days on trial, after which the hiring is a monthly one, but terminable at any moment by either party on the terms of the master or mistress, in the case of a dismissal, paying—or the servant, on voluntarily leaving, forfeiting—eight days' wages. This power of instantaneous leaving, whatever the inconvenience caused, must be a potent weapon in, say, a cook's hands. And it is just this fiery-tempered but prosaically necessary class of servants who alone have an evil reputation for dishonesty at Mentone, where the domestics, though inclined to be lazy, are for the most part honest, and house-doors stand open and unguarded without theft ensuing. The cook, here as elsewhere, has a passion for perquisites, and is unweanable from illicit

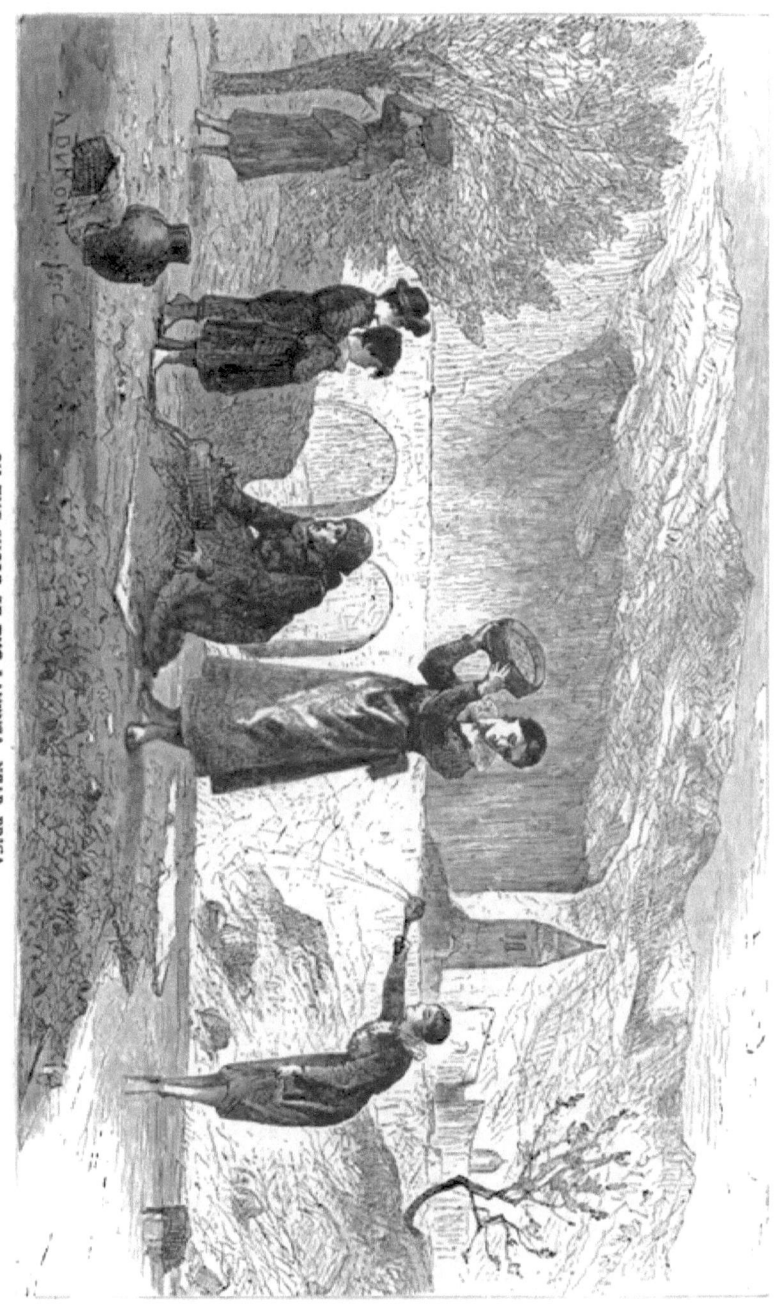

ON THE SHORE OF THE LAVENZA, NEAR BRIGA.

traffickings with the butcher and *charcutier*. She persuades herself that the lard which she resells to them amounts to a quite unappreciable trifle on the kilo, and if she is found out will tranquilly assure her mistress that she "considered it not *comme il faut*" to serve all the fat with the beef. As for certificates of character, they are about as trustworthy as a batch of formal testimonials. The best servants are found in Briga, a picturesque village some distance inland in the hills, where mountain air and simple living have made hardy industry a second nature.

But the number of foreign propriétaires occupying houses and lands of their own at Mentone is very small. The great body of the temporary residents for the season (which extends from October to April) are housed in the many large and prosperous-looking hotels and pensions which, bearing the names of wellnigh every country under heaven, line the shores of both the bays and occupy the neighboring knolls and slopes. No less than thirteen hundred and thirty-six families came from different parts of the world to pass the winter of 1876–77 at Mentone. The English-speaking element was, as usual, the strongest, consisting as it did of three hundred and seventy-four families from Great Britain, fifty from the United States and two or three from Canada. Next came the French visitors, with two hundred and forty-five families, and after them the Germans with one hundred and ninety and the Russians with one hundred. Representatives of every other European country, and several families of Brazilians and Japanese, made up the cosmopolitan tale.

The number and variety of the excursions that may be made on foot, on muleback and by carriage from Mentone make it pre-eminently good head-quarters. It is an easy day's walk to visit one or more of half a dozen mountain-villages almost indistinguishable in general color from the rocks to which they cling, and from which in old days the inhabitants descried betimes the pirates who were apt to pay them unwelcome visits. Roccabruna is a fairly typical sample of these villages, and the stroll up through olive-woods (where, according to the amount of light upon the leaves and the nature of the background to them, they vary bewilderingly in predominant tone between green and blue and gray), with occasional bits of green sward decked with narcissus, till through groves of lemon you suddenly emerge upon the houses pendent on the precipitous crag, is as charming a way of spending a long afternoon as need be desired. The professor, scorning to waste shoe-leather and economize francs, began the ascent on a mule steered by a woman holding on to the beast's tail; but, whether it was that the motion was uncomfortable, or that its incompatibility with pedestrians' pace engendered a feeling of solitariness, or that the proceeding struck him as a trifle ludicrous, it was not long before the professorial lips mildly whispered, "*Ho avuto assai : vuolo descendere*" (the professorial Italian for "I've had enough, and want to get down"), and our friend exchanged the saddle for a convenient wayside wall, whereon he sat and discoursed to us upon many things till time and the hour had worn out so much of the afternoon that we had scarcely daylight enough left to achieve the object of our walk. Roccabruna is a close-packed nest of houses, pierced by narrow, tortuous lanes arched over here and there, sorely perplexing to a stranger enemy no doubt, and superlatively defensible, crowned and dominated by an ancient moated castle, from the battlements of which one might throw a stone down on to any one of the weatherworn, bamboo-looking tile roofs of the little town. The church is relatively spacious, and hung with the gaudy red damask so common in Italy. Through the doorways of their dark cellar-like houses the housewives are visible, engaged in roasting coffee, chopping wood and what not, while a good many of the men seem to be content to sit and lounge about smoking. They are not greedy of high wages, and prefer being masters of their own time to being servants of other people's money. Themselves perched above the route of any thoroughfare,

MONKS PLAYING AT BOWLS.

they look down upon no less than four lines of road passing between their eyrie and the sea. Topmost, the famous Corniche road from Mentone to Nice winds along the mountain-sides; below it runs the road to Monaco; below that, again, the steep gradients of the old Roman way; and lowest of all the level railroad-track.

A shorter walk, suitable for the fag-end of a rainy day, when the sand-path will be firm, and all the way up there will be a grand view of jagged crests standing out dark and clear-cut from wreathing clouds, leads to the top of an isolated conical hill on which stands the monastery Dell' Annunciato. The walls of the little chapel of the Capuchin brothers are thickly hung with ex-voto and *vœu-fait* pictures, rudely-drawn but highly-colored and sensational representations of manifold accidents—shipwrecks, firework-explosions, crushings under diligence wheels and falling olive trees, and so on—from which the offerers gratefully acknowledge themselves to have been saved alive by the special interposition of Our Lady; while other still more realistic votaries have brought here memorial relics of their disasters—crutches, rope-ends and gun-stocks—to dangle

CASTLE OF MONACO.

perennially from the rafters. The wayside "stations" on the approach-path would be the seemlier for a charitable coating of the paint that the votaries daub so liberally upon the records of their own sufferings. Meanwhile, placidly unconscious, one hopes, of these incongruities, the monks pace up and down the pleasant promenades of their level yard. Vines cover the slopes of their sunny hill, and contribute, maybe, to the monasterial purse like the famous produce of the Chartreuse. At present the brethren are merely conversing in pairs, with gesticulations appropriate to the old men in *Faust;* but there is a smooth stretch of ground under the trees that is suggestive of a snug game of bowls now and then, when no troublesome visitors are about.

Then, again, it is only a five-miles' journey, by road or rail, to Monaco, to which diminutive principality, indeed, both Mentone and Roccabruna belonged till about thirty years ago, when, goaded beyond endurance by a petty tyranny which obliged every subject to deal only with the butcher, baker and olive-presser holding the prince's monopolies, they rebelled and joined themselves on to what then was Savoy, and has since, by purchase, become France.

Monaco is assuredly a thing (it is really too small for the big word principality) to be visited and remembered. Upon a diminutive peninsula of rock rising sheer out of the sea the narrow-streeted little capital hangs on to as much of space as was left after the pirate-princes of the house of Grimaldi had taken what they wanted for their castle, gardens and parade-ground. The castle—or rather palace—a really fine bit of Italian Renaissance-work, is a thorough showplace, and apparently exists for the benefit of a corps of sleek personages in livery, each of whom does a strictly limited portion of the lionizing and expects a separate fee. One shows the state apartments, distressingly stately and gilded, with canopied bedsteads, ornamental chairs and shiny floors, quite unassociable with any idea of actual use and habitancy; another descants upon Caravaggio's frescoes in the gallery of the court; and a third picks up the visitor at the staircase foot and acts showman to the garden. Escaping at last, an easy descent—first across the palace *place*, where, as likely as not, the only living beings in sight will be a couple of the superfine-blue-cloth-dressed warriors of the princedom listlessly pelting one another with the gravel, and then through streets honored by the consular escutcheons of a surprising number of useful and important states of the Hayti and Ecuador class—leads down to a narrow slip of land, the Condamine, which, skirting the shore of the harbor, connects Monaco with its all-important suburb and complement,

HARBOR OF MONACO.

the promontory of Monte Carlo. "Facilis ascensus Averni." An excellent wide road leads up to the plateau, where, surrounded by lovely gardens and looking out upon such a panorama of mountain, wood and water as hardly another spot even on the Riviera can show, the gaming-saloons of the late M. Charles Blanc (he died a few months ago, worth, it is said, some ninety millions of francs) stand invitingly open to the stranger public. Yes, here is indeed in all seriousness a veritable "Cercle des Étrangers." No subject of the prince is allowed to set foot within its doors: such is the paternal care of His Highness the prince sovereign for the pockets of his people, who moreover, thirty-four hundred souls in all, enjoy the unique felicity of paying absolutely no taxes at all, the demands upon the public revenue being complaisantly met by the Monte Carlo authorities out of the moneys daily left in their cashier's hands by visitors. The theory of the gaming-house being a private club is kept up by a regulation (not very strictly insisted upon) requiring every visitor, before entering the saloons, to obtain, in exchange for his (or her) visiting-card, a ticket of membership for the day. That formality complied with, the whole building, with its rouge-et-noir and roulette tables, its concert- and reading-rooms, is at your service; and if you have been prudent enough to come provided with a return ticket (ensuring your retreat to Mentone, Nice or wherever you may be staying), a hearty antecedent meal (ensuring you against starvation till you are at home again), and no more cash about your person than you could afford to lose in the course of an evening's whist without annoyance, a single day at Monte Carlo will probably do you no very lasting harm. Indeed, if a gambler goes farther and fares worse to the extent of staking and losing his all at the tables, the "administration," keenly alive to the policy of avoiding scandal, will be generous enough to dole out to him the price of a railway-ticket to—almost anywhere—provided he takes himself off out of the principality without fuss or outcry. A short time ago, though, they were finely caught at their own game. One afternoon, when the play was at its fiercest, a stranger was seen to rush out of the saloons with despair apparent in his excited strides, wild-staring eyes and ruffled hair, and to hurry out of sight into one of the secluded corners of the adjacent gardens. Soon the not unfamiliar bang! bang! of a revolver rang through the air: one of the attendants ran in the direction of the sound, found the stranger stretched motionless, the smoking revolver in his hand, upon a path; and at once, with much presence of mind and obedience to the standing orders of the administration, stuffed the pockets of the fallen with bank-notes enough to convince the most prejudiced anti-Blancite that the catastrophe could not have been the result of ruin at the tables, and then sped off to give the alarm. A few minutes and a cloud of would-be witnesses were on the spot; but, lo and behold! there was nothing for them to witness. The stranger and the notes had vanished.

Seriously, though, this flaunting Monte Carlo establishment is a curse to the whole neighborhood. Not only does it lead directly to a yearly tale of suicides and find infatuated victims in chance visitors from all countries under heaven, but it fills all the neighboring towns with swarms of profligates, and tempts such people as local station-masters, petty tradesmen, and even domestic servants, to embezzlement, bankruptcy and theft. The inhabitants of the principality itself being, as I have said, strictly debarred from entering the *Cercle*, the chief sufferers are the residents in the French departments surrounding it; and these have lately presented a vigorous memorial to the senators and deputies of France praying them to take steps to abate the nuisance. They argue, not unreasonably, that France has the right, as well as the might, to do so. Even if Monaco, with its right princely and (on paper) imposing array of courtly functionaries and its army of seventy men, is to be accounted an independent state (though in truth the telegraph, post-office, railway and customs services are all entirely under French control), still the maxim "Sic utere tuo, ut alienum non lædas," must apply to it, and its neighbors cannot be bound to submit to such a pest as Monte Carlo is to them, merely that His Highness of Monaco may live in luxury at Paris as the pensionary of a gaming-house director. It is to be hoped that the death of M. Blanc will soon be followed by the extinction of the establishment so disastrously associated with his name.

But enough of this disagreeable subject. Let us shake off from our feet the dust of Monte Carlo, and follow the Riviera eastward from Mentone.

It is a perfect morning, as indeed morn-

BORDIGHERA.

ings commonly are hereabouts. Our open carriage is early at the villa-gate, and proves good-humoredly accommodating in the disposal of our very miscellaneous belongings — oranges, chocolate-cakes, rolls, newspapers, Baedekers, a bottle of Bordeaux, sunshades, overcoats and the professor's *cache-nez*. But where is our host? At last he emerges, laughing, from the house, to tell us how, while he was sitting alone in the breakfast-room finishing his coffee, a well-to-do but penurious old lady of the neighborhood, finding the house and room doors open, had coolly walked in upon him, and, pinning him down with some cock-and-bull story about her son, had reduced him to purchasing his escape by giving her a five-franc piece, which she had condescendingly pocketed with an intimation that she would return in a fortnight to finish her story and borrow something more.

After crossing the Italian frontier just beyond the outskirts of the town the road gradually ascends, sheltered here by magnificent olives, between which one gets delicious peeps downward of bright lemon-groves backed by lustrous sea. Then comes a succession of sudden zigzag bends and ups and downs in plenty, following the contour of the mountain-sides, and then a brisk rattle down a long slope ends in the steep streets of the picturesque fortress of Ventimiglia. Here it is *de rigueur* to halt and visit an old church in whose crypt one of the supporting pillars is an undoubted Roman milestone, bearing the inscription, "ANTONINUS PIUS IMPERATOR AUGUSTUS CURAVIT, DXC." And the veriest Gallio in the matter of such relics will feel well repaid for having given in to this bit of sightseeing by the memorable view of a row of snow-capped giants of the Maritime Alps that is commanded from a little square hard by the church.

Our *cocher* is in no particular hurry; so, before making a fresh start, we stroll through the narrow (and, if truth be told, not too savory) streets on the prowl for something characteristic to buy. We scorn the professor's prosaic purchase of a three-franc comforter, and invest in some specimens of roughly-glazed red pottery—tiny pipkins at a sou apiece, that, whatever they may have been intended for, will serve aptly for cigar-ash trays—and oil-cruets of the coarsest glass, but noteworthy for the grace of their long slender necks and curved spouts.

Ventimiglia passed, the road drops sharply almost to the sea-level, and stretches across an unctuous expanse of water-meadows to the promontory on which Bordighera basks sleepily in the sun. Here is the Paradise of palms, combining, as it does, the two conditions—"its feet in the water and its head in the sun"—under which the palm best flourishes. In the gardens of the French consulate and other villas fine specimens have been gathered together in showy profusion; but all about the outskirts of the town they are cultivated on strictly commercial principles, the young shoots being covered up and hidden from the light to keep them white, as required in the market for which they are destined, that of the purveyors of palms for the Palm-Sunday observances of Rome. To most visitors, though, the neighborhood of Bordighera has its chief associations in being the scene of Ruffini's famous novel *Doctor Antonio*, and they will be trying to pick out the wayside house in which that Admirable Crichton of a doctor healed and loved as they drive along the shaded road beyond the town, and will perhaps feel rather annoyed by the obtrusive self-assertion with which the big white villa of M. Garnier (the architect of the new opera-house at Paris), with its gossamer tower, dominates the view; which indeed, as we open out La Colla nestling on the mountain-side and Ospidaletto on the bay below, is surpassingly beautiful. It is not much farther to San Remo. The wealth of fleshy plants and mesymbrianthemum with its pink and yellow flowers that fill the gardens of the Hôtel de Londres bears eloquent testimony to a geniality of climate which recommends this spot above all others to many of the health-seeking visitors to the Riviera. The lover of the picturesque will perhaps find his chief attraction in the close-huddled buildings of the old town, which covers the steep sides of an isolated hill crowned by the invariable castle. High up in the air the narrow alleys are bridged at short intervals by slender arches of brickwork, the meaning and use of which become apparent when one learns that the place is from time to time disturbed by earthquake-shocks, which this clamping together of the houses gives them the best chance of weathering. As to the products of San Remo, the present writer's most vivid recollection is of a variety of smells unequalled even by Cologne; but it must also be recorded to its honor that here,

NEAR BORDIGHERA.

at last, the professor chanced upon and purchased the ideal Hat that he had sought in vain for many a weary day—a soft, broad-brimmed, conical prodigy, the like of which, gentle reader, I venture to assert you will not see until you have the good fortune to come across our professor. The local red wine, too—by name Dolciacqua—may fairly claim a good mark for San Remo.

It is not a little entertaining and instructive to occupy the seat beside the driver on a Riviera excursion. If he is a Frenchman, he will, as likely as not, have served in the disastrous campaign of 1870, and will have plenty to say about the selfishness of the Second Empire and the abuses in army organization that were revealed in the war and have since been corrected. "Ah, *now*," he will tell you, "every one is a soldier: no substitutes are allowed. *C'est juste.* The young subalterns now-a-days have to look after their work, and have no servants. As for Germany— Well, every Frenchman *has something in his head.*" And then he will go off into anecdotes and scraps of information suggested by passing objects, and gossip about local customs—as, for instance, that at Mentone it is forbidden to plant timber-trees—

VIEW NEAR SAN REMO.

the eucalyptus, for example, within two and a half mètres, and oranges within two mètres, of a neighbor's boundary—and practical hints as to where one may best buy the *dolce* tobacco of Italy for five-and-fifty centimes the packet.

It is perhaps one of the many "things not generally known" that the district of Mentone possesses quite a distinct Romance dialect of its own, in the investigation of which the philologically inclined may find a very interesting field of study. The ground has recently been broken by two diligent and careful works by Mr. J. B. Andrews, an American gentleman resident at Mentone, who has for the first time reduced Mentonese to grammar and exhibited it in a printed vocabulary. But much yet remains to be done in settling the orthography and orthoepy of the dialect, and there is reason to believe that any one who is ambitious to be the founder of a literature may find a virgin opportunity in Mentonese. W. D. R.

A MONTH IN SICILY.

PART I.

LA FAVORITA.

EARLY on the morning of the first of February we stood on the deck of the steamer for Palermo, watching the sun rise over the water. Far away in the south the blue edge of the sea began to grow bluer with the rising of the distant land. A fresh breeze blew from the shore—not a pleasant feature in February weather at home, but suggesting comparisons with the warmest morning of a New England May. With the swift advance of the steamer the blue line in the south rapidly rose above the level of the sea into the definite shape of a rugged mountain-range; gradually the blueness of distance changed to rich shades of brown and red on the jagged, treeless summits, and to deepest green where long orange-farms border the bases of the mountains.

Who has not longed to see Sicily? Every one who loves poetry, romance or the history of ancient civilization must often turn in thought to this beautiful and famous Mediterranean island. To the most ancient poets it was a mysterious land, where dwelt the monster Charybdis and the bloody Læstrigones; where Ulysses met the Cyclops; where the immortal gods waged battles with the giant sons of Earth, and bound Enceladus in his eternal prison. No doubt it was the terrific natural phenomena of Sicily—the earthquakes and the outbursts of Etna—which rendered it so much a land of horrors to the early Greek imagination. But in that far-distant age it was not only the terrors of the place that had worked upon the imaginative Greeks: the almost tropical luxuriance of the country, the unrivalled scenery, the brilliancy of the sky, made it a fitting ground for the adventures of nymphs, heroes and gods. In the fountain of Sicilian Ortygia dwelt Arethusa, the nymph dear to the poets; beside the Lake of Enna, where rich vegetation overran the lips of the extinct volcano, was the spot called in mythology the meeting-place of Pluto and Proserpine —the power of darkness and the springing plant personified; and so through all the country places were found made sacred by the presence of the great divinities, and temples were erected in their honor.

When the age of fable had passed away, far back in the early dawn of European history begins authentic knowledge about Sicily. While wicked Ahaz reigned in the kingdom of Judah, and Isaiah had not ceased to utter his prophecies, the Greek colonization of Sicily began. Seven hundred and thirty-five years before Christ, Theocles with his band of Greeks from Eubœa founded Naxos on the coast, hard by the fertile slopes of Etna. Within three centuries from that time the whole Sicilian coast had been studded with Greek cities, and to such wealth, power and splendor of art had they attained that all succeeding epochs of the island's history seem degenerate times when compared with that early golden age.

It has been truly said that "there is not a nation which has materially influenced the destinies of European civilization that has not left distinct traces of its activity in this island." Phœnicians, Greeks, Romans, Saracens, Normans, Spaniards, French and English have successively occupied the island, and noble monuments of the varied civilizations are standing to this day. Scattered through the island, their architectural remains crown the mountain-tops or lie in confusion along the Mediterranean shore, a series of ruins extending through twenty-five centuries, unmatched in any other country for variety of age and style.

At ten o'clock our steamer entered the Gulf of Palermo, passing near the base of Monte Pellegrino, a wild promontory which towers up two thousand feet from the sea. On the day before I had entered for the first time the famous Bay of Naples, but with less delight than I now looked upon the beauties of this Sicilian gulf. Flanked with lofty mountains, colored with the matchless blue of the Mediterranean, studded with picturesque lateen sails, the bay is a fitting entrance to this fair historic island: a more beautiful approach could hardly be imagined even to the Islands of the Blessed.

The Italians call Palermo *la felice* ("the happy"). It is most happy in its climate, its situation and its noble streets and gardens. Below the city lies the lovely bay: behind it stretches back for miles, between converging mountain-chains, the fruit-producing level of the Golden Shell (*La Conca d' Oro*). The plain is one vast orchard of oranges and lemons which every year distributes its huge crop over half the habitable globe. The city is worthy of its position. The chief streets are broad, clean and handsomely built—a contrast to the universal

CATHEDRAL OF PALERMO.

shabbiness and squalor we had found in Naples.

A traveller is sure to be put in a good humor with the place by the many and unusual comforts which he meets in the great sea-fronting hotel; and the first look from the windows of his apartment confirms the opinion that Palermo is the fairest of Southern cities. The outlook is upon the grand seashore drive, the Marina, as gay and pretty a sight as can be found in any European capital. The broad, tree-shaded avenue, bordered on one side by hotels and palaces, on the other by the waters of the bay, is thronged with private carriages. Beginning at the sea-facing gate of the city, the road commands through all its length a view of the mountains, the bay and the open sea: at its terminus lie the public flower-gardens—acres of our choicest hothouse plants growing in tropical profusion.

In Palermo, as in so many European towns, the cathedral is the chief architectural attraction. To approach it from the bay the whole length of the city must be traversed on the Corso Vittorio Emmanuele, the chief business street. This corso is crossed at the centre of the town by another of equal width, which also commemorates by its name Italian unity—the Corso Garibaldi. There is one other broad and important street which no American can enter without remembering that even in this distant land the interest and sympathy of the people have been with our country in its struggles and successes: it is the Via Lincoln.

The drive up the Corso gives an opportunity for seeing a remarkably handsome street lined with gay shops, and for studying the peculiar and often fine faces of the Sicilian people; but nothing of striking interest appears until, near the centre of the town, a street opening on the left discloses a vista ending in a small forest of white marble statues. On a nearer view it is found that the statues belong to the immense fountain of the Piazza Pretoria, a work erected about A. D. 1550 by command of the senate of Palermo. It is perhaps the largest and most elaborate fountain in Europe, and, though it is easy to criticise the countless sculptures that adorn it, the whole effect of their combination into an architectural unit is most imposing.

Continuing the drive up the Corso, a broad piazza suddenly opens on the right, flanked by the cathedral. The abruptness of the transition from between the dark lines of buildings into the sunlight of the square adds to the first strong impression produced by the beauty of the vast duomo. In its external architecture the church is unique: the charm of it to one who has been travelling through Italy is its utter dissimilarity to all the Italian churches. Architectural writers call it a building of the "Sicilian Gothic style;" and, though the expression does not convey a vivid image except to the student of art, any one can see its essential difference from the style of the North, and can recognize the rare grandeur and beauty of the church. The form is simple, but the dimensions are grand. Without the boldness of outline of true Gothic churches, the walls are so covered with ornaments of interlacing arches, cornices and arabesque slightly raised on the masonry as to produce an effect of wonderful richness. The style is peculiarly Sicilian, yet every observer of mediæval churches will at once detect the Norman, Italian and Saracenic influences blended in an exquisite harmony. Connected with the church by light arches, but separated from it by a street, stands the campanile, a mass of enormous solidity, terminating in many pinnacles and one slender and graceful tower rising above them all. Four other lofty towers, springing from the corners of the church, give additional lightness to its elegant design: they were added to the building nearly three centuries after the Norman conquest of Sicily, and yet their minaret-like form and pointed panel ornaments show how strong and lasting had been the influence of Arabian art upon the mediæval architects of Sicily.

It is seven hundred years since the foundations of the duomo were laid. In that distant age, and in a land so remote, it is a curious circumstance that its founder was an Englishman: *Gualterio Offamilio* is the amusing Italian corruption by which the name of Walter of the Mill was suited to the Southern tongue. After Roger and his Normans had driven from Sicily the Arab power which had

GROTTO OF SANTA ROSALIA.

held the land for more than two centuries, and when Christianity had succeeded the Mohammedan religion throughout the island, Archbishop Walter assumed spiritual sovereignty in Palermo, and founded this cathedral on the site of an ancient mosque. Only a part of the original building remains in the crypt and two walls of the present church. All subsequent ages have changed and added to its original simple form, but often have taken from its beauty. Within the church only a part of the south aisle commands close attention: there in canopied sarcophagi of porphyry reposes the dust of Roger, king of Sicily (1154), of Henry VI., emperor of Germany, and of Frederick II., Roger's most illustrious grandson, king of Sicily, king of Jerusalem and emperor of Germany. In a chapel at the right of the high altar, sacred to Santa Rosalia, rest the bones of the saint enshrined in a sarcophagus of silver. Thirteen hundred pounds of the precious metal are wrought into the shrine, and the whole chapel is sumptuous with marble frescoes and gilding, for to the pious souls of Palermo this is the very holy of holies. The cathedral is dedicated to Rosalia, and almost divine honors are paid to her by the city from which she fled in horror at its wickedness.

Every summer a festival of three days is held in honor of this favorite saint; and again in September a day is kept to commemorate her death, when a vast concourse of people from Palermo climb the side of the neighboring Monte Pellegrino to worship at the grotto of St. Rosalia, a natural cavern situated under an overhanging crag of the summit. Here the faithful Sicilians believe that the holy maiden dwelt in solitude for many years; and here were found in 1624 the bones of the saint, which put a stop to the plague then raging in Palermo. The cave has been made a church by building a porch at the entrance. Twisted columns of alabaster support the roof of the vestibule, but within the cavern the walls are of the natural rock, contrasting strangely with the magnificent workmanship of the high altar, beneath which lies the marble statue of the saint overlaid with a robe of gold, while about the recumbent figure are placed a book and skull and other objects of pure gold. It is a figure of a fair young girl, represented by the artist as dying, with her head at rest upon one hand. Though the statue is the work of no very famous artist, Goethe in the narrative of his Sicilian travel has truly said of it, "The head and hands of white marble are, if not faultless in style, at least so pleasing and natural that one cannot help expecting to see them move."

Under the southern precipices of this Mountain of the Pilgrim lies a royal park, and in the midst of it stands a gaudy and fantastic villa called La Favorita. The house is worth a visit for the sake of seeing what a half-crazy fancy will produce when united with royal wealth. King Ferdinand I., during his stay in Sicily early in this century, amused himself by building this country palace in the style of a Chinese villa, and adorned it with innumerable little bells, to be rung by every movement of the wind.

It was in the Favorita that the old king found himself cornered by Lord William Bentinck and his army during the British occupation of the island in 1812. It is said that his faithful subjects from Palermo encamped by thousands in the neighborhood—not, however, for the sake of defending their aged monarch, but to enjoy the fun of witnessing a fight in which both sides were hated by them with equal cordiality.

To an enterprising traveller some of the pleasantest hours of a long tour are those when, cutting loose from all guides and books, he wanders alone through the streets of an old city, enjoying with a sense of discovery the scraps of antiquity not described in any book which he is sure to meet with. Palermo and its neighborhood afford a most fertile field for such researches. The Saracenic villas of the suburbs and the early Norman buildings of the town will repay considerable patience spent in looking up the beauties to be found in the details of their construction. For instance, in the plain old church of S. Agostino there is a doorway and wheel window one sight of which is an ample reward for much wandering and searching.

On a morning too fresh and beautiful for staying in the city we rendered a vivacious cabman ecstatically happy by an engagement to drive us to Monreale. A brisk drive past the royal palace, out of the southern gate and five miles across the orange-covered plain brought us to the foot of an abrupt mountain. Not a half mile away, but far above, on the seemingly unapproachable heights, was perched the quaint village which was our destination: its ancient towering buildings glittered white and hot in the February sun under the canopy of cloudless blue. Ascending for half an hour on the well-constructed zigzag road, we stopped at the gate in the town-wall to buy the luscious-looking fruit of the cactus from a roadside vender, one of those ideal hags, apparently preserved by desiccation under the torrid sun, whom only Italy can produce in perfection. Then onward and upward we pushed through the village street — a street characteristic of these Southern walled villages, narrow, dark, festooned above with interminable lines of drying macaroni, covered below with abundant filth, and bordered by house-walls of enormous thickness, built for resisting heat. At every house-door or on the pavement in front sits the man of the house plying his trade, that all the world may know whether his goods are well made or ill. Up and down the street flow the lines of dark-

MONREALE.

eyed, swarthy people—women robed in rags, occasionally set off by a bit of striking color; children who in their astonishment become rigid at the sight of a foreigner; here and there an officer of the Italian army carefully picking his way through the mud; and everywhere produce-laden asses driven toward Palermo by the most picturesque of cut-throats, for without its ever-present force of soldiers Monreale would at once relapse into a hotbed of brigandage, as its recent history shows.

Almost at the summit of the town, facing a broad, paved square, stands the cathedral and its adjacent Benedictine monastery, both built upon the brink of the precipitous mountain, and both in external appearance severely plain, almost to shabbiness.

William II., king of Sicily, called the Good, founded on this Royal Mount a monastery for the Benedictine friars, and built it up with all the strength of a fortress and the magnificence of a palace. Little is left of that original building, which was finished in 1174, but in its few remains have fortunately been preserved the most splendid of cloisters. This scene of centuries of Benedictine meditations is a large quadrangle surrounded by an arcade of multitudinous small pointed arches resting upon pairs of slender white marble columns, like stalks of snow-white lilies in their grace and lightness. Some of the marble shafts are wrought with reliefs of flowers and trailing vines, while most of them were inlaid in bands or spirals of mosaic in gold and colors, now injured by age. The capitals which crown these shafts are exquisitely carved, and all mythology, the legends of the Church and the book of Nature have been ransacked to furnish subjects for the designs; so that out of two hundred or more no two are similar. All the decaying magnificence of the great building is pervaded by an oppressive silence, for it is one of the innumerable religious houses suppressed by the Italian government.

From the monastery to the cathedral is a walk of but a few steps. All disappointment at the external plainness is forgotten in approaching the chief entrance of the church. Michael Angelo said of Ghiberti's doors at Florence that "they were worthy to be the entrance to Paradise." They have rightly become famous through all the world, and yet these doors of Monreale leave on the mind of the beholder a strong impression of their beauty not less lasting than the Baptistery gates at Florence. In the execution of the biblical reliefs which completely encrust the massive leaves of bronze they must yield, of course, to the mature art of Ghiberti's later age; but the stately height of the solid metal doors, the alternate bands of mosaic and wrought-stone arabesques which flank them and surround over head the Arabian arch, and, above all, the sense that they conceal from view unparalleled splendors beyond, leave on the mind an impression which cannot be effaced.

Perhaps no other building deserves the epithet "splendid" so exactly as the cathedral of Monreale. the whole interior is radiant from the vast extent of its pictured walls. All the walls and vaulting of the nave and aisles, transepts and tribune, are overspread with ancient mosaics on a golden ground. It is natural to compare St. Mark's cathedral at Venice with this church, on account of its immense mosaic-covered surface: its sumptuous interior delights every beholder with the satisfying completeness which belongs to it; yet in all the Oriental splendor of the Venetian church nothing can equal in impressiveness a glance down the nave of Monreale. Wherever the eye turns it rests upon the glowing colors of some sacred picture—scenes from the Old Testament history, bright-robed figures of flying angels, haloed saints in the quaint Byzantine style, apostles and martyrs, patriarchs and prophets, and, high above them all, from a great picture in the vaulting of the apse, a startling face of Christ looking solemnly down through the length of the cathedral. Half the stiffness which characterizes these early mosaics seems to have been cast aside in treating this supreme subject. The colossal size of the figure, the hand raised in blessing the multitude, the sad but awful expression of the countenance, make it an all-pervading presence in the church. Amid all the glittering splendor of the building,

PISA.

while the gorgeous pomp of a holiday mass progressed and rippling strains of organ-music ran echoing through the arches, through all the bewildering brightness of the spectacle, the majesty of that Presence could not for a moment be forgotten, nor could the eyes avoid straying off from the glitter below to answer again and again to that solemn gaze above.

It is impossible, in any ordinary picture, to convey more than a very faint idea of this building, in which the peculiar beauties are dependent upon color, unlike the Gothic churches of the North: nothing but an oil painting of minute details could render the effects produced by the bars of sunshine descending through the twilight of the church and striking on the glowing, pictured walls. The extent of surface covered by the mosaics is said to be more than sixty thousand square feet.

By the bounty of the same pious monarch who endowed the neighboring monastery the cathedral was completed just seven hundred years ago. His body lies entombed in the transept: his monument is the wonderful pile whose construction has made his name to be remembered by succeeding ages more than all his other deeds.

Outside the cathedral, adjoining the monastery-wall, a commanding terrace is built upon the verge of the precipice. Leaning from its edge, we gazed almost vertically into the orange-groves below, where the ripe fruit glowed with the brightness of a flame contrasted with the darkness of the foliage. Far and wide were spread the fruit-gardens over the plain, to where the mountains towered up in the east, and northward to the city and the sea. It is one of those bright and satisfying scenes from which a traveller can hardly turn away without a tinge of bitterness in the thought of never seeing them again.

The drive back to the town was pleasantly varied by a détour which brought us to the Capuchin monastery and the Saracenic villa of La Ziza. The vaults of the monastery are mentioned as one of the interesting sights, but it must be a very ghoulish soul that would take pleasure in them. The horrors of the more famous Capuchin vaults at Rome are tame in comparison with these. There the ornaments are skulls and skeletons in a tolerable state of cleanliness: here the departed brethren have been subjected to some mummifying process, and as they lie piled in hideous confusion their withered faces stare horribly in the twilight of the cellar. Numerous fiery-eyed cats run about with much scratching and scrabbling over the dry bodies, making the place none the pleasanter with their uncanny wails. A very brief visit is sufficient.

La Ziza, the only Saracenic house of this region which is still inhabited, is simply a massive, battlemented tower of unmistakably Arabian appearance. The outside walls are adorned with the depressed panels characteristic of the Saracenic style, but within the Oriental look has almost vanished under the repairs and decorations of many centuries. Only the lofty hallway, arched above with a kind of honeycomb vaulting and cooled by a little cascade of water rushing through it, retains much of the Oriental beauty, and seems like a hall of the Alhambra. Along a wall of the vestibule runs an inscription in Arabic which has been a puzzle to Orientalists, and of which no undisputed interpretation is given. The palace was built as a country pleasure-house by one of the Saracenic princes of Palermo, and can be little less than a thousand years old; indeed, an inscription on its walls, inscribed by one of the Spanish proprietors, claims for the house an antiquity of eleven hundred years.

From the battlements of La Ziza one has the loveliest near view of Palermo and the plain of the Golden Shell. An enthusiastic verse, written over the doorway of the palace, declares it to be the most beautiful scene upon our planet, and while the eyes are resting on the view it is easy to believe the poet; but many of the mountain-views about the city surpass it.

One of the most attractive of the mountain-excursions from Palermo is that to the monastery of San Martino. At a height of seventeen hundred feet above the city, in a lonely spot, the monastery stands on another flank of the mountain on which Monreale is also perched. The mule-path from the suburban village of Boccadifalco to San

PALERMO.

Martino would be worth traversing for its own wild beauty alone. It first enters a gorge between grand cliffs: then, climbing a rocky ascent which commands a superb view of the plain, it runs through a fruitful valley, where the monastery suddenly appears in the front.

The monastery of San Martino has been the wealthiest in Sicily. The entrance-hall is on a scale of regal magnificence, adorned with many-colored marbles. The brethren were all of noble extraction. Though the external architecture of the building is not in the best taste, the grand scale on which it is built, and still more the wild, picturesque site, give to the monastery a beauty which even an Italian architect of the last century could not disfigure. Ascending a grand staircase with balustrades of purple marble, an upper hall is reached, from which the wonderful view may be seen to the best advantage. Turning the eye to the north and east across the savage-looking mountains, a short reach of the coast is seen, and beyond is the boundless expanse of sea, dotted on the horizon by the volcanoes of the Æolian Islands, which lie more than a hundred miles away. The abbey abounds in pictures by masters of the seventeenth century, and there is also a museum of Greek and Saracenic remains, but nothing within the walls compares with the interest of the window-views.

Attractive as are the sights of Palermo, most of them must be passed over or very hastily visited if the tour of the island is to be made in a month, for the Greek cities beyond demand a greater share of time by reason of their immense antiquity and the grandeur of their remains.

Being well prepared for the inland journey, and eager to see antiquities so little known to the outer world, one question arose to give us pause—a question which every year keeps thousands of prudent tourists from exploring a country as full of glorious scenery as Switzerland, possessing more of Greek antiquities than Greece itself, and a far lovelier winter climate than Italy—"Is it safe?" The doubtful question whether this rarely-attempted journey should be accomplished was settled by the friendly advice of the courteous consul of the United States at Palermo. That advice may be of use to travellers in the future: it was to the effect that for two American gentlemen travelling alone and without ostentation through Sicily there is no more danger of capture or violent death than in any civilized country. It is admitted that highway robbery is not impossible, as in many places nearer home, but the simple preventive is to carry as little ready money as possible over the short spaces of unsettled country, and to forward superfluous baggage by steamer. That there are banditti in certain districts of the island no one denies, but their object is the capture of wealthy Sicilians, whose ransom is sure and ample, while that of a foreigner is uncertain and necessarily long delayed.

A dark afternoon found us comfortably established in the best seats of an old-fashioned stage-coach in front of the general post-office of Palermo, whence the stage-lines radiate to the various parts of the island. After the long deliberation which seems to characterize all business (especially official business) transacted outside of England and America, the mail-bags were delivered, and our journey began in the midst of a shower descending with all the tremendous impetuosity of a semi-tropical rainy season. The cumbersome vehicle dashed on with considerable spirit through streets almost emptied by the violence of the shower, and out through the broad arch of the stately Porta Nuova crowded by multitudes seeking shelter from the storm. Late twilight found us at the end of the first stage in Monreale. From thence onward the journey continued for a while through pitchy darkness. The broad highway is engineered with admirable skill along the sides of mountains and over deep ravines, through a region of most uncommon beauty, it is said, but now hidden from us by the impenetrable gloom. However, as the night advanced the clouds rolled away with surprising suddenness, and left a bright moon rising over the mountains. We began to see

CONVENT OF SAN MARTINO, NEAR PALERMO.

something of the beautifully varied country, though viewing it at a disadvantage through the narrow window of a covered coach. Wherever the rugged nature of the country permitted every rood of ground was under exquisite cultivation, and already had its first soft covering of springing vegetation. The night-air was sweet with the spring-like odors of freshly-turned earth and of wild-flowers: from time to time white masses of flower-laden almond trees flashed past the window, looking in the moonlight wonderfully like the snow-drifts which at this season line the roads in New England.

After nightfall the surface of the rich and well-cultivated country seemed as solitary as a wilderness: not a creature was stirring along the road. The intense silence of the night was broken only by the hum of our coach-wheels and the sharp snap of hoofs from our cavalry guard. How unlike were all the surroundings to those of an ordinary modern night-journey over the mail-routes of Europe! The primitive conveyance, the quiet of the lonely road, the arms of the attendant troop of horsemen flashing in the light of the moon,—all the concomitants of an old-time night-journey seemed to carry us back from the age of railroads to an earlier time.

Eleven drowsy hours of staging, and then a long, slow ascent, brought us up to the hilltop where stands the village of Calatafimi. The chief inn of the town is probably not surpassed in Europe in the number of its small discomforts, animate and inanimate, but it must be made the base of operations for visiting the ruins of Segesta. The remnant of the night spent in sleep prepared us for our investigations on the following day. It was pleasant, rising in the cool early morning, to step out from the comfortless interior of the tavern to enjoy on a southern balcony the temperate warmth of the low sun and to look down on the lovely landscape. Before us lay a fertile rolling country clad with verdure, and rising gradually upward toward the south to an elevation deserving to be called a mountain from its great height, yet from its gentle slope and cultivated sides rather to be called a hill. A field near the crest of that distant hill, marked only by a few white crosses, is a spot memorable in Sicilian history, for there lie the heroes who fell fighting with Garibaldi for the unity of Italy on May 15, 1860. Sicily has in all ages been a battle-ground for the contending races of two continents: on Sicilian soil Athens received her most disabling blow, and here too the Punic power was broken; yet there is hardly one among the battlefields of Sicily upon which greater destinies have been settled than on this field of Calatafimi.

Before the morning was far advanced we started out in search of the village curé, the unfailing friend of strangers, that we might inquire of him about the safety of visiting the ruin and in regard to the pleasantest way of reaching it. Picking our way about through the mud of the squalid village, we at length found the old gentleman just coming from his little church on the side of the castle hill at the end of the town. Filled with unfeigned delight that the monotony of his existence should be broken by the advent of two foreigners, especially such living wonders as Americans, the benign priest took a lively interest in our case gave us the information for which we had asked, vouching for the safety of the country, and begged us to walk on with him. For five minutes we followed on together the road cut in the hillside beneath the walls of the Saracenic citadel, our companion all the while talking vehemently, and helping out our lame knowledge of the language with gestures so dramatic that an understanding of his words was hardly needed. Suddenly the road curved round the side of the hill; we stood on the floor of a deserted quarry; the old man ceased speaking and pointed forward: "*Ecco!*" Before us the hill dropped abruptly down in a precipice: far below a deep valley spread out before our eyes, "fair as the garden of the Lord." As the light of the morning sun streamed down through its length bringing out in great brilliancy the fresh green of spring, it looked like a paradise of luxuriant vegetation. The gray of olive trees and the darkness of orange-groves contrasted with the color of springing plants, and everywhere were scattered the pink-and-white plumes of the blossoming almonds. Beyond the valley a rugged, saddle-shaped mountain rose to an imposing height, and upon the summit-line stood in solitary majesty the Doric temple of Segesta, each column in clear relief against the blue of the sky. It is so far removed from all abodes of men, standing alone for thousands of years in the region of the clouds—so grand in its severe and noble outlines—so venerable in its mysterious antiquity—so blended with the natural beauties of the place,—that it seems rather to belong to the power that raised the mountains than to any workmanship of man. The world cannot show a more wonderful example of art exquisitely harmonized with the grandeur of natural scenery.

Eager for a closer view of the temple, we returned immediately to the town, and, being provided with a guide and a beast, were soon on the way down the winding road to the valley. A bridle-path diverged from the main road: an avenue of over-arching olive trees shaded the way, and on all sides here, as everywhere through the country, the orange-crop loaded the trees almost to breaking—the most beautiful of all crops as the fruit hangs upon the branches. As we passed the lower slopes dotted with browsing sheep, and began the rugged ascent of the mountain on which the temple stands, the pathway crept up the edge of a profound gorge: it was a perilous way, clinging close to the edge of the bank, and at some points, where we could look down a thousand feet to the torrent below, the path was so narrow and broken that even our sure-footed mountain-donkeys hesitated to advance. The picturesque but hard climb at length came to an end at the edge of the broad, flattened summit of the mountain. Again the temple suddenly came in sight, but now near at hand. The mountain-shepherds have planted with wheat the level of the summit, and the pale yellow of the volcanic rock from which the temple is built harmonizes well with the color of its surroundings. It cannot be called a ruin. It stands as the builders left it in the fifth century before Christ. Not a column is broken, not a stone has fallen. The interior was never finished, but the outside is perfect.

The pure outlines of a Doric temple are beautiful in any situation, but the impression which this one made upon us in the bright morning sunlight, standing in the midst of verdure and flowers on the brink of that stupendous chasm and overlooking that glorious country, is not a thing to be conveyed in words.

The interest of the temple is comprised in its size, antiquity and beauty, for no mention of it is made in history. Its approximate age is inferred from the internal evidence of the structure. The subjection of the city of Segesta from B. C. 409 to the powers of Carthage and Rome successively, and the subsequent decline of its own power and wealth, render it certain that no such work as this temple would have been undertaken after that date: moreover, the purity of its simple Doric form places it in the earlier ages of Sicilian history. The Carthaginian invasion of the island was doubtless the event which arrested the building. Cicero has described a wonderful statue of Diana in bronze which the people of Segesta showed him with pride as the greatest ornament of their city: it was of colossal size and faultless beauty, belonging to the best period of Greek art. As the statue was in existence before the Carthaginian invasion, it seems to me highly improbable that the citizens of Segesta would have built so grand a temple for any other purpose than to enshrine their most admired and revered statue and to make it a place of worship for Diana. This theory may explain in part the reason why the building was arrested, for it is known that the image was stolen to adorn the city of Carthage,* and its loss, as well as the subsequent poverty of Segesta, would have been a sufficient reason for ceasing to build a temple to contain it. Diana's worshippers of old must have looked upon these lovely mountain-ranges as an abode dear to the queen of the nymphs and the hunter's patron deity. It seems as if nothing less than the presence of the mountain-goddess lingering round her shrine could have kept the temple in its marvellous perfection through the lapse of

* The statue was restored to Segesta by Scipio.

ages in a land of wars and earthquakes. The houses of the neighboring city are indistinguishably levelled with the earth, but hardly a stone of the sacred building is displaced.

The position of the temple was outside and below the limits of the ancient city. The mountain-ridge rises near at hand to a somewhat greater height, and terminates in a peak, on the summit and sides of which the town was built. Warned by the decline of the sun, we turned from the Segestan house of worship and began to climb the slope toward the Segestan place of amusement: the Greek theatre still remains with little loss or change. The ascent was interrupted by many lingering backward looks toward the grand colonnade as it appeared at fresh points of view from above. Hardly a living creature appeared on the lonely heights, except that one wandering shepherd, seeing the dress of foreigners, came forward to offer his little stock of coins ploughed from the earth or found in ancient buildings. As usual, most of the pocketful were corroded beyond recognition, but one piece bore a noble head executed in the Greek style, and the clear inscription, *ΠΑΝΟΡΜΙΤΑΝ*, a coin of Panormus; which is, in modern speech, Palermo. A few coppers were accepted as an ample equivalent for a coin which will not circulate.

The scattered fragments of a fortress crown the peak; and immediately below, cut in the solid rock of the western slope, lies the theatre. It is not large as compared with buildings of its class at Athens and Syracuse, yet I believe that in its seating capacity it exceeds any opera-house of our time. Entering by a ruined stage-door and crossing the orchestra, we rested on the lower tiers of seats. The great arc, comprising two-thirds of a circle, upon which the spectators were ranged, has still its covering of fine cut-stone seats, complete except at one extremity. Every part of the desolate building gains a new interest when peopled in imagination with its ancient occupants, and when we recall to mind the vast multitudes of many generations who have watched with breathless and solemn interest the stately progress of Greek tragedy before that ruined *scena*.

As we lounged upon the lowest seats, whereon the high dignitaries of the town used to sit, and looked across the open space of the orchestra, there at the centre of its farther side lay the slab which supported the altar of Bacchus, where stood the chorus-leader: near it a line of stone marks the front of the stage, and beyond it is spread an expanse of stage-scenery such as no modern royal theatre can boast. The whole broad prospect commanded from the colonnade below is seen across the stage of the theatre, but widened by the greater height and finished in the foreground by the majestic presence of the temple. All the north-western mountains of the island are taken in with one glance of the eye: beneath us the valley of the little river Scamander opens a long vista northward to the Mediterranean Sea, and far away the port of Castellamare glitters, in contrast with the blue, as white as a polished shell upon the shore. Most distant among the group of peaks is Mount Eryx, the lonely rock by the sea on whose summit stood the temple of Venus Erycina, more renowned in the ancient world than all other shrines of the goddess.

We climbed to the brow of the hill in order to descend through the entire length of the city. Hardly one stone is left upon another of all the streets through which the Segestans proudly conducted Cicero. Here and there appear the circular openings of cisterns which occupied the centres of ancient courtyards. The stones once hewn and carved which are strewn over the slope are now reduced to the roughness of boulders, so that one might cross the tract and catch no sign that it was once a city. Little has been done to discover what remains lie beneath the surface, but at one point, where a small excavation has been made, a heap of fallen Ionic columns cover the fragments of a tomb built on a scale of regal magnificence; and a little lower on the mountain two rooms of a house have been exhumed, the floors of which are still covered with beautiful mosaics.

PART II.

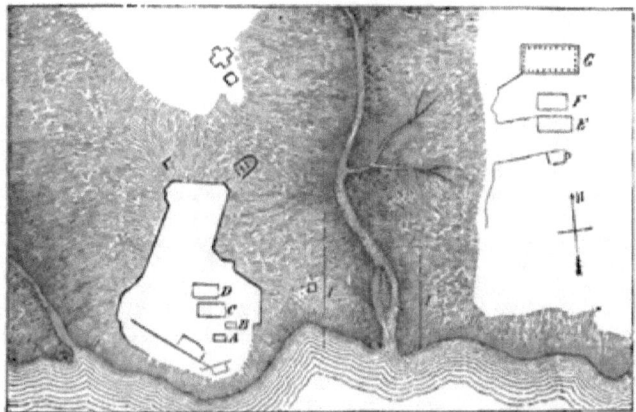

A, B, C, D, temples of the acropolis; E, F, G, temples of the neapolis; I, I, walls of ancient harbor.
SELINUS.

NOT many miles from the western cape of Sicily twin bluffs rise side by side vertically from the southern sea. Their sloping sides are separated by a river: their parallel ridges, running inland, are lost in the high adjacent moorland. On the crests of the cliffs, one hundred feet above the sea, stood the acropolis and the neapolis of Selinus, two divisions of the great and free Greek city which once held sway in all this quarter of the island.

The lapse of two thousand years has so changed the outline of this southern coast that now no natural harbor offers an anchorage safe from the violence of the sirocco; but a deep valley cuts in half the cliff-built city, and in old times an inlet ran up from the sea to meet the valley-brook. This narrow inlet, deepened and improved with all the skill of ancient engineering, was lined with massive quays. Selinus was strong in ships of war, but the citizens of the great commercial town must have looked with not less satisfaction on the multitudinous fleet of merchant-craft that whitened the waters of their bay, and brought to them from all foreign lands the wealth which they lavishly bestowed in adorning their homes and in building up the temples of their gods. Along the edge of the port were ranged, of course, the lines of warehouses essential to an extensive foreign trade, but no vestiges of the ancient town are seen along the valley, for the malarial dampness of the lowlands drove the population to the sides and summits of the enclosing bluffs.

Imagine the beauty of a town thus situated! Range above range on the two hills rose the outlying villas and the more crowded dwellings of the town. We know from one admiring epithet of Virgil's that these ancient houses of Selinus were overshadowed by groups of palm trees. What lovely homes they were! Filled with all luxuries that endless wealth could buy, adorned with the skill of Grecian art—which in our day we wonder at and imitate, but never hope to equal—the houses were so placed upon the hill that the patrician landowner from his shaded roof might watch far up the valley-roads the lines of heavy-laden beasts bringing down for export the products of his estates, and the merchant from the terrace of his home, looking across the sea toward Africa, could catch the most distant glimmer of the sails of his corn-freighted ships bringing back wealth to him from the Carthaginian markets.

By far the greater part of the ancient population gathered around the acropolis on the western hill. Above the dwellings of the slope a theatre and other public buildings rose conspicuously; and higher still, all along the edge of the broad and flattened summit, the massive city-wall enclosed the acropolis, lifting against the background of blue sky its diadem of towers. But the chief features which made Selinus famous for its beauty in the ancient world were its temples.

On the highest crest of the acropolis stood side by side three Doric temples, facing the rising sun, while across the harbor, on the corresponding western height, three other temples, even greater and more splendid, were built to perfect the symmetry of the magnificent city. Some of these temples glittered in snowy whiteness; others, in contrast, were relieved with many bands and ornaments of gorgeous colors — colors so brilliant and enduring that to this day they best reveal to us the beauty of the Grecian polychromic style. Some were of most venerable age, coeval with the colony itself, while others, built with more finished art, were barely completed at the downfall of the city. One bore on its front the earliest works of the Greek chisel which are known in our time; another, on the opposite height, displayed on its lofty frieze the battles of the giants wrought in the archaic but spirited style of a century later. Above the turmoil of the surrounding city the sacred buildings stood apart in two majestic ranks within their own consecrated grounds; the tumultuous noise of the town came from a distance, and, mingling with the roar of the sea that beat the rocks a hundred feet below, echoed through the sacred quiet of the colonnades. All the temples of these two groups towered so high upon the cliffs that peasants laboring on the inland plain or shepherds on the distant hillside might always keep in sight the sacred buildings which symbolized to them the greatness of their gods. Mariners sailing on the African Sea, between the east and the west of the ancient world, might discern, even far out upon the sea, the innumerable columns rising upon the hilltops.

Such was the aspect of Selinus in the time of its grandeur five hundred years before Christ. In the year 409 B. C. a Carthaginian army under Hannibal, son of Gisco, besieged Selinus. For nine days the Selinuntians made a brave resistance, and then the city fell. The people were butchered or sold, the walls destroyed, the temples plundered. Afterward the town revived, and led a feeble existence for another century; but now for two thousand years the ground has been desolate, a terror to all settlers from the miasma which haunts the marshes.

The pleasure of visiting these ruins cannot be attained without paying a penalty. Three times a week a small vehicle connects at Calatafimi with the stage-coach from Palermo, carrying the mails to the southern parts of the island. "Darkly at dead of night" we were suddenly transferred—out of the frying-pan into the fire—from the poor consolation of a Sicilian bed to the utter discomfort of a nondescript conveyance bound for Castelvetrano. However, much travelling teaches how to sleep through all circumstances, and broken repose came in spite of much lurching and many bumps. When at last we were roused by the breaking day, our road had already passed from the mountainous interior into a rolling country. The sun rose into the cloudless and pure brilliancy of a winter sky, and lighted up a land carpeted with soft green. The slopes became by degrees more gentle as we approached the southern coast, till at last we reached a plain, and came to the queer old town of Castelvetrano standing in the midst of it. It would be hard to find in all Europe another large town as much cut off from the world. As we alighted from the coach in the central piazza the throng of men in outlandish costumes politely made room for us to pass, but attempted no concealment of their curiosity at the sight of foreigners. An inspection of the hotel-book in the only *locanda* of the place showed that for nearly a year no American or English traveller had visited this region, so powerful is the danger of banditti and the certainty of bad lodging to keep away visitors from the grandest group of temples in Europe.

There is a peculiar pleasure in passing from the chief lines of travel into the less-frequented parts of the Italian kingdom, for otherwise it is hardly possible to meet familiarly with the educated middle class and to understand the best side of the Italian character. In the cities of the Peninsula the better class of inhabitants shrinks from contact with the promiscuous horde of foreigners which every winter pours down upon them from the North; but in these remote towns of Sicily the freemasonry of good-breeding is strong in the narrow circle who share in it; and an educated foreigner, even though he may have no introductions, can hardly remain long without receiving many kind attentions. A pleasant instance of this national courtesy we met in Castelvetrano. A gentleman of the town volunteered to take the walk of eight miles to Selinunto that we might have his guidance through the ruins. His thorough acquaintance with the place gave additional interest to the excursion.

A flourishing notice posted in the town declared to travellers that the government had just completed a highway to the ruins. It was a pleasing surprise, suggestive of an hour's drive in an easy carriage instead of a long jog on donkey-back; but no such pleasure was in store. In all the town of twenty thousand inhabitants no wheeled vehicle could be had for love or money. The only conveyance for passengers or freight is on the backs of animals.

I have dwelt upon the beauty of Selinus as it was, yet it must be acknowledged that now its buildings are inferior in beauty to the perfect temples of Girgenti, Segesta or Pæstum. They cannot boast of colonnades unharmed by the lapse of ages, but even though prostrated the Selinuntian temples are a more interesting study than even those of Pæstum, and display more richness of ornament and more grandeur of design than any other Sicilian ruins.

The temples seem to have outlasted the sieges and vicissitudes of the city: even its final destruction left them still standing in desolation upon the heights. At last some terrible but unrecorded earthquake shook these hills to their foundations, and the columns which had withstood the wear of ages fell by hundreds in one catastrophe. Not one remained unbroken.

For seven miles we plodded across the plain. The road runs straight through a succession of olive-farms, and is bordered here and there with cork trees, but there are few habitations or other signs of life. Far away we hear the roar of the surf, and soon a lovely column without a capital rises above the dark foliage against the darker sky: then half an hour more of tramping brings us to the summit of the eastern bluff and into the ruins of the neapolis. There is a curious irony in the name of the place—the *neapolis*—the "new city"! It has been a desolate heap of ruins for two thousand years, yet the neighboring acropolis was old when even this was new.

I am glad to have seen Selinunto as it was on that day. The gloomy landscape was in keeping with the aspect of the desolated city. The sea bellowed loud on the rocks below, and, stretching away southward to an horizon indefinite with mist and rain, its whole expanse was lashed into white-caps. To the east the coast extended in curves of yellow beach miles away to the heights of San Marco, half hidden from sight by a transparent veil of showers. The plain and the inland mountain-ranges were black with the shadows of low-brooding clouds, while around us on the cliffs were strewn the tokens of departed splendor, completing the grim desolation of the prospect.

The temple which we first approach is the most northern of the neapolis, by long usage designated by the letter G. It is the most ruinous, the most recent, and by far the greatest, of the Selinuntian temples. No sacred building in the Greek world surpassed it in size except the temple of Diana at Ephesus and that of Jove at Agrigentum. It is the only one of the group which seems to have been wrecked by human agency: probably the Carthaginian army, made furious by long

TEMPLE OF SELINUS.

resistance, spent their rage in overthrowing the greatest pride of the humiliated city. In the other temples drums and capitals lie in long lines side by side, as they fell levelled by one blow, and their plan can easily be traced; but here everything has toppled down in a confused mound of ruins: the walls and columns, formed of some of the hugest masses of stone ever wrought by men, pediments, entablatures, capitals and triglyphs, have been hurled into a shapeless heap, while a lofty but imperfect column stands alone in the midst of the wreck. We stopped by the side of the ruin to notice one of the capitals which lies flat upon the ground with the square abacus upward. Our companion called it "the dancing-floor." The peasants from the country around come here to the Pillars of the Giants, as they call them, and hold their rustic jollifications. This is the dancing-ground. The huge slab lies nearly fourteen feet square, making room for a country-dance of several couples.

The drums which compose these tower-like Doric columns lie scattered about: their diameter is so great that as they lie upon one side one can scarcely reach their centre, and as they stand upright one's back fits comfortably to the curve of the enormous flutes. The difficulty of transporting such masses of stone must have been enormous, and yet scores of such columns supported the roof, making a colonnade one thousand feet in circuit.

It would have been occupation enough for a day to study this one ruin and puzzle out the plan of the building; but the brooding clouds broke at last, and the irresistible violence of the shower sent us flying to the next temple, where a shelter is made by broken masses of stone piled up at the rear of the edifice. In a kind of cavern walled and roofed with Doric fragments we sat down to pass a rainy half hour over the cleanest and most delicate viands that the restaurateurs of Castelvetrano could furnish—hard-boiled eggs, olives and wine. It was a curious dining-room. The rubbish of ages has only of late years been cleared away, exposing the long-buried surface of the stones, which still retains uninjured the coating of fine-grained stucco, and bears many traces of the red and green colors which relieved the whiteness of the surface.

This central temple of the eastern hill is very similar in size and shape to its near neighbor on the right—so much so that it is natural to regard them as a pair.

They are commonly designated by the letters F and E respectively. An inscription lately exhumed on the spot indicates that the former was sacred to Hera: what divinity was worshipped in the latter is unknown. Both were of pure Doric architecture, and lacked but a few feet to equal in length the Parthenon of Athens. Both were adorned with metopes sculptured in relief representing, with the vigor of the archaic Greek style, the battles of the gods and giants. Both were finished with many ornaments of color, and bear to this day on their delicate mouldings much of the red, black and yellow with which they were adorned.

As we have come to the threshold, enter with me one of these Greek temples. We descend by a slight incline from the present surface of the ground to the old level, and stand at the foot of the temple-steps. A flight of magnificent breadth ascends to a stone-paved level, and beyond that another flight, as wide as the temple-front, brings us to the colonnade. We pass between the bases of two fallen columns: on either hand rise the broken shafts of unequal heights, but the position of even the fallen one is clear from some standing fragment. We are within the porch of the temple. Through another line of columns we pass within the cella, the holy place of the temple. There is much sombre picturesqueness about the interior. On the right and left shafts rise in broken gray ranges, and beyond the walls are seen other columns lying on the ground, prostrate but perfect. There is no vestige of a roof overhead, but the low-driving clouds match with the color of the masonry and seem almost to rest upon the ruins. The floor of the sacred apartment by the zeal of antiquaries has been cleared of its long accumulations, except that some fragments, thrown inward by the earthquake, lie as they fell. We walk without obstruction through the great length of the consecrated room, though around us fallen triglyphs and fluted drums lie here and there upon the pavement. We reach at last the farther end of the sacred hall, where we find the altar of the goddess in its old position, while beyond it is the pedestal from which her image is gone. Beside the altar we stoop to notice the channels cut in the floor to collect the streaming blood of the victim.

Some feeling of awe in this place is irresistible. The impression of solitude and hoary antiquity brought a sense of reverence for the place almost like that which the suppliant of old times might have felt when advancing through the temple to throw himself before the altar. To stand in the temple and at the very altar of Hera, to see the spot where, carved in marble, the haughty goddess stood, brings up with wonderful vividness all the old heathen worship. Even a dull imagination can picture the priest at the altar, the burning victim, the bending worshipper. Men, struggling and tempted, have come here to seek from Heaven redress of wrong, expiation of sin, divine aid for human weakness. And who can know that their cries were not heard and answered from Heaven? They worshipped ignorantly, but they perished from the earth centuries before the Child was born in Bethlehem of Judea.

The interest of this temple was so great that it was hard to allow a fair share of time for the acropolis, but it must be seen "now or never." So we were obliged to turn our backs on the neapolis, and hurry down the precipitous slope across the valley for half a mile, and then up through a gateway in the prostrate city-wall to the summit of the western cliff.

Here, as on the other height, Doric remains lie in confusion about us, and on all sides is spread out the same wild landscape. The buildings are so utterly overthrown that a general view is only perplexing; but as we stood gazing there emerged from the ruined temples the man whose presence is most to be desired in this place — Signor Cavallari, the best authority on Sicilian antiquities.

A careful excavation of the acropolis has been carried forward by government within the last year under the superintendence of Signor Cavallari. From the point of excavation to the edge of the cliff a little railroad was laid in order that the débris might be discharged into the sea; and already the digging had so far advanced that the old chief thoroughfare of the town, passing at the rear of the temples, was laid bare for many rods. It was a privilege adding vastly to the interest of the place to explore the ancient city under such guidance, to walk over the pavement trodden by the conquering army of Hannibal, to wander among the temples where every stone was known to our leader, to notice the appliances of the heathen worship still remaining, while we listened to the story of Cavallari's rich discoveries from his own lips.

There is so much similarity of design in all pure Doric temples that a description of each one upon the acropolis would become tedious. The chief claim to special interest which these possess is their extreme antiquity, for it is believed that no trace exists of any older Doric temple, unless it be in one group of columns standing on the Plain of Corinth. Certain peculiarities of architecture in the temples marked upon the plans by the letters C and D show that they were completed before the establishment of the Doric canon in architecture. Their age is plainly greater than that of the other buildings, and C is probably the older of the two, for the hideous sculptured metopes exhumed among its fragments are the earliest and rudest works of the Greek chisel which have ever come to light. No doubt it is almost coeval with the city, and was founded twenty-five centuries ago.

The temporary home of the venerable antiquary is in a little stone cabin, snug but primitive in its arrangements, which is perched on the very edge of the crag. Under its roof, while we were fortified with hot coffee to face again the chilly storm, we were feasted with our host's discourse of his travels and discoveries —of ancient Greece and Young America; of adventures in Yucatan, and uneasy nights passed in the crater of Etna while aiding Baron Sartorius in preparing his work on that volcano. All the pauses of the conversation were filled with the solemn music of the sea rhythmically beating on the crag far beneath our feet. With the fading of light we passed outside the city-wall and down across the old harbor, which is now dry land. There we parted from our entertainer, leaving him standing on the seashore in the light of the low sun, which broke from the clouds at setting. It was a venerable but erect figure, clad in a graceful Italian cloak; a fine face and head, beautified by snow-white hair—a presence in harmony with the hoary grandeur of the buildings among which he dwells and labors.

To penetrate the country lying east of Castelvetrano is no easy matter. There is no steam communication, no diligence, no carriage to be hired, no road, nor can anything deserving the name of a saddle be obtained. Two flattened lumps of white rags were bound to the backs of two raw-boned horses: on the top of these our baggage, ourselves and our two drivers were stacked up in a manner peculiar to the country. For twenty-seven weary miles we rode with unstirruped feet across wild moors, through fords made dangerous by the recent storm, and over long reaches of sea-beach, till, mounting the promontory of San Marco, we came under the walls of Sciacca.

The mediæval remains of Sciacca are worthy to receive some attention from a traveller, but with the light of the next day came a clear sky and west wind, making it possible to continue the journey toward Girgenti by a sailboat—too good a chance to be lost by delay. A zigzag path, steep as a stairway, descended from the city to the sea. Attended by two wizened fishermen, who bent beneath a load of boat-supplies, we came down to the shore, and then, without delay, our pretty little craft rushed impetuously out to the open sea. It was only a rough fishing-boat, yet the grace of the lateen sail and the quaint costumes of the skipper and his man seemed got up for scenic effect. An exhilarating wind blew fresh out of the west, sending us on our course with the speed of a bird.

We continued looking back on the town we had left until it faded in the distance. I have not seen in any country so beautiful a site as that of Sciacca. A range of bare stone peaks, which glowed with many tints in the morning light, rose behind the city from bases of rich verdure; on either hand promontories shut off the violence of the waves; the sea was blue with that brilliancy not known in our Northern waters. In the centre of the scene towers the city, built on the edge of an enormous rock, the massive and battlemented town-wall pierced by imposing gateways; and the towers and palaces rising above it give an impression of majesty which is enhanced by the height of the cliff. It is like one of those ancient fortresses that we see in Doré's fantastic pictures—a citadel of the Middle Ages, fit to be the home of crusaders. For many miles at sea the gleam of its white walls is unmistakable.

> Far beneath a blazing vault,
> Sown in a wrinkle of the monstrous hill,
> The city sparkles like a grain of salt.

The whole sail of forty miles from Sciacca to the port of Girgenti, following the line of the coast, is a panorama of delightful pictures. Cliffs and beaches, mountains and rolling country, flew past us alternately as we ran along steadily at nine knots. Our skipper was a man of incomprehensible tongue, but at the start he pointed significantly to the figure 2 on my watch-dial, and, true to his word, before that hour we came to Porto Empedocle, the harbor of Girgenti, and, riding ashore on the fishermen's shoulders, were unceremoniously dumped on the beach.

As viewed from the sea, the town seemed near at hand, for it is most conspicuous, standing on a ridge a thousand feet above, yet even by rail it is almost an hour's journey, for the grades are tremendous and the road of course winding. This railway will soon be completed to Palermo, and then it is to be hoped that Girgenti will become familiar to travellers; for, excepting Athens, there is hardly another place which so abounds in Greek antiquities. Now the remote ruins of Egypt are better known to the travelling public than the remains of Acragas.

The present town of Girgenti occupies

the height which was the citadel of the Greek Acragas and the Roman Agrigentum. Below the town, on the south, lies an undulating plateau which was overspread by the ancient city, and beyond that the mountain-side slopes abruptly to the sea. When at last our train had climbed the mountain and we were run-

COAST NEAR SCIACCA.

ning at better speed across this plateau, the early winter sun was already setting, and here and there lovely pictures, framed with rocks and green trees, flashed before our eyes, visions of majestic Greek buildings casting across the green sward the long shadows of evening, and, most beautiful of all, one superb Doric temple, unmarred by time, with the soft yellow of its colonnade transformed to the brilliancy of gold by the flood of dying sunshine. From the station there is yet a long ascent by carriage to the town, and it was dusk when we passed the city-gate and drove up through the length of the main thoroughfare—a dark street, rather narrow and less clean than could be desired, but at every corner the eye was charmed with glimpses down the sloping side-streets, for each glimpse revealed a view bounded only by the horizon: the eye runs beyond the town-walls, across the fields and down the slope to the sea, a thousand feet below.

Girgenti is picturesque when you are a few miles from it, but the enchantment of distance is needed to enjoy it: within the walls it is agreeable neither to the eye nor nose. The population is mewed up within the limits of the mediæval fortifications, and therefore all buildings are closely packed and run high in air, making the streets appear like the poor quarters of a dense metropolis. There is hardly a trace to be found within the town of the ancient citadel which stood upon the same hill.

To the vast majority of readers whose classical studies are rusty the name of Acragas conveys a rather vague image. Perhaps the thought arises that some such town, whose situation is but half remembered, was a rival of the more famous Syracuse: perhaps with it are associated thoughts of Theron, the ideal despot, or of Phalaris, most infamous of tyrants. The city which men of our age have so much forgotten was in its time vast, populous, rich, magnificent. Half a million of souls, it is thought, dwelt within its walls: in luxury it rivalled Sybaris; in power it was second only to Syracuse among the Greek colonies. It was of the citizens of Acragas that Empedocles said that they built as if they hoped to live for ever, and lived as if they thought to die to-morrow. Pindar rapturously calls Acragas "the fairest of mortal cities." Nor was its glory that of mere barbaric magnificence and power. The boundless wealth of its rulers and citizens was spent to advance high art.

Except Athens, hardly another Greek city could boast of more perfect culture. Here was the home of famous statesmen, artists, philosophers. Theron and Empedocles were men of Acragas: works of Zeuxis and Myron adorned the line of temples which were the glory of the city.

The rise of Acragas to the zenith of its power was astonishingly rapid. Founded by colonists from Gela in the year 580 B.C., in little more than one century it advanced to a degree of influence which in later times it could never equal. It can hardly be doubted that the swift advancement of the young colony was due in a great degree to the skilful government of the tyrant Phalaris. When the city was but ten years old he usurped the supreme power by the appropriation and free use of funds entrusted to him, and ruled the people with a rod of iron for twelve years. That he governed with skill is certain from the great material prosperity of the city under his control. He seems to have been a patron of letters and the fine arts, and in his time Acragas grew in power and magnificence; but this is almost forgotten by the ancient writers, who rarely mention him except in connection with the brazen bull in which he is said to have roasted his enemies.

Acragas owed much to Phalaris, but more to Theron, who extended the dominions of the city across the island to the Tyrrhene Sea, and in company with Gelon destroyed the vast fleet of Carthage on the day most memorable in the history of Greek civilization; for on that day, it is said, the strength of the African city was shattered by Theron, while, unknown to him, Themistocles was conquering the Asiatic hordes of Xerxes at Salamis.

The victory of Himera brought Acragas to the highest point of her grandeur: wealth poured into the city, luxury increased. The army of Carthaginian prisoners reduced to slavery was employed by the government in building the temples and other public works which made the city one of the most splendid that have ever existed, and which even after two thousand years astonish every visitor to their ruins. For nearly a century more the prosperity of Acragas was uninterrupted, but in the year 406 B. C. the Carthaginian army, fresh from the destruction of Selinus, came upon the city, and after a fearful siege it fell. Some years afterward Timoleon rebuilt Acragas, and again it became flourishing, but never recovered its former greatness; and in the Roman period it was a town of small importance.

A warm evening and a full moon were strong temptations to make a visit to the temples on our first night in Girgenti, for first impressions of a ruined city can never be so charming as in the full moonlight; but the distance to the old southern wall by which the ruins stand seemed too great after a fatiguing day of travel-

TOMB OF THERON.

ling, and a prudent citizen strongly advised against venturing out of the city-gates at night. The value of the warning appeared on the following morning, for some event drew a multitude of countrymen into the town, and the main street was half full of the most savage-looking ruffians I have ever met.

Grote expends some pity on the defeated Agrigentines, because, in addition to the horrors of the siege, they were driven from their homes on a December night. If their sufferings were from cold, it must have been a very different winter day from that on which I first walked through the ancient city. Under a blazing afternoon sun we followed a rough footpath which leads most directly from the town to the ruins, down over ledges of bare rock which radiated an intense heat. Here, as elsewhere about the city, a vast extent of the shelving rocks is honeycombed with graves. They have long been emptied of their contents, but the myriads of them that are found give a clew by which the huge population of Acragas can be estimated. So about Selinus, Syracuse and other ancient cities the graves and memorials of the dead are always amazing in multitude.

After this first declivity our path for two or three miles undulated across the rolling land once wholly covered by the city. It is a well-cultivated country, planted with olive, orange and almond trees, but there are few antique remains to arrest the attention. A lofty ruin, which stands on a height to the west, we passed without a visit: it is a Saracenic bath, and can claim an antiquity of only one thousand years, which in this part of the world is a very insignificant age. The farm-walls which border our way seem to be largely built of antique materials: much of the stone is wrought, and here and there an elegant fluted column is piled on roughly, like the glacial boulders around our Northern farms. As we approach the southern boundary of the Greek city the evidences of ancient life are seen more and more: around the wayside convent of Santo Nicola are strewn architectural fragments of great beauty which have been dug from the fields. But while traversing for miles the site of Acragas hardly a standing wall or column of its ten thousand buildings is seen till we come upon the temple of Juno Lucina, situated at the southeastern angle of the plateau.

The position of this temple was quite the most beautiful in the city. The great natural platform on which Acragas was built is bounded on the seaward side by a short precipice, beyond which the mountain slopes steeply to the shore. This long, low cliff extends from east to west for more than a mile, and, turning inland at right angles, formed the strongest natural defence on three sides of the lower city. On the brow of this cliff five of the Agrigentine temples stood in line, overlooking, like the temples of Selinus, a wide extent of country, and, like them, seen far out at sea.

It is at the angle where this precipitous boundary turns from east to west that the ruined temple of Juno stands. Its remains are full of dignity and beauty. It is ruined, but not prostrate. Earthquakes and other destroying agencies of time have shattered the walls, and the pavement and cornice have disappeared, but all the columns of the northern line are perfect, still bearing the architrave upon their capitals. The shafts of the southern side, roughened by centuries of the south wind from Africa, are less regular: many have lost their capitals, and some have fallen. So much remains of the building that the plan and dimensions are evident at a glance, and yet the marks of time are so unmistakable that even when seen at a distance of miles, towering upon its pedestal of rock, the rugged outline of the ruin always suggests the thought of its immense antiquity.

The building belongs to the best period of Doric architecture, and must have been erected little less than five hundred years before Christ. It is called the temple of Juno, and, though we have not the best reasons for giving that name to the temple, it is not improbable that this was the building which contained the picture of Juno for which, as Pliny relates, Zeuxis chose as his models the five most lovely damsels of Acragas, combining their several beauties in one feminine figure of superhuman perfection. The picture of Juno was the great artist's masterpiece.

The second temple of the line upon the cliff is seen to stand at a considerable distance. The pathway to it follows the ancient city-wall, which in this part is a low parapet of enormous thickness crowning the verge of the precipice: it is not built up of stones, but is formed of the natural rock scarped on both sides. Along the wall are curious sepulchres of many chambers hewn in the rock.

A walk of several hundred yards brought us near the so-called temple of Concord, a building of nearly the same age as the first temple. Unlike the other Greek structures of Sicily, the temple of Concord is not a ruin, nor is it, like the temple of Segesta, unfinished. The front, which is first approached from the east,

RUINS OF THE TEMPLE OF HERCULES, NEAR GIRGENTI.

seems to be without flaw or blemish of any kind: there is but one other building on the earth which has stood for twenty-four centuries with so little injury. The temple is a perfect example of the best Doric order—simple, yet full of grandeur.

In coming upon an edifice so imposing and without any appearance of dilapidation, it is a strange sensation to find only solitude and silence; it seems but natural to hope that some priest or worshipper may descend the steps; but hardly a habitation is in sight except the white houses of the city gleaming far away upon the hill; only the strong sea-wind, shaking the trees, breaks the quiet of the place; no living creature is visible but passing flocks of birds. The temple cannot be approached without commanding the deepest admiration of the beholder: the perfect symmetry of the structure, the look of repose and of unshaken strength, the simple majesty of Greek art, the thought of its changeless existence through a score of centuries, give to it a sublimity equalled by few architectural works. Yet, standing before the faultless portico, it is not easy to realize that its columns were reared when the long drama of European history was just opening: they are still so unyielding in their strength that they seem destined to stand while the solid cliff below remains unmoved.

To pass within the shade of the portico, and follow around the temple the long walk of the peristyle which runs between the wall and the outer colonnade, increases the feeling of wonder at the marvellous preservation of the building. It explains in some degree the reason why it has been preserved to note the exquisite finish of the mason's work: every stone is so finely fitted to its neighbors that a needle would hardly slide between them.

In passing from the portico to the cella of the temple the absence of a roof is first noticed: as it was supported in its place by beams of wood, it must have disappeared when the building was comparatively new; but within, as without, the completeness of the temple is wonderful. The only alterations which have been made seem to be the removal of a partition which anciently divided the interior, and the cutting of arched openings in the walls for the admission of light. These changes were the result of adapting the heathen temple to the purposes of Christian worship. The extraordinary preservation of this most perfect monument of antiquity we owe to the mediæval Christians, who dedicated it in honor of St. Gregorio delle Rape. A curious feature of the interior is the pair of spiral staircases at the corners of the edifice. They afford a safe and unbroken means of ascent to the top of the building, but the hard stone of the steps is worn almost to a continuous slope by the tread of eighty generations of men. Seated upon the top of the cornice, we lingered long to enjoy the most beautiful view that can be obtained in this region: it embraces the rolling country with its ruins, the modern city, the mountains and the sea.

Continuing westward from the temple of Concord, we soon came upon the highroad leading to the port. It descends through the cliff from the plateau to the slope below by a broad inclined plane cut in the rock. It is a cutting of ancient origin, for this was the great seagate of Acragas. Standing before the gateway, it is not hard to imagine it the most splendid entrance that any ancient city could boast, for on the one hand the ruined temple of Hercules lies on the verge of the cliff: on the other are the fragments of the Olympieum.

As we stood before the gateway some solitary armed horsemen at long intervals, and now and then a group of loaded mules toiling up toward Girgenti, were the only reminders of the roaring tide of traffic which in old times rushed through it. In those days the road to the sea was bordered by the mausoleums of the Agrigentine nobles, but the destruction of them began as far back as the Carthaginian siege of Acragas, when Hannibal the elder used them as quarries to aid his military operations. Some were spared, but the only trace of them all that now remains is a lonely tomb in the form of an Ionic tower, commonly called the "tomb of Theron." The magnificent mausoleum of Theron mentioned by old writers probably stood near this spot. It is said that its destruction, when commanded by Hannibal, was arrested by a sign from Heaven; but it is no longer standing. That which is called Theron's tomb is a graceful but plain structure: the walls are simply adorned with sunken panels, and at the corners are four slender columns of the Ionic order; but it corresponds in no way with the royal grandeur of Theron's tomb as described by Diodorus.

The two temples which overlook the sea-gate, flanking it on either side, were the grandest architectural works of the city. That which stood upon the eastern side is believed to be the temple of Hercules, referred to by Cicero in his charge against Verres. Its remains show it to have been a temple built after the usual Doric pattern, but with proportions of remarkable grandeur. It was little inferior to the Parthenon in size; but, great as this building was, it was so dwarfed by the neighboring temple of Jupiter that we hear more of the works of art preserved in it than of its own beauty. In regard to the statue of Hercules which it contained, Cicero, living among the collected art-treasures of Rome, gave this testimony: "I cannot say that I have ever looked on a thing more beautiful." Another work of even greater fame, enshrined in this edifice, was the picture of Alcimene by Zeuxis. He painted it for the Agrigentines without recompense; "For," he said, "the painting is priceless, therefore I will receive no price." The ruins of this temple are disappointing to one just coming from a Greek building in perfect preservation. At first sight it seems but a mound of fragments, heaped about one lonely column, but a walk across the stylobate or stone platform of the temple gives an idea of the grand scale of the building, and is interesting for the sake of the associations of the place.

The Olympieum, or temple of Olympian Zeus, which flanked the sea-gate on the western side, was one of the greatest architectural wonders of the world. Among all the temples reared by the Hellenic race it was inferior in size only to the temple of Diana at Ephesus. The dimensions of the building were equal to those of a large mediæval cathedral. It was referred to by the ancients in terms which show that they regarded it as a thing little less astonishing than any of the world's Seven Wonders. The design was peculiar: unlike the other Sicilian temples, which were usually surrounded by a colonnade, the external walls of the Olympieum were adorned only with engaged columns of enormous size. Diodorus, in a passage often quoted regarding the ancient splendor of Acragas, thus describes these columns: "Their circumference in the outer portion is twenty feet, so that a man's body can be contained in one of the flutes; and the breadth of the part within is twelve feet. The size and height of the porticoes are amazing. In the part looking toward the east was represented the battle of the gods and the giants, excellent for size, beauty and fine workmanship. In the pediment toward the west was represented the capture of Troy, in which each one of the heroes, elaborately sculptured, can be known by his own characteristics."

The interior decorations of this building were of a peculiar character. Against the four walls it seems that huge pilasters rose two-thirds the height of the building, and each was surmounted by the figure of a giant supporting the roof on his uplifted hands. These ranks of colossal figures were the most original and perhaps the most impressive feature of this temple's architecture. They seemed to bow beneath the weight imposed upon them, and symbolized to the worshippers of Zeus his conquest of the giants, who, as tradition said, reigned in Sicily until the power of Zeus became supreme.

I wandered about among the ruins of the Olympieum in a state of simmering indignation, unable to forgive or forget the stupidity of the mediæval inhabitants of Girgenti. They wanted a mole to improve their bad harbor, and found materials for it in this building, though stone in abundance may be quarried at half the distance from the sea. In consequence of this devastation the remains of the edifice are comparatively scanty, though enough is left to afford material for more than one temple of moderate size. Several acres are strewn with the wrought stones, each of which weighs many tons; but nothing stands except the basement-walls, which rise above the surface of the ground to the level of the temple-floor. Even the stone flooring is torn up, and the space enclosed by the foundations is overgrown with wild flowers.

As we climbed up into the area of the temple the one object which seized and held our attention was the monstrous figure of a giant in stone which lies stretched out upon the floor: it is the only one which remains of the roof-supporting colossi, and indeed the only

TEMPLE OF CASTOR AND POLLUX.

remnant of the wealth of sculpture which once adorned the building. Flocks were cropping the pasturage of the temple-floor, and the figure of their shepherd, resting against the statue, set off by contrast its huge proportions. The length of the recumbent form is twenty-six feet: it lies with arms upraised, as if the giant slept with his clasped hands for a pillow. The stone is exceedingly worn by ages of exposure, yet the altitude and size of the figure are full of grandeur, and it aids the imagination more than all the other remains in conceiving what must have been the original beauty of the edifice.

In the range of buildings that overlooked the city-wall the fifth and last goes by the name of the temple of Castor and Pollux. A statue of Leda found on the spot makes it probable that it was built in honor of her, rather than of her sons. It is a picturesque ruin, standing near the western angle of the wall, close to the brink of the precipice, which here is high enough to give grandeur to the site. Of the thirty-four columns that surrounded the peristyle, only a pretty group of four remains, surmounted by the cornice and one angle of the pediment. Though this was one of the smallest of the sacred buildings, its position was one of the loveliest of the town. A large artificial lake filled the ravine on the western side of the city, and washed the base of the cliff on which this temple stands, so that a picture of the white colonnade was reflected from the water far below.

The less important ruins about Girgenti are very numerous. Four days were overcrowded with interesting work in exploring the other temples, aqueducts and tombs, and in revisiting the great ruins.

The fifth day found us hurried reluctantly away, over a most tempestuous sea, toward Syracuse: longer delay was impossible, for Girgenti has but weekly steam communication with the outer world.

A MONTH IN SICILY.

CONCLUDING PART.

THE OLYMPIEUM.

THE steamer which carried us toward Syracuse was small, the sea was rough, our fellow-travellers were officers of the Italian army; therefore, as we rounded the south-eastern cape, the stormy Pachinum, and a drenching rain forced me to leave the deck, the ship's cabin presented a doleful spectacle to my eyes. "How were the mighty fallen!" The stalwart officers, to a man, lay pallid and motionless as if some conquering foe had cut off the flower of the Italian army. On every lounge and berth was seen a pale and woebegone face, made the more ghastly by the contrast with a beard of intense blackness.

Their hair drooped round their pallid cheeks
Like sea-weed round a clam.

The sight strengthened my opinion that the dark-haired people of Southern Europe are more invariably and more severely affected by sea-sickness than fair-haired men of the Anglo-Saxon race.

There are few positions which give to the human soul such a feeling of calm superiority, of deep self-satisfaction, as that which is experienced by a man sitting with a clear head and smiling countenance in the midst of a sea-sick company. Nevertheless, even the dignity of that position became irksome with time, and I could sympathize with the sighs of relief which burst in chorus from the military gentlemen when, sooner than seemed possible, the rolling ceased, we heard the anchor drop, and knew that our voyage was at an end.

The view which greeted our eyes on returning to the deck was of a different character from any which we had met before in Sicily. The steamer was at anchor in the beautiful great harbor of Syracuse. The country on the north, south and west of the bay is prettily varied by low, rolling hills, but would seem tame if compared with the rugged scenery of all other parts of the island except for one grand feature, the superb snow-covered pyramid of Etna, which, though forty miles away from Syracuse, is the most striking object in sight.

Across the eastern side of the bay, dividing it from the open sea, lies the island of Ortygia, covered by the houses of Syracuse. The buildings rise from the edge of the water, and the symmetrical shape of the island gives a singular grace to the city viewed as a whole. Seen from a distance across the water, it is like a great white waterfowl resting on the surface of the sea.

The city was founded twenty-six centuries ago on Ortygia, but in the course of ages it covered many square miles of the adjacent coast: now, in its old age, it has shrunk again within the narrow limits of the island.

A man who in his school-boy days has toiled over the *Æneid* and the *Bucolics*, changing the lovely Latin verses into bad English prose, and has felt even a little appreciation of the poetry, cannot rest long in Syracuse without looking about him for the famous Arethusa, the sacred fountain whose praises are sounded by Virgil, and which was the subject of so much poetry and legend through the classical ages. After we had landed upon the quay before the sea-gate of the city, and had passed up through the gate to one of the adjacent hotels overlooking the bay, enough of daylight remained to us for a little sight-seeing. Our thoughts naturally turned first to Arethusa. The fountain is most pleasantly approached by going back through the sea-gate on to the Marina, a beautiful seashore drive which runs for half the length of the island between the town-wall and the shore of the harbor, and is laid out in imitation of the grand Marina of Palermo.

At the southern end of this avenue we descended a stairway of stone to the shore of the harbor. The custodian of Arethusa threw open an iron gateway on our left, and we stepped down to the edge of the fountain. A large semicircular space, which is bounded on its curve by a wall of massive masonry and faces toward the bay, is quite filled by the pool of Arethusa, except that a narrow flagged walk runs by the water's edge. The clear water bursts in a torrent from many openings in the rock underlying the wall, and, rushing across the pool and through a short channel, falls into the bay with almost the volume of a river. The pool is so close to the surface of the harbor that if it were by any sea but the tideless Mediterranean it would be daily overflowed even by a rise of a few inches.

The fountain is adorned with the papyrus brought from the marshes beyond the harbor. As we paced the flagging along the edge of the water the plumes of the papyrus nodded in the wind high over our heads. It seemed the most stately and graceful of plants, even in the midst of the luxuriant vegetable life of Sicily.

The fable of Arethusa and Alpheus is well known: Virgil has expressed it in a few words:

> Alpheum fama est huc Elidis amnem
> Occultas egisse vias subter mare; qui nunc
> Ore, Arethusa, tuo Siculis confunditur undis.

LATOMIA DEI CAPPUCCINI.

The story goes that the nymph Arethusa, pursued by the river-god Alpheus in Greece, implored the aid of Diana, and was changed by her into a fountain which sank into the earth, and, flowing together with the waters of the river a hundred leagues under the sea, rose to the light again in this Ortygian pool.

The story has this foundation in truth, that the waters of Arethusa really flow under the sea. The fountain is the last outlet of one of the ancient aqueducts, which has its origin far away in the hills of Sicily, north-west of the city. The conduit is carried for several miles under the plateau occupied by that district of Syracuse called Epipolæ: thence it descends under the small harbor, and at last emerges in the island.

It is a charming excursion for half a

day to cross the harbor and visit the remains which lie outside the ancient walls upon its western shore. On a morning when the harbor lay calm and brilliant among its encircling hills, 'looking like a magnified blue flower among green leaves, we descended to the quay and engaged boatmen for the trip across the bay and up the river Anapus. We were rowed due west across the harbor to the mouth of the little river, but we had hardly entered the stream when the boatmen began to insinuate that the gentlemen would find walking more agreeable: the dryness of the winter had rendered the Anapus too low for comfortable navigation. A rough walk through salt marshes and over rocky fields brought us in ten minutes to the top of the low but commanding knoll on which the scanty ruins of the Olympieum stand in perfect solitude.

This temple was one of the richest, oldest and most revered of all Greek fanes. The statue of Olympian Jove which was adored here was ranked by Cicero among three statues of the god which he esteemed the most perfect in the world. Gelon, returning from the spoliation of the Carthaginians at Himera, commemorated the greatest victory of the Sicilian Greeks by clothing this statue in a robe of solid gold; but a century afterward Dionysius the Tyrant appropriated the gold to his own use, apologizing for his greed only with the grim joke that "gold was too heavy a mantle for summer and too cold for winter, but wool was well adapted to both seasons."

The site is interesting rather for its old celebrity than for existing remains. Only two tall Doric columns stand, showing by their wide separation the length of the building. They have a circumference of about eighteen feet, and yet each column was hewn from a single stone.

Near the Olympieum, at a point where the Anapus receives the tributary waters of the famous Cyane—"*celeberissima inter Sicilias nymphas*"—begins a great thicket of papyrus bordering the stream on both sides. The gigantic reeds, bending under the weight of their bushy heads and rising in some cases to a height of nearly twenty feet, are mirrored from the sluggish stream below. Amid such vegetation it is as easy to imagine one's self sailing along the head-waters of the Nile as on a river of temperate Europe; for I believe there is no country nearer than Abyssinia where this famous plant now grows. It long ago disappeared from Egypt, nor is it found elsewhere in Europe than here. It is hard to account for its isolated growth in this marsh, but probably its introduction into Europe was due to the Arab conquerors of Sicily.

Ancient Syracuse had great beauty, both natural and architectural, yet its position cannot compare with the mountainous height of Acragas, conspicuous far away over land and sea; nor had it any such natural beauty as the sea-washed cliffs of Selinus, serving as pedestals for sublime buildings. Nevertheless, the situation had a peculiar loveliness. The buildings of the island, the oldest portion of the town, rose, Venice-like, from the very waves of the sea. The four other districts—Acradina, Tyche, Epipolæ and Neapolis, sometimes called distinct cities—occupied a low table-land which overlooks from the north two fine harbors of Syracuse, and spread to the adjoining plain.

Fine as was the site of Syracuse, its reputation for extraordinary beauty in old times rested chiefly on its architectural grandeur; so that even at a time when the greatness of Syracuse had declined and Rome was in her prime, a Roman, addressing Romans, said, "You have often heard that Syracuse is the largest of Greek cities, and the most beautiful of all cities."

By far the greater portion of the existing remains of Syracuse is found in those districts which lie north of the harbor. Early in the morning we rode through the powerful fortress which defends the island upon the north, and crossed the bridge connecting Ortygia with the Sicilian shore, to pass a delightful day among the ruins.

All along under the brow of the Syracusan plateau the rock is deeply penetrated by old quarries called *latomie*. It

LATOMIA DEL PARADISO, NEAR SYRACUSE.

was from these quarries that ancient Syracuse was built, and their size and number indicate how great the city was. The first of them which is approached on the east is called Latomia dei Cappuccini, from its proximity to the Capuchin convent. It is a vast pit sunk in the earth between scarped cliffs which rise perpendicularly around it to a height of eighty or a hundred feet. In the midst of it two monstrous masses of stone like fortified towers have been left standing. The floor of the quarry, many acres in extent, is partly covered with a garden of oranges and pomegranates, and a wild growth of roses and acanthus runs between the trees: over the fallen masses of rock and from the cliffs above hang ivy and wild vines matted into graceful curtains which soften the rough aspect of the crags.

Looking from above upon this luxuriant garden, which lies below so peaceful and solitary and silent that the flight or chirp of every bird is noticed, it is hard to revive in imagination the tragedy of which it was the scene. In this quarry, amid unutterable horrors, toiled and perished seven thousand Athenians, all that remained of the forces sent forth from Athens under Nicias and Demosthenes in an armada greater and more splendid than any Greek state before had equipped.

A number of the most important remains of the city lie in a group not far from the main northern highway, a mile to the west of the Capuchin monastery. The first great ruin which we meet is the Roman amphitheatre. The dimensions of this amphitheatre, as compared with the neighboring Greek theatre, indicate a great decline in the population of Syracuse during the earlier ages of the Roman empire, for it is hardly larger than the amphitheatre of Verona. The seats are partly excavated from the natural rock, but as the hillside slopes rapidly toward the south, the lower part of the building is constructed of solid masonry. A traveller who has studied the great amphitheatres of the Peninsula will find little of fresh interest in this; nevertheless, it was to me a half hour full of interest which I spent in exploring the labyrinth of vaulted corridors for entrance and exit, the innumerable stairways of stone, and the passages and gateways through which wild beasts and gladiators were introduced upon the arena; in noticing the curious arrangements for supplying the place with water; in searching for inscriptions on the marble trimmings, which show to what families the best sittings in the theatre belonged.

A Greek historian has mentioned that Hieron II., tyrant of Syracuse, built an altar a stadium (one-eighth of a mile) in length. It has been suggested that its incredible dimensions would long ago have been found incorrect by those acute German critics whose mission it is to set the classical authors right in their figures and dimensions, except for the troublesome fact that the altar was dug up in 1839. We came to this altar next among the ruins. It is a vast platform hewn from the natural rock, but supplemented at its southern end with masonry, like the amphitheatre. It is approached on each side by a flight of three steps. There could hardly have been much use for this altar except once in the year, when the Syracusans offered to Jupiter their annual sacrifice of four hundred and fifty oxen—a remarkable example of the lavish scale on which public affairs were conducted at Syracuse both in peace and war.

Above this altar the ground rises first in a gradual slope, then perpendicularly, to the level of the plateau at that part occupied by the district called Neapolis. In the vertical face of this cliff are the entrances of two latomie worthy of special notice. The first is a cavern approached through the vast open quarry called Latomia del Paradiso. Beside its entrance stands a pinnacle of rocks crowned with mediæval ruins. The grotto was anciently used as a prison, but has no special historic interest: it is attractive only for its beauty. The walls of rock about the opening, and even for some distance within the cave, are half concealed under a quivering tapestry of the maiden-hair fern, which clings to every crevice of the rock. The roof rests

RUINS OF THE ANCIENT THEATRE AT SYRACUSE.

upon innumerable piers roughly hewn from the natural rock, and between them are seen, far back in the twilight of the cavern, the forms of men and women moving back and forth as if in the stately figures of a minuet. They are working at the very ordinary business of making ropes, but the surroundings make it an exceedingly picturesque occupation.

The second latomia is called the Ear of Dionysius—a name not flattering to the tyrant, for the shape of the ear is far more asinine than human. The acoustic properties of this cave are very remarkable. It is one room, as long and high as the nave of a large mediæval church. Every sound made near the opening of the cavern is echoed from the farther end, and astonishingly magnified. The noise from a bit of paper crumpled in the hand, after running a distance of five hundred feet, returns to the ear increased in volume; and the crack of a tiny pistol is so multiplied that it seems like the simultaneous roar of a hundred distant cannon.

The last and the most remarkable in this group of remains is the Greek theatre. We descended from the quarries under the arches of an aqueduct to the highway. A few minutes' walk brought us to the theatre. A most impressive first sight of the building is obtained by turning from the road into a vaulted passage on the right, which emerges upon the orchestra just in front of the stage. On three sides the seats in the vast curve of the auditorium rise in receding ranges. To the eye, confused by emerging from the dim light of the vault, they seem like the countless ripples from a stone falling in calm water. No traces of the stage remain except the foundation of the *scena* at the back, and a trough of masonry at the front to contain the curtain; for, contrary to the custom of the modern stage, the curtain rolled *down* at the opening of the play.

This theatre is one of the largest ever built. Among the Greek theatres of which traces remain probably only two equalled it in seating capacity. The entire population of the modern city would find room on the seats which remain, yet many of the upper tiers are gone. The theatre used to accommodate twenty-four thousand persons: the new Grand Opera-house at Paris will seat less than four thousand. Standing in the orchestra and considering the great distance of the remoter seats, it is easy to understand why the ugly and unnatural masks were always retained in the Greek plays, for without the reinforcement of the voice given by the mouthpiece it would have been impossible on the higher tiers to distinguish the words of the actor.

The *cavia*, or excavation, extends from the top to the bottom of the hill. Above the fifteenth row of seats a broad corridor divides the lower seats of the aristocracy from those above occupied by the common people. On the wall of the corridor are inscribed, in large Greek capitals, the names of Zeus, of Hieron the Tyrant, and of Philistis and Nereis, queens of Syracuse, giving titles to the great divisions of the theatre.

A visit to this group of remains usually completes the sightseeing of a traveller to Syracuse, but three miles to the west there stands another ruin, the fortress of Euryalus, which was to me the most interesting building of Syracuse, for it is the finest existing specimen of the military engineering of the Greeks, or perhaps of any other ancient people.

Ascending one of the long stairways of the theatre, and entering the rock-hewn street of tombs, the fortress may be reached by following the course of the old aqueduct westward for a league across the table-land occupied by the Epipolæ.

The lines of cliff which bound the plateau on the north and south converge to a sharp angle at the western end of the town. At this extreme point of the city stood the fortress, powerfully defending the western gate in the town-wall. In looking at the ruin from its western side only the gray bases of four stone towers are seen. All that remains of the fortress above ground is in a state of extreme ruin, but below the surface of the ground the immense fosses, the magazines hewn in the rock, and especially the labyrinth of subterranean passages running in all

STRAIT OF MESSINA.

directions from the fort, are of the highest interest, as throwing light on ancient modes of warfare. From these underground corridors many stairways of stone ascend to concealed openings in the country about. They were to be used for surprising the enemy by sallies from the fortress at unexpected points. There is good reason to believe that we see in Euryalus the work of Archimedes, or at least that the fortification, if older, was greatly improved by him.

Syracuse is connected with the other cities of the eastern coast by the only completed railroad in Sicily: for that reason this part of the island is becoming more familiarly known to foreigners than other regions, and I need not dwell upon the charms of a country so often described by others. The remaining towns of special interest are Catania, Taormina and Messina.

At Catania we paused long enough for a vain attempt to scale the almost impenetrable winter-snows of Etna. At a height of six thousand feet a wind was encountered against which neither man nor beast could stand, and the attempt was abandoned.

I cannot here describe at length the extraordinary grandeur of the view from the ruined Greek theatre of Taormina; but after a year of European travel, when a gentleman acknowledged as a judge in æsthetic matters said to me among the Alps, "There is no other view in Europe so beautiful as that from the theatre of Taormina," I could respond with an unhesitating amen.

After a few days spent in Messina we bade good-bye to Sicily. Messina is a handsome, busy, commercial place, well built and surrounded by wild mountain-scenery. Its cathedral is one of the finest churches of Sicily, but, considering the ancient importance of the place, it is remarkable how few remains of antiquity are to be found.

On a brilliant afternoon, when long shadows from the Sicilian mountains were already beginning to fall across the sea, we took the returning steamer for Naples, and sailed northward slowly against the powerful current which sweeps between Scylla and Charybdis. A month before we had been charmed with the scenery on first approaching the island, but now, as it faded from our eyes, the impression which remained upon the mind was of a view more beautiful.

The Strait of Messina is here no wider than a broad river. On either side the Italian and Sicilian mountains rise so near at hand that the waters of the strait seem to wash their bases. Out of the vivid blue of the sea they tower up through zones of soft green vegetation, lifting to a height of many thousand feet bare shoulders of rock, while here and there the highest mountain-heads are snow-capped, glittering against a blue so deep and so undimmed by any cloud or haze that the reflected light from the summits is almost too dazzling for the eye to bear.

I believe that there cannot be found elsewhere, even on the Mediterranean, a more sublime harmony of sea and mountain-scenery than these views on the Strait of Messina, whether looked at from the water or the adjacent heights. It is a kind of beauty especially fresh and charming to American eyes, from the fact that along our Atlantic coast the mountain-ranges nowhere approach the sea.

A little white town nestling under the mountains on the Italian shore still bears the name of Scylla. After the steamer passed it we were beyond the strongest current, and progress was more rapid. In less than two hours the Sicilian mountains were growing very dim in the south, and on our left the volcanoes of the Lipari Islands were outlined in black against the yellow of the western sky. The sun set into the smoke-cloud from Vulcano, and in the deepening twilight we watched the rugged mass of Stromboli rising higher out of the sea, but with many lingering backward looks at the island whose matchless beauty had in a journey of one month kindled a sort of loyal attachment akin to a feeling of patriotism.

ALFRED T. BACON.

GLIMPSES OF SWEDEN.

PART I.

GÖTEBORG.

THERE is hardly any spectacle in the European world more animated than the field of glorious water that runs like a vein of green malachite between Copenhagen and the Swedish coast. It is filled with innumerable sea-craft of every description, going and coming, tacking and tugging, in every direction, while the water so beautifully ripples and rolls and covers itself with an infinite water-lily of foam that the artist's eye is delighted and the poet's imagination fevered with the spangled and tumultuous motion. The strait is like a mighty trumpet through which immeasurable wind blows—a huge pneumatic tube drawing in draughts from the Atlantic and pouring them up the Baltic, sometimes with resistless force. There is continual agitation in the Cattegat and Skager-Rack. The water seems to take on a human joyousness, and leaps and laughs with living light. It is exquisitely sensitive water to impinging sunlight or to wan and wasting cloud. It is sometimes so black in gloomy weather that the ships that sail on it seem sailing on a thunderstorm; but in a moment a marvellous transformation takes place, and the thunderstorm is smiled away into the loveliest sunlight. I have noticed the same volatilization of thunderstorms— so to speak—in Scotland, where a few rays of shattering sunlight will scatter themselves like luminous quicklime over half an horizon of cloud, and eat it almost instantaneously away.

Although the Sound is thus replete with sea-vessels of every sort trafficking and travelling to the ends of the world, the Danes, like the English in their Channel navigation, have no passenger-ships of any great size to take tourists across to the Swedish coast. Many of such passenger-boats as they have are mere coasting steamers, small, dirty, uncomfortable, seesawing like a political newspaper first to one side and then to the other—a sort of oscillating dungeon rocking you into unutterable nausea. The results of such oscillations are not to be described. The weak, weary and tremulous pilgrim is only too glad to catch sight of huge looming shores that in the lens of the evening light look strangely spectral. Our plan was to cross to the south-west of Sweden and land at Göteborg, go from there by rail to Stockholm, and then return—arterial blood-like—through the heart of Sweden, visiting the lakes and making pilgrimages along the canals to various places of interest. As we steamed on in the dim dilating evening light we could catch glimpses of the mountains veiled in tremulous gauzes of mist that occasionally melted into weak rain, and then opened and revealed the most beautifully vivid green. Some time in the night we dropped in at some remote port on a fjord, anchored for a few moments in a sluggish canal, and then put to sea again in our steam-churn. The same evening we ran into a delightful breezy little Swedish watering-place and took on a Swedish bridal-party. They had a band of musicians, and the tremulous sweetness of the soft and pathetic music has remained with me as a souvenir of the trip. There is something peculiarly sad, joyous and strange in this Swedish music. Perhaps there are reminiscences of the vikings and the old heroic life and the vanished sagas, mingled with a throb or two of that passionate pagan clinging of theirs, that come to melodious resurrection in these bright harmonic sound-pictures, and touch the listener with

TYSKA KYRKAN, GÖTEBORG.

mirth and mournfulness. If, however, I remember aright, our oscillating dungeon soon proved fatal to the newly-initiated pair, and sounds not of "revelry by night" came from their state-room. What an ogre is the sea, that turns the honeymoon into a moon of gall, and blows all the sweet breath out of life!

As we steamed up the Cattegat we caught sight of seals lying among the

NORRA HAMNGATAN, GÖTEBORG.

rocks, but on our approach they disappeared. Early in the morning we ran up a long gray tongue of fog-hidden water, and braced ourselves to the Göteborg dock while the rain and the sea-spray scattered plentifully in our faces.

It is not a particularly delectable sight to see a new and strange land for the first time through a mist. Not even a London fog can idealize away all the immense oppression that a stranger feels on slipping like a drop into the sea of unimagined existence that awaits him. Had my first glimpse of Sweden been a sunlit glimpse — as it was afterward when I visited Göteborg again — how different would have been the first impressions! As it was, we saw people groping about in a sort of mud twilight, waterproofed and umbrella-ed from head to foot, dripping in the chill air of Arctic summer and submerged in the oozy inundation of the mist. It seemed to us like a lacustrine, amphibious world, with seal-like men and women energetically moving about on what looked like land, but proved on nearer acquaintance to be unfathomable mud. To increase our perplexities, we could not find a hotel, or the hotel that we did find—with its sad little rows of Siberian firs firmly planted in green boxes set in rows in front like a sort of make-believe forest—was full. We were told we might dine there if we pleased, but we didn't please, and had to trot off to some outlandish part of the town in search of other lodgings. And here began a series of grimaces, gesticulations, broken Swedish, wild despair, unutterable misunderstandings, but final triumph. They stared and we stared, and then we were carried up flights of stone stairs and along brick-paved passages into a room like a parish prison. There was no water, no towel, no basin; and as for the bed, I think it was still warm with somebody that had just left it. We looked through dingy windows into a stable-yard, but did not dare lift the windows. We could not get a drop of coffee or anything else in the house. Strange men and stranger women came mincing and mouthing in, admiring our outlandish ways and perhaps taking us for a brace of convicts. I felt forlorn. A feeling of utter disappointment crept through my numbed senses. Outside it was hideous—inside it was diabolical. I

GUSTAF ADOLF'S STATUE, GÖTEBORG.

summoned all I had of Swedish up from the vasty deep, but I found they had no more idea of what I was saying than if I had been a Samojede. We were grateful, however, that they did not drive us out of the house into the street. After a while, when we had parted with certain reminiscences of the steamer, we sallied forth to see what was to be seen, or rather to eat what was to be eaten, for a mighty hunger had come upon us meantime since we had stormed the Swedish citadel and found it swept and garnished.

All Göteborg, I found—or all the unclaimed, un-familied, old-bachelor part— led a sort of Bohemian life, and while they slept at what they called "home," seemed to breakfast, dine, and sup at the various restaurants. This seems to be a peculiarity of Swedish life. What the women live on I cannot imagine. The restaurants are of every class and fashion. Our eyes opened at the enormous eating and drinking. The Eskimo are said to consume daily two gallons of blubber and to have a pelvic capacity equal to forty pounds of veal at one meal. The Swedes almost startled us into believing this; or were we bewitched? When we were at dessert our companions would still be wrestling with soup. No nation grapples with dinner like the Swedish. The delicate birdlike appetite of an Italian, satisfied as he is with a string of macaroni and a glass of sunlight, must be absolutely phenomenal to these people. Pounds of food seemed to disappear under their magical mastication—food, too, well mellowed with wine. The Swedes are famous drinkers, and one of the national traits is an abounding conviviality. From this perhaps it comes that they are a somewhat loose people.

I found Göteborg extremely modern and extremely commercial, but I was surprised when the mist lifted to find what an environment of charming scenery it is set in. It is only a place of sixty thousand inhabitants, but it is in some respects superior to Stockholm. It is very rich in manufactures of all kinds. The town lies in a luxuriant valley between bare rocks that lift themselves in fantastic ruggedness about its outskirts. It is a place of ancient memories, with a history—burnt, besieged and rebuilt as the town has been several times—extending into a misty antiquity. The place is not healthy, in spite of the beauty of its situation. Charles IX. in 1607 constructed the new city of Göteborg after the model of the Dutch cities, and peopled it with strangers. There are numerous canals bordered by trees and palatial residences. Looking down the Södra Hamngatan, which is the finest street in the city, there is a striking perspective toward the east. The canal with its migratory population of boats lies before you, with the broad street bordered on both sides by a fringe of palaces; then the bridges, the quays and the avenues; on the right the Great Square (called nearly always *torget*, or market-place), with the elegant bourse, the residence of the commandant, and the German church (Tyska Kyrkan), where the great Rutger von Ascheberg reposes. In the distance is the Göte-Elf (River *Elbe*). There are many bright and busy streets, prominent among which is the Norra Hamngatan with its canal, quays and handsome houses. Fogelberg's great bronze statue of Gustaf Adolf, erected in 1854, adorns the principal square. The graceful Engelska Kyrkan (English church), constructed under the superintendence of Major Edelsvärd, is a pretty object in the Göteborg landscape.

There are lovely gardens in the suburbs, and the same long delightful roads and lanes bordered by limes and elms that I had noticed in Denmark. The Swedes are a simple-hearted, laughter-loving people, and they make as much as possible of their short summer. The town abounds in commercial enterprises of every sort, full of ships, canals and factories —a busy, unpoetic life, relieved on Sundays by theatres and operas, to which everybody goes as a matter of course. I remember a delightful evening passed in one of the pleasant gardens, while a band played soothingly and the long light fell out over luxuriant green shrubberies and bewildering flowers—a garden full of happy people, full of a sort of old Greek Anacreontic spirit, sweet and sunny as any picnic party in Italy. It is in these brilliant bits of summer that the Swedes lay up stores of sunshine for the long and relentless winter—a winter which is a sort of hyperborean twilight illumined by the dazzling shadow-dance of the aurora borealis.

ENGELSKA KYRKAN, GÖTEBORG.

The Swedes are constitutionally sunny-tempered. There is lurking in their constitution that drop of golden light which transforms a dew-drop into a lens —a highly imaginative, sociable, sensuous people, supplementing their bleak climate by every resource of art and culture. Swedish poetry abounds in rich pictorial effects, and yet it has the silvery spirituality of the most unsensuous German ballad. We may look almost in vain through the Greek and Latin poets for any recognition of the superb Mediterranean landscapes that must continually have impinged on their physical consciousness, and yet did not result in the multiplicity of imagery and image-making that we are rainbowed with in the modern school of poets. Their words do not give off that oblique iridescence which is as much a matter of the spirit as any other occult delight, but which the hard texture of their words and thoughts is unfamiliar with. In Theocritus there are delicious hints and buds of landscape painting always *about* to blossom into pictures—a warm, sensuous, silken glamour of sea and sky—an occasional but entirely incidental intrusion of the magical Sicilian scenery by which his life was enatmosphered. But there is none of the elaborate consciousness of the manifold brightness and beauty of the outside world that we gather from any poet of the nineteenth century.

Swedish literature is penetrated with this love of scenery. It is the same with the Norwegian writer Björnson and the Norwegian writers in general. We see the same feeling morbidly intensified when Danes or Swedes journey from their own pale climate to the lands of the South—Hans Andersen, for example, who in his *Improvisatore* shows that he was so bewitched by Italy, and throws off his impressions in pages of impassioned description. The *Improvisatore*, in fact, is a divine Dionysiac sort of book, full of spiritual brilliance and frenzy, full of the supreme effervescence of deified youth. Montaigne said that the simple gazing on a healthy person communicates health. So it seems to me the mere opening of their eyes on Italy endows Swedes and Danes with rare imagination.

The part of Sweden in which Göteborg

ON THE GÖTEBORG AND STOCKHOLM RAILROAD.

lies is full of grain and green fields, and a culture so soft and luxurious that it reminds one of parts of France. The country is mountainous, but everywhere up the mountains there run curving valleys full of rye and wheat that leave behind their lines of sinuous and suggestive green. There are a South and a North to Sweden as different as the South and the North with us. The Lapps and Finns in the extreme North dream of this, to them, delicious Arcadia of the South of Sweden as of something fairylike and unattainable. In the North life is so hard, so bitter, so hopeless: it is a life shared with wolves, bears and reindeer —a life that reduces people to live or the ground bark of trees, grovel in huts two-thirds of the year, and become stunted, abject and miserable. For centuries —and centuries strangely near ours—these northern provinces were strongholds of paganism. The vivid hereditary prejudices of the Finns and Lapps crop out in sharp controversies with the Swedes and Norwegians. A Swedish or Norwegian woman who marries one of these people has to learn his language, there being sounds in the Scandinavian, simple as these sounds are, unpronounce-

SÖDERTELGE.

able to the mountaineers. They possess a plaintive ballad literature and a language that has fifteen cases. Our words *fiend* and *fiendish* are said to be connected with *Finn* and *Finnish*—a designation derived from the homeliness of the nation. Their swart skins, blue-black eyes and squat figures make a *tout ensemble* that richly justifies the etymology. It is said to be difficult to get into their confidence, so suspicious and sinister are they in many cases—a race upon whom the radiations of Christianity have played but faintly. Their country is a country of vast voluminous mountains, frozen and inaccessible except to them—a strange scene of elemental glory and grimness, where the most vivid magnetic storms light up the horizon and startle even the drowsy Lapp with their ghostly magnificence. These displays of electric phenomena resemble a huge æolian harp turned into light, so infinitely still and fitful are they as they flash out into sudden seas of light.

The Swedes are blissfully unconscious of American luxuriousness in railway travelling. They at least seem to remember that *travel* and *travail* are one and the same word. I remember with feverish vividness the night we spent in going from Göteborg to Stockholm—the strange cries, the frequent stoppings, the uniformed conductor with a tiny oil-lamp fixed on his breast like a *boutonnière*, the dim lines of vanishing mountains, the fantastic-looking people and villages we passed, the melodious accents of the Swedish tongue with its intonations voluptuous almost as the Tuscan, the swift, silent rivers the train sped over, and the great number of lakes we passed,—all blending as in the febrile phantasmagory of an opium-dream. It was a bouquet of confused impressions. When we meandered out into daylight, after a while we saw a country almost perfectly bald of trees—a peculiarity which Sweden shares with Italy—thinly populated, with vast stretches of weary, watery horizon and a scantiness of evidences of life that surprised me. The houses were principally one-storied, thatched and low: there seemed to be few or no fences—which is the case also in Germany—and the culture was rude and primitive. The Italian peasant still drags about the plough we read of in the *Georgics* of Virgil, and combs the ground with his superficial harrow precisely as when he sunned himself in the *aurea regna* of Augustus. So the Swedish peasant, mixing his meal with ground beech-bark and eating five or six times a day, clings to

STOCKHOLM IN THE SIXTEENTH CENTURY. (FROM AN OLD ENGRAVING.)

the barbarous implements of the Vasas as he does to their memories, and finds it hard to give up the ancestral mode of agriculture. The wonderful advances the Swedes have recently made in civilization were amply illustrated last year at Philadelphia. We have all heard of their astonishing success in mining, their vast iron- and copper-mines, their silver and lumber, their model school-houses and their pauperism. A specialist would no doubt find much in their foundries and manufactories that would show the utmost scientific spirit. The biting air has kindled science in them, and forced it to a thousand ingenious applications. But in travelling over the face of the country there is an apparent and oppressive absence of all this. The interior of Sweden looks like a country just harvested. Great richness, except mineral richness, is not in the soil, and cannot be brought out of it except by the most thorough fertilization.

The lakes are immense: one of them is ninety, another fifty, miles in length. Yet Switzerland can throw more beauty into a few furlongs of magical water than we find in all these desolate miles. The water is that shallow, sandy-haired sort without depth enough to make it luminously blue, and with that interminable gray in horizon and sky that fatigues the eye. I was disappointed in the great lakes of Sweden. In the far North there are bits of exquisite water full of eerie and savage beauty—mountain-locked Undines that have gathered their shining spiritualities under the curves of enormous cliffs, and are hidden away from the blowing sunlight. There is laughter of fern and gleam of sea-bird about them, while the wild shock of the rain impinges on the septentrional sunlight and suffuses the heavens with orange mist. These atoms of beauty tucked away among the fjelds and fjords are remote from summer pilgrims, unless like true knights they brave the heroic mountains and snatch them from their isolation. As we journeyed on to Stockholm, one after another of the larger lakes came in sight, as gray and gaunt as a Scottish moor, and not even with that silver sidelook that most water has when seen

THE ROYAL CASTLE, STOCKHOLM.

aslant. There appeared to be few waterfowl, though in the mountain-lakes of the North they are countless — just a flat, dull prairie of water. How the Swedes can be so poetic with all this load of fog-producing water is a psychological problem. Of course the exhalations from these waters are full of malaria. They haul up an endless fog, and spread it thick as butter over the whole land. To have one's life thus overlaid with fog would certainly create discontent with us.

A constitutional monarchy like the Swedish, however, can exist as well in fog as in sunshine — perhaps better. There are no nervous revolutionary tendencies, no spasms of sudden self-consciousness, no flaming and fulminat-

NORRBRO.

ing. The Swedes quietly convoke their Diet, or their "Big Thing" (*Storthing*), as they call it—the other provincial ones suggesting by contrast the title "Little Things"—in the winter of every year, and dream of no revolution except to keep down gynocracy. Their experience of Queen Christina appears to have made a profound impression, for by their new constitution of 1807 they relentlessly established the Salic law. The succession is hereditary, though they can elect a foreigner in case of extinction of the reigning race. The king is put under solemn oath to be a Lutheran; which Church no sooner found itself enjoying pre-eminence than it began to persecute, turning Catholics out of doors, elevating its own archbishop into a sort of pope, excluding Protestant dissenters from many important offices, and going about with bell, book and candle to fumigate (so to speak) other pestiferous churches. For centuries the bishops have been true spiritual sovereigns, genuine tetrarchs mayhap, not at all averse, when circumstances permitted, to order a murder of the innocents. The Catholics were emancipated five years ago—a little later than our slaves—and may now be elected if anybody would vote for them. The Jews are, I think, still knocking at the social and political door. Since Norway and Sweden were united in 1814 the Norwegians have rid themselves of a titled class, and their constitution is now the most republican in Europe. The king made a vain attempt to inflict a noble order on the people when their own nobility became extinct; but this stalwart people in a fit of splenetic exaltation rebelled, and there is now not a sprig of titled pedigree in the land.

When the king goes to visit his Norwegian subjects he is often received and entertained by the grand peasants who date their lineage from the vikings and receive their king on terms of equality. It is a beautiful patriarchal relation—a relation full of the hoariness and the homeliness of antique times, full also of a grand but unconscious recognition of human dignity. It is a fine illustration, too, of the etymology of the word king—*i. e.* "one who is the kinsman of all his people."

In Sweden education is compulsory from the age of nine, and in case of persistent neglect the children are taken from their parents and sent to boarding-schools, while the parents are made to pay their board. The Swedish government is determined—and very properly determined—to extinguish ignorance. It has established a complete hierarchy of schools, at all of which tuition is free, from the lowest elementary schools up to the two great universities of Upsala and Lund. The school-houses are quite famous for neatness and completeness. It has been hard, however, to keep down a certain French flippancy that has pervaded and perverted the literature for more than a hundred years. The modern Swedish literature, indeed, may almost be said to have quickened and germinated from the French, just as the great school of modern Germans received in the eighteenth century its chief stimulus from Shakespeare, Milton and Goldsmith. Every Swede has a crumb or two of French which he is particularly proud of, but through this veneering looms the wild, fresh Scandinavian imagination, as sharply individualized as the infinite breath of their heather-bloom.

The bills one gets at the Swedish hotels are truly polyglot, as much French and English and as little Swedish as possible. One always has an uneasy feeling that one is being cheated, and cheated, too, in two or three different languages in one and the same bill. It is really necessary to carry a variety of small pocket dictionaries to work one's way successfully through a Swedish bill of fare. On the right hand there is always a formidable array of what look like dollars and cents, but this is always ingeniously couched in Swedish, in order perhaps that the foreigner may understand as little of it as possible. Although when you arrive you may look

KARL. XII.'S BILDSTOD.

like a millionaire, you are, unless you make voluminous objections, relentlessly consigned to a garret up five flights of stairs, the servant comforting you on the way up by describing the charming view. The view from the Kung Carl, after we had passed the pretty station of Södertelge on the lake and arrived at Stockholm, *was* charming. Europe from an attic is not at first blush so alluring, but when the preliminary indignation and humiliation at being taken up so high have evaporated, then comes in the most enjoyable part of the trip—inspection of the quaint furniture, reading the quaint regulations, linguistic combats with the unintelligible waiter, and gazing down into the delightful streets.

Stockholm lacks the magnificent sunny sweep of the Bay of Naples: it lacks, too, the voluptuous light of Italy that so wonderfully gilds and soothes an Italian landscape into a scene of silken beauty. But with the exception of Naples and Edinburgh it is the most nobly-situated capital of Europe. The Mälar Lake, on whose pregnant emerald slopes it lies— or rather in and about which Stockholm runs like an incrustation of rare repoussé-work—is, on a limited scale, a miniature St. Lawrence, full of islands, turreted and twisted into a thousand insular eccentricities, fantastic with foam and firs, covered with the richest umbrage, bright with castles and châteaux, and made alive by a singularly vivacious population. Stockholm itself is a string of islands linked together by bridges. The crowning architectural feature of the town is the Slottet, or royal residence, built upon a lofty islet and commanding the whole scene with its massive square walls. A beautiful causeway, the Norr-

THE RIDDARHOLMS BRIDGE, STOCKHOLM.

bro, lined by low shops and leading down by a stairway to the famous Strömparterre, connects it with the great square and royal theatre. It is one of the finest sights imaginable to stand on this causeway and watch the tide of people drifting over, the thronging ships and steamers in the winding lake beneath, and the brilliant and buoyant life all around.

The royal castle is a many-sided monster: a vast library, a museum, splendid state apartments and a sumptuous hall are contained within its huge quadrangle. European palaces are not prepossessing in general: they look like immense jails —penitentiaries for princes—with no end of cobwebbed window-glass, and habitable only here and there in certain suites of rooms, like oases in a desert. The quays around and beneath the Slottet are lined with Russian, Danish, Dutch and English ships. Statues of Gustavus Adolphus, Gustavus Vasa and Charles XII.—a remarkable one of the latter by Molin, surrounded by four mortars captured in his wars, stands in the Place Charles XII.—are as numerous as the bronze dukes of Wellington in London, prancing to battle in every square and charging unimaginable enemies on brazen steeds. This apotheosis of brass is really becoming intolerable. One can hardly take a step in continental towns but heroes and martyrs are grimacing and pirouetting from pyramids of granite. The statue of Charles XII., though striking enough in itself, is on a singularly low pedestal. A fine fountain, also by Molin, and a statue of Charles XIII. adorn the same sunny and sylvan square. A little alley leads to the square commemorative of the great chemist Berzelius.

The beauty of Stockholm is its blending of rushing melodic water, towering islands and rich umbrageous suburbs. Its island-clusters are girded by a perpetual sinuous sunlight of changeful water.

GLIMPSES OF SWEDEN.

CONCLUDING PART.

HASSELBACKEN.

THERE are delicious gardens all about Stockholm—gardens full of summer and summer theatres and Arcadian walks everywhere bordering on bright rushing water and filled with mighty beech trees and Norwegian firs. One of the most famous of these resorts is Hasselbacken, a bit of the celebrated Djurgården, which commands an unrivalled view of panoramic Stockholm. Near by is the magnificent old oak called Bellman's Oak, from Bellman, the national Swedish poet, who used to sit here in the gray hours of the last century and play his inimitable guitar. There is a statue of him in the grounds of the Djurgården, and the whole place is garrulous with his bacchic spirit. The air is gay with music. Omnibuses and vapeurs-omnibus carry you everywhere for a mere trifle. There is a hectic flush in the summer of Sweden. The flowers are feverishly bright, and one may well believe there is no lack of them in the land of Linnæus.

The Djurgård which I have mentioned is a town of restaurants, concert-houses, puppet-plays and pavilions, full all the summer long of pedestrians and promenaders. After the long chrysalis slumber of winter the Swedes emerge brilliant as butterflies, smitten with a sort of fury of pleasure brief and vivid as a flower whose whole autobiography is its perfume. This yearning for color, passion and pleasure is what strikes the traveller particularly in them. It may be turned into the Attis-like spiritual inebriation of Swedenborg, whose catalepsy, like Mohammed's, has become a religion; or into the purely scientific passion of Berzelius; or into the exquisite outlining of Tegnér's poetry—a poetry pale and pregnant and perfect as the silver thread of the new moon. It is always distinctly and recognizably there. I felt it as I walked through the ancient house in Upsala where the great Linnæus had dwelt thirty-five years delving among the herbs and flowers, and receiving the paltry title of knight of the Polar Star in recognition of his *System of Nature*. The same enthusiasm leaps up into flamelike exaltation in the wonderful achievements of the Swedish generals.

I have never seen a place that had so many striking situations for churches and public buildings as Stockholm, while the island altitudes and isolated heights, the perpetual shimmer of sunny water everywhere, the long railway bridges leaping the Mälar, and the incessant steaming to and fro of miniature propellers conveying passengers from one part of the town and from one island to another, give motion and variety to every view. The streets are narrow, and frequently interrupted by windings of the Mälar Lake. Much of the architecture has a Cinque-cento look. There is no lack of handsome modern buildings, however, such as the Technological Institute and Blanch's café, where the Stockholmers go for the excellent after-dinner music. There is an air of the Middle Ages in the famous Riddarholmskyrkan (the Westminster Abbey of Sweden), the Svea Hofrättet and the strange-looking inns and wharves. Charles Lamb would have been delighted with their rubbish, their antiquities, their embalmed memorials of a great past and their odd incon-

BELLMAN'S OAK AT HASSELBACKEN.

gruities of the present. We could feel that we were in the land of Jenny Lind and Christine Nilsson, for the August air seemed full of nightingales, and there was a suavity and a sweetness in the manners of the people that sprang from an unseen depth of rhythmic sensibilities.

There float about in my memory many pleasant days spent in rambling about the old town; gazing in at the bookstalls and print-shop windows; wondering at the marvellously artistic way in which the butchers dress up their meats; strolling into dim seventeenth-century churches; stopping at old-fashioned inns to get a cup of coffee, and peeping and poking about after the fashion of a weasel. The fine new National Museum, with its elegant vestibule and rich treasures, came in for its share of attention, and a glamour of delightful pictures, statuary and engravings hovers before my mind's eye still. I have never seen a more beautifully arranged museum, a museum more full of cheerfulness and luminousness, with the bright sun streaming in on the antique armor and kindling all the relics of the dusky past into vivid and silent life. The portico is of green Swedish marble, with ornaments in bas-relief, statues of Tessin

BELLMAN'S STATUE.

and Sergel and busts of Fogelberg, Ehrenstahl, Linnæus, Tegnér, Berzelius and

TECHNOLOGICAL INSTITUTE.

Wallin. There are elegant columns of Italian marble in the great vestibule and salles within. The cost of the structure was two million two hundred thousand rixdalers. Collections of engravings and original drawings, majolica and antique vases, galleries of sculpture ancient and modern, collections of models and plaster casts, galleries of paintings and historical costumes, colossal statues of Odin, Thor and Balder, valuable antiquities from the Stone, Iron and Bronze Ages, mediæval objects of art, coins, armor, are some of the things gathered into this fine building. There are some beautiful modern sculptures, chiefly of the Swedish school

STOCKHOLM, FROM MOSEBACKE.

—among them the *Wrestlers* of Molin. There are also many vivid glimpses of old Swedish life and legend dramatically thrown on canvas. The Swedish school seems particularly rich in landscapes, most of which are a rich reflex of that Southern tropic life that has built its nest among the lilies of Florence or found its types in the bazaars of Constantinople. There are also many scientific and tech nological schools. The old theatre where Jenny Lind made her first appearance stands in the great Gustave Adolphe Place, opposite the crown-prince's residence, with the Hôtel Rydberg on one side and the Castle beyond the Norrbro on the other.

Miss Bremer lived at Stockholm, and with her sister Agathe dispensed a liberal hospitality, after they had both fossilized into something like heroic old-maidhood. Swedish literary annals are full of such remarkable women, working wondrously to reform their people. In fact, the general public know the Swedes chiefly by their celebrated women, by their singers and novel-writers. Many delightful bits have

himself. The old Icelandic *sagas*, written in a language common at the time of their composition to Danes, Swedes and Norwegians, have been finely trans-

BLANCH'S CAFÉ.

lated into German by Simrock, and have given to Carlyle much of his most bizarre imagery. It is a weird, wild, half-demonic poetry, the infinite babble of talking and toiling jötuns—the rhythm of the sea and the sharpness of death. The Sibylline books must have been such Edda-utterances. I know of nothing in the glittering mythologies of the South so fine as the grand allegory of Yggdrasil, the Tree of Life.

Thirty-five years ago there were few hotels in Sweden. Before one's day was done one had to visit three or four places for one's meals. The hotels, such as they were, were called "cellars" (*källare*). You seldom dined where you slept. One had to go to a con-

NATIONAL MUSEUM.

been translated by Longfellow, Mary Howitt and others, but the language is so easy of acquisition that any ordinary linguist can easily learn it and judge for

fectioner's for one's coffee and chocolate, to a wine-merchant for one's drinks, and to a restaurant for the midday meal This trotting about resulted in a fine appetite. Wherever you went were the fumes of the national drink, a sweet, potent punch, put up in dainty little bottles and thick and clear. "Swenska punsch" soon makes the head swim. It and macadamized roads run in all directions. There are all the modern and improved ways of losing your life—bursting reservoirs, collisions, explosions and capsizings. A universal suffrage of death has been established here as elsewhere. Rotten boilers, snags in rivers, boats brilliant with kerosene light, headlong speed and careless pilots are not unknown in Sweden.

The habit of lunching in the very presence of dinner, of going to a side table and eating your fill of anchovies, raw herrings, smoked beef and cold eel-pie while dinner is on the very table, still prevails, and is hardly conducive to health. It is said that the habit of taking "a sup," as the Swedes call it, arose from the scarcity of delicacies. It was hard to get enough of any one nice thing to make a meal of; so you were first delicately innuendoed off to the brandy-table (as it is called), and then allowed to sit down to dinner. The practice is universal in Sweden. Private houses, hotels and boarding-houses, all feed you on preliminary scraps, and woe be to you if you innocently turn away from the proffered luncheon! You fare like an ascetic and feed yourself on odors. The ordinary routine of dining seems in Sweden to be in wild confusion. Soup sometimes ends instead of beginning the dinner. Iced soups and cold fish are dainties to the Scandinavian palate. Much of the soup is nauseously sweet, flavored with cherries, raspberries

LOWER VESTIBULE OF THE NATIONAL MUSEUM.

is sweet as squills, odorous as rum. Before railroads were built passengers were forwarded by post-horses and carrioles, the animals for which had to be furnished in seed-time and harvest by the peasantry under pain of fines. Provisions had to be carried by the traveller, and still have to be in some parts of the peninsula. Generally, however, things are now very different. Canals, railroads, steamboats and gooseberries, often with macaroon cakes and spikes of cinnamon floating wildly about in it. This is eaten as a sort of dessert, and is cold and often beautifully clear. If Heine bitterly reviled the English for bringing vegetables on the table *au naturel*, there is no such complaint to be made here. Heaven, earth and hell are eaten with sauce — s a u c e s red, white and blue, green, yellow and black — s a u c e s celestial and s a u c e s infernal. Strange combinations of ice-cream heaped over delicious appletarts, or strange dishes of berry-juice boiled down and mixed with farina, sugar and almonds, then cooled, moulded and turned out into b a s i n s of cream, to be eaten with c r u s h e d sugar and wine, appear at the end of dinner. The Swedes share with the Danes and Arabs a passionate f o n d n e s s for sweetmeats. Everything is slightly sweet: e v e n green peas are sugared, as well as the innumerable tea- a n d coffee-cakes, so that long before the unhappy tourist has finished his tour he is a hopeless dyspeptic or a raging Swedophobe.

The manners of the people are exceptionally affectionate. The Danes object to the Swedes because they are so gushing. The language is full of pet names, terms of endearment, titillating diminutives and tender synonyms. In no language, not even in Greek, can a man be so covered with a sweet icing of flattery, and the Swedish women are adepts in this art. The language is very musical. There is an undulation of intonation, a rising and falling of silvery inflections, a predominance of soft, silken-footed vowels, which give a peculiar suavity to intercourse and stand in bold contrast with the heroic cast of the Swedish historic achievements. The love of music

"THE WRESTLERS" OF MOLIN (NATIONAL MUSEUM).

has taken deep root among the people. Everybody sings, fiddles, dances and belongs to a musical club.

Travellers have noticed the clumsy household arrangements of the Swedes — the loose and careless building, the rough woodwork and primitive implements — all pointing to indifference engendered by long habit and inaccessible to artistic influences. This, however, is gradually disappearing, and the Swedish houses are no longer, as they used to be, heaps of miscellaneous lumber crazily put together. French taste under Bernadotte and his successors has softened the barbarism of the Vasas, and one finds one's self in apartments as luxuriously and tastefully furnished as anywhere else in the world. Improvements are going on in hotel-life. Stockholm contains half a dozen fine hotels, and one of great elegance, the Grand Hotel, rivalling in beauty and extent the magnificent mass of the royal castle. Watering-places, baths, spas and seaside resorts are numerous. A visit to the baths is not only an essential element in the life of Miss Carlén's and Miss Bremer's heroines, but a general annual habit with the better-conditioned classes. Of course there is nothing to compare with the gorgeous châteaux on the Mediterranean, the lovely half-moon of the Bay

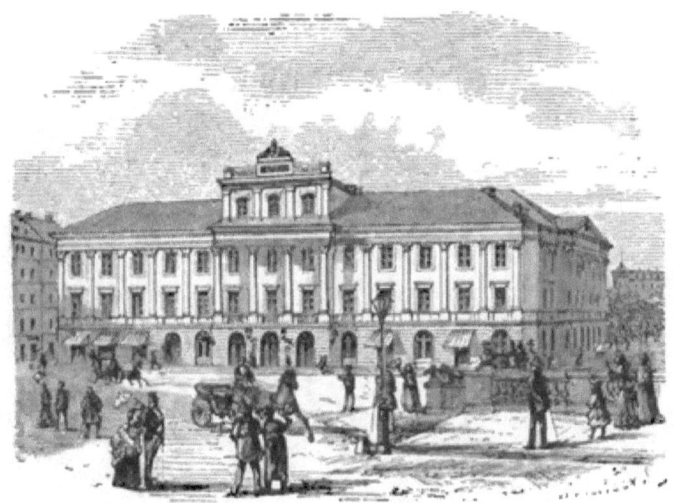

ROYAL THEATRE.

of Naples or the Arcadian snugness of a Swiss water-cure; but neither are the Swedes so critical. They content themselves with unpretentious accommodations, a bit of cultivated Eden to promenade in, a band of music and quantities of gossip. With these a month is agreeably passed, and then the return-journey takes place.

If England is the most aristocratic of European nations, Sweden is the country most exuberantly devoted to titles, to minute exactions of etiquette and to all their attendant absurdities. It is said that the title "Your Ladyship" is given even to the wives of second lieutenants and clerks. Your Excellency, Your Grace, Your Serenity, Your Transparency, succeed one another in bewildering profusion at a metropolitan ball. There will be bitter disputes as to whether an American minister, for example, has the right to the title Excellency. Amusement for an entire evening will be culled from the controversy whether Mrs. Chose is *Fru* or *Fröken* or Madame or Mademoiselle or Grace. And the poor woman may be left dangling in the seventh heaven of beatific expectation for months before her place in society is finally settled.

Among the nobility pride and pedigree exist in all their rigor, but the traveller notices a singular lack of those ancestral châteaux which so picturesquely overhang the rivers of France and everywhere embellish the delightful rural scenery of England. The red, turf-covered cabins of the peasants, with their one story and small garden, are unrelieved by quaint Gothic villas or towering Elizabethan mansions. The fanciful and picture-like costumes of the Middle Ages have almost disappeared.

The condition of the lower orders in

Sweden has long excited the notice of political economists. Drunkenness and debauchery and criminality have long prevailed among them, wedded to an external decency that renders these vices still worse. Few countries are more opulent in figures that tell against itself. The archives are stored with statistics that present a singular self-revelation. The Delphic injunction is carried out with a vengeance, but the self-knowledge seems of little avail. Still, great improvements have taken place since the classification of crimes a few years ago and the estab-

GRAND HOTEL.

lishment of penitentiaries by the late king, Charles XV. Lunatic asylums, asylums for blind and deaf and hospitals for sick and indigent abound. In 1870 there were over two hundred thousand paupers in a population of little over four millions. The peasants make their own household implements, clothes and tools. Special provinces are renowned for special things —furniture, watches, cotton and woollen tissues, cut stone and marble, and mining industries. As soon as you set foot in Sweden you are saluted with the odor of fish. Salted salmon—the famous *Halensta-lax*—is a universal tidbit, and herring, cod and other fish impregnate the air. Of course game abounds in the northern provinces: bears, foxes, reindeer, hares, partridges, woodcock and wild duck contribute to the animation of the vast forests. Six or seven canals, of great length sometimes, meander through the heart of Sweden, and, as in Holland, the eye is seldom without the pleasing sight of bright or fantastic sails threading their way through the landscape. Telegraph-wires stretch everywhere, and internal improvements are progressing rapidly.

From Stockholm we took a small steamer and went to the ancient University of Upsala, passing on the way the lovely château of Drottningholm. Upsala was the old pagan capital of Sweden, and in the vicinity are still shown three immense mounds where tradition says Odin, Thor and Balder are buried. A strange old ruinous church of great age stands near the spot, looking as if it might have been built by Odin himself. There was a pleasant little thatched inn near by, with a garden full of gillyflowers, where we stopped and drank some genuine Scandinavian mead out of huge drinking-horns presented by Bernadotte. There was a legend on them telling how many illustrious folk had drunk from their mammoth sinuosities — dukes, princes and what not. We soon satisfied our curiosity with the

CHÂTEAU KÄRNAN.

mead, and went to visit the house of Linnæus, the large, two-towered cathedral and the famous library of the university. The chief treasure—and a veritable *chef d'œuvre* it is—is the *Codex argenteus* of Ulfilas, a translation of the New Testament into Gothic on purple parchment in letters of silver. The university maintains fifteen hundred students, and has a famous glee-club which won the prize at Vienna.

Upsala is reached from Stockholm by rail or by canal, the latter of which passes part of the time through charming scenery. The summer twilight of this high northern region seems almost endless, ending at midnight, with daybreak at two. Our experience on the steam canalboats was delightful. We took one at Stockholm, and went down through the heart of the country in and out of what appeared innumerable lakes and islands to our original starting-point, Göteborg. The canal-boats are "Tiny Tims" of water-craft, with three decks, handsome state-rooms, dining-room and hurricane-deck, and move swiftly, without much washing of the banks. These banks are lined with mountain-birch, just then crimson-spotted everywhere with bright warm bunches of berries. This canal is, in fact, a series of canals which connect the Mälar, Wener and Wetter lakes. The greatest height attained is one hundred and thirty-four feet, and there are numerous admirably arranged locks.

The interior of Sweden is unpicturesque. The great central railroad traverses a region replete with mines and mining industries, and ends finally at Helsingförs, in whose vicinity lie the lovely ruins of the Château Kärnan, and over the Sound the low-looming flats of Copenhagen and Elsinore. Not until the canal debouches into the Göta-Elf does the canal-scape wake up. Then there is a glorious bit of parenthetic scenery. The canal is constructed round the falls of the Göta-Elf (Trollhätta), the glimmer of whose beautiful white tumbling water is a radiant vision in these gloomy woods. It is a scene of exquisite savageness, gloom and beauty. The fall is one hundred and twelve feet, extending in four breaks over thirty-six hundred feet in length. At the bottom it subsides into the glasslike Göta River, which we follow down to Göteborg. On the way the steamer passes Kongelf, formerly the capital of Norway, and the ruins of the château of Balmö, the most romantic and the most colossal in Sweden.

JAMES A. HARRISON.

TRY NORWAY!

PEASANT-WOMEN.   HAYMAKER OF ELFDAL.

A JOLLY party of Americans stepped off the deck of a steamer at Liverpool the other day, so to speak, full of warm enthusiasm and high glee at the pleasant prospect of a three months' holiday life abroad. They were to "do" London and Paris, of course; Switzerland and Italy, maybe; Scotland, sure. To some of them all these localities were quite familiar; others of the party were novices in foreign travel, and knew neither the half-moon slope of Regent street quadrant nor the gaslit arcades of the Rue de Rivoli. There was novelty enough before these persons, of course, and they would not have been willing to spare the sight of one shop on the Boulevards for the promise of a view of Schliemann's site of ancient Troy. Paris, London, Lucerne and Florence were places of enough interest for them, said these saucy young folks, with each a self-sufficient toss of his or her good-looking head. But while the elders certainly looked forward with great pleasure to visiting these delightful places again, they nevertheless yearned after fresh fields to follow.

We were talking about it as we rode to London in a railway-carriage which we had occupants enough to fill, and which therefore we were privileged in ticketing "Private"—the word written

A GIRL-ROWER.

in blue pencil on the back of one of our Chicago friend's business-cards, and stuck up defiantly in one of the plate-glass windows. "I wonder where we *could* go," said one of my friends, "that would furnish us with a new sensation?"

"*Try Norway!*" said a great, big-lettered poster stuck up at the station which we were that moment passing.

The result was a trial of Norway. But what is here written is only partly derived from that experience.*

* See A. Vaudal's *En Karriole à travers la Suède et la Norwège.*

The tourist-mania has lately driven so many summer travellers from Great Britain into Sweden and Norway that these once secluded regions are becoming like nothing more than an extension of Scotland, and are quite the proper thing to "do" after a rapid run through the storied but well-trodden ground of *Marmion* and the *Lady of the Lake*. The first sounds which greet the traveller's ear when he strikes Scandinavian soil are not those of the language of the skalds and vikings: they are the crisp syllables of the Strand and Fleet street. Every summer steamers from Hull and Leith bring over to the port of Trondhjem parties of British sportsmen and lady travellers. Your English are a race of born sportsmen, and the rivers of Norway are crammed with salmon, thousands upon thousands of trout play in the leaping torrents, while in the almost unbroken woods abide red-deer, reindeer, grouse, woodcocks, elks. The Norwegian fjords, which cut so deeply into the coast, offer to pleasure-yachts a safe harbor and easy navigation. The Englishman who is neither a hunter nor a fisherman nor a sailor becomes a tourist, at least for a few months each year. He conscientiously climbs every mountain-peak in the vicinity of the route he is travelling, drives his karriole with the ardor of performing an expected duty in a thorough manner, and persistently talks English to the natives without the slightest regard to the fact of their not understanding it. And his laudable efforts are having their effect. "Yes," has almost dethroned "Ja" in Norway, even among natives talking together. A proverb has it that when founding a colony Spaniards begin by building a church, the Yankees a factory, the British an hotel. In the gorge of the Romsdal, the journey toward which is one of great difficulty, there is to be found an English hotel which is quite in the London style, even as regards its prices, and where the smiling proprietor spreads before you the latest numbers of *Punch* and the London *Times*. Sailing around the Northern Cape to Bergen, the summer traveller sees on one of the islands of the lonely fjord a British flag flying from the top of an elegant cottage, whose dainty construction recalls the coquettish villas of the Isle of Wight. The steamer touches the shore, and the English colony is found to consist of a single house which was brought here direct from London, with its pretty pointed roof, its green shutters, its tiny tower and its graceful bow-window. Every summer it is erected on the banks of some Scandinavian fjord, and in the autumn it is taken down, board by board, and returns to London to pass the winter in a storehouse. The proprietor is a jolly gentleman, a passionate lover of the forest and the stream, who receives his visitors in a room hung with emblems of his prowess as a fisher and a hunter, with tents easy to pitch, and the last new thing in fowling-pieces and fishing-rods. Outside, a flourishing kitchen-garden is the result of the planting of the seeds he brought from England. His little house is an exact model of the one he lives in in the suburbs of London—a jointed toy easily fitted together. In the spring this eccentric gentleman boards his yacht, embarks his house upon it, takes with his baggage a collection of seeds, a cellar of wines, tinned provisions, tea, coffee and sugar, and turns prow toward the east. When he arrives on the Norway coast he takes possession of a deserted islet in a fish-haunted fjord, puts up his house and plants his salads. By day he hunts the deer and fishes for salmon: in the evening he eats the fish he has caught, the deer he has killed, the vegetables he has sown. The rare steamers which pass before his windows bring him his only news of the world. As soon as the first cold weather comes he folds his baggage, takes to sail again, returns to London and plays the other half of his life—fashionable gentleman during the winter, Robinson Crusoe during the summer.

At the railway-station of Malmö an ambulatory merchant runs along by the car-windows and offers travellers a toy,

COSTUMES: PARISH OF MORA.

a diminutive representation of the karriole. It is a little arm-chair mounted on large wheels and hung between long shafts. You put the karriole in your pocket and take the express-train for Stockholm. In the train the aspect of your fellow-travellers differs in no respect from that cosmopolitan character which you would expect in any express-train near large cities in Europe. All countries seem represented in the dress of these tourists, which varies sufficiently to include the plaid of the Highlander and the Castilian sombrero. As yet you see nothing unmistakably Swedish except perhaps a few tall and extremely blond army officers, wearing the severely-plain uniform of the Royal Guards or the black and gold dolman of the Charles XV. Hussars.

Ten years ago Stockholm was only accessible by sea. Even now it is called the Venice of the North. The streets are arms of the sea. A fleet of war-ships could defile in battle array under the palace-windows of the Swedish king. The sole vehicle of Stockholm is a light steamer, a microscopic affair propelled by a miniature steam-engine. It pulls up at the curb frequently, disembarks the passengers and rings its bell for an-

COSTUMES: PARISH OF LEKSAND.

other load. Captain, engineer, helmsman and fireman are all embodied satisfactorily in the person of one small boy. He collects the fare from the passengers, gives the signal for leaving, and obeys it—slows up or crowds on steam. On these boats you may study at your leisure the peasant girls and women wearing their picturesque provincial costume. Their short skirts disclose stockings of a brilliant red; a brown or green bodice imprisons their waists; quaint, stiffly-starched caps cover their heads. The physical aspect of the Swedish population is blond, large, tall: in repose the face denotes great placidity, but in speaking the blue eyes lighten up with intelligence and the language becomes rapid and full of color. There is much in them which recalls the German character, and yet they are more like the Germans as depicted by Tacitus than the Prussians of our day. The Germans of antiquity built neither towns nor villages. Every family lived isolated, with its servitors, under the absolute authority of the chief. This is the case in Scandinavia to-day. Every family owns and inhabits its own *gaard*, a little miniature state, where the father of the family is the king.

The Scandinavian *gaard* or *gord* is not a farm, neither is it a hamlet; for, though it sometimes consists of many buildings, one man only is their proprietor. It is a collection of eight or ten wooden houses, generally painted in the most brilliant colors, and still further adorned with contrasting bands of color around the doors and windows. These buildings are erected around a square, so as to form a more or less irregular courtyard: one is used as a storehouse, another as a dairy, another as a work-room where the women spin and sew, for the colony must clothe itself. The chief of the family often keeps several buildings for his own private use: one is his dining-room, another his bedroom, another his kitchen. The other cottages are used by his serving-men, whose position is more that of vassals than the ordinary domestics of our day. A second line of buildings encircles the first: it is composed of stables, barns, etc.; and beyond these lies a broad zone of cultivated fields, where the grain grows yellow under the warm sun of summer, and farther on beautiful green prairies dotted with flocks. The lord and master of this little empire, though a peasant, is often a member of the Diet and helps to rule the land. "There is only one state in

Europe which from the political point of view can be compared to Sweden," said a young Scandinavian officer: "it is the canton of Uri in Switzerland. Like our country, it is governed by peasants." The peasant influence has been powerful in Sweden for centuries. This laborious and independent class of men has never

THE KARRIOLE.

known what it is to perform servile work for any master; on the contrary, during the Middle Ages the Swedish peasants themselves held serfs, but to Sweden belongs the honor of being the first country in Europe to abolish serfdom, and to another Scandinavian state, Denmark, belongs the glory of first freeing negro slaves in our times.

The love of bright color is universal

in Scandinavia. The houses are painted every hue of the rainbow; the costumes of the people are as high-colored as those worn by the figurantes of the opera; and even the most ordinary tools and instruments are as flaming in color as a barber's pole. At Leksand the boats which ply on the lakes and rivers are painted red, blue and yellow, and are guided by girl-rowers as gayly dressed as possible. These variegated boats bring down almost the entire population of the four parishes nearabout Leksand to the rendezvous which God gives each Sunday to the faithful. Every gaard possesses a bark of its own dedicated to this special usage, and the family relic is transmitted from generation to generation. The company of peasants attired in their Sunday costumes is a brilliant sight—curious too, for the cut of the garments is several centuries old. It is a real delight to the eyes to contemplate these strange costumes, where red, blue, green and yellow are married so happily and without a jar, for taste and harmony dominate the whole. What more graceful, more elegant, than these white skirts trimmed with red which seem to be the uniform of the girl-rowers? The white jacket opening over a scarlet vest seems the thing of all others to set off the beauty of a handsome young man. This father of a family, with his square-cut coat with enormous skirts, his buckled shoes and his long jabot of lace, looks like a bailiff of the good old times. And these peasant-girls, with striped skirts, bodices adorned with jewels, and odd head-dresses, look for all the world as if they had just stepped out from between the illustrated pages of a mediæval missal. The worship of color is universal. The oars of the boats are sculptured and colored, and in the fields you see harvesters wearing embroidered breeches and scarlet stockings, and whole battalions of haymakers their long rakes painted half red and half yellow. Every parish, every family, has its favorite colors.

The karriole is a Norwegian institution, but some provinces of Sweden have borrowed it. It resembles a cart, a drosky, a tilbury, a sulky, yet differs from all. It is composed of a circular wooden seat for one person, ornamented with a hard flat cushion like a pancake, and perched on a pair of large wheels. Between the seat and the axletree two half hoops of wood serve as springs and make a base pretence of modifying the violence of the jolting. Between the long shafts stands a rusty little horse with unkempt mane, quick eye, prominent ribs and a nervous and steely ankle. The harness is as strange as the vehicle, as wild as the horse. One of the reins is a rope, the other a leather strap rusty with age and weather. But even here the Scandinavian love of color comes in. The horse's collar is ornamented with carved wood painted in brilliant hues, and to it hang a half dozen or more sleigh-bells. You swing up into your rolling chair, your valise fixed between your feet: your young conductor hands you the reins and jumps up behind, and kneels on a narrow board there, his hands holding on to your back. When you are ready he utters a sibilant sound something like this: *pr-pr-pr;* and to the horse this is a magic utterance. He shakes his mane, starts off at a gallop, plunges down hill with his belly to the ground, and takes the ascents by storm. The karriole follows him, jumping, bounding, dancing, describing unheard-of zigzags over the bosom of Mother Earth. Relays are made at certain stages. The traveller leaves not only horse, but karriole, and enters another, bag and baggage. The boy who accompanied the preceding relay receives the stipulated price of the conveyance, shakes hands cordially with the traveller and returns home with his horse and karriole. One of his youthful compatriots succeeds him on the fresh karriole, and thus the traveller passes in review the coming generation of Scandinavia. Though the karrioles vary little in appearance, no one of your young companions resembles the other. One, timid and fearful, crouches behind on the board, hangs tightly by your shoulders and never utters a word; another, wide awake to an astonishing degree, carries on a ceaseless discourse in his own language, and seems quite indignant that you do not understand Swedish like a native. Often the boy jumps to the ground, trots beside the vehicle, springs up again with a bound on to the shafts, stands there astride like a circus-rider, jumps, dances and turns

CATARACT OF THE SKEGGEDAL-FOSS.

summersaults, without the pony relaxing his headlong pace for an instant. Sometimes your young postilion, anxious to show the superiority of Swedish horse-flesh over all other in the world, stimulates the courser of the karriole. You hold the reins, it is true, but the animal pays no attention to any one but his fellow-countryman. It is he who urges him on by a gesture or stops him by a word.

For the most part, however, the best energies of the gamin are devoted to sparing the horse, which is perhaps the only treasure, and certainly the friend

A TOFTÉ PRINCE.

and companion, of the family. The whip is an instrument almost unknown in Sweden, and if you venture to caress the backbone of your horse with a switch, the poor boy behind will groan at every stroke as if he were being switched himself.

The diligence of France and the stage-coach of England are replaced in Scandinavia not by one but a whole procession of karrioles, the column headed by the post-carrier. It is great fun to meet a joyous, noisy caravan like this, with bells ringing, laughter and chat resounding, in the stillness of these great solitudes. Conversation is carried on by the travellers jumping down and running alongside of one another's karriole. All karrioles upset once or twice a day—this is the expected average—in which case the horse, trained by long custom, stops: all the other karrioles in the procession

do the same; the gamin in charge of the conveyance examines his harness and vehicle to see if anything is broken; the traveller picks himself up; and away goes the caravan again at a lively gallop.

Although their religious faith does not encourage belief in the heathen gods their ancestors worshipped, good Lutherans as they are, the common people are superstitious. In the pale dusk which is their night strange figures are seen to float on the surface of their steel-blue lakes: enchanted palaces rise slowly before their eyes. Mirage is a common sight to the sailor, but your Scandinavian explains not such fairy visions by prosaic reasoning. The airy palace seen to rise from the lake is the home of the Scandinavian siren with the glassy eyes and the seductive and perfidious voice. Rising

A NORWEGIAN BRIDE.

upon the narrow plank behind, the karriole-boy in a frightened voice cries out, "Elf! elf!" and points eagerly toward the blue vapor which lifts from the waters on a summer night. In it the Scandinavians think they behold sweet faces and transparent forms. The fairies dance upon the water without ruffling it, and whosoever approaches too near to them will surely be inflamed with love for them. But when an elf timidly approaches the bank and allows the mortal to press her

FISHERMEN OF LOFODEN.

to his breast, she casts a pitiful look into his eyes and expires in his embrace. Then slowly she vanishes in the wave, and unknown disturbances are in store for that wretched lover in the future.

The guide of the karriole is not always a boy. Girls not infrequently perform the office. When it is remembered that necessity obliges them to hang on to the gentlemen's shoulders with their hands, and even sometimes to lay their heads on the gentlemen's backs to get a little rest, it can easily be conceived that the spectacle is an amusing one.

One of the most thrilling sights in Scandinavia is the cataract of the Skeggedalfoss, beside which the favorite Swiss falls of Staubach and Giesbach are but trifling cascades. From the neighboring heights the tourist beholds a panorama composed of sixty leagues of mountains, glaciers and eternal snows. On these heights blooms a special vegetation, brilliant and poisonous. Here aconite exhibits its pale bunches, belladonna reddens the bushes with its scarlet berries, and the tourist brings back as a souvenir of his visit a monster bouquet of poisons. The ascent of the heights near the gorge is very trying: difficult from the base, as the apex is approached it becomes almost impossible. But the climb is well repaid. A fairy spectacle is spread out below, above and around. Three or four torrents as large as rivers fall together from the height of a thousand feet into a lake, where they mingle their waters in foam, roar and fury.

The descendants of Harold with the Fine Hair, the first king who ever reigned over Norway, still exist. They have inhabited an estate called the Tofté for many centuries, and they are known as the Toftés. They still preserve their ancient parchments and their genealogical tree. They are rich too, owning three hundred cows, and to visit all their estates takes a week's time, and to receive their farmers' accounts the entire space of a day. They intermarry among themselves, and have little intercourse with those whom they consider beneath them. Proposals of marriage have frequently come from outsiders, and it has been urged upon them that their race will soon be extinguished unless it is replenished with new blood. They answer that they know this, but prefer to have no sons at all rather than sons less noble than themselves. The chief or king of the Toftés is a vigorous old man, but his only son is a pale and feeble youth who plainly shows the poverty of a blood which is never rejuvenated by new currents. This prince wears the square-cut coat, knee-breeches and buckled shoes used in France in Madame de Pompadour's time, but his cap is a revolutionary bit of headgear such as would hardly have been tolerated at the elegant court of Versailles. The Toftés show the genealogical tree. Near its roots appear the names of those kings to whom affectionate surnames have been given—Harold of the Fine Hair, Hardrath with the Bare Feet, Harold the Red, Bjorn with the Sparkling Eyes. The topmost branch bears the name of the two Toftés who exhibit the precious document. One branch is broken off rudely, and the Toftés explain that this is a scion of the race who no longer belongs to the family, having disgraced himself by an alliance with a woman not of the blood-royal. Among the curious relics exhibited to the visitor is a tall, heavy crown rising into points, upon which silver bells are hung which ring at every touch. This crown has nothing especially royal in it, although it has been for many centuries the property of this princely family. Every family in good circumstances in this locality owns a similar one, and places it on the heads of its daughters the day they marry. The precious relic is transmitted from generation to generation. The bride is hung with ornaments when she walks to the altar. She marches slowly to the ceremony, as pretentiously tricked out as a Spanish Madonna.

A dashing vessel is lying at anchor in one port, getting ready for an expedition to the Lofoden Isles, there to fish for herring and cod. One of its masts is broken short off, and many indications show its recent fierce battle with the tempests. The shape of the ship is truly Norwegian, and announces plainly its descent from the pirate vessels, those dragons of the sea. The prow rises above the wave and twists about like the neck of a serpent: behind is a sort of tower which serves as a shelter for the sailors during a tempest. Formerly, this was a sort of block-house, where the defenders of the ship received the enemy when they attempted to board her. Now her only sea-fights are with cod and herring, which every spring invade the waters about the Lofoden Isles in myriads. The master of the bark wears cowskin boots, a fur-lined jacket, a leathern apron and thick woollen mittens. He looks like a bear back from its hunt and satisfied with its booty. His wife lives with him in his damp home; and if she had not on a

OLD CHURCH IN THE THELEMARKEN.

thick green skirt bordered with red over her boots and her pantaloons, it would be difficult to assign the proper sex to the two spouses. Two or three sailors accoutred in the same guise make up the crew. The boss has navigated the North Sea many years, and has made the ocean-journey on the Atlantic. He has seen England and the United States, and speaks the English language quite fluently. He was doing well "off there," but he got homesick for his Norwegian fjords, and returned to them. These Norwegian fishers prepare for sea as soldiers make ready for the battle-field: no man knows whether he will ever return. In the month of March word reaches them that cod have arrived in the West Fjord, near the Lofodens, and they set out. From the North Cape to Bergen the whole coast is alive: barks of every size and shape, schooners, brigs, luggers, yachts, all set sail. When they arrive at the isles the fishing-area is divided. Four or five hundred boats cast their nets at once, and draw them in full of the squirming prisoners. The remainder of the crew have landed in a sheltered place, and await the arrival of the fish to cure them. As soon as a net casts its living cargo on the rocks the executioners advance: each seizes his victim, hits it, despatches it with a stroke of his knife, cuts off its head, which he slings into a tunnel of oil, drags out its entrails, and then bites greedily into the yet warm liver of the creature as if it were a ripe fruit. This is the battle of the fishers. They have on their side skill and audacity, but the fish have on theirs the tempest, the Maëlstrom which draws in ships and sucks them down, the icy currents of the North Sea. So reasoned the boss when the subject of cruelty to cod was broached to him. The Norwegian sailors are reputed the best in the world. A British admiral once said, "To rule the seas I should like a fleet of English ships manned by Norwegian sailors."

Bergen is the principal port where all this wealth of fishing industry goes. Every year Bergen receives six hundred thousand cod from the Lofoden Isles, and sends to the European markets two hundred thousand barrels of salted fish and oil. The little town is perched in a most uncomfortable situation on a rocky steep incessantly beaten by terrific rains and at the mercy of all the storms which gather and break on the North Sea. Why the town is not washed away seems a marvel. But, such as it is, it has been perched there for six hundred years.

The Norwegians claim the discovery of America of course. In the year 1000 the navigator Leif with thirty-five companions sighted the Isle of Newfoundland, and pushing on to the westward he found a vast country covered with vines, to which, like our temperance neighbors in their New Jersey town, he gave the name of Vineland. This was North America, near the mouth of the St. Lawrence River. A Scandinavian colony established itself on the banks of the river, and soon pushed onward to the New England coasts: it is claimed that a company even ventured as far as the bay whereon Boston now sits so proudly. Regular communication was established between Norway and the New World. The pope appointed bishops in America four centuries before Las Casas. About 1350 the civil wars which raged among the Scandinavian peoples and the terrible black pest—a scourge not yet forgotten in Norway—seem to have caused an interruption of communication between the two continents. It was nearly a century and a half later before the New World was definitely discovered. The spirit of Norwegian adventure showed Europeans the route to America; chance lost it; genius brought it to light again. Such is their tale.

The Thelemarken province is a corner of Norway almost unknown to tourists. The English go to the North Cape, to the Lofoden Isles, but have not yet quite discovered the Thelemarken, probably because it is nearer home than Lapland and Norrland. The manners and customs of past ages seem to have taken refuge in this valley imprisoned on all sides by lofty mountains. It presents a curious sample of Norway as it was two centuries ago: costumes, manners, characters, all have a primitive savor. The chairs are but trunks of trees coarsely hewed out, with a part of the trunk left to form a back. The table is another tree-trunk, and on it are plates, cups and spoons made of sculptured wood painted in bright colors. Both furniture and walls are ornamented with proverbs, moral sentences, quotations from the Bible—sometimes in Scandinavian, sometimes in Latin. Around a wooden milk-bowl you read, "Drink, and thank God;" at the bottom of a wooden platter these words of the Psalmist: "Eat with thy friend: let thine enemy eat;" over the

THE HOUSE OF THE STRANGER.

door: "If the Lord does not guard the house, he who guards it will guard in vain;" and on the bed-tester: "Man sows: God prospers the seed." In the bed sleep sometimes mother, father and half a dozen children. Your karriole guide, though an urchin but four or five years of age, has his waist encircled by a stout leather belt in which hangs an unsheathed dagger. All the inhabitants of the Thelemarken wear this arm, and use it with dexterity.

After a long twilight the night falls. It is the first time for six weeks that you have known what darkness is. You greet the stars as old acquaintances who have been long absent. By this romantic light you discern in the distance a strange black mass whose size and unusual form almost frighten you. It looks like an immense monster with shining scales, humpbacked, stretching out long weird arms which terminate in grimacing heads. At sight of it the karrioleboy extends his tiny hand, and indicating a point beyond it, says, "Priestergaard"—the gaard or farm of the priest. This explains the monster. The curious old mass is simply one of those ancient Norwegian churches which are imitated to some extent in all parts of Norway, but in the Thelemarken are undoubted originals. Imagine a squat wooden edifice nearly rectangular, surrounded by galleries open to the air and daylight, and surmounted by a tangled mass of slate roofs which pile themselves one above the other, run up into spires or round out in cupolas, and from every angle of which and on every frontage jut out dragon-faced gargoyles. These churches, essentially Scandinavian, are three or four centuries old. The cold of the North, which disagrees with stone, respects their wooden walls. There is scarcely anything stranger in building than this disordered architecture, which defies symmetry and is strikingly effective in spite of all rules to the contrary, and especially in the steel blue of the northern moonlight makes a fantastic and impressive silhouette against the azure background of the atmosphere.

At the door of the pastor's house a knock brings a venerable patriarch to open. The priest knows neither French, English nor German, but being asked for a few minutes' rest and shelter in Latin, replies fluently in that language, and presses the traveller to stop all night.

Sometimes your karriole will bring you to the gate of a sort of rustic castle, the mistress of which comes out herself to meet you, surrounded by a whole population of children and servants. The hostess wears a pair of trousers of black woollen stuff which reach quite over the feet and are tucked into her sculptured wooden shoes, and around the ankle are beautified with embroidery in brilliant colors; a short skirt, not reaching to the knees, something like the Greek petticoat; the bodice open in front and ornamented with a double row of jewels; a multi-colored scarf twisted several times about her waist; and on her head a sort of cape, falling on the shoulders and embroidered to match the trousers. On a sign from this lady the traveller is conducted into "the house of the stranger" —a house specially reserved for hospitality. In it are antique beds overhung with embroidered phrases in illuminated letters, arm-chairs with more sculpture than stuffing about them, and walls adorned with consoling maxims from the Bible painted in Gothic characters. Servants busy themselves silently to provide for your wants without waiting for a request or asking a question, in obedience to the motto inscribed over the door of the stranger's house: "One must not fatigue the guest one receives. He needs repose, dry clothing, and not to be questioned."

The southern part of Sweden is pierced with canals, grand works which have immortalized the name of Ericsson, the civil engineer. These canals link the lakes, and, putting these great floods into communication, offer to commerce as well as to tourists a means of transport which facilitates the journeys and shortens distances. In twenty-two hours the Dalsland Canal takes the traveller from the Norwegian frontier to Lake Wener. It opens a passage through solid rocks, climbs mountains by means of sluices cut in granite, glides among wooded heights, crosses lakes and boldly passes over a cataract, the Hafverud falls. The boat, floating in an iron aqueduct, a sort of gigantic gutter suspended in air, sees below it torrents of water and foam precipitating themselves into an abyss. Near the Hafverud Cataract is Lake Wener, an immense interior basin whose waters are often as tumultuous as those of the ocean. It is the largest lake in Europe after Ladoga in Russia. A quaint little town called Wenersborg is situated on the southern extremity of the lake. It is merely a group of houses without streets or squares. Sheep nibble unconcernedly before the very door of the hotel, where the smiling proprietor complacently

THE LOCKS OF TROLHÄTTA.

stands awaiting the customers whom every steamer brings him in the summer-time. He is a man who understands his business and means to make himself agreeable. Addressing the French travellers, whose Parisian air and speech announce their nationality, he bows to the ground and says with an accent which would do no discredit to a Boulevard lounger, "Messieurs, it is with a real pleasure that I place my services at your disposition." Without waiting for an answer, he turns to a group of English people and repeats the same phrase in English. A Viennese family complete the list, and to them Boniface proffers the same remark, word for word, in German. But when an effort is made to pursue this happy opening to more extended converse, relating to something to eat and drink, bath, soap and towels and a bed, English, French and German being in turn tried, all is found to be in vain. Boniface speaks no language but Swedish, and has only learned a single phrase in the other tongues, which he uses out of compliment to his patrons.

Near Wenersborg are the celebrated falls of Trolhätta. For many miles the Göta-Elf River, held in by two steep banks, rushes from cascade to cascade, throws itself from cliff to cliff; now pours down an abyss, now beats against a menacing rock; boils, bounds, launches in the air great volumes of foam, and finally finds a calm and green limpidity in a basin two hundred feet below which lies in everlasting repose. The boat—which cannot very well navigate a body of water so restless as this—finds a pleasant journey in a neighboring canal; and the travellers, who have gone ashore to see the falls, are surprised to suddenly behold their boat at a distance of three hundred feet above their heads, at the top of a giant staircase cut out in a mountain's flank. Each step is an immense trough which alternately empties and fills in order to raise or lower the water for the boat's descent—the locks of our own Niagaran Lockport on a wilder scale. OLIVE LOGAN.

HUNGARIAN TYPES AND AUSTRIAN PICTURES.

PART I.

VIEW OF WAITZEN.

AN old gentleman whom I had known in other climes, and when he was seeing better days, accompanied me through the darkened streets of Pesth to a garden in the suburbs, and, seating me before a green table under a mass of vines, he knocked loudly and cried out, "Now I am going to show you something very curious."

A sleepy-looking waiter shuffled in and took the venerable gentleman's order for a flask of the very best red wine. At that moment a little curtain amid the foliage rolled up, and a dashing young fellow, with a sinister look about the eyes, came forward to the smoking footlights of a tiny stage and began to sing a song.

"That's it!" cried my friend. "He always sings the brigand ballad at this hour. You shall be delighted. Listen!"

I did. It was the most remarkable song that I ever heard. In it the brigand of the steppes related the savage joys of his adventurous life — the peril, the assault, the battles with herdsmen and travellers, as well as his rustic love. The Hungarian language sounded extremely poetic as this stage-brigand sang it. In the music there was the wild wail, the intense passionate earnestness, the rude poetry which you can understand when you have heard Remenyi play upon his violin or Liszt upon his piano. What is this wonderful, this fascinating echo in a minor key which is heard in the music throughout South-eastern Europe? Whence comes it?

Brigands still flourish in some parts of Hungary, but when caught they are so severely dealt with that many are abandoning the career for the safer ones of shepherds or nomadic fortune-tellers and tinkers. The peasantry have a dangerous tendency to make popular heroes of them. Among these brigands have now and then appeared adorable types of beauty, of exquisite manly grace, which made many fair ladies' hearts ache. In a few years the last brigand will have vanished, in company with the remaining bits of costume to which certain people in Hungary still fondly cling. Let the artist who would catch the picturesque aspects of peasant-life in this country hasten, for the young generation is getting into the hideous black clothes, slouch hats and sombre petticoats that offend the eye in Northern Germany. Munkacsy has painted a few bits from sketches made among the lower classes of his fellow-countrymen: how fresh, original and sympathetic they are! And what a noble head the artist himself has! It is a real Hungarian type, symmetrical, strong, framed in handsome beard and crowned with finely-colored hair. When Munkacsy walks on the Paris boulevards passers who do not know him turn to stare at him. "If he is not something exceptional, he ought to be," they say to themselves. One sees dozens of striking faces in the course of a day's walk in Pesth. Sometimes they are deceptive, and the lad whom one takes for an incipient poet is only a vulgar schoolboy, with few ideas above his dinner and his geography, or the man of noble and stately port is a waiter in a restaurant. Beauty has been lavished on many people without respect to class or fortune. Yet the ugly types are so hideous that I doubt if they can be equalled elsewhere. The gypsies at the Kaiserbad and around the other "oven"-like heated grounds from which *Ofen* takes its name are as fantastic as the beggars in Doré's illustrations to Balzac's *Contes Drolâtiques*. The old peasant-women who beg on the fine bridge over the Danube are such wrecks of humanity that one vainly endeavors to discover in them any remnants of past grace or beauty.

The Esterhazy Gallery is so well known that I will only mention the extreme pride which the Hungarians take in it—a pride heightened, perhaps, by the fact that the beautiful collection was ceded by Vienna to Pesth. There are Hungarians who would willingly take the Grand Opera-house, the Belvidere, the Votive Church and the Palace of Schönbrunn from Vienna if they could, although they have an admirable opera of their own, and palaces enough to house the memories of all their kings. The Hungarians are good Wagnerites, and bestow much attention upon the music of the erratic and immortal Richard.

Up river, toward Vienna, the intelligent traveller who will not be dictated to by Murray or Baedeker, and who scorns haste, can find dozens of interesting excursions. He will not think the Hungarian village very impressive, especially if he happens into it on a rainy day. The streets have no sidewalks, and are speedily transformed into mud-puddles under the furious rains which now and then beat across hill and plain. The houses are low, blessed with but few windows, and the doors are narrow. The inn has some wooden benches in front of its principal entrance, and there wagoners sit and drink, even in the rain. Solemn processions of geese promenade the muddy ways, now and then indulging in sinister cries rather more discordant than any accents to be heard in the human dialects thereabouts. Bare-limbed peasant-girls stare at the strangers and laugh at them. Even an Austrian excites their attention and their critical remarks.

The extensive fleet of Danube steamers is built at Old Ofen, but a short distance above the newer and principal town of that name. Old Ofen is charm-

VIEW OF GRAN.

ingly situated among vineyards, and the activity of the fresh-water dockyards and the beauty of the vine-clad slopes are only made more striking by contrast with many ugly and tumbling hovels in which a rabble of low Jews herd together. The Jews have been so ambitious to build a fine synagogue that they have quite forgotten decency in housing themselves. Their church at Alt Ofen exceeds any other of its religion in Austria-Hungary in grace of design and beauty of decoration. Hundreds of workmen are employed in the yards of the Danube Steam Navigation Company, for the number of barges, towboats, rafts and express steamers required for the commerce of the great stream is legion. Destruction of property is rare, but the company has found it necessary to increase its stock steadily for many years, and in the winter harbor at Pesth there is a veritable flotilla when ice has formed on the stream.

Waitzen, Gros-Maros, Wissegrad and Gran are all so unlike any towns in Middle Europe that the traveller whose æsthetic sense has been dulled by too much sameness in France and Belgium and Northern Germany will feel his heart leap up with a sense of gratitude when he sees them. Waitzen is full of quaint monuments left by the Romans or constructed in the Middle Ages; and in the episcopal palace especially—for it is the seat of a see—there are great numbers of curious relics. The cathedral is not more than a hundred years old, but is a noble monument, resembling its mighty brother at Gran above. Perhaps the most noticeable peculiarity of Waitzen is the manner in which the town is divided into quarters. In one lives a Roman Catholic population, which has little or nothing to do with the Protestants, who are ensconced in a section by themselves; and both these peoples consider that they have a right to look down upon the Servians, who of course profess the Greek Protestant rite. Waitzen is like many other towns in Austria-Hungary in the variety of its populations and the diversity of their beliefs, but unlike most of them in the manner in which its peoples keep apart.

Wissegrad (the "high fortress"), where Matthias Corvinus built many a pleasant château and embellished numerous gardens, is a monument to the stupid mania for destruction which characterized the Turks' entry into Europe. In the eleventh century Hungarian kings had already established themselves there, and the peasants in the vineyards can tell the lingering pedestrian any quantity of legends, more or less authentic, but all, to their thinking, solidly founded on the eternal rock. The old walls of the fortress, twice dismantled — once by the Turks, and once by the emperor Leopold—are bathed by the smoothly-flowing Danube, which here is exquisitely beautiful. A lofty ruined tower, the most conspicuous object at Wissegrad, was once a state prison, and many a victim of royal caprice languished here for long years, hearing no cheerful sound save the gurgling of the Danube when a storm came, or an occasional shout from a passing boatman. The rocks rise in the wildest fashion on every side, and the brilliant southern sun beats fiercely upon their peaks of porphyry and limestone.

Raab is a town which merits attention, and, turning aside from the high road of travel, the visitor may speedily reach it by a fascinating route. It was there that Francis Joseph gave evidence of his thorough pluck during the siege in 1849, when he signified his determination to lead the assault on the insurgents in Raab in person. It was with difficulty that General Schlick dissuaded the emperor from the hazardous adventure. Raab has a handsome twelfth-century cathedral, and the guides also show strangers some horrible dungeons into which the Turks, when they were there, used to throw their prisoners.

Gran is one of the most ancient towns in Hungary. The Hungarians call it *Esztergom*, and a hundred ballads sing its praises. Its cathedral has a huge dome, which the pious folk of the locality are fond of likening to that of St. Peter's at Rome; and one can scarcely summon up courage to undeceive them. An altarpiece in the cathedral represents the baptism of St. Stephen, the first Christian king of Hungary and founder of the bishopric at Gran nearly nine centuries ago. The Turks have left their marks on the sacred edifices here. It provokes a smile to wander through Hungary, noting this evidence of Turkish barbarism and rage, and at the same time hearing everywhere from Hungarian lips most enthusiastic praise of the invading Mussulman.

From Pesth to Presburg the journey up the Danube by river or by the railroad, which keeps close to the stream's bank, is charming. The mountains are with you, grave, majestic; from Presburg the view of the far-away chain of hills is ravishing. You are in a land of

WOMEN GARDENING IN THE ENVIRONS OF PESTH.

sunshine and song, where blood runs quickly, yet is so hot that it almost burns the veins; where faces are swart and limbs are round and eyes sparkle; where the vines in the lusty autumn are loaded with millions of clusters of exquisite grapes; where the plains are rich in a hundred colors; where legend has consecrated every stone; where men talk in heroic terms, and every fellow, even though he be but a sorry one, may boast of the glorious deeds of his ancestors.

This is the land of Strauss's "Danube:" this is the country whence comes the bewitching, maddening music which has affected us all. Here the venerable towns, half hidden under moss and vines, seem to protest against the tooting horn of the railway-porter and the shriek of the locomotive: they appear to frown upon the present, or to pray it to pass them by as gently and with as little ostentation as possible. Here and there, however, the present has given an added interest to the glories of the past, as at Komorn—ancient Komorn—at the junction of the Waag with the Danube. Under Matthias Corvinus the fortifications of Komorn sprang into existence, and they were, even in his day, one of the glories of Hungary. At the beginning of this century they were immensely enlarged and strengthened, and the Austrians little dreamed that they would be used to sustain an Hungarian army against Austrians during the bloody and perturbed hours of 1849. Komorn made a successful defence at that time, and might perhaps do so again. If the noble Magyars should have no other means of defeating an Austrian army in any future complications, they could send out to the besiegers a few wagon-loads of the potent wine of Neszmely, which grows on the hills near by, and that would have the desired effect. Your Austrian cannot drink wine moderately, as your delicate Southern Hungarian does: he must guzzle it in large quantities, and the effect is disastrous to his sobriety.

On many a peak of mountain or slope of hill one sees rich abbeys surrounded by carefully-tilled lands, and also great castles, reminding one that the feudal epoch has not yet entirely passed away in Hungary. The friar and the master of the manor are still important figures there. The servile peasant does not realize his condition here, although in some sections of the country he has begun to think. But he is not oppressed. If it were not for the spectre of military service, he might with justice consider his lot enviable by comparison with that of the peasantry in certain lands less favored by Nature than his own. He is devout, and would not like to see the clergy or nobility deprived of their privileges, no matter how they obtained them. I do not mean to have it understood that landlords have legally any of the old-fashioned feudal control over their tenants. The legislation of 1848 abolished all *droits du seigneur*, which had already lasted longer in Hungary than in most European countries; and the "lords of the soil" were indemnified for any losses which they might incur, by funds taken from the state revenues. But there has never been any such great and general redistribution of land in Hungary as came in France after the great Revolution, and as must some day come in England. The lawmakers of 1848 hoped for more radical results than have been achieved. The peasant has not made the best use of his opportunities. Small farmers are still the exception, and one sees the vast estates tilled by a humble tenantry that seems curiously unconscious of its emancipation. The Slavs and the two millions of Roumanians in Hungary are jealous of their rights, but the peasant born on the soil does not share their jealousy. He sows his summer and winter wheat, his grass-seed and his tobacco, contentedly; cultivates the vine; tends the hive of the industrious bee; raises cattle and horses; toils in the forest right manfully, and accepts the wages dictated. His policy is that of his employer and of his village priest.

The train which brings one to Presburg whirls along the edges of steep banks which are crowded with fat vineyards. In autumn the spectacle is amazing. As far as the eye can reach in every direction except the site of the town a sea of vines salutes the view. Presburg people are fond of their own wines, as the traveller speedily discovers by a short sojourn among them. They talk as glibly of the virtues of some special vintage as of the proud days when the Hungarian monarchs came to be crowned in the town. The ancient capital has a somewhat neglected air: the citadel, on an imposing hill, is partially ruined, and the royal palace, which looked down on the Danube from a high plateau, was burned about fifty years ago. This palace was in a beautiful spot. Climbing up through the crooked and ill-smelling Judengasse, and passing under a massive gateway, one gets from various vantage-grounds among the ruins a superb outlook over the fertile plains and the old city lying calm and silent at one's feet; over the villages scattered along the slopes of the Little Carpathians; and over many a rustic merrymaking in pleasant grove or inn-yard, for the Hungarians have as many fête-days as the French, and make quite as liberal use of them. It is a trial to one's nerves to wander through the Judengasse, for the amiable Hebrew of the lower classes seems determined in Presburg, as in many other cities in the dual empire, to pay as little attention as possible to cleanliness in his dwelling. Sunshine does not penetrate his haunts: it makes one shudder to peer into the black holes in which he lives, and then to gaze up out of the vile lane at the luminous sky, and to remember the vineyards, the river, the orchards, the perfumed thickets, from which the children of Abraham seem voluntarily to have shut themselves out.

Presburg is not far from Vienna, and the cookery at one of its inns is so renowned that hundreds of excursions yearly go out from the Austrian capital to dine on pheasants and to drink the ruddy wine in the old town. Then the lanes and the pleasant roads by the riverside resound with the uproarious merriment of the Austrian who has dined well, and some of the graver of the inhabitants sneer at his antics, for they do not like him, even when he is sober. Two American friends informed me that, having once sent a telegraphic order from Vienna for a dinner at the inn in Presburg—kept by a landlord rejoicing in the classic name of Paluygay—they found such a gorgeous repast awaiting them that they began to feel some misgivings about the size of the bill. But when it was brought they were agreeably surprised to discover that it amounted to but six guldens, *or a dollar and a half*

apiece! Pheasant and white wines would have cost a trifle more than that in America, England or France.

THE DANUBE NEAR RAAB.

The sights of Presburg are not numerous. There is a beautiful Gothic church over which various architects toiled for four hundred years. Therein the kings were crowned; and not far from the river was the *Krönungshügel*, like that now in Pesth—the mound of earth whence the king brandished his sword against the four quarters of the globe, menacing all humankind with destruction if it dared to scowl at Hungary. The museums, the old seat of the imperial diets, the lines of the bulwarks, now converted into handsome promenades, arrest the attention for a day or two only. There is many a finely-wooded hill in the neighborhood dotted with monasteries, some of which are in ruins, others still prosperous and tenanted; and he who understands Hungarian may amuse himself well by wandering among the rustics and the monks. The peasantry is hospitable in the highest degree, and extremely civil, and the local authorities are the same, if they do not take it into their heads to fancy that you are a Russian spy.

Theben, on the left bank of the Danube, above Presburg, is very striking in appearance. The Hungarians often speak of it as the gateway to their kingdom. It is at the point where the Morava River, which forms a kind of natural boundary between Austria and Hungary, empties into the Danube, and there once stood a fortified work near the junction of the streams, but the French destroyed it in 1809. The castle, of wild and straggling architecture, still exists. Who knows what sanguinary battles may not yet be fought near Theben? History, it is said, repeats itself, but the present Habsburg dynasty doubtless disbelieves that it will do so in the case of Theben. The journey to Vienna by boat is far preferable to that by rail from Presburg, for on the river one has a chance to observe the famous "Hat Hill," near the church of St. John, at Deutsch Altenberg. This hat hill is a mound sixty feet high, constructed, it is said, with hatsful of earth which the worthy burghers contributed to celebrate their joy at the expulsion of the Turks. The boat also passes near Lobau Island, and one can see the villages of Aspern, Essling and Wagram, after the last two of which the French, when they were flushed with victory, named two of the elegant avenues of new Paris, without even taking the trouble to consult the Austrians' feelings on the subject. Near Lobau the Danube flows swiftly, and its current is rough and boisterous. It seems hastening away from the scene of national humiliation to more smiling and peaceful scenes below. Napoleon I. once had his head-quarters on the low, narrow wooded islet, and for four days sent forth those terrible orders which resulted in frightful carnage at the battle of Wagram and in the signing of peace by the Austrians shortly afterward. There are still some traces of fortifications on the Lobau, and every year thousands of curious visitors go to see them and to trace the battle-ground according to the legends of the oldest inhabitants. It is needless to say that in the immediate vicinity of Essling and Wagram the French visitor is not looked upon with friendly eyes, although throughout Austria generally Frenchmen receive plenty of that sympathy which springs from the common hatred that two unfortunate nations feel for successful Prussia and her victorious armies.

The largest Danube steamers — those which descend as far as Galatz and the Black Sea — do not go nearer Vienna than a point just above Lobau Island. Travellers are brought up in small and swiftly-running steamboats under the great bridges into the "Danube Canal," and are allowed to disembark only a few minutes' ride from the heart of the "Kaiserstadt," as the Austrians fondly like to call their beautiful capital.

Vienna is a city of delights, and one never regrets a sojourn in it; but this does not appear at first sight to the newcomer. The older portions of the town have a stern and almost forbidding aspect. There are great numbers of narrow streets, mysterious passage-ways, which bring you face to face with low, sombre buildings, black with age, and so dreary that you fancy them prisons. The iron bars or gratings at all the windows of the lower stories do not aid in dispelling this illusion. Just as you are beginning to fancy that you must retire and seek out a new route, you see a road leading under an arch or beneath a house, and, boldly pushing forward, find yourself perhaps in a main avenue, perhaps in a public square, or possibly

THE PRATER-STRASSE, VIENNA.

in a new labyrinth. Surprises await you on every hand. The Prater-Strasse, wide, well paved, with horse-railroads traversing it in all directions, and with houses of brick or brownstone or immense stuccoed mansions, reminds you of the better portions of Fourth or Sixth avenue in New York. A glimpse of the magnificent "Ring," as the circular street running around the whole of the old city is called, is a forcible reminder of the Paris boulevards. A peep into the Judengasse recalls to you the slums of Frankfort-on-the-Main, as well as those of Pesth. The Graben, a smart promenade in a central section, gives you a queer sensation of being on the border-line of the Orient, because of the odd statues which adorn it—statues such as one sees in smaller towns near the frontier of Turkey-in-Europe. The splendor of a goodly number of the principal edifices astonishes you: here is new Europe springing into life close beside the old and decaying Europe. Vienna is so rich in exterior sights, the out-of-door life is so abundant and variegated, there is such a never-ending procession of interesting figures in every street and alley, that you speedily become fascinated, although your first walk of an hour or two disappointed and, mayhap, vexed you. If you arrive in autumn, you are almost certain of finding a cold wind abroad to worry you, and to explain why it is that so many of the cafés and beer-houses have double windows, and why such a small number of people sit out of doors. It may be remarked here that the Austrians, and especially the Viennese, share the German prejudice against fresh air, and exclude it whenever and wherever they can. To throw open a window in a horse-car or in a public room, even on a moderately warm day, would be to encounter a certain torrent of reproaches. The Grand Opera-house is the only properly ventilated building in Vienna. In summer and in the early autumn thousands of people dine and sup daily in the open air, but the moment that there is a suspicion of rawness in the breeze they fly to close rooms.

I left the huge building which serves as an office for the Danube Steamboat Company one summer evening just as the swarms of workers were beginning to leave their shops and get home to their suppers, and wandered carelessly until I came to the venerable cathedral known as St. Stephen's. In the information-office of the steamboat company I had had an excellent opportunity to judge of the cosmopolitan nature of the populations. Each notice was printed in Polish, Slavic, German, Servian and Italian. The dialects of the Slavic language are so essentially different from each other that several versions in this lively tongue were printed and affixed to the wall. Interpreters stood ready at hand in the cabinet of the chief businessman. I fancied that the odd mixture of peoples which I saw there was observable only in the currents of travel, and that I should find Vienna solidly German in appearance. Nothing of the sort; and that which was still more striking was that the Vienna speech did not seem at all like the harsh and guttural language of Northern Germany, where German only was spoken. I strolled along the bank of the Danube Canal, whose current flowed impetuously past low and ancient-looking houses, gray in color, on one bank, and on the other past the splendid edifices which ornament the new "Ring." Fences separate the bank of the canal from the streets, and on the sloping green sward there was a motley gathering. The humble folk from the back streets had come out to repose there and to watch the current, dangerously near which any number of small bald-headed babies were playing. The mothers, stretched at full length on the grass, gossiped in loud, shrill voices, and seemed to take no heed for their darlings. Great hulking men sat here and there, smoking pipes and eating bits of bread and meat alternately. Your true Viennese of the lower order cannot refrain from smoking for a long time: he grudges the moments of sleep, for they deprive him of his favorite pipe. A few of the loungers on the canal's shores were evidently regular visitors there for professional purposes. Among them was a very old woman with purple face and bulbous eyes, whose livelihood was laboriously gained by washing poodles and shearing them. The spectacle of this old creature plunging the cringing and whining animals into the water, then drawing them out and scrubbing them with a coarse towel, was comical in the extreme. Another "professional" was the toy-seller, a bushy-haired youth in a leathern jerkin and very dilapidated hose, with a frowzy fur cap placed on his locks and a basket filled with cheap wooden toys on one arm. A few *commissionaires* in red caps were beating carpets in a lazy way under an arch of one of the bridges. A little group of vagabonds, dirty and disconsolate, was crouched not far from this bridge, and seemed to shrink into the shade whenever the imperious policeman, with his hand on his broad sabre, stalked near them.

Crossing the Ring-Strasse—of which more anon—I plunged into the side streets, and speedily found myself confronted by a huge flight of steps leading up among houses which appeared to have been on a prolonged drinking

THE "GRABEN."

bout, and were tipsily endeavoring to keep their equilibrium. Serving-maids, with hats set upon the extreme verge of topknots of straw-colored hair, and wearing red gowns, dark gaiters and yellow basques, tripped down by me, impudently grinning as they passed. Gretchen, Netti and Katti are fond of a joke, especially if it be at the expense of a stranger. I would I could speak well of their taste in dress, but I cannot. Candor compels me to state, however, that among these toiling women of the people there are some wonderful types of beauty. Are the most beautiful German, Slavic or Hungarian? I know not. They are all witty, light-headed, ignorant, and the real Vienna serving-girl thinks that the world is bounded by the Kahlenberg, a high mountain-peak which looks down upon the lofty tower of St. Stephen's. Their merry laughter is heard in every street, and they always seem to be going somewhere in great haste, much to the delight of soldiers and loungers in general.

Once at the top of the stairs, I found my way without much difficulty to the cathedral. I passed through many an ill-smelling alley, and was not a little amazed at the absence of the animation usual in a large city. In some of the sunless and dreary avenues not a soul was to be seen, unless, perchance, a fluffy face emerged from a beer-cellar: in others people sat silently—looking, as I chose to fancy, rather morose—in their shops. Had I gone back to the canal or into any of the principal parks, as it happened to be a very warm and sunshiny day, I should have found the people whom I looked for in vain in their homes. Presently I came to the dark and gloomy avenue monopolized by the sons of Abraham, who sell old and new clothes and clocks, watches, bones and rubbish. It had the appearance of a miniature exchange. The Jews, nearly all dressed in extravagantly long coats which came down to their heels, and in flat caps which only set off to great advantage the ugliness of their faces, and their abundant hair combed in front of their ears in uncouth fashion, were chaffering with each other, and now and then their voices rose into that pleading shriek which signifies that the Hebrew has said his last word in a bargain. As I came in they all looked at me as if I were an intruder, and one of them, laying a skinny hand upon my arm, endeavored to arrest my course as well as my attention. Anxious to see the interior of his shop, I pretended to be persuaded, and looked in among the extraordinary specimens of cheap clothing which garnished the doorway. The stench of stale sewage, of beer and food, was revolting. I doubt if a ray of health-giving sun or a breath of anything like pure air had been known in that infected avenue for fifty years. All the men were frightfully dirty, but seemed sweetly unconscious of their degraded appearance. It is in the morning that the Jews congregate most numerously in front of their houses for the purposes of traffic, and I came after the business of the day was over. Still, I have a most lively recollection of the manner in which I was tormented to purchase articles to which I would have given houseroom on no condition whatsoever. I suppose that dozens of the wretched-looking objects whom I passed were millionaires, but they seemed fit for a chorus to the *Beggars' Opera.* All is grist that comes to their mill: it may be a brass watch, or a servant's livery, or a silk dress, or clothes stripped from a drowned person: they buy for little and sell for a great deal. They are harmless creatures, but I defy any stranger to find himself suddenly surrounded by them, to gaze upon their haggard and unwashed and unshaven faces, and to feel them nervously pulling him this way and that, without for a few moments experiencing strange misgivings which he is afterward at a loss to account for to himself. And it is but a step from such forbidding places as this to the brightness, the cheerful elegance, of some principal street, where never an unkempt Jew shows his face! Heaven bless the Hebrews! They are, after all, the most influential folk in Vienna, and it is no discredit to them that a certain number of their race will not wash their faces and have a resistless passion for dealing in rubbish. The Jews own the finest palaces in Vienna; they manage and dictate the policy of the Vienna press; they control the Viennese banking business; and they could crumple up in a day, if they were not too kind and considerate to do so, two-thirds of the members of the Austrian, Hungarian and Galician nobility, who in society pretend to be infinitely their superiors. As for the Jews engaged in high finance and in the liberal professions, they are as dandyish as their brethren of the lower classes are negligent. Paris and London tailors have nothing which is too good or too costly for them. The Hebrew who now and then confiscates the goods and chattels of some wealthy Christian must feel a grim satisfaction when he remembers that up to 1856 his race had almost no privileges in Vienna, and that in 1849 no Jew could remain in the city over night without a passport, which he was obliged to have renewed every fifteen days. Four hundred and fifty years ago five-score Jews were burned alive in the Austrian capital because the rumor ran that some son of Israel had purchased a consecrated wafer, and had made use of it in parodying the forms of the Catholic high mass.

It was refreshing to get out of the Judengasse into decent air, and at last to find myself before the old cathedral, around which the busy life of commer-

THE RING-STRASSE, VIENNA.

cial Vienna flowed and roared as a noisy stream breaks at the base of a majestic rock. St. Stephen's cathedral is entitled to the traveller's keenest admiration. Legend and history and poetry have done their utmost to make it interesting, and its beautiful proportions at once enlist one's sympathies. The Viennese have a positive affection for it, and stop in the midst of their morning hurry to look lovingly upon it. The old southern tower of the noble limestone edifice dates from 1359, and it was nearly a century before it was completed. From that tower the weary Austrians saw the glitter of the spears and helmets of the Christian army approaching to deliver them from the besieging Turks in those dread days when the Burg bastion was already in the hands of the infidel, and when it seemed certain that he would be able to pillage the town; and from the same tower, with sinking hearts, Viennese high in power watched the progress of the battle between French and Austrians at Essling when this century was young. The thorough restoration which the church has undergone in the last fifteen years has detracted no whit from its picturesqueness. The Giant's Door, opened only when some great religious festival demands the use of every portion of the cathedral, is extremely imposing. It is not the custom of the Viennese to mention that the tower has been entirely restored; but such is the fact, as the ancient one had become so shaky that it had twice undergone very extensive repairs. The common people in Austria are exceedingly devout, and the Protestant traveller feels almost as if he were guilty of indelicacy in stalking before the rows of worshippers who may be found at nearly every hour of daylight kneeling at the shrines or thumbing their prayer-books or loudly responding to the intonations of the priests. The lovely faces of the adoring women are not raised as their shoulders are brushed by the heretic who has come to spy out the wonders of the church. Whether or not the religion be more than skin-deep, it is certainly apparent to a considerable degree on the surface. The richly-carved choir-stalls, the ornate stained glasses of fifteenth-century workmanship, the stone which closes the entrance to the old vault in which the sovereigns of Austria were long buried (the present receptacle of dead royalty is in the church of the Capuchins), the altar representing the stoning of Stephen, the Adlerthor and the Bischofsthor, the groined vaulting supported by eighteen massive pillars,—are all worth many hours of careful study. So are the beggars, deputies from the under-strata of all Austria's nationalities, who lay in wait for me—and I dare say will for you when you go to Vienna—both within and without the sacred edifice. Old women, importunate as witches, heap imprecations in the *Wiener* dialect upon the luckless wight who does not drop a kreutzer-piece into their trembling hands.

High up in the tower swings a noble and melodious bell called "Josephine," cast in the reign of Joseph I., and rung for the first time when Charles VI. fastened the imperial crown upon his brows at Frankfort. Black days have come to Austria since that time: the house of the Habsburgs—noteworthy because it has been so full of almost blameless princes—has seen bitter humiliation, and profound discouragement has knocked at the doors of the "Burg," as the Viennese call the monarch's palace. But steady toil at reconstruction has done good both to men's spirits and to their prospects, and some day Josephine's mighty tongue will clamorously announce a great victory. The peasants in the far-away Styrian Mountains sometimes stop suddenly in their work, and, calling to each other, say, "Do you hear Josephine in Vienna? What can have happened?" The bell is of immense power. An ingenious fire-alarm is also managed from the belfry in which Josephine is housed. St. Stephen's is so central that the numbers of the streets are reckoned from it.

From the venerable church it is but a short walk through handsome streets lined with fine business-blocks, the lower stories of which are devoted to attractive shops, to the Graben, the broad but not long avenue which the eye hails gratefully after resting on narrow lanes on many sides of it. The most bewildering effect is produced on the visitor by constantly stepping from brilliant thoroughfares into mean and unattractive ones. The arcades which branch out from the Graben are much finer than the "passages" of

Paris. It is astonishing that they have not been adopted in our American cities, where the extreme heat in summer and the cold and snow in winter render them very desirable. The Graben—which derives its name from the fact that it is on the site of the moat of the old fortifications existing in the twelfth century—is a dangerous place for people with slender purses, for in the windows are displayed all the tempting specialties of Vienna, such as delicious Russia leather goods, ornamental bindings for books and albums, bronzes and *bijouterie*, photographs—for which the Viennese artists seem to possess especial talent—and carvings from the Tyrol and from the Styrian Alps. There are no striking architectural features in the famous avenue; the red-nosed hackmen group around a peculiar-looking monument erected in 1693 to commemorate the cessation of the plague; and, in the season, hundreds of tall, elegant ladies, equipped in the latest Paris fashions, besiege the shops. "The season" is an unfortunate moment for the stranger who is not rich. In autumn and winter every hotel, every suitable apartment-house, every palace, is occupied by the country nobility, who flock in from their estates, where they have been economizing for seven months, to lead a merry life in the capital for the other five. Princes, archdukes and counts are as plenty as blackberries in an American pasture. The respect for title is carried to an exaggerated point in Austria unknown even in Great Britain. The porter at a grand hotel speaks with bated breath of his titled guests. Hat-raising, genuflexion and hand-kissing salute the nobleman from the moment he leaves his bedchamber until he returns to it at night. These courtesies cost money: each noble lord is severely fleeced by his retainers, by shopkeepers and by hotel-men; and before he leaves for home he is frequently compelled to call upon some Hebrew friend for a tremendous loan. Vienna is a very expensive capital: it is safe to say that fifty cents there will not buy more than twenty in Paris.

CONCLUDING PART.

THE Ring-Strasse was a happy thought. Vienna would have been but a second-rate capital without it. But it was a terribly expensive conception, and Austrian finances could not stand the strain which it placed upon them. To-day the project is incomplete, but it is splendid, even in its unfinished condition. When all the great edifices, which now look melancholy and forlorn surrounded with ugly palings and scaffoldings, are complete, Paris must look to her laurels. The Viennese is proud of his "Ring," and as soon as his business is done he hastens from his dingy office in an ancient and unsavory street to promenade in the immensely broad avenues or to view other promenaders from behind the windows of a café or *restauration*.

Until the early years of this century Vienna possessed a double line of fortifications. She did not propose to be again caught napping by the Turks. In 1704 the exterior line was built to protect the city against Rakoczy's Hungarians, who were exceedingly troublesome. This still exists, but the city has gone beyond it, and the traveller is not a little surprised to find himself confronted by the guard whose task it is to levy duty upon passengers and freight coming in to town when he thinks that he is in the very centre of the capital. After 1858 the inner fortifications, which were gradually crumbling into unsightly ruins, were mainly removed, although some of the massive walls may still be seen, and the new Ring-Strasse was built on the site of the old rampart and fosse. The builders were mindful of coming generations, and laid out the avenue on such an ample scale that the present population cannot fill it. Even on fête-days it has a suburban air. But a century hence the wisdom of the plans will be apparent.

Starting from the new and magnificent Exchange, in front of which crowds are always pressing as tumultuously as is possible for people who are not especially excitable, a walk around the Ring is exceedingly impressive. The Exchange is a rather sad-colored structure, with a superb portico. The interior is finer than that of any other Exchange in Europe. The public cannot view it from convenient galleries, as it can those of Paris and London: the speculators who frequent it even pay an annual subscription for their entries. Each businessman of importance has a small room opening on one of the three grand naves of the central hall. There he receives his visitors and makes his sales. Clouds of smoke rise up to the stately ceiling, and from the corridors below come odors of invigorating beer. In the basement the flour exchange is located, besides a colossal restaurant, where much of the principal business of Vienna is done between the discussion of two *bocks*. After the terrible crisis of 1873 there were some stormy scenes outside this Exchange. Several prominent financiers were brutally beaten, and the government was compelled to send troops to restore order. Now the men who were then doing business by millions are contented with the safer game of hundreds, and are every way more rational than during the days of inflation.

Not far from the Exchange, and on a side street, is the new telegraph-office, which is, as a recent writer has expressed it, "a finer palace than that of the emperor." The telegraph service in Austria is admirable and cheap, and apparently restricted by no more formalities since the epoch of liberalism arrived than in America. A porter, imposing in costly uniform, meets you on the steps and directs you to any office which you may designate. Every palace, church and establishment of importance, even the bank and the wholesale dry-goods house, boasts one of these porters, dressed far better than a general and of most extravagant manners. These gentry date from the time when Charles VI. introduced the most extraordinary luxury into Vienna, and when it was not uncommon for a single nobleman to have a hundred servants in his household.

The Ring is dotted with beautiful structures from the Exchange to the Grand Opera. The police head-quarters is installed in a mammoth hôtel built just before the crash—an hôtel devoid, however, of any special architectural features. The days have passed away when the police was Austria's principal and most formidable organization, and when no man's secrets were safe; but the famous body still has great authority. The men, in their short jackets and navy hats, and with their broad sabres dangling at their sides, are prompt and efficient, as now and then they need to be, for Vienna has a *canaille* among its lower classes as dangerous as that of London. Not far from the police-office are the Comic Opera, the Hôtel de France and the unfinished Parliament Palace, City Hall and University. Heaven alone knows when these latter will be finished. The present Chamber of Deputies is a temporary structure, insignificant in appearance and inconvenient. If these great buildings are ever completed, the government intends to build near them a vast museum, in which the rich collections of the Belvedere and of the Museum of Natural History will be united. Near the site selected for this museum are the stables of the emperor, in which six hundred noble horses are housed; and among the treasures in these stables are saddles and rich housings taken from the Ottomans whom John Sobieski chased from under the walls of Vienna. At this point of the Ring the splendors of the Austrian capital will culminate, unless new wars and financial embarrassments for ever swamp the designs. The Votive Church, a memorial of Francis Joseph's gratitude to Heaven for his escape from assassination in 1853, is, to my thinking, the prettiest church in Austria. It is a triumph of Gothic art. The delicious lightness of its lines, the ethereal colors of its windows, the quaint effect produced by its sharply-pitched roof ornamented with variegated tilings,—all give a pleasurable sensation to eyes long offended by heavy and ungracious edifices. I doubt if there is a single church in the United States as beautiful as this

STATUE OF THE EMPEROR FRANCIS I. OF AUSTRIA.

"votive" shrine, which springs as daintily and naturally from the ground as does a slender and graceful elm.

There are many lovely gardens in Vienna, but none more handsome than the Hofgarten, which the promenader around the Ring finds at his left as he goes on toward the Grand Opera. This Hofgarten, which has in it a statue of Francis I., is the resort of the court, and has for its neighbor the humbler but even more attractive Volksgarten, where stands an imitation of the temple of Theseus at Athens, with sculptures by Canova within. A new court theatre is springing up just north of the Volksgarten. In summer and autumn thousands of Vienna burghers wander among the flowers here, listening to the music furnished by orchestras and bands such as Johann and Eduard Strauss know how to assemble. In winter the gardens look uninviting, and not even occasional sunshine can tempt the burgher and his family to risk a promenade in them. In spring, when the fountains are plashing, the great ranks of flowers sending out their perfumes, the orchestras playing, hundreds of children and nursemaids romping and laughing, knots of brilliantly-uniformed officers promenading arm-in-arm with the exquisitely-pretty Viennese girls, the Stadtpark and the Volksgarten present a spectacle gayer than any to be found in more northern capitals. There is more spontaneous and natural ebullition of merriment, more pleasure in the fact of mere existence, than the North will permit of. Life seems pleasant indeed to these large lustrous-eyed Italian beauties, to the slender and passionate-faced Hungarian daughters, to the haughty young Slavs, whose loveliness is powerful as a spell over the man of German blood. It is on the Ring and in these gardens that one discovers that Vienna is not a German city in the strict sense of the word. German is heard no oftener than at least three other languages, and Francis Joseph is beloved of all classes because he has never endeavored to force the diverse national elements in his empire into one groove or to make one language flourish at the expense of another.

The ladies of Vienna are in some respects almost as independent as those of New York or Philadelphia. They wander about the streets unattended, on foot, morning and afternoon, and feel none of the influence of those absurd conventionalities which cripple the French and the Italians.

Not far from the Hofgarten, and attached to the archduke Albert's palace, is a matchless gallery of designs and engravings, founded by that duke Albert who was a son of Frederick Augustus, king of Poland, elector of Saxony. Here are grouped together one hundred and forty-seven designs by Rembrandt alone, and a vast number of studies by Rubens and Van Dyck. Here also are nearly four hundred original designs by Albrecht Dürer, the legacy of the enthusiastic Rodolph II. The artistic riches of Vienna may be guessed at from the fact that important as is this Albertina Collection—as it is called—it is nearly equalled by five others, which give an admirable idea of the old Dutch, Italian and German schools. These five collections belong to Prince Liechtenstein and to Counts Breunner, Schönborn, Czernin and Harrach; and to these must be added that of the Belvedere, renowned throughout Europe. The Ambras collection in the Belvedere and the Museum of Weapons are among the brightest memories of American tourists. The "Hall of Fame" in the last-named museum is a colossal plan badly carried out. The scenes from the earlier history of Austria in the dome are good, but many of the other paintings are decidedly inferior. The Academy of Art, founded in 1705, likewise has some noteworthy pictures, and the emperor has promised to add to them, now that the new Academy is in order. This institution is in the Schiller Platz, and is ornamented with a bronze statue of that poet, as well as of many other demigods of literature and art. The cynical German of the North likes to say that there is no culture in Vienna, but this is very far from the truth. Goethe, Schiller and Shakespeare are as passionately adored in the Austrian capital as in Berlin, and the Bard of Avon is especially cultivated.

The "Opern Ring" and points near it are among the most interesting in Vienna, and in summer they are very animated until a late hour. But Vienna has no such night-life as Paris. By eleven o'clock the majority of the streets are almost deserted, and the porter who opens the door of your house is entitled to levy a small fine—ten kreutzers, I think—because you disturb him after his day's duties are supposed to be over. Apartment-houses are the rule, and each house has a vast outer door opening into a court, whence the various stairways diverge. There is also a variety of vast edifices, each containing hundreds of apartments and tenements, which are the property of the great ecclesiastical foundations and abbeys, and some of these are so extensive as to be mistaken by strangers for public institutions. The Schottenhof, once the property of some Scottish Benedictines, who were invited to Austria by the first duke in 1158, and the Melkerhof, which belongs to a picturesque old abbey not far from Vienna, are good illustrations of this. Many of these caravanseries have passage-ways through them, and the ground-floors within the courts are occupied by small shops. The friendly beggar also ensconces himself in the shelter of a wall, and begs of the hundreds of inmates as they go out and in, without ever being

THE BELVEDERE.

troubled by the police, so far as I could discover.

But let us come back to the Opern Ring. Naturally, the most conspicuous object upon it is the Grand Opera, whence it takes its name. This edifice is by no means of so fine exterior as that of Paris, but as an opera-house is far superior. It is long and low, its arcades are not very impressive, and the few statues which it possesses are not works of genius. But in the theatre portion of the house it is the ideal of a well-ordered structure for musical spectacles. A Swiss author, whose stories need to be taken with a grain of salt, says that the principal architect of the Opera died of chagrin because of the numerous unfavorable criticisms which his work excited. The building was completed only in 1869, and still has an atmosphere of newness environing it. The façade fronting on the Ring-Strasse is so low that when one views it from that point one can form no adequate idea of the immense size of the building. Everything within is arranged with the most exquisite order and good taste. Entering the marble corridor, which is nearly level with the street, and from which a superb marble staircase ascends to the boxes, one finds that there are plenty of ticket-offices, so that there need be no crowding. A vast and brilliantly-uniformed beadle, a stupendous creature, evidently born expressly for the purpose of creating mingled admiration and fear in just such a place as he occupies, parades to and fro, striking the marbles with his brass-pointed staff. He is "one having authority," and when there is any necessity for orders he gives them freely to a staff of more soberly dressed officials. Cloak-rooms abound; the ushers are civil to a degree unknown elsewhere; and, ushered into an audience-room which contains three thousand people, and from each section of which every part of the stage can be distinctly seen, one realizes for the first time in his life the real solemnity of theatre-going. To the orchestra-seats ladies and their cavaliers enter in the same dignified way that they would go into a fashionable church. They feel that they have come to be moved and inspired by art: the opera is an institution which they are proud to sustain, and at which they are delighted to be seen twice or thrice weekly. There are habitués who never miss a night during the whole long season. Among them I remember well an aged officer who always arrives just as the curtain is about to rise, settles slowly and painfully into his seat, and then devotes himself until the close to every detail with the most painstaking attention. The beautiful hall is so thoroughly and perfectly ventilated that one never experiences the slightest discomfort. Employés can at any moment, by touching electric bells, procure you a current of warm or of cool air. The ventilating machinery in the capacious cellars is so complicated as to seem magical. The whole building is lighted at once by an electric apparatus, and all the colossal scenes on the stage are moved up, down or away by steam. So fine is the organization in this latter department that twelve men manage the whole business of scene-shifting and produce effects which are marvellous. I have never seen anything to surpass the metamorphosis in the first act of *Tannhäuser*. In the twinkling of an eye the vast grotto in which the knight has been spellbound by the lurid lady and her attendants—a grotto filled with cascades, with cool recesses crowded with shells and translucent waves, with fantastic retreats in which sea-monsters are basking—fades away and leaves Tannhäuser trembling at the foot of a rocky hill, on which stands a lofty abbey. The beams of dawn are faintly touching the towers, and the leaves of the trees are tremulous in the morning breeze. To the left, on a moss-grown rock, one sees a shepherd lad playing upon a rustic pipe a bewitchingly pastoral air. A hunting-horn is heard: a party of huntsmen advance, and Tannhäuser awakes from his dream. This is poetry sublimated, and reconciles one with Wagner. Meantime, the grand orchestra of one hundred and fifty musicians unrivalled in Europe interprets the unspeakable and especially unsingable things which Master Wagner evolves from his soul. *Aïda*, as given at this Opera, is a touching, tender, inexpressibly lovely poem from first to last. From the moment that it begins until it ends the seer and hearer is transported into ancient Egypt, and his senses are intoxicated by a wealth of artistic detail which is unrivalled elsewhere. Frau Materna, as Zelika in *L'Africaine*, courting death beneath the poisonous manzanilla tree, while the orchestra interprets the splendid symphony on which Meyerbeer bestowed genius enough to make half a dozen composers immortal, can never be forgotten by those who have seen her. She appears to less advantage in some of the rôles in Wagner's mythical operas, where the action passes in the clouds, and where she is condemned to wear an ill-looking helmet and to unloose her locks. Seven hundred persons are employed by the administration of the Opera, and the institution has its own establishment for making properties and costumes. Shams are despised, and dresses are made of rich materials. The arsenals and museums of the state are drawn upon whenever they can be of service in the production of an opera. Herr Richter, who conducted the orchestra which interpreted Wagner's works at Bayreuth, holds the *bâton* at the Vienna Opera, and devotes himself with the greatest earnestness to popularizing the master in the Austrian capital. I confess that not even the luxurious appointments of the stage nor the exalted character of the

THE OPERA-HOUSE.

orchestration succeeded in convincing me that *The Valkyrior* was sufficiently dramatic to be interesting as an opera; but the manner in which mechanical skill had overcome the difficulties which I had supposed to prevent representation of supernatural things was quite stupefying. The chorus and the ballet are as admirable as every other essential feature of the performances is. Ballets, as given in Vienna, are worth travelling hundreds of miles to see. They are frequently in two or three acts and last for an hour or two, and villages, forests, armies and troops of beautiful women pass before the vision like phantasms in a dream. *Cappelia* is the name of a ballet first produced in Paris. When it was taken to Vienna it was so much improved and amplified as to be scarcely recognizable. The fact that ballets are given as separate pieces at the Grand Opera does not hinder the administration from embodying them in the musical works also. Nothing can exceed in idyllic beauty the scene in the temple where the priestesses of the Sun are performing their sacred rites, while Aïda and her lover are dying suffocated in the vault below. The Viennese have made this the *ne plus ultra* of dramatic contrast.

The director of the Opera is an ambitious man. He does everything thoroughly, and is so anxious to have it done better than elsewhere that he rehearsed Wagner's *Valkyrior* one hundred times before he allowed it to be presented to the public. Not very long ago one of Mendelssohn's symphonies was "set to scenery" and produced on this stage. There is a yearly season of Italian opera alternated with the regular German repertoire from March until May. It is then that such stars as Nilsson, Patti and Lucca appear. The Viennese are very faithful in their affection for their own stock company, which is exceptionally rich in good voices. Certainly, excellent singing may be expected in an opera which receives a large subsidy from the state, and which pays its first tenor twelve thousand florins for nine months' service. The Vienna people are, curiously enough, more interested in Wagner than the Prussians are. The court has, I fancy, contributed somewhat toward the enthusiasm of the Austrians for a composer who is the especial pet of Francis Joseph's son-in-law, young Louis of Bavaria.

The imperial family has its "box at the opera," a huge, richly-blazoned loge in the middle of the dress-circle, and sometimes the emperor in uniform may be seen there. He evidently comes to the music for relaxation and rest, and not merely to be seen and to lend glory to the occasion. The opera and promenades in the Prater are about the only amusements in which he indulges during "the season." He listens intently, and applauds like a connoisseur, not ostentatiously, but discreetly and "in the proper places." The emperor has a sad face — not bitter nor cynical, but worn and weary. It is not strange, for he has had trouble enough to kill men of less sturdy stock. He is an earnest man, anxious for the consolidation of the empire-kingdom committed to his keeping. It would be difficult to recognize in him now the dainty "Prince Charming" who danced with the Hungarian beauties when he was first made emperor, and whose elegance in fashionable life was on every one's tongue. Now he is a loving husband and father and a sober man of hard work—out of bed, summer and winter, at five o'clock in the morning, and busy in his library while his functionaries—even the astute Andrassy—are recovering from the fatigues of rout and reception in the diplomatic world, or ball. He takes coffee early, lights a long cigar, and smokes it while reading his despatches. About eleven o'clock he drinks a glass of beer, and at one he dines with his family. The rest of his day is spent either in the saddle or in the council-chamber. The Habsburg family is very devout, and has a great many religious duties to perform, which consume a good deal of Francis Joseph's time. To be emperor of Austria and king of Hungary implies being an apostolic as well as an imperial majesty. The emperor and all the members of his family are rigid Catholics. On Holy Friday Francis Joseph follows, bareheaded and humble, behind the archbishop who leads the procession, surrounded by swarms of priests, who revive the sacerdotal splendor of the Middle Ages, to and from the old cathedral. Austria still allows the Catholic street-displays which are forbidden in so many other countries. The state lends all that it possesses of dazzling to dignify the ceremonials of the Church. Artillery thunders, trumpets sound, heralds advance clad in fantastic garments. After religious rites have been celebrated in the interior of the imperial palace, the cortége promenades the principal streets. The archbishop bears the holy sacrament, round which rise clouds of incense from censers swung by the hands of acolytes. The emperor wears the uniform of a general, and is followed at a respectful distance by his staff of marshals and officers, the German Guard resplendent in scarlet and gold, and the Hungarians in brilliant tunics, with leopard-skins hanging from their shoulders and their breasts aglow with precious stones. The number of lackeys, pages, court chamberlains, gentlemen of the household and musicians is only exceeded by the friars, black, white, red, gray, yellow and green, who spring up on this day of days from the hundreds of religious institutions in the neighborhood of the capital, and who vanish as quickly as they came when the ceremonies are ended. All work is suspended: people who without exaggeration may be counted by hundreds of thousands flock from church to church and render the streets impassable for vehicles. Later in the day the emperor and empress enter the reception-room of the palace, and there wash the feet of twelve old men, who come clad as pilgrims to receive this touching homage and memorial of humility from the hands of their sovereigns. Then the old men are seated at table and the emperor and empress serve them food and wine. When the meal is finished Francis Joseph hangs about the neck of each venerable man a little purse filled with gold,

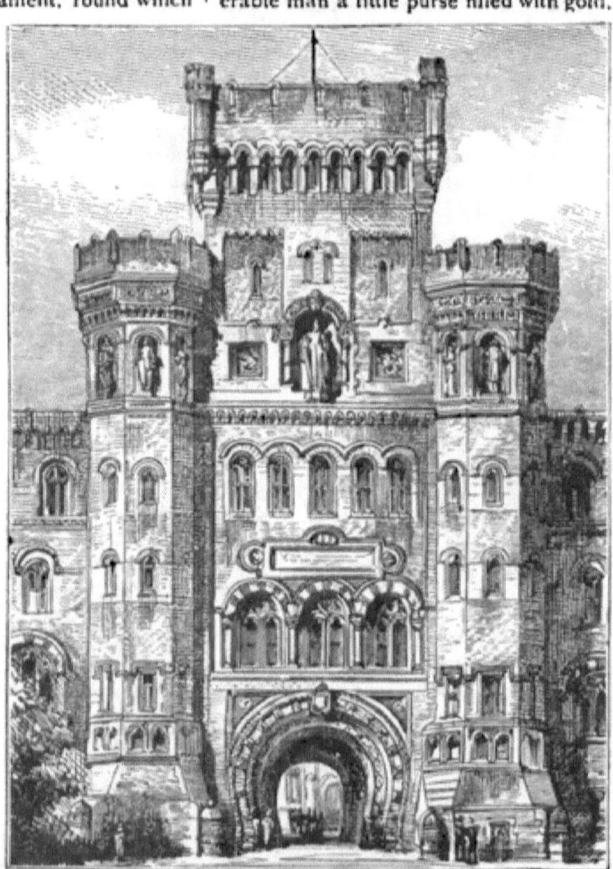

THE IMPERIAL ARSENAL.

and proceeds to inquire tenderly about his wants and those of his family. This scene never fails vividly to recall, as it is intended to do, the acts and words of Jesus at the Last Supper. There are no signs that these processions and observances will ever fall into disuse. Hungarians, Slavs, Italians and Southern Germans have a profound affection for religious pomp, and the shopkeepers would growl were they to be deprived of the income which they draw from the necessary preparations for these festivals. But many of the customs which prevailed during the last century are no longer observed. Then the mystery of the "Passion" was represented in the churches; Judas was burned in effigy at the door of the cathedral; and a "benediction of the wolves" was given in memory of the time when wolves used to venture even into the streets of Vienna, and when their howlings troubled pious souls who were engaged in their devotions. All Saints' Day and "the Day of the Dead" are observed with the same earnest fidelity as in Paris and throughout France. There is still a large fund of superstition among the lower classes in Austria, and religious fanaticism is sometimes carried to a startling pitch, as in the case of a stableman who crucified himself a year or two since, and who was found bleeding slowly to death with a rosary about his neck.

The emperor is able to speak in their own language to all his varied subjects, and it is not unusual for him to receive Slavs, Hungarians, Germans and Poles in one morning. He never makes the slightest pretensions to unapproachable dignity in public, and is as democratic as General Grant or President Hayes. The entrance to that portion of the palace in which he resides is in a vast courtyard, through which there is a public passage-way, and the humblest cobbler or corporal may stand close beside the emperor as he comes in or out. He is always affectionately saluted by baring of the head on the part of men and profound bows from women.

The old "Burg," or palace, is a mass of buildings of different styles and epochs— none of them especially striking—united by courts. Once upon a time it was defended by fortifications, but now the populace could invade it in five minutes. Within, there are splendid apartments, libraries, collections of armor and hundreds of costly portraits. In the imperial treasury are the famous globe surmounted by a cross, the sceptre crowned with an eagle and the massive crown which the Habsburgs have so long worn. The crown which the archdukes of Austria wore when they went to Frankfort to be crowned is also in this treasury: it is in fine gold, ornamented with diamonds, pearls and rubies, and cost countless thousands. The diamond crown worn by the empress on state occasions cost nearly eight hundred thousand dollars. Neither the receptacles of the Vatican nor the museums of Dresden contain such a miraculous store of riches as is shut within the treasury in this sombre old Burg. Add to this unrivalled museum the imperial library, which contains three hundred thousand volumes and twenty thousand manuscripts, the museums of natural history, the cabinets of antiquities and precious stones, galleries devoted to mineralogy, zoology and botany, a vast riding-school for the use of the ladies and gentlemen of the court in winter, and you have some faint idea of the diversity of the Burg's interior.

Passing through the gallery leading to the zoological museum during a visit to Vienna some years ago in company with an eccentric American friend, a curious episode occurred. At a dark point in the long corridor we came upon a white-coated sentinel, grim, silent, hugging his gun as if he fancied that we desired to take it from him. This sentinel, if he be still alive, has probably never recovered from the stupefaction into which he was thrown by what then and there occurred. My friend walked up to him, and with a quick motion of his hand turned the soldier round as if he had been a wooden manikin swinging on a pivot. When he had thus taken a good look at him he apostrophized him as follows: "You must get awful tired of this standing about; and it is a dreadful poor business for a big, handsome fellow like you. When you get through, you'd better emigrate to Ameriky. Never heard of Ameriky, mebbe. Well, never mind: you jest take my advice and go to Ameriky." Then he turned the sentinel round once more, gave him a playful dig in the ribs with his fore finger, and moved on. What the sentinel thought it is impos

ST. CHARLES CHURCH.

sible to imagine. Perhaps he was afraid to resent it, for fear that it might be some imperial joke. If my friend had ventured thus cavalierly to treat a Prussian sentinel, he would infallibly have been skewered with a bayonet.

Near by is the tomb—as here, in the Burg is the cradle—of the Habsburgs. A subterranean alley unites the imperial palace to the church of the Augustines, where the members of the family are in these later times buried, or, rather, where their hearts are preserved in funereal urns. There is the magnificent tomb which Maria Theresa's daughter erected to her husband, Duke Albert: Canova's richest marbles are lavished on this monument. The tombs of the emperor Leopold II. and of the great marshal and general Daum are also in this church. But the powerful emperors of the elder days sleep in the church of the Capuchins, in the centre of the city, and among them lie Joseph II. and Maximilian, the two unhappiest in the line which rules over *infelix Austria*. Even to this day the good people of Trieste and Vienna cannot speak without emotion in their voices of the gentle prince whose life was sacrificed in Mexico to the necessities of a cruel situation for which he was in no measure responsible.

Sunday church-going is a prime feature of Viennese fashionable life, chiefly because of the superb concerts given in the principal religious edifices on that day. On great festivals like those mentioned above the ladies of aristocratic circles frequently sing in the choirs. The court chapel, the church of the Augustines, and those of the Scotch and of St. Anne of the Jesuits, are thronged with elegant gentlemen and ladies, who come to listen in the same enraptured manner that they do at the opera, and doubtless for the same reason—the gratification of the æsthetic sense. In the Carlskirche, built in the reign of Charles VI. to commemorate the cessation of the plague, remarkable concerts are also given. On each side of the portal of this church rises a colossal column nearly one hundred and fifty feet in height, the effect of which is singularly imposing.

Opposite the Opera-house stands an edifice which serves to illustrate the luxurious habits of modern business-men in Vienna. It is a veritable palace, built by a brickmaker in which to house himself and his fortune. On the upper portion of the front are numerous frescoes by Rahl on a gold ground. Not far away to the right one strays upon the banks of the little Wien, the picturesque stream which flows in a deep channel through the Wieden quarter. There is a polytechnic school in this part of the town which has a thousand students, and with it is connected a technological museum which contains more than sixty thousand specimens of manufactures in various stages of production. In the Albrechtsgasse, and not far from the Opera, is the elegant new palace of the archduke Albert, connected by a covered passage-way with an older and less commodious house which was the archduke's former residence. Of the Albertina Library I have already spoken. The Albrechtsbrunnen, a fountain adorned with marble statues of the principal rivers of the empire, is an attractive work, and relieves the eye, which becomes a little fatigued by the acres of yellowish stuccoed fronts on the Ring. Beyond the Opera the broad circular thoroughfare is ornamented with palatial dwellings, hotels large enough for asylums, a commercial academy, the elaborate building of the "Society of the Friends of Music," the palaces of various potentates, several clubs frequented by the nobility, and a new academic gymnasium. Here in pleasant afternoons Count Andrassy may be seen riding or walking with his daughter, a stately Hungarian of the most bewitching type. Andrassy is a remarkable figure, and wherever he goes is well stared at. He has come perilously near to the verge of defeat in his policy many times, but has held his own with most consummate ability, keeping decently in check the Magyars, who are inclined to be overreaching, and at the same time contenting, in at least a reasonable degree, jealous Slavs and Germans. Andrassy's delicate, spirituel features are aglow with an intelligence admirably fitted for diplomatic encounter with able adversaries. His wit is like a rapier: it cuts severely before one feels the sting. The number of his *mots* on the complex Eastern Question is legion. Bismarck affects to laugh at Andrassy and his policy: the mighty Prussian chancellor speaks of Austria as the "sick woman," just as Turkey's sultan has long been called the "sick man of the East," but in his heart of hearts he realizes that the wily Hungarian would be a dangerous enemy. Andrassy is precisely the man for the epoch of "dualism" in Austria.

This word *dualism*—so often used to express the present period in the history of the country—possibly needs a bit of explanation. Victor Tissot says that when he visited Vienna the situation was explained to him by an able Austrian as

THE TOWN PARK.

follows: "From 1851 to 1859 we were ruled by absolutism; from 1859 through 1860, by federalism; from 1861 to 1865, by centralism; and now, for some time past, we have dualism. The empire is divided into two great groups of states —on the west, Cisleithania; on the east, Transleithania, separated by the little river Leytha a few leagues south of Vienna. Cisleithania comprises Lower and Upper Austria, the duchy of Salzburg, Styria, the Tyrol and the Vorarlberg, Carinthia, Carniola, the Littoral, Dalmatia, Bohemia, Moravia, Galicia, and the Bukovina. The deputies of these provinces meet in Vienna: the Germans are in the majority, and the Tchechs, Slavs and Poles complain that they are oppressed. Transleithania is composed of three states—Hungary, Transylvania, and Croatia and Esclavonia. The deputies of these provinces meet at Pesth, where the Croatian deputies refuse to go, just as the Tchechs refuse to sit in Vienna. The two central chambers of Vienna and Pesth each elect a superior delegation, whose seat is in Vienna, and before which the common ministers of Foreign Affairs, War and Finance are responsible." It is easy to see that there must be much trouble in satisfying all these discordant elements, and in shaping out of them a real *Austrian* policy. Count Andrassy has certainly endeavored, although he has by no means been negligent of his countrymen in Hungary, to take a broad and national view of matters—*national* in the sense of being in some measure representative of all the peoples scattered up and down the broad land over which the house of Habsburg rules. That he has shown large-heartedness in dealing with the condition of the unhappy populations that were lately groaning under the Turkish yoke is more astonishing when one considers that he is an Hungarian than it would be if he were of German blood. The emperor has always had full confidence in him, even in hours when the Germans grumbled loudly against him. He appears to be for ever meditating something important, and when he rides in the Prater people are more anxious to see him than to gaze upon the emperor or young Rodolph, the prince imperial.

The Stadt Park, the Kursaal and the Blumensaal are resorts in which the *beau monde* of Vienna loves to show itself, and where it comes to worship at the shrine of the Strauss brothers winter and summer. The Stadt Park on a May morning, when hundreds of people are taking their coffee under the trees or in the pleasant arcades of the restaurants, is as agreeable a spectacle as one could well expect to find in a large city. What a sharp contrast with the dull, sodden streets of London, with their gloomy house-walls reeking with smoke, and the shops with their small windows and inhospitable doors! The birds are everywhere, and the sunshine riots on the trellises, the bosquets of symmetrically-trimmed trees, the yellow walls and the noble fronts of palaces and halls near by. Eduard Strauss gives concerts with a perfect orchestra in the profusely-ornamented halls near this park when the musical season is at its height. Vienna will never tire of the Strauss brethren, nor of the delicious music which has sprung from their brains. Johann — who is a positive genius, and whom Americans have judged for themselves, since they have had an opportunity to hear him and see him—appears rarely in public as a leader now. He is the imperial chapel-master, and court duties and the composition of new operas absorb his attention; but Eduard is ubiquitous, sometimes appearing at as many as five popular concerts in an evening—here presiding at a polka, there at a waltz, and yet elsewhere beating time to a ravishing mazurka. The Strauss music is indeed, as Meyerbeer said it was, the "echo of the life of Vienna." There is in it an immense fund of passion, a flood of tears, gay and innocent laughter, the tender minor chords of despairing love, of death and sorrow; the wild and voluptuous abandonment of the Orient, the nervous vigor of the Hungarian song and dance, the noble form and rhythm of Italian poetry; and a certain German humor and grotesqueness which belong to no other national character. There is a certain delicate and refined taste which coldly rejects the Strauss compositions as unworthy attention, but no Viennese would do so if he could, or could if he would. Strauss the father had to run away from home to become a musician. He began by playing in public balls: by and by he made a triumphal tour of Europe, and died loaded with princely honors. Johann has become his principal successor, although some of the Viennese pretend to prefer Eduard, who composes fewer operas, but mingles more with the people.

Supper is a joyous festival with a very large class of the Viennese. The theatres are closed and the audiences are on their way home by half-past nine or ten o'clock, and father, mother, sons and daughters stop to sup in one of the immense underground restaurants which so astonish the stranger. Stairways, broad, beautifully decorated and illuminated, lead down into the very bowels of the earth, and there are spacious saloons where thousands of people may be seen supping together. The smoke-clouds rise from innumerable cigars, but mysteriously disappear. The beer-boys, little pale-faced fellows in black dress-coats, shout and run until it seems to the looker-on as if their legs would come

THE NORTHERN RAILWAY-STATION.

off. Laughter is universal, but never rude or repulsive. All classes meet in these basement restaurants, but never clash. Prices are moderate and food is good. The Viennese cuisine is as excellent as that of Berlin is atrocious. The Frenchman who accused the Prussians of putting sugar on their beefsteaks and beating their wives could not repeat his criticism in Vienna. The Austrian is much more refined in his taste and manners than his conquerors are. I regret that he imitates them in one particular: he persists in eating with his knife. How he manages to do it so dexterously without cutting his throat is a puzzle. The quantities of beer consumed are startling, but the climate seems to allow of more drinking than would be possible in America. Intoxication is almost unknown, at least in public.

In some restaurants above ground a variety performance is carried on upon a vast stage from seven until eleven in the evening. Officers and their wives, family groups, strangers and children, go to take their suppers at the Orpheum, the most unique restaurant it was ever my fortune to enter. A favorite comic singer makes his appearance at about ten each evening, and sings local ditties, in the choruses of which the audience—if audience it may be called—joins with a gravity and an unction which are extremely amusing. The timeworn ballads of Augustin, one of the ancient street-singers of Vienna, are still repeated with affection, and sturdy voices roll out in the most natural and unaffected manner the words,

> O du lieber Augustin,
> Alles ist hin,

while the comic artist on the stage beats time and says, "All together." When the chorus is over he adds, "Now you can go on with your eating."

The Viennese workman enters a restaurant of the lower class, and orders one of the savory dishes compounded of veal or goose of which the Austrians are so fond. As it is generally more than he can eat at once, he asks for a bit of paper, and picking out the available morsels, makes a bundle of them and stows them in his pocket. No false delicacy interferes with his determined frugality. An American workman would die before he would do such a thing. The laboring classes in the capital, as a rule, get enough to eat, but they have simple fare, which our laborers of the humblest kind would turn away from in disgust. The street-merchants, hackmen, porters and commissionaires, all manage to earn decent livings. The Vienna coachman is a furious driver, is enthusiastically devoted to beer—of which he can consume enormous quantities without appearing any the worse for it—and is very honest if he thinks that you are familiar with the prices, which are much higher than they ought to be. The little one-horse coupé is a favorite mode of conveyance for people in easy circumstances, but the populace takes to the "tramway," as horse-cars are called throughout Europe. These vehicles are divided into compartments for smokers and non-smokers, and in them every one talks to his or her neighbor in the most cordial and off-hand manner. The English and French sit glaring and scowling at each other, but the Austrians are much too good-natured to do that. If one asks a question a dozen voices are pretty sure to be heard in answer, and I had almost said that the response would be in as many languages. There is a little of the democratic crowding to which we are accustomed in horse-cars in the United States, and although the ladies do not ask you for your seat nor expect you to give it, a black-haired Jewess may very possibly give you her baby to hold, and a market-woman may set a heavy basket upon your toes.

One would scarcely think, in the United States, of going to a railway-station restaurant in pursuit of an elegant dinner, but the restaurants in the Vienna dépôts are so good that it is quite fashionable to do exactly that thing. At the Südbahn station game is cooked in the most exquisite manner. The great dépôts of Vienna are excelled by none in the world in elegance and beauty. Order and comfort are found in them, combined with spaciousness and grace. Swarms of attentive employés accost the traveller, but do not attempt to tear him to pieces. They accept modest remuneration in a polite manner, and do not ask you for "another penny" for drink, as the English porters do. A good essay on the enviable management of the Austrian railways was recently furnished our government by our efficient consul in Vienna, General Philip Sidney Post, but I believe that the facts have never found their way out of the obscurity of the State Department's reports. EDWARD KING.

ODD CORNERS IN AUSTRIA.

MONTENEGRIN POPE OF PEROI.

HE who fails to perceive that he is approaching the East as he enters Vienna, and who, as he wanders round in the gay and brilliant capital, sees no signs of Oriental manners and architecture, must indeed be dull of apprehension. I remember the startling effect which the sight of a certain church-tower between Vienna and Gratz once produced on me. I was on the road to Trieste, and, worn out with protracted journeying, fell asleep in the comfortable coupé as the train rolled out of Vienna in the early morning. When I awoke the sun was scorching my face; the train was at a standstill; and directly in front of me, surrounded by vineyards and fields where a profusion of flowers bloomed and multitudes of birds sang, I saw a—mosque! At least, it seemed to me exactly like the pictures of Oriental mosques that I had so often seen. There was the bulbous spire, the slender point at the top: the resemblance was complete. I rubbed my eyes, and could not believe that I was in Austria; and the illusion was heightened by the fact that, leaning from the carriage-window, I heard the peasants in the road below speaking the smoothly-flowing Sclavic tongue: not one word of German could I distinguish. As we went on to Gratz I looked in vain for other churches with this curious outcropping of Eastern architecture, but I did not find it again until we had travelled more than a hundred miles.

The impression of the immediate proximity of the East is of course more striking as one descends the Danube below Vienna. The dark faces of the wandering gypsies, the loose and flowing garments worn by the peasants who are tending their floating flour-mills, and the imperturbable gravity of the masses have very little that is European in them. One cannot help fancying that Asia is about to begin at some boundary arbitrarily stretched near at hand. In contrast with the heavy, blonde, voluptuous and voluminous types of womanhood in Vienna, one sees the swart, lithe, dark-eyed women from the Sclavic provinces held under the odious dominion of Turkey. There is something nameless and inexpressible in the demeanor of these latter which at once betrays their origin. On the Austrian shore of the Danube, opposite Belgrade, one sees people who are so utterly different from the Germans of Vienna, or even the Bohemians of Prague, that he cannot imagine them to be of the same country or continent. Austria's Sclavic folk are wonderfully varied: it is almost impossible to believe that they can understand one another or have a community of ideas and common national dreams and ambitions.

The variety of type in Austria is of course far greater than in most other Eu-

TRIESTE: GENERAL VIEW.

ropean countries. In the course of many journeys up and down the land I have met persons who I could have sworn were Italians, Americans, Turks, Servi-

TRIESTE: THE EXCHANGE.

ans, Frenchmen, but they always proved to be Austrians. Going one day from Trieste to Pola, the principal naval station of Austria, in the little bark Jonio, I was vastly entertained by a surgeon who was about to join his ship, and whom I should never have believed an Austrian had he not given me his word that he was a native-born subject of the House of Hapsburg. He appeared like an Italian when he was conversing in the pretty Venetian dialect so universally used along the Adriatic coast; like a Frenchman when talking rapidly and well in French; he might readily have been mistaken for a person born in a Sclavic province when he talked with the merchants from Fiume or Agram; but when he joked with the officers on the boat and swore robust Teutonic "Donnerwetters!" and "Potztausends!" he seemed to me like a foreigner talking German. Yet he was born in Vienna, and German was his native tongue.

Nowhere does one get so remarkable a panoramic view of these varied populations as during the journey from Vienna to Trieste. The good-natured and perhaps a trifle boorish German peasant; the graceful, civil and gentle-spoken representative of the German upper classes; the Styrian laborer in his quaint costume; the stolid, plodding mountaineer, with his green hat ornamented with the feathers of the heathcock; the peasant-women in their curious headdresses of long white cloths; the rotund, placid farmers; the stiff and haughty retired generals of Gratz,—all these are one by one left behind, and in their stead one passes in review the many and polite Sclaves from the towns of Agram and Sissek, or their ferocious-looking fellow-citizens, the Croatish shepherds and wood-cutters from the neighboring plains and mountains; coming at last to the Italian types at Adelsberg, and finding them everywhere until one arrives at lovely Trieste on the shores and cliffs of the Adriatic. The brown-eyed, oval-faced, chestnut-haired maiden who brings wine to the visitor at Prosecco, the little town on the great hill which overhangs Trieste, seems an alien. What does she in Austria? Is not this Italy into which we have suddenly, by some subtle magic, been conveyed? Surely, the architecture of this roadside inn, with its curious mediæval courtyard, its wooden galleries and its deep window-seats, is Italian; and so is yonder chapel, over whose door sits a woe-begone saint whose battered visage seems covered with lamentations for his lost country. Italian is the language spoken by the brown-eyed maiden; by the old woman who sprawls at the roadside, and seems to menace you with the evil eye unless you accord alms; by the stealthy-looking rascals who spring up a by-path among the rocks as you return to your carriage—fellows with rings in their ears and long knives in their belts; by the very driver of the carriage— No, he is a German, and is cursing you, perhaps, in his thick, uncouth way, because you have not sent him a draught of beer while he has been waiting for you.

The beauty and quaintness of Trieste are all the more surprising because the traveller approaches them from the landward side through such a broken and desolate country. Who does not remember what a pang the desolate and forbidding scenery of the Karst, that rock-strewn country which stretches from Adelsberg to Trieste, brought to him, coming as it did so soon after the luscious panorama of fertile fields at the bases of the Carniolan and Julian Alps, after the rich lands studded with fine barns and comfortable dwellings, and inhabited by the merry, frugal, sober, contented Sclavonians? I arrived at Adelsberg for the first time just as a beautiful September day was drawing to a close. The twilight cast a weird mantle over the masses of grayish rock which rose everywhere in the treeless plains. It seemed a land of ambush, of surprises: I could fancy that the train might be attacked there. At the station little Italian damsels, bare-headed and bare-legged, ran to and fro, melodiously crying "Fresh water!" which cooling draught they carried in earthen jars poised daintily on their shapely heads. Up a rude road which climbed a tiny hill among the piled rocks a group of maidens was slowly climbing: each girl held another by the hand, and together they were singing a tender Venetian ballad. Again I rubbed my eyes, yet I was not dreaming. Only two hours before, however, I had left Steinbrück, the comfortable restaurant-station at the junction of the roaring Sann and the noble Save, and there, among the lofty mountains and the savage and gloomy forests, I had found no trace whatever of Italians or Italian manners.

TRIESTE: A CICI FAMILY.

From Adelsberg to Trieste one is apparently in the midst of Italian civilization, although great numbers of the inhabitants in all the surrounding country are Sclavonians. Nothing can be more enchanting than this evening ride beyond Adelsberg, after the most barren portion of the Karst is passed. The vegetation in the gardens which are bestowed among the stones is rich and luxuriant: the vine shows its lithe form everywhere. Sometimes the terrible *borra*, which works such mischief along the Adriatic coast, descends on these plains, and sweeps across them with such force as to overthrow loaded wagons. When a wandering peasant sees the cloud of dust raised by the borra he throws himself flat on his face, pulls his cloak over his head, makes the sign of the cross, and waits for the unwelcome visitor to go by. In the Karst there are numerous caves and funnel-shaped cavities which the old Romans, when they were thereabout, doubtless thought were the abodes of the mischievous winds.

At Nabresina, a pretty town, thoroughly Italian in aspect, the road begins to descend the crags at the foot of which Trieste lies. The twilight had deepened into darkness ere we arrived there, and from the car-windows there was little to be seen except the edges of rocks and occasional "section-houses" by the track overgrown with vines. But presently a "large low moon" stole out of a dull horizon, and began to invest even the most prosaic bits of scenery with her proverbial witchery. I leaned out from the window, regardless of the sharp admonition of the guard, who was clambering from carriage to carriage on the narrow outer platform, and who espied me. As the moon pierced the thin veil of clouds which at first seemed anxious to rob her of her glory, the train came slowly and carefully round a great pinnacle and rolled along the edge of a high precipice. Below, in the distance, were the blue waves of the placid Adriatic, now illuminated by the chaste moonbeams, so that I could see a long path of silver, over which merrily slipped little barks bound inward to Trieste. The effect was exhilarating, delightful: in fancy I already saw those headlands of the Istrian coast which in the words of the old poet "brood o'er the sea;" and I strained my eyes to catch a view of the lights of Trieste. But the train wound on and on under jagged masses of rock which seemed certain to fall upon and crush us; beside yawning gulfs into which had we been plunged there would have been no earthly resurrection for any one of us; through sleepy villages which appeared just on the point of committing suicide by sliding into the Adriatic; over bridges and through tunnels, all high in air; constantly descending—descending slowly but surely. At last a line of dancing lights seemed suddenly to spring from the bosom of the waves: far below us they beckoned, pirouetted, vanished, reappeared. I looked at them steadfastly for half an hour, yet we did not seem to come nearer them. Just as I was beginning to despair of ever reaching them our engine shrieked, and we rolled into a long tunnel. When we came out I could find the lights no longer, but in ten minutes we were in the huge railway-dépôt at Trieste.

The night was lovely: each touter for each hotel gave me such a bad opinion of every other that I stored my baggage in the station and set off alone for a walk, while the rattling omnibuses, with their polyglot conductors chattering in German, Italian, French, English, Sclavic and Greek, whirled away to the various caravansaries. It was ten o'clock, and in the harbor basin, along whose edge I took my way, the air was melodious with the ringing of ships' bells sounding the hour. A solemn rich note from the tower of some far-away church added harmony and beauty to these chimes. I saw but few people: here and there a belated sailor was sidling toward his bark, keeping his eyes warily fixed on the promenading watchman, who seemed half inclined to make him halt and declare his name and qualities. Now and then I passed a little café, in front of which, under broad awnings, showily-dressed Montenegrins and Greeks were drinking sugared water or coffee and playing simple games. At last I came to a hostelry facing the quay, and, entering, ordered the Italian porter to send for my baggage. Then I sat down on a bench in the moonlight, and watched the rows of fishing-boats symmetrically ranged against the stone sides of the quay, their stained sails showing out in bold relief in the moonlight; watched the great fiery eyes of the steamer just coming in from Constantinople, and another departing for Venice; and watched the blue water on which all these craft were so silently and securely cradled. Finally, I betook myself sleepily to an exquisite and diminutive room, from whose windows I could look out over the Adriatic, and could hear the musical resonance of the bells from hour to hour until, at midnight, the air was verily burdened with it; and then — and then I slept.

Nothing was stranger to me next morning, as I wandered through the narrow and antique streets of old Trieste, than that I belonged to this day and generation. It seemed to me that I had somehow gone back three hundred years — that perhaps I was a Dalmatian sailor returning from some venturesome excursion in far Levant, and had landed here in Trieste to repose my weary bones, or that I was a Venetian merchant or adventurer strayed away from my own proud city for a little airing, and amusing myself in fair Trieste. There was nothing to suggest the present century in the massive walls, black with age, which reared themselves on either side of the lanes, so near together that only the most infinitesimal bit of blue sky was visible between them at the top. There was no hint of the nineteenth century in the tiny shops stowed into the most miraculously picturesque corners, up the most sombre blind alleys and in the most forlorn basements. I found a shoemaker directly over my head, and a primitive-looking barber's shop almost under my feet. I peered into a cabaret, whose door was pierced with a half window protected by a thin curtain, and there, on wooden benches, I could see sailors with long knives in their belts talking uproariously and gambling furiously. Climbing a dozen ancient, well-worn stone steps to get into the next street, I came upon half a dozen bald-headed little babies squatted together, crooning and laughing in all the recklessness and impudence of helpless babyhood in the path of men and women passing with heavy burdens on their broad backs; yet no baby was smashed to a jelly under the splay feet of any of the porters, and no infant rolled down the steep and dangerous flight of stairs. On a long wall overhanging a courtyard a hundred feet below a bevy of round-armed, black-haired girls were perched, swinging their feet, munching fruit and making mock of timid passers-by. An unlucky movement would have precipitated these untrimmed beauties on to the cruel stones below; but they balanced themselves as if they had been birds, while they responded gayly to the mockeries of two young soldiers who, in the window of a tall house forty feet above them, were looking out on the world and making free comments upon it after their own fashion. Tired of seeing these towering masses of grayish stone always above me, I climbed persistently. At last I blundered into a blind alley, where a party of young maidens, not specially encumbered with clothing, were dancing merrily to the music of a hurdygurdy, whose owner had just happened that way. The hurdygurdy-man's monkey was of a sociable turn of mind, and came up to chatter in my ear and to examine the texture of my silk umbrella. As he betrayed an intense anxiety to tear the umbrella in pieces, I was compelled to chastise him with it. He retreated, howling and chattering, to his master: the maidens, looking up from their sport, perceived a stranger and hastily dispersed in all directions, and the hurdygurdy-man stood contemplating the hapless wanderer who was the innocent cause of the sport's interruption with an expression of mingled rage and disgust which it would be quite impossible for me to describe. I retreated precipitately, and did not look round until I found myself on a broad plateau near an ancient church. From this plateau I could overlook the port of Trieste and the adjacent mountains. Away across the bay, and sheltered from the rude winds of winter, as well as from the torrid summer suns, by projecting crags, I saw the historic château of Miramar, world-famous since one of the former occupants died an usurper's death in Mex-

PEASANT-WOMAN: NEIGHBORHOOD OF POLA.

ico, and the other met a more horrible fate in losing her reason. Poor stately, generous Maximilian! Trieste has a good statue of him now in one of her squares fronting on the bay; and looking at it, and remembering the principal points in his character, one cannot help a thrill of pity for him, for he was emphatically a man. Perhaps the Italian population here in Trieste would not share in this sympathy; for, although they are loyal and wear an outward air of content, they are never weary of criticising the Germans, whom they dislike. I was not a little amused to note that some of the most intelligent merchants in Trieste share the absurd belief of the Italian lower classes, that the central Austrian government does all it can to prevent the prosperity of Trieste. When asked why such a peculiar course of conduct should be maintained, they shook their heads gloomily, and were, I fancy, really at a loss for a reason.

Business habits in Trieste are notably different from those in other portions of the Austrian empire, and the climate demands the difference. In summer the bankers and principal merchants enter the cool darkened rooms in which they transact their affairs at an early hour in the morning, and work until the sun grows hot. The middle of the day is given to breakfast and to a visit to the corridors of the Exchange, where a cosmopolitan throng is always gathered. The Polish Jew, with his incomparably filthy great-coat and the slovenly locks of hair pulled down in front of his ears, shuffles by; the Greek and the Montenegrin, in their white and green petticoats, discuss

PARENZO.

financial matters amicably; the rotund and spectacled German and the refined Italian argue questions of trade-policy with the Sclaves and Croats; and the shippers and skippers represent every nation under the sun. After the visit to the Exchange, and a cup of coffee or an ice in one of the pleasant cafés which abound in the vicinity, the merchants disappear from public view until three o'clock. At that hour banks and wholesale establishments are reopened, and work goes on uninterruptedly until six. Then the streets are filled with people taking the air before supper: they flock to the principal promenades and gardens to hear music, they stroll on the piers or they loll in the shade of their own courtyards until twilight or dark, when they refresh themselves copiously after the day's fatigue.

Looking seaward from the terrace, old Trieste seems in some miraculous fashion to disappear, and the new town, with its handsome piers, its wide and well-paved streets, its pleasant hotels, and its main avenue, the "Corso," comes into view. The German element is so thoroughly subordinated here that one sees almost nothing of it. The apothecary, the bookseller, the photographer, the silk-merchant, all advertise their articles of merchandise in Italian; the newspapers, printed in black, heavy type on thick, muddy paper, are in Italian; the "commissionnaire" who offers to show you the sights of Trieste addresses you in English with a strong Italian accent; the black-eyed ladies languidly promenading wear lace veils thrown loosely over their beautiful heads and talk in high Italian key. The playbill, in Italian, announces a most extraordinary season of comedy: if you attend the theatre in the evening, you will find that the audience is almost entirely composed of women, all of whom have the inevitable black lace veils or at least coquettish black bonnets; the play will doubtless be highly spiced with allusions to domestic infelicity and to the failings of the representatives of Mother Church; the ladies will manifest their enthusiasm by tears, sometimes by tapping upon the backs of the chairs in front of them with their fans. At the opera—which is often extremely good—the *haut ton* of Trieste is to be seen—the German officials and their wives, the Italian merchants and the upper crust of the Hebrew social fabric. These same people also frequent the huge and beautifully decorated halls in which the best of classical music and moderately good beer are served up together. Hundreds of elegantly-dressed ladies and gentlemen are sometimes seen in one of these halls at supper, while the orchestra in the gallery plays the dreamy music of Donizetti or startles the ear with audacious refrains from Wagner's Tetralogy.

On this terrace stands the cathedral of San Giusto, a sombre edifice filled with memorials of the Romans. It is an odd collection of basilicas, baptisteries and Byzantine churches, representing all grades of architecture from the fifth to the fourteenth century; and Roman columns aid in supporting the principal tower. Underneath a stone in front of this venerable edifice lies Fouché, who played such a singular and important rôle under Napoleon I. as minister of police, and who gave up the ghost at Trieste in 1820. Winckelmann, the great German archæologist, is also buried near by, not far from a museum of antiquities which is appropriately located in a venerable burying-ground. Winckelmann was robbed and murdered in a tavern in Trieste more than a hundred years ago. To-day the traveller's life is as safe in the well-ordered town as it is in Paris. The Austrian police understand how to enforce the law in a seaport; and when a Montenegrin comes to town he has to lay aside the small arsenal of weapons which he usually carries in his belt before he is permitted to land.

Landward, seaward, the view is entrancing. In winter the mountains now and then take on a bleak aspect, for the wind is sometimes unkind at Trieste; but in summer the exquisite effects of light and shadow on the tall crags, the wide expanse of the placid blue water, the sleepy headlands that seem to hide such mysteries behind them, and the rows of colored sails gliding in and out among the large craft, make a fascinating picture. There is wealth of curious costume in the market-places, for the Istrian and Dalmatian peasants still keep to their an-

PARENZO: THE CATHEDRAL, A RELIC OF THE EARLIEST AGES OF CHRISTIANITY.

cient dress. The great square of the Pescheria, the fish-market of Trieste, is filled from early morning till noon with a crowd of babbling girls and women dressed in glaring colors, bare-headed, and sometimes bare-footed. The fruit-venders sit lazily all day behind stands piled with luscious grapes, figs, melons and pomegranates, and do not even take the trouble to cry their wares. Late in the afternoon a little steamer comes bustling to a wharf near the Pescheria, and the gossiping women flock to it with their baskets on their heads. As soon as all are on board a whistle blows, and the noisy freight is whisked off to Capo d'Istria, where these worthy fishmongers live, and whence they draw their supplies.

Capo d'Istria! An odd corner indeed! Old Trieste is modern compared with this: the past seems to have got a firm hold in Istria; there is no hint of modernism, unless it be a huge state prison, which stands on an eminence overlooking a breezy estuary. No! the prison accords well with the ancient walls, the curious Venetian gateways, the alleys so narrow that one cannot help thinking that the houses have just been jostling each other, the forbidding passages where it seems as if assassins, lying in wait with long sharp daggers, must be the inevitable and fitting accessories. The inhabitants of all this region were once greatly given to piracy and brigandage, but now they are peaceful and law-abiding, as they may well be under the shadow of the great frowning prison. This was the *Justinapolis* of the Romans, and there are many traces of the dominion of those hardheaded old conquerors in all the territory. The Venetians came to Capo d'Istria nine hundred years ago, and stayed there long after other portions of Istria had passed into the hands of the Austrians. The central square of the town is as Venetian as the great plaza of St. Mark: into the dimly-lighted cathedral which stands in a recess at one extremity the peasant men and women daily flock and fall on their knees in prayer. They wander about under the olive trees, and never seem to do any work except at prayer-time. The hotels in Capo d'Istria are repulsive-looking stone structures, through whose lower stories long and narrow passages lead into pretty gardens where waiters serve the foaming Asti, the delicious Prosecco, and the dark-red traitorous Istrian wine, which is pleasant to the palate, but dangerous to the brain. The good German burghers from the more Teutonic portions of Austria greatly enjoy a journey to Capo d'Istria and deep draughts of its wine.

Outside the gates of the town — for Capo d'Istria has gates and walls — the country looks as wild and uncivilized as it was a thousand years ago. A poorly-graded road leads over some rolling hills to the adjacent town of Pirano, a picturesque place as seen from the sea, but common and dirty when approached by land. A few poorly-clad women, driving donkeys laden with grain, fish or vegetables, and one or two swineherds, followed by their snorting, burrowing charges, are the only living objects which greet the eye, unless perchance a blind, halt or lame beggar looms up before the visitor, insisting with outstretched skinny hand upon immediate alms. The Istrian peasantry in the interior are not over fond of the stranger: they laugh at his European clothes, and find his modern refinements repulsive; they understand him and his new notions as little as they do the colossal remains of the fortified towns of the people of the Stone Age which are scattered through Istria. But these good folk are nevertheless far from wishing the wanderer any harm: they will not throw a brick at him, as an English farm-laborer might do. And if they do not understand hospitality very well, it is because they so rarely have any occasion to practise it.

These little Istrian towns, Capo d'Istria, Omago, Cittanova, Parenzo, Orsara, Rovigno, scattered along the pretty coast from Trieste to Pola, know nothing of railroads, and many of them have no regular steamer communication with the outer world. The people who live in the smaller towns by the water-side furnish fine recruits for the Austrian navy: the women rarely leave home. Many of them have never been twenty miles from their native towns in their lives, and their only amusement is rambling among the rocks or making pilgrimages to the neighboring monastery. The pilgrimage is a great feature of life in all these southern Austrian provinces: on the wild Dalmatian border, among the rugged rocks, the traveller may any day come upon a long procession of men and women carrying candles or branches of trees or rudely-fashioned crucifixes, and all on the road to a cross placed high on some wooded hill or to a church on a pinnacle.

POLA: THE ARSENAL.

It is said that a quarter of a million persons annually visit the pilgrimage church of Marienzell in the Styrian Mountains; and in every mountain-region the numbers might be counted by thousands. Some of the small Istrian towns are scourged by malaria, which the inhabitants bow down before without the least endeavor to escape from it. Much of the ill-health is due to the wretched drainage of the houses and to the poor food eaten by these folk, but he who should attempt to teach them new and better ways would run the risk of being burned as a sorcerer.

Pola, with its grand Roman amphitheatre, with its fine hills and its excellent basin, where the Austrian government generally keeps a large fleet stationed, is well enough known to the traveller who has made the journey to Antivari or Corfu. The Austrians are proud of their naval station, which they have fortified, and are continually fortifying, with consummate care. The town is a shrine filled with great memories. Augustus built a fine resort there, enriched it with superb monuments and called it *Pietas Julia*. Belisarius went out from Pola with the fleet which was destined to assemble before Ravenna. A royal Roman road led from Pola to Trieste. The Venetian republic took the town in the twelfth century, and kept possession of it until its fall. So rich was Pola in Roman memorials that the Austrians, when they wished to build a citadel on an advantageous point of land, were compelled to destroy the remains of a beautiful ancient theatre. One of the present gates of the town is the *Porta Aurea*, which the magnificent Sergius erected in honor of his victory. The temple of Diana has been transformed into a block of dwellings, as has the superb palace of Diocletian at Spoleto. Your landlord is liable to tell you that you are lodged in the temple of Jupiter, and he may possibly invite you to crack a bottle of wine with him in the palace of Justice. One treads upon dust of antique monuments at every step, and under the foundations of the breweries, arsenals and shiphouses of the Pola of to-day lie the ruined tombs and sarcophagi of which Dante has sung in his *Inferno*.

He who voyages on the Adriatic in autumn needs courage, especially if he sails along the Istrian and Dalmatian coast. The borra sweeps down without warning, and straightway the sea is transformed from a tranquil sheet of lovely blue water into the veriest whirlpool and mad vortex of waves imaginable. The rugged coast which must be skirted before the entrance to Pola harbor can be reached becomes a constant danger: the small steamers rock down to their rails, and now and then seem just on the point of sinking. Soldiers *in transitu* swear, peasants howl, friars count their beads and pray, travellers from other climes, accustomed to the buffetings of a dozen oceans, suffer and are silent. Although this coasting seems but child's play to the inexperienced observer, it is fraught with great danger, and requires accurate and immediate judgment on the part of the captain, as any one journeying from Trieste to Cattaro or Antivari will readily discover.

Southward from the southernmost point of Istria stretches along the coast a garland of small islands, many of which are inhabited by only a few fishermen and friars. For two hundred miles the steamers can make their way tranquilly between these islands and the mainland, feeling but little of the inconveniences of storms which lash the sea just outside the islets. In summer and in autumn a journey through these long canals, past these pretty islands, on whose reddish-brown rocks the resplendent sunlight of these latitudes produces the most entrancing and bewitching effects of color, is an experience never to be forgotten. Land is never lost sight of: on either side there are houses, gardens, peaks capped with monasteries, peaceful villages, fertile fields, valleys rich with vines, gulfs as tranquil as broad rivers. At night the steamer cautiously picks its way into the dozens of small ports, and chattering throngs of boatmen, lighting up the dark water with torches, row out their little barks to receive the mails and the merchandise. In every large port one comes upon a variation in dialect, in dress and in features.

One almost forgets that Austria is not Italian as he wanders for days in these towns and among these mountains, where the signs on the shops and rustic inns and the manners of the people are all Italian in tone. The Sclavonic population, although numerous in all these regions, does not give any surface evidences of its existence. But it is easy to find within a night's journey from Trieste towns and sections where the Sclavic is spoken almost exclusively, and where there is not an Italian sign to be found over a single shop. I made an excursion in 1875 from Steinbrück, which is on the direct railway-line from Vienna to Trieste, down the valley of the Save River to Agram and Sissek and the towns beyond on the Turkish border. The Save—or *Sau*, as the Germans call it—is a capricious and charming stream, born of pure springs far in the recesses of the lofty Carniolan Alps. It rushes down through the forests, now breaking, a veritable torrent, through some frightful chasm, now flowing smoothly through rich meadows, and now—as at Steinbrück, where it receives the waters of the Sann—becoming broad and shallow as it finds room in a valley at the bases of the great hills. Around Steinbrück the scenery is grand, imposing, in some of the

AGRAM.

gorges awful. The precipices are majestic in their beauty. The road thence to Agram leads high above the river, along beetling crags, around corners where an unskilful engineer would throw his train hundreds of feet on to rocks below, and through villages lying under the walls of some vast château, whose owner is doubtless spending his income in riotous living in Vienna. Agram has no specially remarkable architectural features: the autumn climate there reminds one of the charms of Indian summer in New England and in the Middle States; and I found myself imagining several times during my stay there that I had been transported by magic into some quiet New England city of twenty-five thousand inhabitants. Yet I was possessed of this illusion only when I looked at some of the comfortable mansions, in whose wide yards children were rollicking and spectacled maidens sat reading books hour by hour. The white-gowned peasant-women, with their flaming-red head-dresses, who served in the market; the men, with their square-brimmed Hungarian hats, their amply-flowing white trousers, their girdles filled with knives, and their clownish manners, certainly furnished no reminders

VILLAGE NEAR CAPO D'ISTRIA: THE CLERGYMAN'S RESIDENCE.

of New England. Agram is a rich and thriving town, and, like Belgrade in Servia, one of the centres whence come the great propelling forces now at work in the interests of Pansclavism. Agram has universities, fine schools of upper and lower grade, and a hundred organizations for culture and refinement: it has subtle and active politicians also, and the central Austrian government keeps a strong garrison there, ready to declare it in a state of siege if at any time the sympathies of the leaders should bid fair to lead the country into war or disagreeable diplomatic negotiations. These Sclaves of Croatia hate the Hungarians and the influence which they possess in Austria to-day as bitterly as the Servians do. The people of the aristocratic and commercial classes are refined, polite and hospitable. They live much in the open air, and gather for supper in the evening in the courtyards of the large hotels to listen to music and to chat together.

Round about Agram the plains stretch out, seemingly limitless as the prairies of Illinois, after a few fertile hills are passed. Agram itself lies on a hill, the top of which is occupied by a handsome square, surrounded with cafés and pretty mansions. In early autumn the waving grain and the dark green of the trees along the banks of the Save contrast prettily with the gay colors of the garments worn by the peasant-women trudging afield and doing a large share of the heavy farmwork. The road to Sissek leads through a level land dotted with moss-grown villages. In the narrow streets of these ancient dorfs wild-looking children watch flocks of screaming geese, and a few old women sit spinning or knitting in the sun. The young people make profound obeisances, and the old ones repeat the traditional formula, "I kiss your hand," when addressed by a stranger. Sissek is a rambling village, divided by the Save into military and civil quarters: a strong garrison is always maintained there, as in most of the towns on the Austrian side of the river. A little below the town stands an old stone castle which has been often besieged by the Turks when in their wild wars they set their faces toward Vienna. To-day this historical château is —alas for the romance of association!— a cheese-factory!

To Sissek and to many other towns on the Save, which here begins to be a broad and navigable stream, refugees from Bosnia have been flocking in great numbers for the last eighteen months. Nothing has done more to excite to fiery pitch of indignation the Sclavic populations of this interesting and influential section of Austria than the sight of these unhappy thousands driven from their homes by the cruelty of the rapacious and bloodthirsty Turk. Centuries of enforced degradation have done their work on these unfortunate masses, these timorous and dependent Christians, who are themselves harmless, laborious and frugal when not driven to desperation. The Austrian government has not been hard-hearted enough to send the cowering wretches back across the boundary to a fate which is worse than death, and hundreds of them are settling in Croatia and Sclavonia. Some day, when they have learned the difficult lesson of independence, they will arise and turn their weapons against those who have beaten them down into the very dust; and then let the oppressor tremble! But up to the present time they have not been allowed to have any weapons: an ignorant and malicious Mohammedan police has watched them with the most untiring care, and has succeeded, by terrible punishments inflicted upon the few daring ones who have attempted to conspire, in frightening all the others into passive endurance. It seems now as if the hour of deliverance has sounded; yet no man can venture to prophesy what is to be the rôle of the Sclaves in Austria in the settlement of the Sclavic question. EDWARD KING.

ALONG THE DANUBE.

SOMENDRIA.

ADA-KALÉ is a Turkish fortress which seems to spring directly from the bosom of the Danube at a point where three curious and quarrelsome races come into contact, and where the Ottoman thought it necessary to have a foothold even in times of profound peace. To the traveller from Western Europe no spectacle on the way to Constantinople was so impressive as this ancient and picturesque fortification, suddenly affronting the vision with its odd walls, its minarets, its red-capped sentries, and the yellow sinister faces peering from balconies suspended above the current. It was the first glimpse of the Orient which one obtained; it appropriately introduced one to a domain which is governed by sword and gun; and it was a pretty spot of color in the midst of the severe and rather solemn scenery of the Danubian stream. Ada-Kalé is to be razed to the water's edge — so, at least, the treaty between Russia and Turkey has ordained — and the Servian mountaineers will no longer see the Crescent flag flying within rifleshot of the crags from which, by their heroic devotion in unequal battle, they long ago banished it.

The Turks occupying this fortress during the recent war evidently relied upon Fate for their protection, for the walls of

Ada-Kalé are within a stone's throw of the Roumanian shore, and every Mussulman in the place could have been captured in twenty minutes. I passed by there one morning on the road from Orsova, on the frontier of Hungary, to Bucharest, and was somewhat amused to see an elderly Turk seated in a small boat near the Roumanian bank fishing. Behind him were two soldiers, who served as oarsmen, and rowed him gently from point to point when he gave the signal. Scarcely six hundred feet from him stood a Wallachian sentry, watching his movements in lazy, indifferent fashion. And this was at the moment that the Turks were bombarding Kalafat in Roumania from Widdin on the Bulgarian side of the Danube! Such a spectacle could be witnessed nowhere save in this land, "where it is always afternoon," where people at times seem to suspend respiration because they are too idle to breathe, and where even a dog will protest if you ask him to move quickly out of your path. The old Turk doubtless fished in silence and calm until the end of the war, for I never heard of the removal of either himself or his companions.

The journeys by river and by rail from Lower Roumania to the romantic and broken country surrounding Orsova are extremely interesting. The Danube-stretches of shimmering water among the reedy lowlands — where the only sign of life is a quaint craft painted with gaudy colors becalmed in some nook, or a guardhouse built on piles driven into the mud — are perhaps a trifle monotonous, but one has only to turn from them to the people who come on board the steamer to have a rich fund of enjoyment. Nowhere are types so abundant and various as on the routes of travel between Bucharest and Rustchuk, or Pesth and Belgrade. Every complexion, an extraordinary piquancy and variety of costume, and a bewildering array of languages and dialects, are set before the careful observer. As for myself, I found a special enchantment in the scenery of the lower Danube — in the lonely inlets, the wildernesses of young shoots in the marshes, the flights of aquatic birds as the sound of the steamer was heard, the long tongues of land on which the water-buffaloes lay huddled in stupid content, the tiny hummocks where villages of wattled hovels were assembled. The Bulgarian shore stands out in bold relief: Sistova, from the river, is positively beautiful, but the now historical Simnitza seems only a mud-flat. At night the boats touch upon the Roumanian side for fuel — the Turks have always been too lazy and vicious to develop the splendid mineral resources of Bulgaria — and the stout peasants and their wives trundle thousands of barrows of coal along the swinging planks. Here is raw life, lusty, full of rude beauty, but utterly incult. The men and women appear to be merely animals gifted with speech. The women wear almost no clothing: their matted hair drops about their shapely shoulders as they toil at their burden, singing meanwhile some merry chorus. Little tenderness is bestowed on these creatures, and it was not without a slight twinge of the nerves that I saw the huge, burly master of the boat's crew now and then bestow a ringing slap with his open hand upon the neck or cheek of one of the poor women who stumbled with her load or who hesitated for a moment to indulge in abuse of a comrade. As the boat moved away these people, dancing about the heaps of coal in the torchlight, looked not unlike demons disporting in some gruesome nook of Enchanted Land. When they were gypsies they did not need the aid of the torches: they were sufficiently demoniacal without artificial aid.

Kalafat and Turnu-Severinu are small towns which would never have been much heard of had they not been in the region visited by the war. Turnu-Severinu is noted, however, as the point where Severinus once built a mighty tower; and not far from the little hamlet may still be seen the ruins of Trajan's immemorial bridge. Where the Danube is twelve hundred yards wide and nearly twenty feet deep, Apollodorus of Damascus did not hesitate, at Trajan's command, to undertake the construction of a bridge with twenty stone and wooden arches. He builded well, for one or two of the stone piers still remain perfect after a lapse of sixteen centuries, and eleven of them, more or less ruined, are yet visible at low water. Apollodorus was a man of genius, as his other work, the Trajan Column, proudly standing in Rome, amply testifies. No doubt he was richly rewarded by Trajan for constructing a work which, flanked as it was by noble fortifications, bound the newly-captured Dacian colony to the Roman empire. What mighty men were these Romans, who carved their way along the Danube banks, hewing roads and levelling mountains at the same time that they engaged the savages of the locality in daily battle! There were indeed giants in those days.

When Ada-Kalé is passed, and pretty Orsova, lying in slumbrous quiet at the foot of noble mountains, is reached, the last trace of Turkish domination is left behind. In future years, if the treaty of San Stefano holds, there will be little evidence of Ottoman lack of civilization anywhere on the Danube, for the forts of the Turks will gradually disappear, and the Mussulman cannot for an instant hold his own among Christians where he has no military advantage.

But at Orsova, although the red fez and voluminous trousers are rarely seen, the influence of Turkey is keenly felt. It is in these remote regions of Hungary that the real rage against Russia and the burning enthusiasm and sympathy for the Turks is most openly expressed. Every cottage in the neighborhood is filled with crude pictures representing events of the Hungarian revolution; and the peasants, as they look upon those reminders of perturbed times, reflect that the Russians were instrumental in preventing the accomplishment of their dearest wishes. Here the Hungarian is eminently patriotic: he endeavors as much as possible to forget that he and his are bound to the empire of Austria, and he speaks of the German and the Slav who are his fellow-subjects with a sneer. The people whom one encounters in that corner of Hungary profess a dense ignorance of the German language, but if pressed can speak it glibly enough. I won an angry frown and an unpleasant remark from an innkeeper because I did not know that Austrian postage-stamps are not good in Hungary. Such melancholy ignorance of the simplest details of existence seemed to my host meet subject for reproach.

Orsova became an important point as soon as the Turks and Russians were at war. The peasants of the Banat stared as they saw long lines of travellers leaving the steamers which had come from Pesth and Bazros, and invading the two small inns, which are usually more than half empty. Englishmen, Russians, Austrian officers sent down to keep careful watch upon the land, French and Prussian, Swiss and Belgian military attachés and couriers, journalists, artists, amateur army-followers, crowded the two long streets and exhausted the market. Next came a hungry and thirsty mob of refugees from Widdin — Jews, Greeks and gypsies — and these promenaded their variegated misery on the river-banks from sunrise until sunset. Then out from Roumanian land poured thousands of wretched peasants, bare-footed, bareheaded, dying of starvation, fleeing from Turkish invasion, which, happily, never assumed large proportions. These poor people slept on the ground, content with the shelter of house-walls: they subsisted on unripe fruits and that unfailing fund of mild tobacco which every male being in all those countries invariably manages to secure. Walking abroad in Orsova was no easy task, for one was constantly compelled to step over these poor fugitives, who packed themselves into the sand at noonday, and managed for a few hours before the cool evening breezes came to forget their miseries. The vast fleet of river-steamers belonging to the Austrian company was laid up at Orsova, and dozens of captains, conversing in the liquid Slav or the graceful Italian or guttural German, were for ever seated about the doors of the little cafés smoking long cigars and quaffing beakers of the potent white wine produced in Austrian vineyards.

Opposite Orsova lie the Servian Mountains, bold, majestic, inspiring. Their noble forests and the deep ravines between them are exquisite in color when the sun flashes along their sides. A few miles below the point where the Hungarian and Roumanian territories meet the mountainous region declines into foot-hills, and then to an uninteresting plain. The Orsovan dell is the culminating point of all the beauty and grandeur of the Danubian hills. From one eminence richly laden with vineyards I looked out on a fresh April morning across a delicious valley filled with pretty farms and white cottages and ornamented by long rows of shapely poplars. Turning to the right, I saw Servia's barriers, shutting in from the cold winds the fat lands of the interior; vast hillsides dotted from point to point with peaceful villages, in the midst of which white churches with slender spires arose; and to the left the irregular line of the Roumanian peaks stood up, jagged and broken, against the horizon. Out from Orsova runs a rude highway into the rocky and savage back-country. The celebrated baths of Mehadia, the "hot springs" of the Austro-Hungarian empire, are yearly frequented by three or four thousand sufferers, who come from the European capitals to Temesvar, and are thence trundled in diligences to the water-cure. But the railway is penetrating even this far-off land,

SISTOVA.

where once brigands delighted to wander, and Temesvar and Bucharest will be bound together by a daily "through-service" as regular as that between Pesth and Vienna.

I sat one evening on the balcony of

the diminutive inn known as "The Hungarian Crown," watching the sunbeams on the broad current of the Danube and listening to the ripple, the plash and the gurgle of the swollen stream as it rushed impetuously against the banks. A group of Servians, in canoes light and swift as those of Indians, had made their way across the river, and were struggling vigorously to prevent the current from carrying them below a favorable landing-place. These tall, slender men, with bronzed faces and gleaming eyes, with their round skull-caps, their gaudy jackets and ornamental leggings, bore no small resemblance at a distance to certain of our North American red-skins. Each man had a long knife in his belt, and from experience I can say that a Servian knife is in itself a complete tool-chest. With its one tough and keen blade one may skin a sheep, file a saw, split wood, mend a wagon, defend one's self vigorously if need be, make a buttonhole and eat one's breakfast. No Servian who adheres to the ancient costume would consider himself dressed unless the crooked knife hung from his girdle. Although the country-side along the Danube is rough, and travellers are said to need protection among the Servian hills, I could not discover that the inhabitants wore other weapons than these useful articles of cutlery. Yet they are daring smugglers, and sometimes openly defy the Hungarian authorities when discovered. "Ah!" said Master Josef, the head-servant of the Hungarian Crown, "many a good fight have I seen in mid-stream, the boats grappled together, knives flashing, and our fellows drawing their pistols. All that, too, for a few flasks of Negotin, which is a musty red, thick wine that Heaven would forbid me to recommend to your honorable self and companions so long as I put in the cellar the pearl dew of yonder vineyards!" pointing to the vines of Orsova.

While the Servians were anxiously endeavoring to land, and seemed to be in imminent danger of upsetting, the roll of thunder was heard and a few drops of rain fell with heavy plash. Master Josef forthwith began making shutters fast and tying the curtains; "For now we *shall* have a wind!" quoth he. And it came. As by magic the Servian shore was blotted out, and before me I could see little save the river, which seemed transformed into a roaring and foaming ocean. The refugees, the gypsies, the Jews, the Greeks, scampered in all directions. Then tremendous echoes awoke among the hills. Peal after peal echoed and re-echoed, until it seemed as if the cliffs must crack and crumble. Sheets of rain were blown by the mischievous winds now full upon the unhappy fugitives, or now descended with seemingly crushing force on the Servians in their dancing canoes. Then came vivid lightning, brilliant and instant glances of electricity, disclosing the forests and hills for a moment, then seeming by their quick departure to render the obscurity more painful than before. The fiery darts were hurled by dozens upon the devoted trees, and the tall and graceful stems were bent like reeds before the rushing of the blast. Cold swept through the vale, and shadows seemed to follow it. Such contrast with the luminous, lovely semi-tropical afternoon, in the dreamy restfulness of which man and beast seemed settling into lethargy, was crushing. It pained and disturbed the spirit. Master Josef, who never lost an occasion to cross himself and to do a few turns on a little rosary of amber beads, came and went in a kind of dazed mood while the storm was at its height. Just as a blow was struck among the hills which seemed to make the earth quiver to its centre, the varlet approached and modestly inquired if the "honorable society"—myself and chance companions — would visit that very afternoon the famous chapel in which the crown of Hungary lies buried. I glanced curiously at him, thinking that possibly the thunder had addled his brain. "Oh, the honorable society may walk in sunshine all the way to the chapel at five o'clock," he said with an encouraging grin. "These Danube storms come and go as quickly as a Tsigane from a hen-roost. See! the thunder has stopped its howling, and there is not a wink of lightning. Even the raindrops are so few that one may almost walk between them."

I returned to the balcony from which the storm had driven me, and was gratified by the sight of the mountain-side studded with pearls, which a faint glow in the sky was gently touching. The Danube roared and foamed with malicious glee as the poor Servians were still whirled about on the water. But presently, through the deep gorges and along the sombre stream and over the vineyards, the rocks and the roofs of humble cottages, stole a warm breeze, followed by dazzling sunlight, which returned in mad haste to atone for the displeasure of the wind and rain. In a few moments the refugees were again afield, spreading their drenched garments on the wooden railings, and stalking about in a condition narrowly approaching nakedness. A gypsy four feet high,

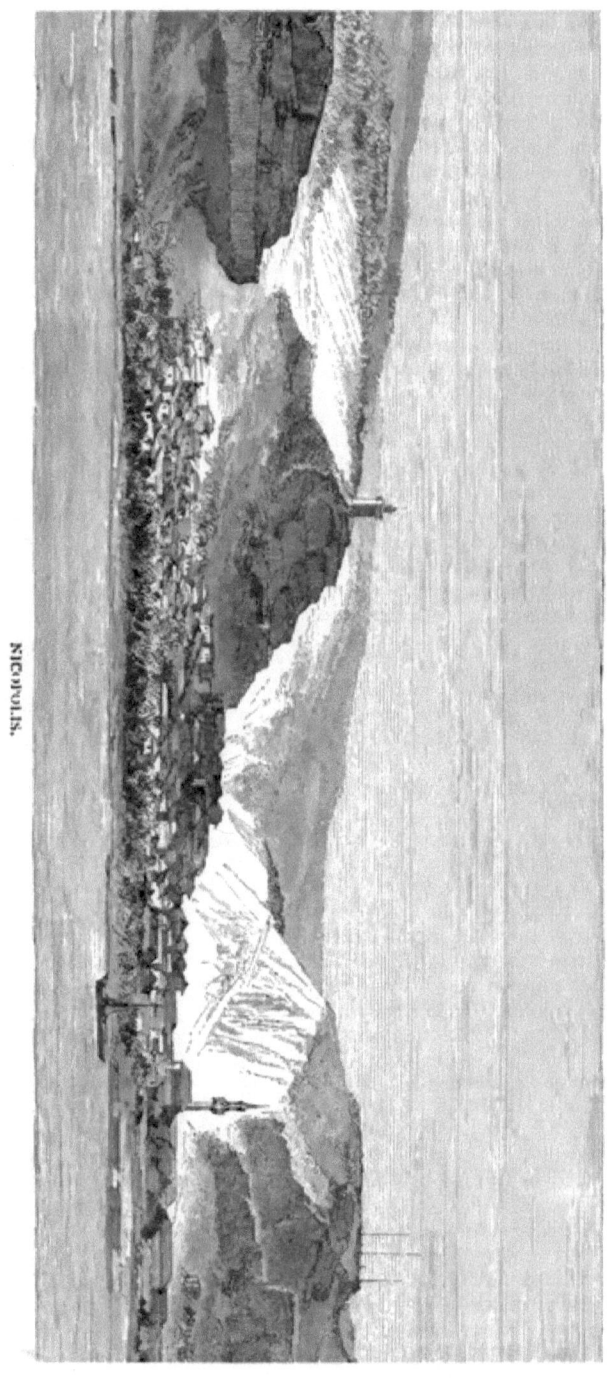

NICOPOLIS.

clad in a linen shirt and trousers so wide as to resemble petticoats, strolled thoughtlessly on the bank singing a plaintive melody, and now and then turning his brown face skyward as if to salute the sun. This child of mysterious ancestry, this wanderer from the East, this robber of roosts and cunning worker in metals, possessed nor hat nor shoes: his naked breast and his unprotected arms must suffer cold at night, yet he seemed wonderfully happy. The Jews and Greeks gave him scornful glances, which he returned with quizzical, provoking smiles. At last he threw himself down on a plank from which the generous sun was rapidly drying the rain, and, coiling up as a dog might have done, he was soon asleep.

With a marine glass I could see distinctly every movement on the Servian shore. Close to the water's edge nestled a small village of neat white cottages. Around a little wharf hovered fifty or sixty stout farmers, mounted on sturdy ponies, watching the arrival of the Mercur, the Servian steamer from Belgrade and the Sava River. The Mercur came puffing valiantly forward, as unconcerned as if no whirlwind had swept across her path, although she must have been in the narrow and dangerous cañon of the "Iron Gates" when the blast and the shower were most furious. On the roads leading down the mountain-sides I saw long processions of squealing and grunting swine, black, white and gray, all active and self-willed, fighting each other for the right of way. Before each procession marched a swineherd playing on a rustic pipe, the sounds from which primitive instrument seemed to exercise Circean enchantment upon the rude flocks. It was inexpressibly comical to watch the masses of swine after they had been enclosed in the "folds"—huge tracts fenced in and provided with shelters at the corners. Each herd knew its master, and as he passed to and fro would salute him with a delighted squeal, which died away into a series of disappointed and cynical groans as soon as the porkers had discovered that no evening repast was to be offered them. Good fare do these Servian swine find in the abundant provision of acorns in the vast forests. The men who spend their lives in restraining the vagabond instincts of these vulgar animals may perhaps be thought a collection of brutal hinds; but, on the contrary, they are fellows of shrewd common sense and much dignity of feeling. Kara-George, the terror of the Turk at the beginning of this century, the majestic character who won the admiration of Europe, whose genius as a soldier was praised by Napoleon the Great, and who freed his countrymen from bondage,— Kara-George was a swineherd in the woods of the Schaumadia until the wind of the spirit fanned his brow and called him from his simple toil to immortalize his homely name.

Master Josef and his fellows in Orsova did not hate the Servians with the bitterness manifested toward the Roumanians, yet they considered them as aliens and as dangerous conspirators against the public weal. "Who knows at what moment they may go over to the Russians?" was the constant cry. And in process of time they went, but although Master Josef had professed the utmost willingness to take up arms on such an occasion, it does not appear that he did it, doubtless preferring, on reflection, the quiet of his inn and his flask of white wine in the courtyard rather than an excursion among the trans-Danubian hills and the chances of an untoward fate at the point of a Servian knife. It is not astonishing that the two peoples do not understand each other, although only a strip of water separates their frontiers for a long stretch; for the difference in language and in its written form is a most effectual barrier to intercourse. The Servians learn something of the Hungarian dialects, since they come to till the rich lands of the Banat in the summer season. Bulgarians and Servians by thousands find employment in Hungary in summer, and return home when autumn sets in. But the dreams and ambitions of the two peoples have nothing in common. Servia looks longingly to Slavic unification, and is anxious to secure for herself a predominance in the new nation to be moulded out of the old scattered elements: Hungary believes that the consolidation of the Slavs would place her in a dangerous and humiliating position, and conspires day and night to compass exactly the reverse of Servian wishes. Thus the two countries are theoretically at peace and practically at war. While the conflict of 1877 was in progress collisions between Servian and Hungarian were of almost daily occurrence.

The Hungarian's intolerance of the Slav does not proceed from unworthy jealousy, but rather from an exaggerated idea of the importance of his own country, and of the evils which might befall it if the old Serb stock began to renew its ancient glory. In corners of Hungary, such as Orsova, the peasant imagines that his native land is the main world, and that the rest of Europe is an unnecessary and troublesome fringe around the edges of it. There is a story of a gentleman in Pesth who went to a dealer in maps and inquired for a *globus* of Hungary, showing that he imagined it to be the whole round earth.

So fair were the land and the stream after the storm that I lingered until sunset gazing out over river and on Servian hills, and did not accept Josef's invitation to visit the chapel of the Hungarian crown that evening. But next morning, before the sun was high, I wandered alone in the direction of the Roumanian frontier, and by accident came upon the chapel. It is a modest structure in a nook surrounded by tall poplars, and within is a simple chapel with Latin inscriptions. Here the historic crown reposes, now that there is no longer any use for it at Presburg, the ancient capital. Here it was brought by pious hands after the troubles between Austria and Hungary were settled. During the revolution the sacred bauble was hidden by the command of noblemen to whom it had been confided, and the servitors who concealed it at the behest of their masters were slain, lest in an indiscreet moment they might betray the se-

THE DANUBE AT TRAJAN'S BRIDGE.

cret. For thousands of enthusiasts this tiny chapel is the holiest of shrines, and should trouble come anew upon Hungary in the present perturbed times, the crown would perhaps journey once more.

It seems pitiful that the railway should ever invade this out-of-the-way corner of Europe. But it is already crawling through the mountains: hundreds of Italian laborers are putting down the shining rails in woods and glens where no sounds save the song of birds or the carol of the infrequent passer-by have heretofore been heard. For the present, however, the old-fashioned, comfortless diligence keeps the roads: the beribboned postilion winds his merry horn, and as the afternoon sun is getting low the dusty, antique vehicle rattles up to the court of the inn, the guard gets down, dusts the leather casing of the gun which now-a-days he is never compelled to use: then he touches his square hat, ornamented with a feather, to the maids and men of the hostelry. When the mails are claimed, the horses refreshed and the stage is covered with its leathern hood, postilion and guard sit down together in a cool corner under the gallery in the courtyard and crack various small flasks of wine. They smoke their porcelain pipes imported from Vienna with the air of men of the world who have travelled and who could tell you a thing or two if they liked. They are never tired of talking of Mehadia, which is one of their principal stations. The sad-faced nobleman, followed by the decorous old man-servant in fantastic Magyar livery, who arrived in the diligence, has been to the baths. The master is vainly seeking cure, comes every year, and always supplies postilion and guard with the money to buy flasks of wine. This the postilion tells me and my fellows, and suggests that the "honorable society" should follow the worthy nobleman's example. No sooner is it done than postilion and guard kiss our hands; which is likewise an evidence that they have travelled, are well met with every stranger and all customs, and know more than they say.

The Romans had extensive establishments at Mehadia, which they called the "Baths of Hercules," and it is in memory of this that a statue of the good giant stands in the square of the little town. Scattered through the hills, many inscriptions to Hercules, to Mercury and to Venus have been found during the ages. The villages on the road thither are few and far between, and are inhabited by peasants decidedly Dacian in type. It is estimated that a million and a half of Roumanians are settled in Hungary, and in this section they are exceedingly numerous. Men and women wear showy costumes, quite barbaric and uncomfortable. The women seem determined to wear as few garments as possible, and to compensate for lack of number by brightness of coloring. In many a pretty face traces of gypsy blood may be seen. This vagabond taint gives an inexpressible charm to a face for which the Hungarian strain has already done much. The coal-black hair and wild, mutinous eyes set off to perfection the pale face and exquisitely thin lips, the delicate nostrils and beautifully moulded chin. Angel or devil? queries the beholder. Sometimes he is constrained to think that the possessor of such a face has the mingled souls of saint and siren. The light undertone of melancholy which pervades gypsy beauty, gypsy music, gypsy manners, has an extremely remarkable fascination for all who perceive it. Even when it is almost buried beneath ignorance and animal craft, it is still to be found in the gypsy nature after diligent search. This strange race seems overshadowed by the sorrow of some haunting memory. Each individual belonging to the Tsiganes whom I saw impressed me as a fugitive from Fate. To look back was impossible; of the present he was careless; the future tempted him on. In their music one now and then hears hints of a desire to return to some far-off and half-forgotten land. But this is rare.

There are a large number of "civilized gypsies," so called, in the neighborhood of Orsova. I never saw one of them without a profound compassion for him, so utterly unhappy did he look in ordinary attire. The musicians who came nightly to play on the lawn in front of the Hungarian Crown inn belonged to these civilized Tsiganes. They had lost all the freedom of gesture, the proud, half-savage stateliness of those who remained nomadic and untrammelled by local law and custom. The old instinct was in their music, but sometimes there drifted into it the same mixture of saint and devil which I had seen in the "composite" faces.

As soon as supper was set forth, piping hot and flanked by flagons of beer and wine, on the lawn, and the guests had assembled to partake of the good cheer, while yet the afterglow lingered along the Danube, these dusky musicians appeared and installed themselves in a corner. The old stream's murmur could not drown the piercing and pathetic notes of the violin, the gentle wail of the guzla or the soft thrumming of the rude tambourine. Little poetry as a spectacled and frosty Austrian officer might have in his soul, that little must have been awakened by the songs and the orchestral performances of the Tsiganes as the sun sank low. The dusk began to creep athwart the lawn, and a cool breeze fanned the foreheads of the listeners. When the light was all gone, these men, as if inspired by the dark-

BOATS ON THE DANUBE.

ness, sometimes improvised most angelic melody. There was never any loud or boisterous note, never any direct appeal to the attention. I invariably forgot the singers and players, and the music seemed a part of the harmony of Nature. While the pleasant notes echoed in the twilight, troops of jaunty young Hungarian soldiers, dressed in red hose, dark-green doublets and small caps sometimes adorned with feathers, sauntered up and down the principal street; the refugees huddled in corners and listened with delight; the Austrian officials lumbered by, pouring clouds of smoke from their long, strong and inevitable cigars; and the dogs forgot their perennial quarrel for a few instants at a time.

The dogs of Orsova and of all the neighboring country have many of the characteristics of their fellow-creatures in Turkey. Orsova is divided into "beats," which are thoroughly and carefully patrolled night and day by bands of dogs who recognize the limits of their domain and severely resent intrusion. In front of the Hungarian Crown a large dog, aided by a small yellow cur and a black spaniel mainly made up of ears and tail, maintained order. The afternoon quiet was generally disturbed about four o'clock by the advent of a strange canine, who, with that expression of extreme innocence which always characterizes the animal that knows he is doing wrong, would venture on to the forbidden ground. A low growl in chorus from the three guardians was the inevitable preliminary warning. The new-comer usually seemed much surprised at this, and gave an astonished glance: then, wagging his tail merrily, as much as to say, "Nonsense! I must have been mistaken," he approached anew. One of the trio of guardians thereupon sallied forth to meet him, followed by the others a little distance behind. If the strange dog showed his teeth, assumed a defiant attitude and seemed inclined to make his way through any number of enemies, the trio held a consultation, which, I am bound to say, almost invariably resulted in a fight. The intruder would either fly yelping, or would work his way across the interdicted territory by means of a series of encounters, accompanied by the most terrific barking, snapping and shrieking, and by a very considerable effusion of blood. The person who should interfere to prevent a dog-fight in Orsova would be regarded as a lunatic. Sometimes a large white dog, accompanied by two shaggy animals resembling wolves so closely that it was almost impossible to believe them guardians of flocks of sheep, passed by the Hungarian Crown unchallenged, but these were probably tried warriors whose valor was so well known that they were no longer questioned anywhere.

The gypsies have in their wagons or following in their train small black dogs of temper unparalleled for ugliness. It is impossible to approach a Tsigane tent or wagon without encountering a swarm of these diminutive creatures, whose rage is not only amusing, but sometimes rather appalling to contemplate. Driving rapidly by a camp one morning in a farmer's cart drawn by two stout horses adorned with jingling bells, I was followed by a pack of these dark-skinned animals. The bells awoke such rage within them that they seemed insane under its influence. As they leaped and snapped around me, I felt like some traveller in a Russian forest pursued by hungry wolves. A dog scarcely six inches high, and but twice as long, would spring from the ground as if a pound of dynamite had exploded beneath him, and would make a desperate effort to throw himself into the wagon. Another, howling in impotent anger, would jump full at a horse's throat, would roll beneath the feet of the team, but in some miraculous fashion would escape unhurt, and would scramble upon a bank to try again. It was a real relief when the discouraged pack fell away. Had I shot one of the animals, the gypsies would have found a way to avenge the death of their enterprising though somewhat too zealous camp-follower. Animals everywhere on these border-lines of the Orient are treated with much more tenderness than men and women are. The grandee who would scowl furiously in this wild region of the

Banat if the peasants did not stand by the roadside and doff their hats in token of respect and submission as he whirled by in his carriage, would not kick a dog

ORSOVA.

out of his way, and would manifest the utmost tenderness for his horses.

Much as the Hungarian inhabitants of the Banat hate the Roumanians, they do not fail to appreciate the commercial advantages which will follow on the union of the two countries by rail. Pretty Orsova may in due time become a bustling town filled with grain- and coal-dépôts and with small manufactories. The railway from Verciorova on the frontier runs through the large towns Pitesti and Craiova on its way to Bucharest. It is a marvellous railroad: it climbs hills, descends into deep gullies, and has as little of the air-line about it as a great river has, for the contractors built it on the principle of "keeping near the surface," and they much preferred climbing ten high mountains to cutting one tunnel. Craiova takes its name, according to a somewhat misty legend, from John Assan, who was one of the Romano-Bulgarian kings, Craiova being a corruption of *Crai Ivan* ("King John"). This John was the same who drank his wine from a cup made out of the skull of the unlucky emperor Baldwin I. The old bans of Craiova gave their title to the Roumanian silver pieces now known as *bañi*. Slatina, farther down the line, on the river Altu (the *Aluta* of the ancients), is a pretty town, where a proud and brave community love to recite to the stranger the valorous deeds of their ancestors. It is the centre from which have spread out most of the modern revolutionary movements in Roumania. "Little Wallachia," in which Slatina stands, is rich in well-tilled fields and uplands covered with fat cattle: it is as fertile as Kansas, and its people seemed to me more agreeable and energetic than those in and around Bucharest.

He who clings to the steamers plying up and down the Danube sees much romantic scenery and many curious types, but he loses all the real charm of travel in these regions. The future tourist on his way to or from Bulgaria and the battle-fields of the "new crusade" will be wise if he journeys leisurely by farm-wagon — he will not be likely to find a carriage — along the Hungarian bank of the stream. I made the journey in April, when in that gentle southward climate the wayside was already radiant with flowers and the mellow sunshine was unbroken by cloud or rain. There were discomfort and dust, but there was a rare pleasure in the arrival at a quaint inn whose exterior front, boldly asserting itself in the bolder row of house-fronts in a long village street, was uninviting enough, but the interior of which was charming. In such a hostelry I always found the wharfmaster, in green coat and cap, asleep in an arm-chair, with the burgomaster and one or two idle landed proprietors sitting near him at a card-table, enveloped in such a cloud of smoke that one could scarcely see the long-necked flasks of white wine which they were rapidly emptying. The host was a massive man with bulbous nose and sleepy eyes: he responded to all questions with a stare and the statement that he did not know, and seemed anxious to leave everything in doubt until the latest moment possible. His daughter, who was brighter and less dubious in her responses than her father, was a slight girl with lustrous black eyes, wistful lips, a perfect form, and black hair covered with a linen cloth that the dust might not come near its glossy threads. When she made her appearance, flashing out of a huge dark room which was stone paved and arched overhead, and in which peasants sat drinking sour beer, she seemed like a ray of sunshine in the middle of night. But there was more dignity about her than is to be found in most sunbeams: she was modest and civil in answer, but understood no compliments. There was something of the princess-reduced-in-circumstances in her demeanor. A royal supper could she serve, and the linen which she spread on the small wooden table in the back courtyard smelled of lavender. I took my dinners, after the long days' rides, in inns which commanded delicious views of the Danube — points where willows overhung the rushing stream, or where crags towered above it, or where it flowed in smooth yet resistless might through plains in which hundreds of peasants were toiling, their red-and-white costumes contrasting sharply with the brilliant blue of the sky and the tender green of the foliage.

If the inns were uniformly cleanly and agreeable, as much could not be said for the villages, which were sometimes decidedly dirty. The cottages of the peasants—that is, of the agricultural laborers—were windowless to a degree which led me to look for a small- and dull-eyed race, but the eloquent orbs of youths and maidens in all this Banat land are rarely equalled in beauty. I found it in my heart to object to the omnipresent swine. These cheerful animals were sometimes so domesticated that they followed their masters and mistresses afield in the morning. In this section of Hungary, as indeed in most parts of Europe, the farm-houses are all huddled together in compact villages, and the lands tilled by the dwellers in these communities extend for miles around them. At dawn the procession of laborers goes forth, and at sunset it returns. Nothing can give a better idea of rural simplicity and peace than the return of the peasants of a hamlet at eventide from their vineyards and meadows. Just as the sun was deluging the broad Danube with glory before relinquishing the current to the twilight's shades I came, in the soft April evening, into the neighborhood of Drenkova. A tranquil afterglow was here and there visible near the hills, which warded off the sun's passionate farewell glances at the vines and flowers. Beside the way, on the green banks, sat groups of children, clad with paradisiacal simplicity, awaiting their fathers and mothers. At a vineyard's hedge a sweet girl, tall, stately and melancholy, was twining a garland in the cap of a stout young fellow who rested one broad hand lightly upon her shoulder. Old women, bent and wrinkled, hobbled out from the fields, getting help from their sons or grandsons. Sometimes I met a shaggy white horse drawing a cart in which a dozen sonsie lasses, their faces browned by wind and their tresses

BELGRADE, FROM SEMLIN.

blown back from their brows in most bewitching manner by the libertine breeze, were jolting homeward, singing as they went. The young men in their loose linen garments, with their primitive hoes and spades on their shoulders, were as goodly specimens of manly strength and beauty as one could wish to look upon. It hurt me to see them stand humbly ranged in rows as I passed. But it was pleasant to note the fervor with which they knelt around the cross rearing its sainted form amid the waving grasses. They knew nothing of the outer world, save that from time to time the emperor claimed certain of their number for his service, and that perhaps their lot might lead them to the great city of Buda-Pesth. Everywhere as far as the eye could reach the land was cultivated with greatest care, and plenty seemed the lot of all. The peasant lived in an ugly and windowless house because his father and grandfather had done so before him, not because it was necessary. It was odd to see girls tall as Dian, and as fair, bending their pretty bodies to come out of the contemptible little apertures in the peasant-houses called "doors."

Drenkova is a long street of low cottages, with here and there a two-story mansion to denote that the proprietors of the land reside there. As I approached the entrance to this street I saw a most remarkable train coming to meet me. One glance told me that it was a large company of gypsies who had come up from Roumania, and were going northward in search of work or plunder. My driver drew rein, and we allowed the swart Bohemians to pass on—a courtesy which was gracefully acknowledged with a singularly sweet smile from the driver of the first cart. There were about two hundred men and women in this wagon-train, and I verily believe that there were twice as many children. Each cart, drawn by a small Roumanian pony, contained two or three families huddled together, and seemingly lost in contemplation of the beautiful sunset, for your real gypsy is a keen admirer of Nature and her charms. Some of the women were intensely hideous: age had made them as unattractive as in youth they had been pretty; others were graceful and well formed. Many wore but a single garment. The men were wilder than any that I had ever before seen: their matted hair, their thick lips and their dark eyes gave them almost the appearance of negroes. One or two of them had been foraging, and bore sheeps' heads and hares which they had purchased or "taken" in the village. They halted as soon as they had passed me, and prepared to go into camp; so I waited a little to observe them. During the process of arranging the carts for the night one of the women became enraged at the father of her brood because he would not aid her in the preparation of the simple tent under which the family was to repose. The woman ran to him, clenching her fist and screaming forth invective which, I am convinced, had I understood it and had it been directed at me, I should have found extremely disagreeable. After thus lashing the culprit with language for some time, she broke forth into screams and danced frantically around him. He arose, visibly disturbed, and I fancied that his savage nature would come uppermost, and that he might be impelled to give her a brutal beating. But he, on the contrary, advanced leisurely toward her and spat upon the ground with an expression of extreme contempt. She seemed to feel this much more than she would have felt a blow, and her fury redoubled. She likewise spat; he again repeated the contemptuous act; and after both had gratified the anger which was consuming them, they walked off in different directions. The battle was over, and I was not sorry to notice a few minutes later that *paterfamilias* had thought better of his conduct, and was himself spreading the tent and setting forth his wandering Lares and Penates.

A few hundred yards from the point where these wanderers had settled for the night I found some rude huts in which other gypsies were residing permanently. These huts were mere shelters placed against steep banks or hedges, and within there was no furniture save one or two blankets, a camp-kettle and some wicker baskets. Young girls twelve or thirteen years of age crouched naked about a smouldering fire. They did not

THE IRON GATES.

seem unhappy or hungry; and none of these strange people paid any attention to me as I drove on to the inn, which, oddly enough, was at some distance from the main village, hard by the Danube side, in a gully between the mountains, where coal-barges lay moored. The Servian Mountains, covered from base to summit with dense forests, cast a deep gloom over the vale. In a garden on a terrace behind the inn, by the light of a flickering candle, I ate a frugal dinner, and went to bed much impressed by the darkness, in such striking contrast to the delightful and picturesque scenes through which I had wandered all day.

But I speedily forgot this next morning, when the landlord informed me that, instead of toiling over the road along the crags to Orsova, whither I was returning, I could embark on a tug-boat bound for that cheerful spot, and could thus inspect the grand scenery of the Iron Gates from the river. The swift express-boats which in time of peace run from Vienna to Rustchuk whisk the traveller so rapidly through these famous defiles that he sees little else than a panorama of high rocky walls. But the slow-moving and clumsy tug, with its train of barges attached, offers better facilities to the lover of natural beauty. We had dropped down only a short distance below Drenkova before we found the river-path filled with eddies, miniature whirlpools, denoting the vicinity of the gorges into which the great current is compressed. These whirlpools all have names: one is called the "Buffalo;" a second, Kerdaps; a third is known as the "Devourer." The Turks have a healthy awe of this passage, which in old times was a terrible trial to these stupid and always inefficient navigators. For three or four hours we ran in the shade of mighty walls of porphyry and granite, on whose tops were forests of oaks and elms. High up on cliffs around which the eagles circle, and low in glens where one sometimes sees a bear swimming, the sun threw a flood of mellow glory. I could fancy that the veins of red porphyry running along the face of the granite were blood-stains, the tragic memorials of ancient battles. For, wild and inaccessible as this region seems, it has been fought over and through in sternest fashion. Perched on a little promontory on the Servian side is the tiny town of Poretch, where the brave shepherds and swineherds fought the Turk, against whose oppression they had risen, until they were overwhelmed by numbers, and their leader, Hadji Nikolos, lost his head. The Austrians point out with pride the cave on the tremendous flank of Mount Choukourou where, two centuries ago, an Austrian general at the head of seven hundred men, all that was left to him of a goodly army, sustained a three months' siege against large Turkish forces. This cave is perched high above the road at a point where it absolutely commands it, and the government of to-day, realizing its importance, has had it fortified and furnished with walls pierced by loopholes. Trajan fought his way through these defiles in the very infancy of the Christian era; and in memory of his first splendid campaign against the Dacians he carved in the solid rock the letters, some of which are still visible, and which, by their very grandiloquence, offer a mournful commentary on the fleeting nature of human greatness. Little did he think when his eyes rested lovingly on this inscription, beginning—

IMP. CÆS. D. NERVÆ FILIUS NERVA.
TRAJANUS. GERM. PONT. MAXIMUS.

—that Time with profane hand would wipe out the memory of many of his glories and would undo all the work that he had done.

On we drifted, through huge landlocked lakes, out of which there seemed no issue until we chanced upon a miraculous corner where there was an outlet frowned upon by angry rocks; on to the "Caldron," as the Turks called the most imposing portion of the gorge; on through an amphitheatre where densely-wooded mountains on either side were reflected in smooth water; on beneath masses that appeared about to topple, and over shallows where it looked as if we must be grounded; on round a bluff which had hidden the sudden opening of the valley into a broad sweep, and which had hindered us from seeing Orsova the Fair nestling closely to her beloved mountains.   EDWARD KING.

DANUBIAN DAYS.

COSTUMES AT PESTH.

IF it were not for the people, the journey by steamer from Belgrade to Pesth would be rather unromantic. When the Servian capital is reached in ascending the great stream from Galatz and Rustchuk, the picturesque cliffs, the mighty forests, the moss-grown ruins overhanging the rushing waters, are all left behind. Belgrade is not very imposing. It lies along a low line of hills bordering the Sava and the Danube, and contains only a few edifices which are worthy even of the epithet creditable. The white pinnacle from which it takes its name—for the city grouped around the fort was once called *Beograd* ("white city")—now looks grimy and gloomy. The Servians have placed the cannon which they took from the Turks in the recent war on the ramparts, and have become so extravagantly vain in view of their exploits that their conceit is quite painful to contemplate. Yet it is impossible to avoid sympathizing to some extent with this little people, whose lot has been so hard and whose final emancipation has been so long in arriving. The intense affection which the Servian manifests for his native land is doubtless the result of the struggles and the sacrifices which he has been compelled to make in order to remain in possession of it. One day he has been threatened by the Austrian or the jealous and unreasonable Hungarian; another he has received news that the Turks were marching across his borders, burning, plundering and devastating. There is something peculiarly pathetic in the lot of these small Danubian states. Nearly every one of them has been the cause of combats in which its inhabitants have shed rivers of blood before they could obtain even a fragment of such liberty and peace as have long been the possessions of Switzerland and Belgium. It is not surprising that the small countries which once formed part of Turkey-in-Europe are anxious to grow larger and stronger by annexation of territory and consolidation of populations. They are tired of being feeble: it is not amusing. Servia once expected that she would be allowed to gain a considerable portion of Bosnia, her neighbor province, but the Austrians are there, and would speedily send forces to Belgrade if it were for a moment imagined that Prince Milan and his counsellors were still greedy for Serajevo and other fat towns of the beautiful Bosnian lands. Now and then, when a Servian burgher has had an extra flask of Negotin, he vapors about meeting the Austrians face to face and driving them into the Sava; but he never mentions it when he is in a normal condition.

The country which Servia has won from the Turks in the neighborhood of Nisch, and the quaint old city of Nisch itself, were no meagre prizes, and ought to content the ambition of the young prince for some time. It was righteous that the Servians should possess Nisch, and that the Turks should be driven out by violence. The cruel and vindictive barbarian had done everything that he could to make himself feared and loathed by the Servians. To this day, not far from one of the principal gates of the city, on the Pirot road, stands the "Skull Tower," in the existence of which, I suppose, an English Tory would refuse to believe, just as he denied his credence to the story of the atrocities at Batak. The four sides of this tower are completely covered, as with a barbarous mosaic, with the skulls of Servians slain by their oppressors in the great combat of 1809. The Turks placed here but a few of their trophies, for they slaughtered thousands, while the tower's sides could accommodate only nine hundred and fifty-two skulls. It is much to the credit of the Servians that when they took Nisch in 1877 they wreaked no vengeance on the Mussulman population, but simply compelled them to give up their arms, and informed them that they could return to their labors. The presence of the Servians at Nisch has already been productive of good: decent roads from that point to Sophia are already in process of construction, and the innumerable brigands who swarmed along the country-side have been banished or killed. Sophia still lies basking in the mellow sunlight, lazily refusing to be cleansed or improved. Nowhere else on the border-line of the Orient is there a town which so admirably illustrates the reckless and stupid negligence of the Turk. Sophia looks enchanting from a distance, but when one enters its narrow streets, choked with rubbish and filled

SOPHIA.

with fetid smells, one is only too glad to retire hastily. It would take a quarter of a century to make Sophia clean. All round the city are scattered ancient tumuli filled with the remains of the former lords of the soil, and they are almost as attractive as the hovels in which live the people of to-day. What a desolate waste the Turk has been allowed to make of one of the finest countries in Europe! He must be thrust out before improvement can come in. Lamartine, who was one of the keenest observers that ever set foot in Turkey, truly said "that civilization, which is so fine in its proper place, would prove a mortal poison to Islamism. Civilization cannot live where the Turks are: it will wither away and perish more quickly whenever it is brought near them. With it, if you could acclimate it in Turkey, you could not make Europeans, you could not make Christians: you would simply unmake Turks."

BANKS OF THE DANUBE NEAR SEMLIN.

The enemies of progress and of the "Christian dogs" are receding, and railways and sanitary improvements will come when they are gone. Belgrade was a wretched town when the Turks had it: now it is civilized. Its history is romantic and picturesque, although its buildings are not. Servia's legends and the actual recitals of the adventurous wars which have occurred within her limits would fill volumes. The White City has been famous ever since the Ottoman conquest. Its dominant position at the junction of two great rivers, at the frontier of Christian Europe, at a time when turbans were now and then seen in front of the walls of Vienna, gave it a supreme importance. The Turks exultingly named it "the Gate of the Holy War." Thence it was that they sallied forth on incursions through the fertile plains where now the Hungarian shepherd leads his flock and plays upon his wooden pipe, undisturbed by the bearded infidel. The citadel was fought over until its walls cracked beneath the successive blows of Christian and Mussulman. Suleiman the Lawgiver, the elector of Bavaria, Eugene of Savoy, have trod the ramparts which frown on the Danube's broad current. The Austrians have many memories of the old fortress: they received it in 1718 by the treaty of Passarowitz, but gave it up in 1749, to take it back again in 1789. The treaty of

VILLAGE NEAR SEMLIN.

Sistova — an infamy which postponed the liberation of the suffering peoples in Turkey-in-Europe for nearly a hundred years — compelled the Austrians once more to yield it, this time to the Turks. In this century how often has it been fought over — from the time of the heroic Kara George, the Servian liberator, to the bloody riots in our days which resulted in driving Mussulmans definitely from the territory!

Everywhere along the upper Servian banks of the Danube traces of the old epoch are disappearing. The national costume, which was graceful, and often very rich, is yielding before the prosaic — the ugly garments imported from Jewish tailoring establishments in Vienna and Pesth. The horseman with his sack-coat, baggy velvet trousers and slouch hat looks not unlike a rough rider along the shores of the Mississippi River. In the interior patriarchal costumes and customs are still preserved. On the Sava river-steamers the people from towns in the shadows of the primeval forests which still cover a large portion of the country are to be found, and they are good studies for an artist. The women, with golden ducats braided in their hair; the priests, with tall brimless hats and long yellow robes; the men, with round skull-caps, leathern girdles with knives in them, and waistcoats ornamented with hundreds of glittering buttons, — are all unconscious of the change which is creeping in by the Danube, and to which they will presently find themselves submitting. The railway will take away the lingering bits of romance from Servia; the lovely and lonely monasteries high among the grand peaks in the mountain-ranges will be visited by tourists from Paris, who will scrawl their names upon the very altars; and Belgrade will be rich in second-class caravanserais kept by Moses and Abraham. After the Austrians who have gone over into Bosnia will naturally follow a crowd of adventurers from Croatia and from the neighborhood of Pesth, and it would not be surprising should many of them find it for their interest to settle in Servia, although the government would probably endeavor to keep them out. Should the movement which Lord Beaconsfield is pleased to call the "Panslavic conspiracy" assume alarming proportions within a short time, the Servians would be in great danger of losing, for years at least, their autonomy.

The arrival by night at Belgrade, coming from below, is interesting, and one has a vivid recollection ever afterward of swarms of barefooted coal-heavers, clad in coarse sacking, rushing tumultuously up and down a gang-plank, as negroes do when wooding up on a Southern river; of shouting and swaggering Austrian customs officials, clad in gorgeous raiment, but smoking cheap cigars; of Servian gendarmes emulating the bluster and surpassing the rudeness of the Austrians; of Turks in transit from the Constantinople boat to the craft plying to Bosnian river-ports; of Hungarian peasants in white felt jackets embroidered with scarlet thread, or mayhap even with yellow; and of various Bohemian beggars, whose swart faces remind one that he is still in the neighborhood of the East. I had on one occasion, while a steamer was lying at Belgrade, time to observe the manners of the humbler sort of folk in a species of cabaret near the river-side and hard by the erratic structure known as the custom-house. There was a serious air upon the faces of the men which spoke well for their characters. Each one seemed independent, and to a certain extent careless, of his neighbor's opinion. It would have been impossible, without some knowledge of the history of the country, to have supposed that these people, or even their ancestors, had ever been oppressed. Gayety did not prevail, nor is there anywhere among the Danubian Slavs a tendency to the innocent and spontaneous jollity so common in some sections of Europe. The Servian takes life seriously. I was amused to see that each one of this numerous company of swineherds or farmers, who had evidently come in to Belgrade to market, drank his wine as if it were a duty, and on leaving saluted as seriously as if he were greeting a distinguished company gathered to do him honor. That such men are cowards, as the English would have us believe, is impossible; and in 1877 they showed that the slander was destitute of even the slightest foundation in fact.

Morals in Belgrade among certain classes perhaps leave something to desire in the way of strictness; but the Danubian provinces are not supposed to be the abodes of all the virtues and graces. The Hungarians could not afford to throw stones at the Servians on the score of morality, and the Roumanians certainly would not venture to try the experiment. In the interior of Servia the population is pure, and the patriarchal manner in which the people live tends to preserve them so. There is as much difference between the sentiment in Belgrade and that in the provinces as would be found between Paris and a French rural district.

But let us drop details concerning Servia, for the brave little country demands more serious attention than can be given to it in one or two brief articles. The boat which bears me away from the Servian capital has come hither from Semlin, the Austrian town on the other side of the Sava River. It is a jaunty and comfortable craft, as befits such vessels as afford Servians their only means of communication with the outer world. If any but Turks had been squatted in Bosnia there would have been many a smart little steamer running down the Sava and around up the Danube; but the baleful Mussulman has checked all enterprise wherever he has had any foothold. We go slowly, cleaving the dull-colored tide, gazing, as we sit enthroned in easy-chairs on the upper deck, out upon the few public institutions of Belgrade—the military college and the handsome road leading to the garden of Topschidere, where the liliputian court has its tiny summer residence. Sombre memories overhang this "Cannoneer's Valley," this Topschidere, where Michael, the son and successor of good Milosch as sovereign prince of the nation, perished by assassination in 1868. In a few minutes we are whisked round a corner, and a high wooded bluff conceals the White City from our view.

The Servian women—and more especially those belonging to the lower classes

—have a majesty and dignity which are very imposing. One is inclined at first to believe these are partially due to assumption, but he speedily discovers that such is not the case. Blanqui, the French revolutionist, who made a tour through Servia in 1840, has given the world a curious and interesting account of the conversations which he held with Servian women on the subject of the oppression from which the nation was suffering. Everywhere among the common people he found virile sentiments expressed by the women, and the princess Lionbitza, he said, was "the prey of a kind of holy fever." M. Blanqui described her as a woman fifty years old, with a martial, austere yet dreamy physiognomy, with strongly-marked features, a proud and sombre gaze, and her head crowned with superb gray hair braided and tied with red ribbon. "Ah!" said this woman to him, with an accent in her voice which startled him, "if all these men round about us here were not women, *or if they were women like me*, we should soon be free from our tormentors!" It was the fiery words of such women as this which awoke the Servian men from the lethargy into which they were falling after Kara George had exhausted himself in heroic efforts, and which sent them forth anew to fight for their liberties.

At night, when the moon is good enough to shine, the voyage up the river has charms, and tempts one to remain on deck all night, in spite of the sharp breezes which sweep across the stream. The harmonious accents of the gentle Servian tongue echo all round you: the song of the peasants grouped together, lying in a heap like cattle to keep warm, comes occasionally to your ears; and if there be anything disagreeable, it is the loud voices and brawling manners of some Austrian troopers on transfer. From time to time the boat slows her speed as she passes through lines or streets of floating mills anchored securely in the river. Each mill—a small house with sloping roof, and with so few windows that one wonders how the millers ever manage to see their grist—is built upon two boats.

The musical hum of its great wheel is heard for a long distance, and warns one of the approach toward these pacific industries. The miller is usually on the lookout, and sometimes, when a large

THE OXEN OF THE DANUBE.

steamer is coming up, and he anticipates trouble from the "swell" which

FISHERMEN'S HUTS ON THE DANUBE.

she may create, he may be seen madly gesticulating and dancing upon his narrow platform in a frenzy of anxiety for the fruits of his toil. A little village on a neck of land or beneath a grove shows where the wives and children of these millers live. The mills are a source of prosperity for thousands of humble folk, and of provocation to hurricanes of profanity on the part of the Austrian, Italian and Dalmatian captains who are compelled to pass them. Stealing through an aquatic town of this kind at midnight, with the millers all holding out their lanterns, with the steamer's bell ringing violently, and with rough voices crying out words of caution in at least four languages, produces a curious if not a comical effect on him who has the experience for the first time.

Peaceable as the upper Danube shores look, Arcadian as seems the simplicity of their populations, the people are torn by contending passions, and are watched by the lynx-eyed authorities of two or three governments. The agents of the *Omladina*, the mysterious society which interests itself in the propagation of Panslavism, have numerous powerful stations in the Austrian towns, and do much to discontent the Slavic subjects of Francis Joseph with the rule of the Hapsburgs. There have also been instances of conspiracy against the Obrenovich dynasty, now in power in Servia, and these have frequently resulted in armed incursions from the Hungarian side of the stream to the other bank, where a warm reception was not long awaited. In the humblest hamlet there are brains hot with ambitious dreams daringly planning some scheme which is too audacious to be realized.

The traveller can scarcely believe this when, as the boat stops at some little pier which is half buried under vines and blossoms, he sees the population indulging in an innocent festival with the aid of red and white wine, a few glasses of beer, and bread and cheese. Families mounted in huge yellow chariots drawn by horses ornamented with gayly-decorated harnesses, come rattling into town and get down before a weatherbeaten inn, the signboard above which testifies to respect and love for some emperor of long ago. Youths and maidens wander arm in arm by the foaming tide or sit in the little arbors crooning songs and clinking glasses. Officers strut about, calling each other loudly by their titles or responding to the sallies of those of their comrades who fill the after-deck of the steamer. The village mayor in a braided jacket, the wharfmaster in semi-military uniform, and the agent of the steamboat company, who appears to have a remarkable penchant for gold lace and buttons, render the throng still more motley. There is also, in nine cases out of ten, a band of tooting musicians, and as the boat moves away national Hungarian and Austrian airs are played. He would be indeed a surly fellow who should not lift his cap on these occasions, and he would be repaid for his obstinacy by the very blackest of looks.

Carlowitz and Slankamen are two historic spots which an Hungarian, if he feels kindly disposed toward a stranger, will point out to him. The former is known to Americans by name only, as a rule, and that because they have seen it upon bottle-labels announcing excellent wine; but the town, with its ancient cathedral, its convents, and its "chapel of peace" built on the site of the structure in which was signed the noted peace of 1699, deserves a visit. Rumor says that the head-quarters of the Omladina are very near this town, so that the foreign visitor must not be astonished if the local police seem uncommonly solicitous for his welfare while he remains. At Slankamen in 1691 the illustrious margrave of Baden administered such a thrashing to the Turks that they fled in the greatest consternation, and it was long before they rallied again.

Thus, threading in and out among the floating mills, pushing through reedy channels in the midst of which she narrowly escapes crushing the boats of fishers, and carefully avoiding the moving banks of sand which render navigation as difficult as on the Mississippi, the boat reaches Peterwardein, high on a mighty mass of rock, and Neusatz opposite, connected with its neighbor fortress-town by a bridge of boats. Although within the limits of the Austria-Hungarian empire, Neusatz is almost entirely Servian in aspect and population, and Peterwardein, which marks

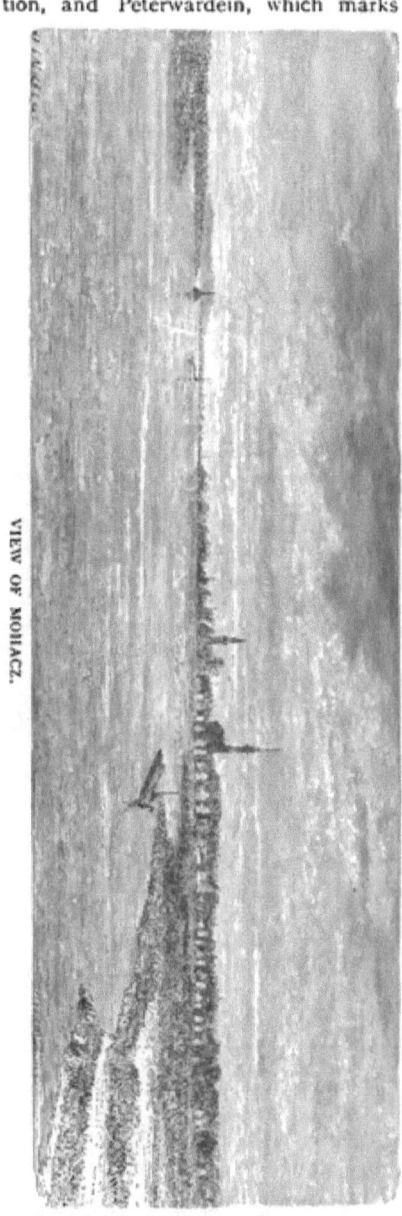

VIEW OF MOHACZ.

the military confines of Slavonia, has a large number of Servian inhabitants. It was the proximity and the earnestness in their cause of these people which induced the Hungarians to agree to the military occupation of Bosnia and the Herzegovina. At one time the obstinate Magyars would have liked to refuse their adhesion to the decisions of the Berlin Congress, but they soon thought better of that. Peterwardein is the last really imposing object on the Danube before reaching Pesth. It is majestic and solemn, with its gloomy castle, its garrison which contains several thousand soldiers, and its prison of state. The remembrance that Peter the Hermit there put himself at the head of the army with which the Crusades were begun adds to the mysterious and powerful fascination of the place. I fancied that I could see the lean and fanatical priest preaching before the assembled thousands, hurling his words down upon them from some lofty pinnacle. No one can blame the worthy Peter for undertaking his mission if the infidels treated Christians in the Orient as badly then as they do to-day. Centuries after Peter slept in consecrated dust the Turks sat down before Peterwardein to besiege it, but they had only their labor for their pains, for Prince Eugene drove them away. This was in 1716. It seems hard to believe that a hostile force of Turks was powerful enough to wander about Christendom a little more than a century and a half ago.

After passing Peterwardein and Neusatz the boat's course lies through the vast Hungarian plain, which reminds the American of some of the rich lands in the Mississippi bottom. Here is life, lusty, crude, seemingly not of Europe, but rather of the extreme West or East. As far as the eye can reach on either hand stretch the level acres, dotted with herds of inquisitive swine, with horses wild and beautiful snorting and gambolling as they hear the boat's whistle, and peasants in white linen jackets and trousers and immense black woollen hats. Fishers by hundreds balance in their little skiffs on the small whirlpool of waves made by the steamer, and sing gayly. For a stretch of twenty miles the course may lie near an immense forest, where millions of stout trees stand in regular rows, where thousands of oaks drop acorns every year to fatten thousands upon thousands of pigs. Cattle stray in these woods, and sometimes the peasant-farmer has a veritable hunt before he can find his own. Afar in the wooded recesses of Slavonia many convents of the Greek religion are hidden. Their inmates lead lives which have little or no relation to anything in the nineteenth century. For them wars and rumors of wars, Russian aggression, Austrian annexation, conspiracies by Kara Georgewitch, Hungarian domination in the Cabinet at Vienna, and all such trivial matters, do not exist. The members of these religious communities are not like the more active members of the clergy of their Church, who unquestionably have much to do with promoting war and supporting it when it is in aid of their nationality and their religion.

One of the most remarkable sights in this region is a herd of the noble "cattle of the steppes," the beasts in which every Hungarian takes so much pride. These cattle are superb creatures, and as they stand eying the passers-by one regrets that he has not more time in which to admire their exquisite white skins, their long symmetrical horns and their shapely limbs. They appear to be good-tempered, but it would not be wise to risk one's self on foot in their immediate neighborhood.

As for the fishermen, some of them seem to prefer living on the water rather than on dry land. Indeed, the marshy borders of the Danube are not very healthy, and it is not astonishing that men do not care to make their homes on these low lands. There are several aquatic towns between Pesth and the point at which the Drava (or Drau), a noble river, empties its waters into the Danube. Apatin is an assemblage of huts which appear to spring from the bosom of the current, but as the steamer approaches one sees that these huts are built upon piles driven firmly into the river-bed, and between these singular habitations are other piles upon which nets are stretched. So the fisherman, without going a hundred yards from his own door, traps the wily denizens of the Danube, prepares them for market, and at night goes peacefully to sleep in his rough bed, lulled by the rushing of the strong current beneath him. I am bound to confess that the fishermen of Apatin impressed me as being rather rheumatic, but perhaps this was only a fancy.

Besdan, with its low hills garnished with windmills and its shores lined with silvery willows, is the only other point of interest, save Mohacz, before reaching Pesth. Hour after hour the traveller sees the same panorama of steppes covered with swine, cattle and horses, with occasional farms — their outbuildings protected against brigands and future wars by stout walls — and with pools made by inundations of the impetuous Danube. Mohacz is celebrated for two tremendous battles in the past, and for a fine cathedral, a railway and a coaling-station at present. Louis II., king of Hungary, was there undone by Suleiman in 1526; and there, a hundred and fifty years later, did the Turks come to sorrow by the efforts of

BRIDGE OF BUDA-PESTH.

the forces under Charles IV. of Lorraine.

Just as I was beginning to believe that the slow-going steamer on which I had embarked my fortunes was held back by enchantment—for we were half a day ascending the stream from Mohacz—we came in sight of a huge cliff almost inaccessible from one side, and a few minutes later could discern the towers of Buda and the mansions of Pesth. While nearing the landing-place and hastening hither and yon to look after various small bundles and boxes, I had occasion to address an Hungarian gentleman. In the course of some conversation which followed I remarked that Pesth seemed a thriving place, and that one would hardly have expected to find two such flourishing towns as Vienna and Pesth so near each other.

"Oh," said he with a little sneer which his slight foreign accent (he was speaking French) rendered almost ludicrous, "Vienna is a smart town, but it is nothing to this!" And he pointed with pride to his native city.

Although I could not exactly agree with this extravagant estimate of the extent of Pesth, I could not deny that it was vastly superior to my idea of it. When one arrives there from the southeast, after many wanderings among semi-barbaric villages and little cities on the outskirts of civilization, he finds Pesth very impressive. The Hungarian shepherds and the boatmen who ply between the capital and tiny forts below fancy that it is the end of the world. They have vaguely heard of Vienna, but their patriotism is so intense and their round of life so circumscribed that they never succeed in forming a definite idea of its proportions or its location. Communication between the two chief towns of the Austria-Hungarian empire is also much less frequent than one would imagine. The Hungarians go but little to Vienna, even the members of the nobility preferring to consecrate their resources to the support of the splendors of their own city rather than to contribute them to the Austrian metropolis. Seven hours' ride in what the Austrians are bold enough to term an express-train covers the distance between Vienna and Pesth, yet there seems to be an abyss somewhere on the route which the inhabitants are afraid of. Pride, a haughty determination not to submit to centralization, and content with their surroundings make the Hungarians sparing of intercourse with their Austrian neighbors. "We send them prime ministers, and now and then we allow them a glimpse of some of our beauties in one of their palaces, but the latter does not happen very often," once said an Hungarian friend to me.

An American who should arrive in Pesth fancying that he was about to see a specimen of the dilapidated towns of "effete and decaying Europe" would find himself vastly mistaken. The beautiful and costly modern buildings on every principal street, the noble bridges across the vast river, the fine railway-stations, the handsome theatres, the palatial hotels, would explain to him why it is that the citizens of Pesth speak of their town as the "Chicago of the East." There was a time when it really seemed as if Pesth would rival, if not exceed, Chicago in the extent of her commerce, the vivacity and boldness of her enterprises and the rapid increase of her population. Austria and Hungary were alike the prey of a feverish agitation which pervaded all classes. In a single day at Vienna as many as thirty gigantic stock companies were formed; hundreds of superb structures sprang up monthly; people who had been beggars but a few months before rode in carriages and bestowed gold by handfuls on whoever came first. The wind or some mysterious agency which no one could explain brought this financial pestilence to Pesth, where it raged until the *Krach*—the Crash, as the Germans very properly call it—came. After the extraordinary activity which had prevailed there came gloom and stagnation; but at last, as in America, business in Pesth and in Hungary generally is gradually assuming solidity and contains itself within proper bounds. The exciting period had one beneficial feature: it made Pesth a handsome city. There are no quays in Europe more substantial and elegant than those along the Danube in the Hungarian capital, and no hotels, churches and mansions more splendid than those fronting on these same quays. At eventide, when the whole population comes out for an airing and loiters by the parapets which overlook the broad rushing river, when innumerable lights gleam from the boats anchored on either bank, and when the sound of music and song is heard from half a hundred windows, no city can boast a spectacle more animated. At ten o'clock the streets are deserted. Pesth is exceedingly proper and decorous as soon as the darkness has fallen, although I do remember to have seen a torchlight procession there during the Russo-Turkish war. The inhabitants were so enthusiastic over the arrival of a delegation of Mussulman students from Constantinople that they put ten thousand torches in line and marched until a late hour, thinking, perhaps, that the lurid light on the horizon might be seen as far as Vienna, and might serve as a warning to the Austrian gov-

CITADEL OF BUDA.

ernment not to go too far in its sympathy with Russia.

Buda-Pesth is the name by which the Hungarians know their capital, and Buda is by no means the least important portion of the city. It occupies the majestic and rugged hill directly opposite Pesth—a hill so steep that a tunnel containing cars propelled upward and downward by machinery has been arranged to render Buda easy of access. Where the hill slopes away southward there are various large villages crowded with Servians, Croatians and Low Hungarians, who huddle together in a rather uncivilized manner. A fortress where there were many famous fights and sieges in the times of the Turks occupies a summit a little higher than Buda, so that in case of insurrection a few hot shot could be dropped among the inhabitants. Curiously enough, however, there are thousands of loyal Austrians, German by birth, living in Buda—or Ofen, as the Teutons call it—whereas in Pesth, out of the two hundred thousand inhabitants, scarcely three thousand are of Austrian birth. As long as troops devoted to Francis Joseph hold Buda there is little chance for the citizens of Pesth to succeed in revolt. Standing on the terrace of the rare old palace on Buda's height, I looked down on Pesth with the same range of vision that I should have had in a balloon. Every quarter of the city would be fully exposed to an artillery fire from these gigantic hills.

Buda is not rich in the modern improvements which render Pesth so noticeable. I found no difficulty in some of the nooks and corners of this quaint town in imagining myself back in the Middle Ages. Tottering churches, immensely tall houses overhanging yawning and precipitous alleys, markets set on little shelves in the mountain, hovels protesting against sliding down into the valley, whither they seemed inevitably doomed to go, succeeded one another in rapid panorama. Here were costume, theatrical effect, artistic grouping: it was like Ragusa, Spalatro and Sebenico. Old and young women sat on the ground in the markets, as our negroes do in Lynchburg in Virginia: they held up fruit and vegetables and shrieked out the prices in a dialect which seemed a compound of Hungarian and German. Austrian soldiers and Hungarian recruits, the former clad in brown jackets and blue hose, the latter in buff doublets and red trousers, and wearing feathers in their caps, marched and countermarched, apparently going nowhere in particular, but merely keeping up discipline by means of exercise.

The emperor comes often to the fine palace on Buda hill, and sallies forth from it to hunt with some of the nobles on their immense estates. The empress is passionately fond of Hungary, and spends no small portion of her time there. The Hungarians receive this consideration from their sovereign lady as very natural, and speak of her as a person of great good sense. The German and Slavic citizens of Austria say that there are but two failings of which Her Imperial Majesty can be accused—she loves the Hungarians and she is too fond of horses. Nothing delights the citizens of Pesth so much as to find that the Slavs are annoyed, for there is no love lost between Slav and Magyar. A natural antipathy has been terribly increased by the fear on the part of Hungary that she may lose her influence in the composite empire one day, owing to the Slavic regeneration.

At Pesth they do not speak of the "beautiful blue Danube," because there the river ceases to be of that color, which Johann Strauss has so enthusiastically celebrated. But between Vienna and Pesth the blue is clearly perceptible, and the current is lovely even a few miles from the islands in the stream near the Hungarian capital. The Margarethen-Insel, which is but a short distance above Pesth, is a little paradise. It has been transformed by private munificence into a rich garden full of charming shaded nooks and rare plants and flowers. In the middle of this pleasure-ground are extensive bath-houses and mineral springs. Morning, noon and night gypsy bands make seductive music, and the notes of their melodies recall the strange lands far away down the stream — Roumania, the hills and valleys of the Banat and the savage Servian mountains. Along the river-side there are

MUSEUM AND SEAT OF THE DIET AT PESTH.

other resorts in which, in these days, when business has not yet entirely recovered from the *Krach*, there are multitudes of loungers. In midsummer no Hungarian need go farther than these baths of Pesth to secure rest and restore nealth. The Romans were so pleased with the baths in the neighborhood that they founded a colony on the site of Buda-Pesth, although they had no particular strategic reasons for doing so. As you sit in the pleasant shade you will probably hear the inspiring notes of the *Rakoczy*, the march of which the Hungarians are so passionately fond, which recalls the souvenirs of their revolutions and awakens a kind of holy exaltation in their hearts. The *Rakoczy* has been often enough fantastically described: some hear in it the gallop of horsemen, the clashing of arms, the songs of women and the cries of wounded men. A clever Frenchman has even written two columns of analysis of the march, and he found in it nearly as much as there is in Goethe's *Faust*. These harmless fancies are of little use in aiding to a veritable understanding of the wonderful march. It suffices to say that one cannot hear it played, even by a strolling band of gypsies, without a strange fluttering of the heart, an excitement and an enthusiasm which are beyond one's control. A nation with such a *Marseillaise* as the *Rakoczy* certainly ought to go far in time of war.

The Hungarians are a martial people, and are fond of reciting their exploits. Every old guide in Pesth will tell you, in a variegated English which will provoke your smiles, all the incidents of the Hungarian revolution, the events of 1848 and 1849—how the Austrians were driven across the great bridge over the Danube, etc.—with infinite gusto. The humblest wharf-laborer takes a vital interest in the welfare of his country, even if he is not intelligent enough to know from what quarter hostilities might be expected. There is a flash in an Hungarian's eye when he speaks of the events of 1848 which is equalled only by the lightnings evoked from his glance by the magic echoes of the *Rakoczy*.

The peasantry round about Pesth, and the poor wretches, Slavic and Hungarian, who work on the streets, seem in sad plight. A friend one day called my attention to a number of old women, most miserably clad, barefooted and bent with age and infirmities, carrying stones and bricks to a new building. The spectacle was enough to make one's heart bleed, but my friend assured me that the old women were happy, and that they lived on bread and an occasional onion, with a little water for drink or sometimes a glass of adulterated white wine. The men working with them looked even worse fed and more degraded than the women. In the poor quarters of Pesth, and more especially those inhabited by the Jews, the tenements are exceedingly filthy, and the aroma is so uninviting that one hastens away from the streets where these rookeries abound. The utmost civility, not to say servility, may always be expected of the lower classes: some of them seize one's hand and kiss it as the Austrian servants do. Toward strangers Hungarians of all ranks are unfailingly civil and courteous. A simple letter of introduction will procure one a host of attentions which he would not have the right to expect in England or America.

The mound of earth on the bank of the Danube near the quays of Pesth represents the soil of every Hungarian province; and from that mound the emperor of Austria, when he was crowned king of Hungary, was forced to shake his sword against the four quarters of the globe, thus signifying his intention of defending the country from any attack whatsoever. Thus far he has succeeded in doing it, and in keeping on good terms with the legislative bodies of the country, without whose co-operation he cannot exercise his supreme authority. These bodies are a chamber of peers, recruited from the prelates, counts and such aristocrats as sit there by right of birth, and a second chamber, which is composed of four hundred and thirteen deputies elected from as many districts for the term of three years, and thirty-four delegates from the autonomous province of Croatia-Slavonia. The entrance to the diet is guarded by a frosty-looking servitor in an extravagant Hungarian uniform, jacket and hose profusely covered with brilliant braids, and varnished jack-boots. The deputies when in session are quiet, orderly and dignified, save when the word "Russian" is pronounced. It is a word which arouses all their hatred.

Buda-Pesth is about to undergo a formidable series of improvements notwithstanding the illusions which were dispersed by the *Krach*. One of the most conspicuous and charming municipal displays in the Paris Exposition is the group of charts and plans sent from Pesth. The patriot Deak is to have a colossal monument; the quays are to be rendered more substantial against inundations than they are at present; and many massive public edifices are to be erected. The Danube is often unruly, and once nearly destroyed the city of Pesth, also doing much damage along the slopes of Buda. If an inundation should come within the next two or three years millions of florins' worth of property might be swept away in a single night. The opera, the principal halls of assembly and the hotels of Pesth will challenge comparison with those of any town of two hundred thousand population in the world; and the Grand Hotel Hungaria has few equals in cities of the largest size.

The Hungarians are a handsome race, and the people of Pesth and vicinity have especial claims to attention for their beauty. The men of the middle and upper classes are tall, slender, graceful, and their features are exceedingly regular and pleasing. The women are so renowned that a description of their charms is scarcely necessary. Beautiful as are the Viennese ladies in their early youth, they cannot rival their fellow-subjects of Hungary. The Austrian woman grows fat, matronly and rather coarse as she matures: the Hungarian lady of forty is still as willowy, graceful and capricious as she was at twenty. The peasant-women, poor things! are ugly, because they work from morning

SLAV WOMAN IN PESTH.

till night in the vineyards, toiling until their backs are broken. The wine which the beauties drink costs their humbler sisters their life-blood, their grace, their happiness. The sunshine of a thousand existences is imprisoned in the vintages of Pressburg and Carlowitz. Poor, homely toilers in the fields! Poor human creatures transformed into beasts of burden! The Hungarian nation owes it to itself to emancipate these struggling women and show them the way to better things.

EDWARD KING.

www.ingramcontent.com/pod-product-compliance
Lightning Source LLC
Chambersburg PA
CBHW030736230426
43667CB00007B/740